Economic Analysis of Law in European Legal Scholarship

Volume 16

The purpose of the book series "Economic Analysis of Law in European Legal Scholarship" is to publish high quality volumes in the growing field of law and economics research in Europe, from a comprehensive theoretical and practical vantage point. In particular, the series will place great emphasis on foundational and theoretical aspects of economic analysis of law and on interdisciplinary approaches in European Legal Scholarship. Following Nobel laureate Ronald Coase's famous essay "The Problem of Social Cost" (1960) fifty years ago law and economics has become the lingua franca of American jurisprudence. In recent decades, law and economics has also gained widespread popularity in Europe and its influence on Legal Scholarship is growing significantly.

Therefore, the economic analysis of law in European Legal Scholarship academic book series illustrates how law and economics is developing in Europe and what opportunities and problems – both in general and in specific legal fields – are associated with this approach within the legal traditions of European countries. Rather than further exploring economic analysis as such, the main focus of this series lies on the implementation of economic methods in legislation and legal adjudication from a European perspective. It takes into account the particular challenges the European legal systems face. Volumes will address law and economics research in Europe from a critical and comparative viewpoint. The studies in this series are strong and bold narratives of the development of economic analysis of law in European Legal Scholarship. Some are suitable for a very broad readership.

Contributions in this series primarily come from scholars in Europe. The purpose is to provide the next generation of European lawyers with the models and skills needed to understand and improve the economic analysis of law in their own legal field. The series includes monographs focusing on specific topics as well as collections of essays covering specific themes.

Rute Saraiva • Paulo Alves Pardal
Editors

Sustainable Finances and the Law

Between Public and Private Solutions

Springer

Editors
Rute Saraiva
CIDEEFF, Law School
University of Lisbon
Lisbon, Portugal

Paulo Alves Pardal
CIDEEFF, Law School
University of Lisbon
Lisbon, Portugal

ISSN 2512-1294 ISSN 2512-1308 (electronic)
Economic Analysis of Law in European Legal Scholarship
ISBN 978-3-031-49459-8 ISBN 978-3-031-49460-4 (eBook)
https://doi.org/10.1007/978-3-031-49460-4

This Springer imprint is published by the registered company Springer Nature Switzerland AG
The registered company address is: Gewerbestrasse 11, 6330 Cham, Switzerland

Paper in this product is recyclable.

Preface

Global sustainability challenges—including climate change, natural resource depletion, and rising inequality—are affecting the commercial environment and the real economy in a way that presents both risks and opportunities for the private and public financial actors. On the one hand, policymakers, investors and financial intermediaries (including banks and pensions funds) increasingly recognize the ESG factors important implications for the financial sector through both physical and transitional risks with impacts in financial services and products as well as in corporate governance. On the other, governments and international organizations are aware of their sustainability mission, the impact of ESG factors in their financial management, and of the power of their actions by regulating and supervising financial markets but also by using their budgetary and tax policies (e.g., carbon tax) and their participation in financial markets (e.g., green bonds and development banks).

Therefore, in a time when ESG matters are becoming mainstream with a very active regulatory agenda, the book aims to understand how the private and public financial systems can be rewired to create better value for society through sustainable initiatives such as the integration of ESG factors in investment, procurement, budgeting, or taxing.

So, its main originality comes from an interdisciplinary approach and linkage between private and public solutions in funding and incentivizing a more sustainable economy, considering both academic and practical expertise, thanks to the close collaboration of professors and professionals.

Consequently, this book is not only for academia but also for rule-makers, decision-makers, practitioners, and civil society to help building a higher and more effective sustainability consciousness.

Finally, the authors would like to acknowledge that this book would not be possible without the support of CIDEEFF at the University of Lisbon Law School, the enthusiasm of its President, Prof. Dr. Ana Paula Dourado and its funding by FCT, and the tireless help of Joana Silva, André Alfar Rodrigues, and Jenny Hill.

Lisbon, Portugal

Rute Saraiva
Paulo Alves Pardal

Contents

Part I Financial Sector, Regulation, Supervision and Sustainability

ESG Factors in Pensions Funds Regulations: Why, How Far Have They Gone, and What Is the Potential for Improvement? 3
Rute Saraiva

Benchmarking of National ESG Banking Regulations: State of Art and Remaining Challenges 27
Luciane Moessa de Souza

The Importance of Practicality: The Role of a Transition Green Asset Ratio for Banks 63
Sofia Santos

EIB Group Climate Bank Roadmap 2021–2025 77
Miguel Morgado

Part II Markets and Climate Change

Evaluating Additionality Analyses: California Cap and Trade and the Regional Greenhouse Gas Initiative 91
Ruthie Lazenby

Paying the Piper: On the Legal Qualification of Carbon Prices 103
Tatiana Falcão

The Economics of Adaptation to Climate Change and Its Main Challenges 139
Miguel Patrício

Part III Green Public Finance, Budgeting and Procurement

When Climate Change Knocks on the Finance Minister's Door 163
Paulo Alves Pardal

The Climate Dimension of Fiscal Policy Sustainability: Best Practices in Green Budgeting and Lessons for Portugal 195
Carlos Fonseca Marinheiro, Amílcar do Rosário e Sousa, and Ana Pinheiro

Government Procurement and Sustainable Development in the WTO . . . 219
Pedro Infante Mota

Part IV Green Taxes

Environmental Taxation and ESG: Silent Partners 253
Janet E. Milne

International Fiscal Cooperation to Better Integrate Public and Private Efforts on Sustainability: The Case of Carbon Offset Credits 281
María Amparo Grau Ruiz

The Use of Windfall Taxes on the Energy Sector to Support the Green Transition in the EU 295
Karolina Tetłak

The European "*Fit for 55*" Package and the Portuguese Tax Benefits System: Prospective Analysis and Reform Proposals 317
Filipe de Vasconcelos Fernandes

"*Fit for 55*": The EU Plan for a Green Transition 333
André Alfar Rodrigues

Jurisdictional Assessment of Environmental Taxation 345
Solange Juvandes

Part I
Financial Sector, Regulation, Supervision and Sustainability

ESG Factors in Pensions Funds Regulations: Why, How Far Have They Gone, and What Is the Potential for Improvement?

Rute Saraiva

Abstract Several countries and regional organizations have basically been developing hard, comprehensive, and flexible regulations and guidelines specific to pension funds and asset managers regarding the integration of ESG considerations into their investment policies. Therefore, the author wants to understand what are the limitations and opportunities considering the particular nature and function of pension funds, their actual extension, and the potential for improvement.

1 Introduction

According to Mercer's latest report on sustainable investment in pension funds,[1] the vast majority of European and British funds currently include environmental, social, and governance (ESG) considerations in their investments. This trend has been reinforced with the pandemic and in relation to concerns about climate change which becomes, together with governance, a key area of fiduciary scrutiny. Furthermore, the data collected reveal that the main driver is the regulatory dimension

This work is supported by national funds through the Foundation for Science and Technology (FCT), I.P. (Portugal), within the scope of the PTDC/DIR-OUT/32096/2017 project – "ART 63: The right to social security and the crisis – social regression as a normalization of the state of financial exception". It was published in a preliminary version in Revista de Direito Financeiro e dos Mercados de Capitais (RDFMC), n.° 3, 2022. With thanks to Luciane Moessa for her contribution and support in the collection and treatment of the main regulations and her critical notes on this paper. See, for all, her repository of worldwide ESG financial regulations, including for pension funds: https://sis.org.br/en/esg-financial-regulations/.

[1] Mercer, European Asset Allocation Insights 2021, Sustainable Investment Survey, 2021. https://www.mercer.com/content/dam/mercer/attachments/global/gl-2021-sustainable-investment-survey-investing-in-the-future.pdf.

R. Saraiva (✉)
CIDEEFF, University of Lisbon, Law School, Lisbon, Portugal
e-mail: rutesaraiva@fd.ulisboa.pt

R. Saraiva, P. A. Pardal (eds.), *Sustainable Finances and the Law*, Economic Analysis of Law in European Legal Scholarship 16,
https://doi.org/10.1007/978-3-031-49460-4_1

(67%), although it has been losing importance compared to previous years (85%). This is followed by the weighting of the financial materiality of risks (40%), reputational risks (35%), alignment with sponsor's corporate responsibility strategy (26%), individuals on the trustee board (14%), and pressure from plan members (13%).[2] Thus, although the value associated with the weighting of ESG factors is beginning to be considered in pension funds' structure and activities, regulation does not cease to play a key role in the paradigm shift.

Indeed, several (developed and developing) countries and regional organizations, such as the EU, have basically been developing hard, comprehensive, and flexible regulations and guidelines. These are specific to pension funds and asset managers regarding the integration of ESG considerations into their investment policies.

Thus, in the following pages, there will be more than just answering the question of whether pension funds should meet ESG issues since the (inter)national principle of integration associated with sustainability imposes it. The author seeks, on the one hand, to understand what are the limitations and opportunities considering the particular nature and function of pension funds. On the other hand, it will be seen how it is being carried out by regulators all over the world in order to leave some policy recommendations at the end given the potential for improvement. To this end, only the regulatory production of financial supervisors will be examined leaving aside self-regulation despite recognizing its value, especially for softly opening the way for harder, more systematic (and public) measures.

2 Conceptually Sustainable

The development of ESG factors associated with investments and, in particular, financial markets, including pension funds, appears as a natural evolution of the principle of integration underlying sustainability that has been extended to all areas of the economy. However, there is a massive and indiscriminate use of the term sustainable, whether or not associated with development and now to sustainable development goals (SDG) and ESG, as if it had the magic power of solving civilizational problems and aligning economic activity with environmental, social, and cultural protection. This has been eroding what should be understood by sustainability and sustainable development. Therefore, this raises the question of whether these are mere terminological strongholds that serve as an umbrella to a complex reality (conceptual, interstitial, principiological, and normative) or if they have a conceptual and normative nature and substance of their own. Now, since the ESG criteria are an extension of sustainability in the corporate and financial universe, it is appropriate to delimit them it in order to understand their impact, in particular legal and in the scope of their application to pension funds especially given their both soft and hard regulatory growth. It is all the more necessary as their

[2]The respondents could choose multiple drivers.

attractiveness lies in the subtle suggestion of a paradigm shift without specifying how, thus allowing the business-as-usual model to continue with a lighter conscience due to the ethical and moral character it contains.

At the economic level, sustainability is related to the continued, long-lasting, and stable production of goods and services in order to ensure at least the satisfaction of needs and avoid situations of extreme imbalances that could affect economic activity.[3] According to neoclassical thinking, and in a simplified way, sustainability is defined by maximizing the utility derived from consumption over time that is associated with an efficient allocation of resources and a discount rate.[4]

The delimitation of the economic sustainability rule depends on the *a priori* adoption of a stronger or weaker concept of sustainability and the acceptance of a greater or lesser fungibility of natural capital and the eventual determination of a minimum safety threshold. From Daly's thesis to Hartwick's rule, positions vary, revealing a greater or lesser sensitivity to moral and ethical imperatives and to arguments referring to a corrective and guarantor intervention by the state. However, even the theses that are intended to be neutral cannot escape a normative element related to the underlying appraisal value (judgement value)[5] and the establishment of a sustainability objective with no merely economic characteristics that call for a multidisciplinary analysis.[6]

Financially, moreover on the pensions topic, sustainability also entails an abiding and steady dimension of ensuring the future fulfilment of needs.

In fact, in this matter, due to its intergenerational dimension and the trade-off between present and future (paying now for a delayed benefit), what is at stake is to ensure, on the one hand, that the exaggerated preference for the present associated with a hyperbolic discount is overcome, and there are savings for later. On the other hand, in the "non-productive" and possibly in the most fragile phase as human beings, there is access to the means put aside that are expected to have been correctly managed and optimized (privately or publicly) to cover the costs of this period. Thus, much of the ideologically biased discussion centres around the financial sustainability of pension systems, that is, whether contributions will be sufficient to pay pensions in the future.[7] In this line of thought,

> the OECD Core Principles of Private Pension Regulation state that the duty of pension providers is to manage the assets in the best interests of their members and beneficiaries [with] the objectives of investment undertaken on behalf of pension fund members traditionally [being] defined by governing bodies and asset managers in financial terms: pension funds are typically expected to maximise the risk-adjusted returns/retirement benefits or to

---

[3] Wolf (2003), pp. 291–292.

[4] Harris (2000), p. 8.

[5] Pezzey and Toman (2002), p. 3.

[6] Harris (2000), p. 11.

[7] Moreira (2019), p. 14.

> preserve the real value of pension assets/retirement benefits. They do so by focusing on financial risks.[8]

Therefore, in terms of the general regulation of pension fund investment, it is verified that the overriding requirement is for the trustees to act in the long-term best interests of beneficiaries, mainly financially. This fiduciary duty also guides the approach to investment even when there are few specific requirements, for example, in relation to ESG issues and climate change.

However, increasingly in the wake of OECD reports,[9] the concept has been extended to a more social dimension of "social adequacy".[10] In other words, will pension systems be able to ensure an adequate standard of living for pensioners, especially by protecting them of an abrupt drop in income and of the risk of poverty?[11] This implies the consideration of specific indicators and measures for the social sustainability of pension systems with consequential impacts on the governance of the funds that may include:

i) To ensure an adequate level of income in retirement considering the evolution of the pension benefit that compares the average value of pensions in the system with the average value of wages;
ii) To prevent sudden drops in income in the transition to retirement, the gross old-age pensions replacement rate will be measured which establishes the average value of new pensions as a percentage of the last salary of individuals; and
iii) To prevent the risk of poverty, it is important to check the evolution of the poverty rate in this group which measures the percentage of pensioners aged 65 or over with incomes below the poverty threshold.[12]

However, as Moreira (coord.) recalls, "contrary to the measurement of the financial sustainability of the system, this type of indicators does not lend itself to clear judgments about its (un)sustainability. It is rather about assessing whether the social sustainability of the system will improve or regress."[13] In other words, despite the quantitative dimension of the indicators, their assessment will be subjective and contextual, focusing on trends.

This concern with the social dimension in pension systems that has not been addressed much as the consecutive OECD reports and the studies by Moreira (coord.) mentioned above point out and which is of interest here for pension funds is actually broader and older. Indeed, as Aubry et al. state:

> Public pension funds have engaged in social investing since the early 1970s, when several states passed laws to screen out "sin" stocks, such as tobacco, alcohol, and gambling. The

[8]IOPS, *IOPS Supervisory Guidelines on the Integration of ESG Factors in the Investment and Risk Management of Pension Funds*, IOPS (2019) 19.

[9]OECD (2015, 2019); Scarpetta and Blundell-Wignall (2015); Queisser and Whitehouse (2005).

[10]Queisser and Whitehouse (2005), p. 16.

[11]Moreira (2019), pp. 14, 69, 75 ss.

[12]Moreira (2019), pp. 70–71, 120 ss.

[13]Moreira (2019), p. 71.

> practice was broadened in the early 1980s in the wake of a major campaign to encourage pension funds and others to divest from companies doing business in South Africa. States have also aimed to achieve domestic goals, such as promoting union workers, economic development, and homeownership. In the mid-2000s, the focus shifted to "terror-free" investing in response to the Darfur genocide and to weapons proliferation in Iran. And, after mass shootings in Aurora, CO and Newtown, CT, some public funds shed their holdings in gun manufacturers. In the last few years, state legislation has renewed the call to divest from Iran and has increasingly targeted fossil fuels to combat climate change.[14]

This trend,[15] not only in public but also in private pension funds, has been extending to the so-called ESG factors, normally classified as non-financial,[16] either through (more or less disinterested) voluntary commitments, or gradually, through regulatory means, all over the world. This translates into different approaches such as economically targeted investments, shareholder advocacy and, more commonly, stock selection (screening out undesirable companies or, more recently, investing in "good" firms).

Now, this paradigm shift forces the consideration of the underlying materiality in its various dimensions (the ESG but also financial) and in its intimate relationship with sustainability. However, it must be considered that not all ESG issues matter equally since their relevance varies industry to industry and firm by firm which forces ESG scores to be more tailor-made.[17]

In these terms, in an attempt to make the sustainability-ESG materiality relationship more concrete for pension funds, some national regulations try to delimit ESG topics generally or by sector or geographical criteria. For instance, the Australian, Indonesian (which comprises key performance indicators as the Japanese guidance issued by the TCFD-Task Force on Climate-related Financial Disclosures Consortium), and Malaysian regulations incorporate, for example, environmental issues such as climate change, GHG emissions, air and water pollution, waste and effluents management, water scarcity, biodiversity or deforestation; social dimensions such as diversity, labour standards (including forced and child labour), human (and particularly, indigenous) rights; and governance topics such as business ethics, anti-competitive behaviour, corruption, board composition, or executive compensation schemes.

---

[14]Aubry et al. (2020), p. 1.

[15]In the United States, however, during the Trump Administration, the social dimension suffered a setback since retirement-plan fiduciaries were held to a "pecuniary" standard when selecting plan investment options therefore questioning the adequacy of social investing in defined-benefit plans covered by the Employee Retirement Income Security Act of 1974. The Biden Administration has suspended enforcement of that policy and a new rule "Prudence and Loyalty in Selecting Plan Investments and Exercising Shareholder Rights" has been proposed, establishing that, when considering projected returns, a fiduciary's duty of prudence may often require an assessment of the economic effects of the ESG and climate factors on the investment.

[16]The IOPS (2019) 19–20, nevertheless, classifies the ESG factors as financial ones since they may materially impact the long-term risk and return of investments, a company's valuation, and reputational risk as well as its operational efficiency (governance).

[17]Steinbarth and Bennett (2018).

Of these specific regulatory examples of an attempt to achieve ESG materiality, it may be observed that its treatment is still incipient but growing in order to overcome the many criticisms of lack of clarity in its delimitation, classification, and densification.[18] This could even be due to the underlying complexity and multifactoriality since that ESG categories are diverse and, in many cases, very distinct from one another. In fact, it is significant that the effort around taxonomy has not yet been carried out by the specific regulators of pension funds but worked transversally or by banking or capital markets regulators (in non-monist or twin peaks systems).

In sum, in respect to sustainability for pensions funds, two factors might converge:

i) Financial sustainability; and
ii) ESG issues.

Nevertheless, in the end, the main goal is to provide the beneficiaries their pensions and, lately, also to ensure a "social adequate" life to them. This means that ESG factors or any other risks should be considered by the funds' governing bodies or asset managers as any other substantial factor that can financially impact a pension fund and therefore integrate ESG concerns into their risk and investment management process. In other words, pension fiduciaries should consider what ESG issues may be important to the exercise of their prudential duty to meet the pension promise.[19] This does not mean, however, that pension funds should assume themselves as motors of ESG sustainable change of the economy and have as a primordial goal the financing of ESG initiatives. In other words, there is a supremacy of the meta-interest of the beneficiaries over ESG generic concerns that both the pension fund managers and sectorial regulators should not forget. That is, the integration of ESG issues in the structure and activities of the pension funds should be conditioned to an ESG financial sustainability.

3 Integrating ESG Standards in Pension Funds

3.1 Linkage Between Pension Funds and ESG Concerns: Advantages and Disadvantages

Given their long-term obligations, pension funds are in a comfortable position to assess long-term risks to their portfolios, and the intergenerational nature of their business model tends to open them to other intergenerational issues such as the ESG, SDGs, or climate concerns. Subsequently, some of these institutional investors have realized that ESG factors represent important material risks in terms of the (financial)

[18] Aubry et al. (2020), p. 4.
[19] Sarra (2022).

sustainability of their investments. Simultaneously, as "universal owners"[20] with large and diversified shareholdings, these funds might play an essential role in advocating the integration of ESG factors along their investment chains through active and responsible ownership. As the EIPOA states: "Given their role as society's risk managers and important long-term investors, insurers and pension funds have a unique opportunity and responsibility to address sustainability-related challenges and facilitate the transition to a more sustainable and resilient economy."[21]

A plethora of studies[22] already exist seeking to determine whether there is a relationship between the financial performance and the ESG performance with an overall conclusion for positive correlation. That is, sustainable investments, especially ESG indexes, behave alike or even better than conventional investments.

However, as Lachance and Stroehle rightfully recall,

> The particular structure of pension funds creates both a set of advantages and disadvantages for the adoption of sustainable finance practices, compared with other institutional investors. While asset owners in general are often hailed as the ultimate enablers of a sustainable transition on the financial market, pension funds often do not live up to that expectation. Although there is an assumption that because of their long-term focus, pensions can take a more systemic perspective than conventional investment products, many feel restricted in integrating ESG due to their fiduciary duty to secure the financial returns of their beneficiaries and related, restraining regulation.[23]

In other words, their "*social origins*"[24] as a combination of the historical and structural characteristics of pensions funds may help explaining the tension around their organizational and institutional enablers as well as the inhibiters of integrating ESG considerations into their structure and activities that mainly consider three major factors.

Firstly, there is an agency problem at two different levels when considering integrating ESG-driven investments:

i) decision-makers and shareholders do not coincide, i.e., trustees on one side and beneficiaries on the other, with asymmetric information; and
ii) decision-makers and the stakeholders are different. The first ones are either the fund board or the state legislature/regulator, or a combination of the two, where the stakeholders are tomorrow's beneficiaries and/or taxpayers. If social investing produces losses either through higher administrative costs or lower returns, future retirees will receive lower benefits or tomorrow's taxpayers will have to ante

[20] On the universal owner theory, see, for all, Lachance and Stroehle (2021), pp. 3–5.

[21] https://www.eiopa.europa.eu/browse/sustainable-finance_en.

[22] For example, Albertini (2013); Brammer et al. (2006), pp. 97–116; Busch and Friede (2018), pp. 583–608; Flammer (2015), pp. 1–20; Friede et al. (2015), pp. 210–233; Margois et al. (2009), pp. 403–441. Defending and proving a negative correlation, at least for public pension funds, Aubry et al. (2020), p. 8.

[23] Lachance and Stroehle (2021), pp. 1–2.

[24] Lachance and Stroehle (2021).

> up. The welfare of these future actors is not well represented in the decision-making process[25]

which, at the end, means that the people who are deciding are not the ones who will bear the burden of any miscalculations attending ESG concerns (mainly in their portfolios and risk management).

Furthermore, the beneficiaries are not necessarily a homogeneous group and may present diverse levels of ESG-sensitivity and valuing. Given distinct inclinations, it would be hard for pension funds to fully integrate the value of ESG factors for all beneficiaries, especially when their preferences (and attitudes) may shift over time.

Secondly, and as pointed out this chapter, there could be a divergence between the fiduciary duties and ESG investment considerations, which is truer if considering the implications of pensions being between public interest and private markets. As a result, there is wide consensus that pension funds must both serve the financial interests of their members and act as institutions of public interest which creates an opportunity to extend their objectives to ESG issues but also makes them vulnerable to becoming political instruments.[26]

After all,

> there are five characteristics of pension funds which have an important impact on whether and how they can integrate ESG. The historical origins of funds and their regulatory embeddedness, their mandate and legal structure, the importance of corporate governance and leadership at the funds, their investment strategies and asset mix, and finally, pensions' ability to engage in collaborative and advocacy activities. In reviewing these characteristics, we emphasize that pension funds are not a homogenous community, as they have different mandates, face distinct legal environments, and have different governance structures. Despite this diversity, pension funds share a common objective, which is to identify the best investments or investment strategies to generate investment returns to be able to pay pensions to their beneficiaries. In doing so, the inherent long-term investment time horizon and the diversified portfolio structures are two of the principle enablers of ESG at pension funds.[27]

Consequently, on the one hand, one-size-does-not-fit-all, that is, the integration of ESG factors in pension funds must ponder their concrete and characteristic specificities; on the other, sustainable opportunities may arise from the link between pension funds' organization and structure and ESG investments, especially when adequately weighing specific ESG factors as materially and financially relevant.

Finally, one major challenge to thoroughly integrating ESG factors in an investment model of pension funds is the barrier around the access to consistent, complete, and comparable ESG information. The growing of a truly digital society occurs with Big Data and crossing and intelligent algorithms. The development of regulated ESG rating agencies may help trustees to better assess the financial materiality of ESG concerns and the fidelity and validity of the information around the market agents'

---

[25] Aubry et al. (2020), p. 7.

[26] Lachance and Stroehle (2021), pp. 5–8.

[27] Lachance and Stroehle (2021), pp. 27–28.

proclamations about their sustainable practices. Additionally, asset owners and asset managers will need to be better prepared in terms of ESG issues, opportunities, and pitfalls when they have a long-term investment horizon. In other words, they need to increase their ESG literacy by either contracting and integrating experts and advisers or by investing in their own skills or both.

3.2 From the Mission to the Governance Structure and Measures for ESG Factors Integration

The first step in the journey of integration of ESG standards in pension funds begins with reorienting their vision to make sustainability a core element of the fund's long-term mission. This ensures, or at least frames, that the strategy, business planning, activities, and the governance structure encompass ESG considerations mainly by committing to integrate ESG concerns in all investment decisions and risk management. It is also essential to adopt long-termism as a guiding principle of fund investments in order to safeguard and create sustainable value and "healthy returns".[28] This is all the more important since the German regulator remembers in what seems a truism attending to transparency and loyalty duties and competition fairness that, if the financial institution adheres to self-regulatory ESG initiatives as a voluntary self-commitment (above all when integrated in its mission), these should be echoed in its strategies and guidelines. This ruling opens the door, in the case of non-alignment, to possible sanctioning by the fund's supervisor, especially because it may reflect greenwashing practices and a breach of the trustees' duties.

Along with the mission statement and probably more relevant, in reality, the governance structure (i.e., oversight structures, processes, and systems regarding an organization's sustainable investment decision making and implementation) should incorporate ESG considerations in order to ensure its effectiveness. Therefore, good governance is the result of having adequate structures and processes in place and conducting continuous monitoring to ensure that they are aligned with the objectives and needs of the funds.[29] This involves not only commitment from the top and across all of the structure but also executive leadership and a dedicated sustainable investment team or at least some personnel with ESG investment knowledge and skills.

The regulators are watchful of the importance of the governance structure for ESG integration in pensions funds. For instance, the Austrian, German, and Singaporean regulators want clear definitions of roles and responsibilities and refer to appropriate staff, budget allocation, and capacity-building. Going even further, the Australian pension funds regulation, in a unique example across the world, includes gender diversity in the fund's board. Moreover, with regards to the governance structure, the German regulator states an important principle that should be

[28] UNCTAD (2020), p. 12.

[29] UNCTAD (2020), p. 13.

accounted for in other countries regulations, i.e. the granularity level of the incorporation of ESG factors in the governance of pension funds should be subject to proportionality. This is because, for example, smaller pension funds that outsource investment management activities may find it, at least at the beginning, more difficult and costly to integrate these factors into their structure and procedures.

In this line, some regulatory authorities are trying to align interests of the governance structure with ESG considerations by establishing rules or guidelines on the selection and monitoring of service providers and the integration of ESG factors into compensation schemes of asset managers and governing bodies. Directive (EU) 2017/828, for instance, states that "performance should be assessed using both financial and non-financial performance criteria, including, where appropriate, environmental, social and governance factors". Its Article 3H establishes the terms of the alignment of the investment strategy of institutional investors and arrangements with asset managers. In Japan, the regulator suggests that remuneration schemes should be constructed in order to nudge sustainable growth in the long-run.

More broadly in terms of governance structure, Directive (EU) 2016/2341 on the activities and supervision of institutions for occupational retirement provision (IORPs), in its Article 25 No. 2 g), determines that the risk-management system shall cover certain risks according to the proportionality principle. These risks can occur in the IORPs or in undertakings to which tasks or activities of an IORP have been outsourced, when applicable, to "environmental, social and governance risks relating to the investment portfolio and the management thereof". Furthermore, once again concerning proportionality, risk assessment according to Article 28 No. 2 h) should include, when ESG factors are considered in investment decisions, "an assessment of new or emerging risks, including risks related to climate change, use of resources and the environment, social risks and risks related to the depreciation of assets due to regulatory change".

Despite the EU regulation, some Member States also provide more ruling and guidance on ESG considerations in pension funds. For instance, in Spain, Royal Legislative Decree 1/2002 determines in its Articles 16 No. 8, 27 No. 1 and 30 bis that, in the case of employment pension funds, it must be indicated whether the socially responsible investment criteria (including the ESG) that affect the different assets of the pension fund are taken into account in the investment decisions. If so, then it must be determined how it is reflected in the governance structure according to the provisions of the declaration of the principles of the investment policy and in the risk management system. Similarly, the Italian Resolution of 16 March 2012, establishes in Article 5 No. 2 c) 5 that, with reference to contractual and pre-existing pension funds with legal subjectivity, the finance function involved in the investment process periodically checks, with support of the consultant for ethical investments (if present), compliance by the parties in charge of management of the indications given in relation to the principles and criteria of sustainable and responsible investment when provided for within the implementation criteria of the investment policy.

On the other hand, giving Article 214 No. 12 of the French Monetary and Financial Code, asset managers should mention in their annual report and in the documents intended for the information of their subscribers the methods of integrating in their investment policy the criteria relating to the respect of ESG objectives. They should specify the nature of these criteria and the way that they apply them. Furthermore, they should indicate how they exercise the voting rights attached to the financial instruments resulting from these choices. Similarly, Article Art. 42. (§ 1) No. 2 of the Belgian law on supplementary pensions and their tax regime and certain supplementary social security benefits of 28 April 2003 requires that pension funds draw up an annual report on the management of the pension commitment. This is to be made available to the organizer who communicates it on request to the affiliates. The report should contain information on the long-term and short-term investment strategies and the extent to which social, ethical, and environmental aspects are taken into account.

Still in terms of the governance structure, the UK Stewardship Code, in its Principle 1, asks asset owners and asset managers to explain their purpose, investment beliefs, strategy, and culture enabling stewardship that creates long-term value for clients and beneficiaries leading to sustainable benefits for the economy, the environment, and society. They should also explain their governance, resources, and incentives support stewardship, their conflicts policy, how they identify and respond to market-wide and systemic risk, and how they review their policies, ensure their processes, and assess the effectiveness of their activities according, respectively, to Principles 2 to 5. The Draft of the UK Code of Practice (which is expected during 2022) is expected to set requirements that are more specific on how trustees should approach ESG issues and climate risk (even for schemes not directly subject to the TCFD regulations) in the investment strategy and how trustees and managers evaluate them.

Other regulators such as the Brazilian,[30] South African[31] and Japanese[32] demand or at least recommend that ESG considerations should be included in the pension funds' investment policies. In Australia,[33] the pension funds should have an ESG risk management policy and strategy, including procedures and diligences, duly disclosed to their members.

Finally, and more generically, Principle 5 of the Malaysian Code for Institutional Investors establishes that they should incorporate corporate governance and sustainability considerations including ESG matters into the investment decision-making process. This is because they are expected to deliver sustainable returns in the long-term interest of their beneficiaries or clients.

---

[30]Resolution No. 4.661, 25th May 2018, Brazil Central Bank.

[31]Financial Sector Conduct Authority Guidance note 1 of 2019 (PFA).

[32]Japan's Stewardship Code, Principles for Responsible Institutional Investors—To promote sustainable growth of companies through investment and dialogue.

[33]FSC Standards (No. 20).

3.3 *Pension Fiduciary Duties*

It is well-recognized in both civil and common law that pension plan administrators are fiduciaries, and their fiduciary duty comes close to imposing on ethical conduct because of the legal requirements to act in good faith and avoid conflicts of interest.

Fiduciaries' primary duty is to take into account financial risks and opportunities when managing plan assets in order to optimize the beneficiaries' interests. Trustees, in their prudential obligation, should act with the standard of care, diligence, and skill in the administration and investment of the pension fund of a person of ordinary prudence in dealing with the property of others (a somewhat more elevated than the reasonable person standard of care applied to negligence or contract cases). The duty of loyalty, translating into standards of honesty, good faith, and impartiality, requires them to behave in the best interests of plan members and to avoid conflicts of interest. They should also ensure even manoeuvrability in dealing with different classes of beneficiaries. Therefore,

> pension fiduciaries have a duty to acquire an understanding of, and then balance their decisions in respect of, current and future intergenerational risk and return over periods that potentially exceed human lifetimes. Pension funds are large diversified institutional investors with long-term investment horizons, so they cannot diversify away from systemic risk such as climate change and income inequality, and that system-level investment lens needs to be keenly attuned to intergenerational responsibilities as part of their fiduciary duties.[34]

In other words, the fiduciary duties of loyalty and prudence require the incorporation of ESG issues since they can be financially material, a source of investment value, and a mark of prudent investment.[35] Moreover, integrating ESG concerns is becoming an investment norm globally, especially in big pension funds, and regulatory frameworks are changing in order to consider and require ESG factors incorporation as a long-term value driver.[36]

In sum, as put before, governing bodies and trustees should defend the beneficiaries' interest, above all maximizing their pensions and ensuring them periodic payments after retirement and until death in respect of their service as employees. This should involve the assessment of financial risks and also the impact of ESG factors into the performance of the fund investments. In other words, ESG considerations can (and should, under fiduciary duties) be taken into account in the pension scheme investment decision-making when they are financially material. This should be done as a sort of "governance duty" that implies obtaining information on ESG factors; assessing, considering, and balancing it with other factors; and developing adequate expertise in doing so.[37] If they are not financially material or based on

[34] Sarra (2022), p. 3.

[35] Bauslaugh (2021), p. 6 ss.

[36] UNEP FI, PRI (2019); Sarra (2022), p. 3.

[37] Lewis and Gilmour (2022).

wider non-financial concerns, they should meet additional tests before being integrated into the investment strategy.[38]

On the other hand, trustees should attend to the (expressed and revealed) preferences, attitudes, and will of the beneficiaries, including on ESG topics. This raises the question around engagement activities and voting policies on ESG issues.

Directive (EU) 2017/828 on the encouragement of long-term shareholder engagement stipulates that institutional investors and asset managers should be transparent on the drivers of their investment strategies, including ESG factors. After all, effective and sustainable shareholder engagement is a cornerstone of the corporate governance model of listed companies and one of the levers that can help improve the financial and non-financial performance of companies, including ESG factors. Therefore, according to Article 3G, No. 1 a), they

> shall develop and publicly disclose an engagement policy that describes how they integrate shareholder engagement in their investment strategy. The policy shall describe how they monitor investee companies on relevant matters, including strategy, financial and non-financial performance and risk, capital structure, social and environmental impact and corporate governance, conduct dialogues with investee companies, exercise voting rights and other rights attached to shares, cooperate with other shareholders, communicate with relevant stakeholders of the investee companies and manage actual and potential conflicts of interests in relation to their engagement.

Therefore, the asset manager should also inform the institutional investor whether and, if so, how he makes investment decisions on the basis of an evaluation of the medium to long-term performance of the investee company, including its non-financial performance and ESG matters.

Some regulators, such as the Australian, British, and Japanese, recommend collaborative engagement with other investors for scaling purposes and require the disclosure of the policies for the exercise of voting rights in line with European guidance.

The question to be asked is what could happen if the pension trustees break their "new extended" fiduciary duties, including identifying and addressing ESG and climate-related financial risks? If they fail to act to address material ESG and climate-related risk, might they be personally liable for breaching their fiduciary obligation?

Concerning the EU, in relation to failing to meet the ESG requirements under the IORP II Regulations, the pensions authority has full monitoring and supervisory powers. Furthermore, Member States must ensure that the competent authorities[39] monitor compliance with the SFDR requirements under its Article 14 with its No. 2 also declaring that the competent authorities shall have all the necessary

[38] In the United Kingdom, additional and very demanding legal tests are required and were partially considered by the Supreme Court in R (Palestine Solidarity Campaign Ldt and another) v Secretary of State for Housing, Communities and Local Government (2020) UKSC 16.

[39] Designated in accordance with the sectoral legislation referred to in Article 6(3) of SFDR and Directive 2013/36/EU.

supervisory and investigatory powers that are for the exercise of their functions under the SFDR Regulation.

In the United Kingdom, breaches of the new requirements can cause trustees to be subjected to discretionary penalties and compliance notices by the supervisor. The existing disclosure penalty regime will apply if trustees fail to inform members where they can find the TCFD report. Fiduciaries may also be subjected to mandatory penalties for not publishing a TCFD report on a publicly available website. In addition, compliance notices can be issued against third parties when the supervisory authority considers that they are wholly or partly responsible for a breach.

In Canada, any breach of the duties set out in pension legislation is an offence under that framework which may include the application of administrative monetary penalties. Additionally, offences may as well be subject to prosecution by the competent regulatory authority resulting in fines. Common law also provides civil remedies including payments to plan beneficiaries and/or the pension fund for breach of fiduciary duties.

In Australia, on the contrary, there are no mandatory rules and, consequently, no penalties imposed in relation to the consideration of climate change risks by fiduciaries. However, there is growing interest in whether consideration of climate concerns is required under the general fiduciary duties as presaged in the ruling of *McVeigh v Retails Employees Superannuation Trust*.[40] In 2019, a member of an Australian pension plan sued pension fiduciaries for failure to identify, manage, and disclose climate risks. The case was settled with

> the trustees acknowledging that climate change is a material, direct and current financial risk to the fund across many risk categories; committing to actively identifying and managing these issues, and to develop systems, policies and processes to ensure that the financial risks of climate change for assets and the fund's portfolio as a whole are addressed; and ensuring that investment managers take active steps to consider, measure and manage financial risks posed by climate change and other relevant ESG risks.[41]

In the United Kingdom, a lawsuit is now pending against trustees of the British's largest private pension scheme for alleged breach of fiduciary duties, conflicts of interest, and failure to create a credible plan for disinvestment from fossil fuel investments.[42] Additionally, a member of the Shell Contributory Pension Fund filed an (unsuccessful) complaint to the Pensions Ombudsman in the United Kingdom concerning the information provided to him on climate risks.[43]

---

[40] Mark McVeigh v Retail Employees Superannuation Pty Limited ACN 001 987 739, NSD 1333 of 2018, Concise Statement filed September 21, 2019, McVeigh v. Retail Employees Superannuation Trust – Climate Change Litigation (climatecasechart.com).

[41] Sarra (2022), p. 9. See also, on this case, Bauslaugh (2021), p. 6 ss; Mark McVeigh v Retail Employees Superannuation Pty Limited settlement statement, (2020), Microsoft Word – Statement from Rest 2 November 2020.docx (climatecasechart.com).

[42] McGaughey et al v Universities Superannuation Scheme Limited and individuals listed, Claim form, USS, 20211027_14857_petition.pdf (climatecasechart.com).

[43] Failure to provide information—The case study of Mr D | The Pensions Ombudsman (pensions-ombudsman.org.uk).

Some litigation over ESG concerns on pension funds is already popping. *Alea jacta est.*

4 ESG Risk Management

When pursuing financial returns, pension fund governing bodies and asset managers should consider all substantial factors that can financially impact a pension fund. However, prudential regulations or rules should not make a separate case for ESG factors or any other emerging risks (...) but encourage pension funds' governing bodies or asset managers to fully integrate ESG factors into their risk management and investment management process. Governing bodies should therefore integrate risk factors that are relevant for a pension fund and its members and beneficiaries and have them implemented in the overall investment process.[44]

Therefore, IOPS Guideline 5 states that:

> Supervisory authorities should require that a governing body and the asset managers involved in the development and implementation of a pension funds' investment policy integrate ESG factors, along with all substantial financial factors, into their investment strategies (analysis and decision-making process) (...) [and that they] should also request that in case these factors are not integrated in investment and risk management process, a governing body and the asset managers provide explanations.

Nevertheless, the IOPS alerts to the level of adequate granularity of the public rulings and guidelines, considering that the

> Supervisory authorities should avoid being overly prescriptive on how governing bodies should deal with ESG factors but rather emphasize the need to document the ways a particular governing body is treating such factors. (...) Integration of ESG factors may be subject to the principle of proportionality, i.e., the scale of the pension funds and complexity of its governing structure.

Assuming the virtue of the IOPS' guideline, the question to ask now is: How have the national and regional regulators ruled the ESG risk management in pension funds? Too little or too much?

For instance, the compliance with Principle 7 of the UK Stewardship Code in the perspective of asset owners and asset managers (on them systematically integrating stewardship and investment, including material ESG issues, and climate change in order to fulfil their responsibilities) requires, as an outcome, that they "should explain how information gathered through stewardship has informed acquisition, monitoring and exit decisions, either directly or on their behalf". For service providers, as stated in their Principle 5 (on them supporting clients' integration of stewardship and investment, taking into account material ESG issues and communicating what activities they have undertaken), they "should explain: how they have taken account of clients' views and feedback in the provision of their services; and

[44] IOPS (2019) 23.

the effectiveness of their chosen methods for communicating with clients and understanding their needs, and how they evaluated their effectiveness".

In terms of target-setting or other strategies at portfolio-level, the Austrian, German, and Singaporean orientations from the regulator recommend management, including stress tests as well as short and long-term scenario analysis, especially for climate risks, similar to those of the EU and British[45] regulatory guidelines. The EIOPA, through its opinion on the supervision of the use of climate change risk scenarios in the Own Risk and Solvency Assessment (ORSA)[46] incorporates quantitative and qualitative matters regarding the portfolio's climate risk analysis and into ORSA.

5 Disclosure and Stewardship of Investments

5.1 Disclosure

For the sake of transparency, accountability and, more importantly, of the confidence required between trustees and beneficiaries, disclosure duties are essential. It should be expected, as the IOPS points out in its Guideline 7, that, "Supervisory authorities should require that a governing body or the asset managers involved in the development and implementation of the pension fund's investment policy will report to supervisory authorities how they integrate ESG factors in their investment and risk management process." Moreover, as in the IOPS' Guideline 8 and 9, respectively,

> Supervisory authorities should issue regulations, rules or guidelines on how a pension fund's governing body or the asset managers, when setting up their investment policy, should report to its members and stakeholders on substantial financial factors, including ESG factors " and they "should require that, in their investment policy statement, a governing body or the asset managers of a pension fund disclose to members and stakeholders information about the pension fund's investment policies in relation to long-term sustainability, including ESG factors, stewardship and non-financial factors. Where appropriate, pension funds should also regularly provide reports on their engagement with investees as well as request companies in which they invest to disclose their ESG-related policies.

In sum, the regulators should regulate or establish guidance on disclosure on the integration of ESG factors in pension funds considering not only the markets, the stakeholders, the investees, and the supervisors but also the members and

[45] Trustees of schemes in scope must, as far as their abilities go, perform a scenario analysis assessing the impact on the scheme's assets and liabilities, the resilience of the scheme's investment strategy, and (when it has one) the scheme's funding strategy for at least two scenarios—one of which corresponds to a below 2 °C temperature rise consistent with the Paris Agreement and one above. A scenario analysis must be carried out in the first year in which the requirements apply to the scheme and at least every three years thereafter.

[46] EIOPA-BoS-21-127, 19 April 2021, opinion-on-climate-change-risk-scenarios-in-orsa.pdf (europa.eu).

beneficiaries of the pension funds. However, how are real world regulators dealing with this topic?

The EU has been investing this topic and presents several rulings that enforce disclosure on the integration of ESG factors.

Firstly, Regulation (EU) 2019/2088 on sustainability-related disclosures in the financial services sector (SFDR)[47,48] requires pensions funds to disclose:

i) Their policies on the integration of sustainability risks in their investment decision-making process (Article 3);
ii) Their remuneration policies information on how those policies are consistent with the integration of sustainability risks (Article 5);
iii) The manner in which sustainability risks are integrated into their investment decisions and the results of the assessment of the likely impacts of sustainability risks on the returns of the financial products they make available (Article 6); and
iv) The adverse sustainability impacts at the financial product level (Article 7).

When a financial product promotes, among other characteristics, environmental or social characteristics, or a combination of those characteristics, provided that the companies in which the investments are made follow good governance practices, the information to be disclosed pursuant to Article 6(1) and (3) shall include, in accordance to Article 8, data on how those characteristics are met and, if an index has been selected as a reference benchmark, information on if and how this index is coherent with those characteristics. On the other hand, concerning Article 9 in which a financial product has sustainable investment as its objective and:

i) an index has been designated as a reference benchmark, the disclosure should also include information on how the designated index is aligned with that objective and an explanation as to why and how the designated index aligned with that objective differs from a broad market index; and if
ii) no index has been selected, the disclosure should include an explanation on how that objective is to be attained.

If a financial product has a reduction in carbon emissions as its objective, the disclosure requirement includes the objective of low carbon emission exposure in view of achieving the long-term global warming objectives of the Paris Agreement. It also gives a detailed explanation of how the continued effort of attaining the objective of reducing carbon emissions is ensured.

[47] Although this regulation does not cover national social security schemes treated by Regulations (EC) 883/2004 and (EC) 987/2009, considering that Member States are opening up parts of the management of compulsory pension schemes to financial market participants or other entities and since they are exposed to sustainability risks and might consider adverse sustainability impacts or ESG investment, Member States should have the option to apply this regulation with regard to such schemes in order to mitigate information asymmetries.

[48] In Portugal, see Circular No. 1/2021 of February 26th, of the ASF.

Furthermore, if the pension fund has more than 500 employees, considering Article 4 No. 2, 3, 4 and the underlying principle of proportionality, it should disclose:

- Information about its policies on the identification and prioritization of principal adverse sustainability impacts and indicators;
- A description of the principal adverse sustainability impacts and of any actions in relation thereto taken or, when relevant, planned;
- Brief summaries of engagement policies;
- A reference to its adherence to responsible business conduct codes and internationally recognized standards for due diligence and reporting and, when relevant,
- The degree of its alignment with the objectives of the Paris Agreement.

Secondly, Directive (EU) 2017/828 mentioned previously asks institutional investors and asset managers to publicly disclose information about the implementation of their engagement policy and particularly how they have exercised their voting rights. The asset managers disclosure should cover, according to Article 3i No. 1, reporting on the key material medium to long-term risks associated with the portfolio investments and its composition. This should include corporate governance matters and other medium to long-term risks, the use of proxy advisors for the purpose of engagement activities and their policy on securities lending, and how it is applied to fulfil its engagement activities if applicable. The asset manager should also inform the institutional investor whether and, if so, how the former makes investment decisions on the basis of an evaluation of the medium to long-term performance of the investee company. This should include its non-financial performance and whether and if so which conflicts of interests have arisen in connection with engagements activities and how the asset managers have dealt with them. Furthermore, proxy advisors shall publicly disclose (on a website) on an annual basis at least all of the information in relation to the preparation of their research, advice, and voting recommendations demanded in Article 3j No. 2.

Thirdly, Commission Delegated Directive (EU) 2021/1270 of 21 April 2021 amending Directive 2010/43/EU regarding the sustainability risks and sustainability factors to be taken into account for Undertakings for Collective Investment in Transferable Securities (UCITS) requires the ordinary integration of sustainability risks into the management of investment funds.

In the antipodes, the Australian capital markets regulator issued, in its Regulatory Guide 65, disclosure guidelines for investment products (S1013DA) on "how labour standards or environmental, social or ethical considerations are taken into account in selecting, retaining or realising an investment" if the financial products claim their integration. Therefore, the guidelines focus especially on the standards, methodologies, and weighting system used.

5.2 *Stewardship of Investments*

The UK Stewardship Code (2020) establishes high stewardship standards aimed at those responsible for investing the assets of UK savers and pensioners and those who support them. According to it, "Stewardship is the responsible allocation, management and oversight of capital to create long-term value for clients and beneficiaries leading to sustainable benefits for the economy, the environment and society." Despite the voluntary nature of this code, it represents a significant shift of the traditional paradigm where the main aim for fiduciaries was typically phrased as the maximization of investment returns for beneficiaries commensurate with an acceptable degree of risk. The long-term, environmental, and social considerations introduce a change and mark a concern with the impact of business on the planet and society.

In regard to legislation concerning stewardship, the EU SRD II Directive will increase disclosure of investment management activities. However, apart from this, there is little legislation in this area, but voluntary stewardship codes have been developed in Australia, India, Japan, Switzerland, and the United Kingdom and have received widespread support.[49]

The Australian Asset Owner Stewardship Code constitutes a comprehensive guide to the reporting requirements of its signatories who are required to make annual reports publicly available, including ESG integration into investment processes and engagement with management (with no specificities for climate change). The code has a broad application, but pension funds seem to be the main drivers.

6 Final Remarks

6.1 *In a Nutshell*

The overall conclusion is that, apart from voluntary commitments and self-regulation, the integration of ESG factors in pensions funds and asset managers' regulations is still limited in many parts of the globe, especially when compared to banking regulations. Nevertheless, it is increasing rapidly, particularly in Europe, which means that, on the one hand, pension fund investments are coming under more granular scrutiny and, on the other, supervisory authorities have a margin to evolve. Hence, actuaries involved with pension funds must be conscious of these trends in order to ensure that their clients or employers address the challenges timely and adequately.

---

[49] Meins et al. (2020), p. 13.

6.2 Policy Recommendations

Considering the author's description and analysis of ESG factors in pension funds regulations around the globe, the time has come to try to establish policy recommendations to governments (in general) and pension fund regulatory and supervisory authorities (in particular) for them to support the involvement of pension funds in ESG initiatives:

1. Regulatory and supervisory authorities should consider and assess: i) what is the best regulation tool for each specific purpose in ESG regulation, i.e. commands, economic instrument, nudges?; ii) what is the adequate level of regulation intensity, i.e. harder or softer?; iii) should there be (or not) sanctions for governing bodies, trustees, and property owners who do not comply?; and, more importantly, iv) how can the sometimes divergent interests of an increasingly disintermediated structure of corporate ownership align with trustees, consultants, external asset managers, beneficiaries, and also the community?
2. The author recommends clear, well communicated, consistent, and long-term policies and regulations so that strategic and financial players have the confidence to integrate ESG considerations into their business model. For instance, regulatory sludges and barriers and contradictory policy signals must be tackled such as the removing of fossil fuel subsidies, quantitative and qualitative investment obstacles in pensions regulations, namely in terms of scaling by, for example, pooling resources to invest jointly. After all, nudging pension funds to move their assets towards ESG initiatives will need stable and secure conditions, such as guarantees, public financing mechanisms, tax incentives, or the help of investment banks. This is even more true since this strategic shift involves risks and costs that may be difficult to the pension funds to assess or to hedge especially in the beginning;[50]
3. In order to ensure clear and transparent criteria and standards, and consequently their monitoring and evaluation, governments or regional organizations should consider sponsoring a rating agency or a standard setter to endorse ESG projects;
4. Governments, regulators, and supervisors should also promote both financial and ESG literacy of the governing bodies but also of the beneficiaries and consider requiring the appointment of trustees with experience in these sectors—particularly when investments are intended to be undertaken in-house, which would improve pension fund governance and oversight;[51]
5. In order to encourage institutional investors to be active, long-term investors, the regulatory and supervisory authorities should more often consider removing obstacles to active ownership and voting (such as taxation, takeover rules, length of mandates given to external managers, the turnover of funds, fees paid) to

[50] Croce et al. (2011), pp. 61–64.

[51] Croce et al. (2011), p. 64.

create incentives (such as requiring voting disclosure) and to encourage collaboration initiatives;[52]

6. Supervisors should embrace the principle of proportionality in its triple test (adequacy, necessity, and not excessive) to regulate and control the integration of ESG factors in pension funds: i) by not forgetting that the main objective of pension funds is ensuring pensions to beneficiaries and not promoting ESG investments *per se*; ii) by recognizing very different types, sizes, and structures of pension funds so one-size-regulation-does-not-fit-all which entails a more granular approach across all of the ESG regulations;
7. Imposing (proportional) external auditing should be regarded as essential for sustainability reporting once it can ensure quality and reliability (preventing greenwashing) while helping to enhance reporting skills and capacities through best practice sharing;
8. Concerning international law evolution, voluntary commitment trends, and the development of taxonomies (e.g., green, social, SDGs), regulators may go beyond ESG concerns and build investment strategies around broader environmental or developmental objectives such as the SDGs;
9. The regulators should be clear on the asset classes to be evaluated;
10. The involvement of stakeholders in the elaboration and enforcement of the Sustainability/ESG policies regarding risk management and positive impact investments should be endorsed by the regulators and supervisory authorities who should also look at the more detailed regulatory solutions for risk management in banking as a benchmark for pension funds and asset managers;
11. The regulators should also be more assertive in the definition and establishment of ESG risk assessment criteria and in guiding risk mitigation strategies;
12. Climate risk identification, monitoring, and disclosure should be emplaced since there are presently no specific requirements concerning pensions funds' climate change risks which is contrary to the spirit of the recommended disclosures from the Financial Stability Board (FSB) Task Force on Climate-related Financial Disclosures (TCFD);
13. The regulators should also consider establishing the disclosure of the proportion of the level of sustainability and of positive impact of the investment portfolio, considering contextual and granular characteristics (e.g., sector, size, level of disclosed engagement);
14. Procedures and criteria to prevent and combat greenwashing should be strengthened; and
15. Finally, tracing and assessing financial returns according to ESG classification should be contemplated, not only for ensuring the goodness of the strategy and activities of the pension funds but also for aligning interests with the trustees mainly through impacts on their remuneration schemes.

[52] Croce et al. (2011), p. 65.

6.3 What Does the Future Hold?

Covid-19, as a syndemic, has shown, in a very salient way, the close interconnections between environmental (including climate), social, governance, economic, and financial issues. If its brutal and unequal distributive impact raises hope in a more holistic, integrated, strengthened, and strategic approach to these concerns, and therefore in a new breath to integrating ESG factors in financial regulation, in particular concerning pensions funds, the ongoing war in Europe with growing preoccupations associated to inflation and food security seems to be deviating the attentions.

Nevertheless, even with a war, some challenges are long-lasting such as climate change, environmental decline, social inequality, and aging. Additionally, ESG risks will remain of crucial concern for pension funds and their advisers. Therefore, and attending to trends in financial and environmental regulations and the persuasive and the almost subliminal drive of soft law, self-regulations, and voluntary commitments, it is most likely that their "hoft" power[53] will frame, influence, and change public ESG regulations of pension funds.

Furthermore, the development of digital governments and regulators with an increasing integration of technology in policy, law, and regulation making opens the door to more precise, calibrated, and rapidly updated ESG regulations of pension funds and to new (technical, political, legal, and ethical) challenges. These are particularly concerning transparency, the quantity and quality of the data used (including their assessment and validation), the design of algorithms, and their determinist and narrowing potential.[54] In other words, the use of technology, especially big data and AI (machine-learning and intelligent algorithms) may help in this (crude) personalization of the regulation and of its definition of objective ESG indicators, making it more effective and fair. Moreover, RegTech, SuperTech, machine-consumable, and self-executing regulations may also improve compliance, especially in terms of disclosure, by decreasing the translation gap between the making and the consumption of regulation.

References

Albertini E (2013) Does environmental management improve financial performance? A meta-analytical review. Organ Environ 26(4)

Aubry J-P et al (2020) ESG investing and public pension funds: an update. Center for Retirement Research, Issue in Brief

Bauslaugh R (2021) Climate change legal implications for Canadian pension plan fiduciaries and policy-makers. McCarthy Tétrault

[53] *Hoft law* as soft law with hard effects. Catarino (2012b), p. 131; Catarino (2012a), p. 158.

[54] For all, see Saraiva (2022).

Brammer S et al (2006) Corporate social performance and stock returns: UK evidence from disaggregate measures. Financ Manag 35(3)
Busch T, Friede G (2018) The robustness of the corporate social and financial performance relation: a second-order meta-analysis. Corporate Social Responsibility and Environmental Management
Catarino L (2012a) A "Agencificação" na Regulação Financeira da União Europeia: Novo meio de regulação?, Revista de Concorrência e regulação, No. 9
Catarino L (2012b) O Direito Administrativo Global na Regulação Financeira Europeia: Alguns Problemas, Revista do Ministério Público
Croce R et al (2011) The role of pension funds in financing green growth initiatives. OECD Publishing, Paris
Flammer C (2015) Does corporate social responsibility lead to superior financial performance? A regression discontinuity approach. Articles in Advance
Friede G et al (2015) Esg and financial performance: aggregated evidence from more than 2000 empirical studies. J Sustain Finance Invest 5(4)
Harris JM (2000) Basic principles of sustainable development. Global Development and Environment Institute, Working Paper No. 00-04, Tufts University, Medford, MA
Lachance S, Stroehle JC (2021) The origins of ESG in pensions: strategies and outcomes. Prepared for presentation at the Pension Research Council Symposium, April 29-30, 2021 'Sustainable Investment in Retirement Plans: Challenges and Opportunities
Lewis A, Gilmour J (2022) ESG law: ESG and UK pension schemes: a matter of governance? ICLG
Margois J et al (2009) Does it pay to be good...and does it matter? A meta-analysis of the relationship between corporate social and financial performance. SSRN Electron J
Meins P et al (2020) Pension fund environmental, social and governance risk disclosures: developing global practice. Discussion Paper, Resource and Environment Working Group, International Actuarial Association
Moreira A (coord) (2019) Financial and Social Sustainability of the Portuguese Pension System. FFMS
OECD (2015) Pensions at a Glance 2015: OECD and G20 indicators. OECD Publishing, Paris
OECD (2019) OECD reviews of pension systems: Portugal, Paris. OECD Publishing
Pezzey J, Toman M (2002) Making sense of "sustainability", RFF, Issue Brief No. 02-25, Washington, DC
Queisser M, Whitehouse E (2005) Pensions at a glance: public policies across OECD countries. OECD, DELSA
Saraiva R (2022) Segurança Social, Direito e Tecnologia: entre rule-as-code e a personalização, RFDUL, special number
Sarra J (2022) Enhancing effective ESG and climate governance in pension fund oversight. Canada Climate Law Initiative
Scarpetta S, Blundell-Wignall A (2015) The next frontier for pension policy: focusing more on social sustainability. OECD
Steinbarth E, Bennett S (2018) Materiality matters: targeting the ESG issues that impact performance. Harvard Law School Forum on Corporate Governance
UNCTAD (2020) How public pension and sovereign wealth funds mainstream sustainability. Practices of the frontrunners and a proposed integration framework. UN
UNEP FI, PRI (2019) Fiduciary duty in the 21st century – Final Report
Wolf C (2003) Intergenerational justice. In: Frey RG, Wellman CH (eds) A companion to applied ethics. Blackwell

Benchmarking of National ESG Banking Regulations: State of Art and Remaining Challenges

Luciane Moessa de Souza

Abstract This article describes the contents of banking regulations that address ESG (environmental, social and governance) issues globally, analyses them critically, points out some inconsistencies and remaining gaps, and concludes with recommendations for further improvement. It includes only regulations or guidance issued by banking regulators/supervisors, not market self-regulatory initiatives. The topics addressed by banking regulations herein described include: (a) the definition of relevant environmental, social and climate issues; (b) the characteristics of a sound environmental and social and climate risk management (encompassing the definition of the universe of relevant transactions and customers, criteria for the identification of the risks, due diligence processes and data sources for the identification of risks, consequences of risk assessment, risk mitigation, monitoring, classification and reporting, risk management at portfolio level and scenario analysis, integration into traditional risk categories, risk assessment for new financial products); (c) the definition of positive environmental and social impacts that can be generated by financial products (without approaching green taxonomies); and (d) governance issues that are required from financial institutions to manage environmental and social risks and opportunities properly (including the definition of roles and responsibilities, staff dimension and capacity-building, budget, integration of ESG factors into compensation schemes, mapping and communication with stakeholders, business strategy and target-setting, principle of proportionality, timeframe for implementation of policies, effects of voluntary commitments, periodic review of policies, environmental and social impacts of banks own operations). It concludes with recommendations for further regulatory actions and for a minimal content of a sound ESG banking regulation.

L. Moessa de Souza (✉)
CIDEEFF, University of Lisbon, Lisbon, Portugal

Sustainable Inclusive Solutions (SIS), Rio de Janeiro, Brazil

R. Saraiva, P. A. Pardal (eds.), *Sustainable Finances and the Law*, Economic Analysis of Law in European Legal Scholarship 16,
https://doi.org/10.1007/978-3-031-49460-4_2

1 Introduction

From the first self-regulatory initiatives (creation of UNEP-FI in 1992) to the first comprehensive banking regulations addressing ESG (environmental, social, and governance) or sustainability factors back in 2011 (China and Bangladesh) and the current state when more than 30 banking regulators have somehow approached the topic, it has been a long journey. Guidelines or binding regulations are becoming more and more specific with a stronger focus on climate issues (since the aftermath of the Paris Agreement in 2015) but slowly moving beyond. The purpose of this article is to describe the contents of these regulatory initiatives (with a lot of good examples, many times coming from emerging economies) and then analyse them critically, pointing out inconsistencies and remaining gaps.

First of all, it is important to clarify that only regulations or guidance issued by banking regulators/supervisors were considered in this paper due to a number of reasons: (1) self-regulations/market-led initiatives are never universal once they depend upon voluntary adhesion, hence reaching only part of the market; (2) usually, there are no monitoring actions to ensure that compliance is actually achieved on the commitments made through self-regulations. The most common approach is reporting, but without any monitoring of adequacy or authenticity of contents of the reports, which are usually not audited and whose content is not verified even through a sample methodology.

Some studies even argue that average market performance is not higher among adherents to self-regulatory initiatives, due to the phenomenon of the "free-riders".[1] This does not mean that value is not recognized in self-regulatory initiatives, either in terms of contents or due to the fact that, in many countries, they arise before any regulatory action, led by market pioneers. Countries where there are self-regulatory initiatives are, for example, Brazil, Cambodia, Colombia, Ecuador, Kenya, Mexico, Mongolia, Panama, South Africa, Thailand and Turkey, as well as a number of European countries.

As of June 2022, it was possible to identify that banking regulators/supervisors in at least 25 countries, plus the European Union, had issued either mandatory regulation or non-binding guidance/principles on the integration of environmental, climate, or social factors into banking. A non-binding approach is more common and was adopted in Austria, Bangladesh, China, Egypt, Georgia, Germany, Ghana, Hong Kong, Kenya, Malaysia, the Netherlands, Nigeria, Pakistan, Paraguay, Australia, Philippines, Singapore, the United Kingdom, the United States, and Vietnam. The issuance of actual regulations (when non-compliance may justify the application of

[1]Unfortunately, it is quite common that self-regulatory mechanisms are distorted to work as greenwashing—what Wörsdörfer and others call "free-riding" and "adverse selection". The free-riders, he says, enjoy the [reputational] benefits without facing the costs of effective implementation—that end up harming those that really make the efforts associated with implementation while, at the same time, harming the global credibility of the initiative because the free-rider behaviour is unmasked after a while. Cf. Wörsdörfer (2013).

penalties) (or other sort of consequence) happened in Brazil, Honduras, Indonesia, Nepal and Peru. In a few countries (like Brazil, China, Bangladesh, and Vietnam), regulations or guidance have been issued more than once—there was more than one "wave" regarding the topic. It is important to clarify, however, that the fact that regulators issue only guidance rather than binding regulation does not mean that they might not verify market adherence to the guidance, as done, for example, by regulators of China, Bangladesh and Vietnam, who were some of the global pioneers in this field and kindly agreed to be interviewed by this author in a project sponsored by the German international cooperation agency GIZ in 2021. All of them have data on impacts of their ESG guidance.[2]

Furthermore, there are the cases of Colombia, Costa Rica, Mexico, Mongolia, Rwanda, South Africa and Sri Lanka, which are unique in the sense that the only regulatory guidance is actually a taxonomy of positive impacts of economic activities focussed on the mitigation and adaptation of climate change (or other E&S objectives, in some cases), mapped per relevant sectors and added by cross-sectoral activities—as such, their contents are not going to be addressed, because taxonomies deserve a specific analysis.

Before moving to the contents of the ESG banking regulations that are going to be analysed, it might be useful to provide a definition of regulation and a few considerations on what motivates regulatory action and what can be considered a good regulation.

As a matter of definition, Martin Lodge and Kai Wegrich provide a comprehensive view: "Regulation is a phenomenon that includes three components: standard-setting (to provide for overall 'direction'), behaviour-modification tools (to provide for means of enforcement to change people's behaviour) and information-gathering (to allow for knowledge about what is 'happening'). Any discussion of regulation that focuses on one component alone needs to be explicit about such limitation as regulatory regimes can only achieve their intended effects if all three regime components operate in non-dysfunctional ways."[3]

On the motivations behind regulation, the lessons of Fiona Haines are insightful. After quoting a couple of examples in which economic or human disasters of our recent history were followed by new regulations, she says: "regulation embodies the promise of modernity. It creates the vision of technical mastery over threats (whether from technology, terrorists or financial mismanagement). It offers hope of learning from the past to control the hazards of the future. (...) Regulation as a modernist project, then, involves the development of processes and styles of enforcement that

[2]For example, the State Bank of Vietnam reported that: (a) in the period 2017–2020, there was an average growth of green credit balance of 22.97% per year; (b) most credit institutions have issued guidelines for the implementation of environmental and social risk assessment in credit granting activities; and (c) the number of outstanding loans assessed for environmental and social risks in 2020 was 5.59 times higher compared to 2017.

[3]Lodge and Wegrich (2012), p. 25.

are argued to ensure greater and greater levels of compliance that will minimise a risk, or avoid a specified harm."[4]

Nevertheless, "the gap between the reforms and what actually happens on the ground, in terms of actual compliance, can be considerable".[5] She points out in her analysis that, to "be successful, regulation must embrace actuarial, sociocultural and political risk reduction through a common regulatory project", in order to create "a positive dynamic where a 'race to the top' in risk reduction occurs".[6] She acknowledges that there is a trend to resist to more regulation for different reasons: (a) "socioculturally based fears often lie behind the perennial demand for a strong command and control regulatory response from government"; (b) "pressing demand for them [regulators] to release the chains around the creativity of the market".[7]

She provides a picture of what type of regulatory action is needed: "Proponents argue that better regulation and enforcement practices, greater coherence, firmer connectedness between various regimes and higher levels of integrity between regime and its actual capacity to achieve set goals need to be established. Then, it is argued, regulation can allow both greater levels of productivity and wealth while reducing the harmful 'side-effects' of competitive markets."[8]

As such, "whatever regulation we do end up with must be the most efficient, sharply defined and transparent set of rules and requirements".[9]

Adding this author's own contribution to this debate, synthetically it can be said that a good regulation is defined by the fact that it pursues the *right goals* (and the acknowledgement of the interconnections and competing demands of public policies is needed for the adequate definition of these goals) in the *most efficient way* (hence, being able to achieve more comprehensive, higher quality, and lasting outcomes with less financial costs, less effort, and faster).

2 Definition of Relevant Environmental and Social Topics

The first topic that raises doubts when integrating environmental and social/governance considerations into banking is which exactly are the issues that fit into this approach, especially in a historic moment when many limit this approach to climate change. Most regulators give examples about it, all of them clarifying that they are non-exhaustive. The mention of examples (especially when the list is quite comprehensive) provides much more clarity, which is certainly needed for banks in order to define their entire strategy, from relevant databases to be consulted to questions to be

[4]Haines (2010), p. 3.
[5]Haines (2010), p. 5.
[6]Haines (2010), p. 6.
[7]Haines (2010), p. 6.
[8]Haines (2010), p. 12.
[9]Haines (2010), p. 29.

made to clients or invested companies, and also regarding financial products to be developed aiming at a positive impact. Of course, it is not possible to develop a consistent strategy to address a problem before defining what the problem actually is.

One first difference that is possible to observe regarding regulators' approaches is that some (like the Georgian) consider that climate issues fit into environmental issues, while others (like the Brazilian) consider it a separate category. There are even cases (like regulations from Kenya and Australia) where the only topics actually covered are climate issues—other environmental and social issues are not included at all.

In terms of listing the topics that are included in each category (environmental, social, and climate), the Brazilian regulation of 2021 is by far the most detailed: even the "excessive use of natural resources" was mentioned (which is a performance issue, going much beyond compliance with environmental rules and implying a clear economic advantage as well) and also economic activities that, even if they are legal might negatively impact the reputation of the institution due to environmental damages. Other examples are more linked to compliance issues, such as environmental violations in general (including illegal deforestation, illegal use of water resources, pollution of air, water, or soil, biodiversity degradation, traffic or cruelty against animals) and non-compliance with environmental permit requirements. Finally, environmental transition risks (changes in environmental regulations that might negatively impact the institution) were also included, following the example of climate transition risks.

For social risks, topics mentioned in the Brazilian regulation include modern slavery; illegal child labour; illegal discrimination; any type of labour harassment or labour traffic; violations of labour regulations (including labour health and safety ones); damages to indigenous people or other traditional communities, damages to historic or cultural heritage, damages to urban heritage, violations of data privacy laws, disasters that cause damages to communities (such as collapses of mining tailing dams); social transition risks due to regulatory changes were also included. The Georgian regulation also exemplifies social topics, i.e., human rights, employment and industrial relations, corruption prevention and consumer issues.

For climate, international standards (such as the Taskforce for Climate-related Financial Disclosures—TCFD and the Taskforce for Nature-related Financial Disclosures—TNFD) with definitions of physical (including extreme weather events and permanent changes in weather patterns or consequences of these changes such as rising sea levels) and transition risks (changes in regulation, market preference, investors' demands, technological innovations, reputational risks) were adopted in all of their comprehensiveness in the Brazilian regulation. Besides banking regulators from Brazil, Australia, Georgia and Kenya, other ones who adopted detailed definitions or provided many examples of climate issues are from the United Kingdom, the Netherlands, Germany, and Australia.

3 Risk Management

Most regulations include some sort of definition of risk management encompassing identification, measurement/assessment, mitigation/control, and monitoring of risks, a full system that is expected to be developed by financial institutions. Many also mention classification and reporting of risks. This item approaches all of these phases and how they can be developed, starting with the definition of the universe to be managed.

Before addressing them, though, it is interesting to refer that the "Principles for the effective management and supervision of climate-related financial risks" published by the Basel Committee on Banking Supervision/Bank of International Settlements (BIS) in June 2022 mention, under Principle 4, that: "Banks should incorporate climate-related financial risks into their internal control frameworks across the three lines of defence to ensure sound, comprehensive and effective identification, measurement and mitigation of material climate-related financial risks." Principles 6 and 7, conversely, explore identification, monitoring and management of risks, while Principle 7 goes further with regards to reporting.

3.1 Universe of Relevant Transactions (Types and Thresholds)/Customers

A few regulators are very clear on the *transactions to be assessed,* such as the Nepal Central Bank, who mentions "project finance", long-term lending (term longer than one year), SME finance and small loans above a certain value (the Nepalese regulator defines the thresholds). It also establishes minimal criteria for "all business purpose loans" (such as working capital) which are: (a) compliance with environmental and social (E&S) regulations and (b) not to be in the exclusion list. The Bangladeshi regulator also defines thresholds. The Nigerian regulator provides examples of all categories of financial transactions to be assessed. The Peruvian regulator requires assessment only for corporate finance above USD 10 million. The Pakistani regulator defines clearly the universe of transactions to be assessed, using as criteria the type, value and term, mentioning also the type of due diligences that should be applied to each category (in a model similar to Nepal).

The Central Bank of Ghana exemplifies relevant financial transactions (corporate and small and medium enterprises—SMEs—lending, project finance, leasing and equity investments) and mentions that each bank might define a threshold transaction value considering the "potential severity of negative E&S impacts associated".

The problem with the definition of thresholds is that it does not consider the FI size, on the one hand (a value that is not relevant for one FI might be for another, and vice-versa), and the aggregated impact of all of the small transactions at portfolio-level and economic/systemic level, on the other hand. It also disregards the level of E&S risks associated to the economic activity.

Many regulators also mention the "principle of proportionality" with regards to the transaction value (such as the Brazilian and the German ones). However, the "proportionality" criterion still does not consider the aggregated impact of the small transactions at portfolio-level and at economic/systemic level.

So, definitions using thresholds and "proportionality" as criteria should at least be added by sectoral/industry consideration (as done by the Nepal Central Bank), which clearly defines the "critical sectors" where transactions should be assessed against E&S criteria, irrespectively of value. In any country that has a sound environmental permit issuance system, a simple criterion for this universe (critical sectors but small transaction values) is to require at least compliance with E&S regulations. This would mean checking the existence of a valid permit and the environmental/social track record (in terms of investigations of violations and application of penalties) for all of the industries that need an environmental permit (once the need of environmental permits is clearly associated with higher community/occupational health and safety risks as well).

The Georgian regulator requires that banks disclose "to which activities its risk management and mitigation approach applies", describing that the universe should include at least "corporate lending and securities underwriting; project-based and asset-based financing; and any other financial or operational activities undertaken by the entity and considered material."

Other regulators prefer to refer to "relevance", such as the one of Honduras, that mentions "relevance to FIs [financial institutions] activities"; the Brazilian, who also refers to the "principle of relevance", and the Chinese, that clarifies it expects all "relevant financial transactions" to be assessed. The Pakistani regulator does the same, mentioning that the only exception are loans to natural persons. However, none of them defines "relevance" and in which sense it must be understood (financial relevance or environmental/social relevance).

Moreover, only a few regulators addressed the issue of the E&S risk assessment of the pending transactions. The regulator of Honduras established this requirement and gave banks a 6-month period for the assessment of their portfolios. Pakistani regulator also required so.

Regarding investment banking, most regulators do not clearly mention the *securities underwriting* activities as included in E&S risk management, but the Georgian and Singaporean ones do. This is definitely aligned with the purpose of a comprehensive E&S risk management system, especially when dealing with larger companies, whose impacts are therefore bigger.

Another way to address that is to require *E&S risk management at customer level*, as mentioned by regulators from China, the Netherlands, Nigeria and Singapore.

In both cases, the industry is key for the definition of the need of assessment that is appropriately linked to the environmental/social relevance. The financial relevance needs to be measured/addressed at portfolio level.

Finally, another key issue often disregarded by regulators is the *environmental assessment of real estate collaterals* which might have environmental liabilities either in terms of soil contamination or illegal deforestation, and these circumstances might undermine their market value. Bangladeshi, Brazilian (2021), Georgian and

Singaporean regulators addressed the topic (as well as the USA regulation, which is focussed solely on this topic). Furthermore, real estate collaterals are exposed to climate physical risks (as a result of both extreme weather events and rising sea levels) as highlighted by Dutch and Austrian regulators. The German and Singaporean regulators also remember that real estate collateral is exposed to climate transition risks as their energy efficiency might affect their market value. The Georgian regulator requires the disclosure of the most relevant ESG risks to which collaterals are exposed.

3.2 *Criteria for Identification/Assessment of E&S Risks*

3.2.1 E&S Legal Compliance as Criterion

A few regulators, such as those from China, Nepal, Philippines, Nigeria, Paraguay, Peru and Honduras, refer to compliance with national E&S regulations as minimal criterion for E&S risk assessment, sometimes clearly prohibiting the loan granting in the case of violations (e.g., China and Paraguay). In the Brazilian regulations (2021), signs of violations (when there is no certainty yet) are clearly considered risks—and, as said, there is also reference to two other relevant risks, lack of compliance with environmental permit requirements and potential/likely risks of more stringent E&S regulations.

On the social side, the regulators guidance in Germany, Austria and Ghana also includes anti-corruption and anti-bribery issues (including facilitation of whistleblowing), as well as tax honesty. German and Austrian guidances also mention labour collective rights. Risks or impacts on tribal people are often forgotten in European regulations, though, which is not justified, as most large European banks operate in other continents where these communities do exist.

A few regulations, such as the ones from Pakistan, Ghana, Malaysia and Nepal, even list the relevant E&S national and international regulations in an annex to the regulation.

3.2.2 E&S Performance/Efficiency as Criteria

Other regulators (e.g., Pakistan, Ghana, Honduras, Nepal: Annex I of regulation, Germany and Austria) add the description of E&S topics beyond compliance such as:

- air emissions;
- GHG emissions (considering both electricity and fuels mix/efficiency);
- soil contamination or erosion;
- water use/efficiency;
- wastewater management;

- solid waste management;
- land use conversion;
- labour health and safety conditions;
- workplace diversity;
- risks of child labour and forced labour in the value-chain;
- community and consumers health, safety and security;
- land use conversion/biodiversity impacts;
- impacts on tribal people;
- resettlement of communities; land conflicts; and
- impacts on cultural heritage.

German and Austrian guidelines even mention the combat to inequality.

The Austrian regulator mentions the need of analysis of the value chain (especially suppliers). The Brazilian regulation, as said, brings a very relevant environmental topic that is related to performance/efficiency, i.e., excessive use of natural resources.

A separate category included in many recent regulations is that of climate risks based on the definitions of transition and physical risks made by TCFD—regulations from Australia, Austria, Brazil, Germany, Hong Kong, Kenya, the Netherlands, Singapore, and the United Kingdom, all include them.

Others simply refer to international/best practices standards (e.g., Nepal, Nigeria, and Singapore) either as safeguards (such as the IFC E&S standards) or as source (e.g., GRI) of relevant key performance indicators—KPIs (water use; energy use; energy mix; GHG emissions; E&S management internal capacity; etc.). The Malaysian regulator clearly recommends a combination of both national and international standards.

It is worth clarifying that, when local environmental and social regulations are below minimal international standards, the adoption of the latter is an example of market best practice—and the relevance of "performance-based (or beyond compliance) approaches" (that might be included in regulations) becomes clear in such cases.

3.2.3 Description of Industry-Specific E&S KPIs

Finally, in terms of criteria, a few regulators (e.g., from Pakistan, Paraguay and Georgia) require that banks/FIs develop industry-specific criteria, while others already indicate minimal (or examples of) KPIs at industry level, such as the banking regulators of Bangladesh, China, Nigeria (agriculture; energy; oil and gas), Honduras, Nepal, Ghana (agriculture/forestry, construction and real estate, manufacturing, oil and gas and mining, energy), Malaysia (agriculture and fishery, forestry, beverage/food manufacturing, mining, metals and chemicals, energy, infrastructure), etc. The Australian regulator mentions that financial institutions should create sector-specific policies, which is essential to assess E&S performance effectively. The Brazilian regulation requires that financial institutions disclose the list of industries to which restrictions exist due to environmental, social or climate factors. CBRC (Chinese banking regulator) reported in an interview in 2021 that ICBC (Industrial and Commercial Bank of China) has specific guidelines for 60 different industries.

Ideally, industry specific KPIs should be followed by weight criteria once each KPI has a specific relevance in the productive process of each industry. For example, the use of energy, water, or land have different weights in mining, agriculture (also varying according to commodity), or for each type of manufacturing. Land use is much less relevant for manufacturing than it is for agriculture—while the opposite is true for energy. However, no regulations have addressed this point thus far, and there are not even many self-regulatory initiatives that do so. The exception is the UNEP-WCMC tool ENCORE (Exploring Natural Capital Opportunities, Risks and Exposure) that assigns ratings of low, medium, or high materiality to impacts and dependencies from water, soil, air, terrestrial and water ecosystems, as well as waste and disturbances to more than 140 different industries,[10] illustrating with examples of each category.

3.3 *Due Diligence Process/Databases/KPIs (for Identification and Monitoring of Risks)*

A few regulators demand a preliminary classification of risks based on industry/ activities to be financed (the Honduras regulator even refers to the environmental agency categorization of risks based on industry) or also on the type of financial transaction or even its value (or a combination of both, as done by the Nepalese regulator). Other relevant criteria are geography/location (once environmental sensitivity is definitely affected by it) and the size of the specific enterprise/project (considering number of employees and/or revenues once the borrower environmental/social governance capacity varies according to it).

This preliminary classification should guide the *level of depth/comprehensiveness of the due diligence process*, varying from a simple documentation verification process (and/or use of public or paid databases) to questionnaires/interviews with borrowers, on-site inspection, sometimes even including the use of external experts for E&S risk assessment. More complex projects might also need a stakeholder mapping and dialogue to identify potential risks and adverse impacts and strategies to mitigate them. While most regulators give examples of diligences to be developed, others (Nepal) already define the diligences to be developed according to the type of financial transaction. While linking the type of diligence to the potential risk level seems to be appropriate, adopting the type of financial transaction as a criterion for that (rather than the industry and the size of the business operations) is arguable.

The Nepalese regulator describes guidance for *site visits*, citing examples of E&S issues to be assessed (such as labour safety conditions, waste management,

[10] https://encore.naturalcapital.finance/en.

production processes) and signs of potential concerns.[11] It also provides questionnaires with relevant KPIs to be used by banks in the E&S risk assessment.

With regards to the sources of information (databases) beyond the borrower itself, the Singaporean regulator mentions the use of both public *databases* or proprietary (provided by private third-parties) ones. The Brazilian regulator mentions the use of public databases, which must be understood as both data provided by public entities (no matter the size of the company or natural person) and data disclosed publicly by listed companies directly or through their adhesion to initiatives like the Carbon Disclosure Project (CDP), Stock Exchanges Sustainability indices, etc. The Chinese regulator created a **platform for sharing E&S information between financial bodies and E&S public bodies**, which is an example to be followed.[12] The Malaysian regulator refers to various databases with geospatial (or other sort of) information, such as tools managed by the World Resources Institute (like Global Forest Watch), the Water Risk Filter (WWF), the Carbon Disclosure Project, the Sustainability Policy Transparency Toolkit (SPOTT). Many others could be added to this list, both at international and national levels. Moreover, it mentions **external certifications and verifications**, such as the ones who check compliance with ISO systems or with sectoral or commodity-level standards (like Roundtables on Sustainable Palm Oil, Beef, Biomaterials, etc, Better Cotton Initiative, Marine Stewardship Council and so on).

A few regulators (Singapore, Germany and Austria) mention as another potential source of relevant E&S information the **ESG ratings** from credit rating agencies. The Austrian regulator emphasizes, however, that different rating agencies achieve different conclusions for the same company. It is possible to add that most rating agencies do not disclose their methodologies, the topics assessed and data sources, so it does not make sense to consider these ratings as a reliable source of information, unless regulations start to demand minimal levels of transparency/consistency (ESG ratings are not even regulated yet).

Finally, it is of foremost importance to consider additional sources of information (even if it might entail a certain degree of uncertainty): **media** (both traditional press and other online sources) and **relevant stakeholders**—the latter especially for projects/activities with higher E&S impacts or risks. The Peruvian regulation makes this very clear regarding stakeholders, requiring not only a mapping, but a dialogue with affected communities, especially because this regulation is focussed on financial transactions over USD 10 million and with high E&S impacts. It is important to

---

[11]Nepal Rastra Bank. 2018. Guideline on Environmental & Social Risk Management (ESRM) for Banks and Financial Institutions, 18. Available at: https://www.nrb.org.np/contents/uploads/2019/12/Guidelines-Guideline_on_Environmental__Social_Risk_Management_for_Banks_and_Financial_Institutions_2018-new.pdf.

[12]In a research interview with this author in 2021, China Banking and Insurance Regulatory Commission (CBIRC) reported that "competent authorities provide CBIRC with a list of companies that violate environmental and labour health and safety legislation every 6 months. This list is shared with banks."

remember that not all information is available online, so stakeholder engagement is also an important strategy.

The Hong Kong regulator asks FIs if they have an appropriate data management framework for identifying, measuring, monitoring, reporting, controlling or mitigating environmental risks. The topic of data collection is also mentioned by the Egyptian regulator.

The Austrian regulator mentions the need of a plan to develop a sound database, qualitative and quantitatively. The Dutch one also refers to the need of identifying and addressing data gaps on climate risks.

Only one regulator (Malaysian) recommends a quantitative-based strategy for the assessment of risks, which is very appropriate and absolutely necessary to define the magnitude of risks: "As far as possible, the IFI [Islamic financial institution] should use data-driven measures. For quantifying the impact and decision-making, the IFI should consider positive and negative impacts for each financing or investment activity, independently, and not offsetting the two."[13]

As a matter of fact, each type of risk should be given a different weight considering the severity of its nature, the likelihood of its materialization, and the size (in terms of E&S impact) of the financed activities.

The Georgian regulator stands out as the only one that requires banks to disclose their due diligence approach. This is actually one of the four key elements that make it possible to evaluate the consistency of the risk management of each bank—the other three are the data sources, the topics covered, and the decision-making process (including the consequences of the risk assessment that is addressed in the next item). It is also worth highlighting that this regulation mentions that the assessment should include the supply-chain, the "identified areas of significant risks", and the KPIs to assess progress and trends—all of them to be disclosed as well.

3.4 Consequences of Risk Assessment

The final outcome of the risk assessment process is not addressed by all regulators, but a few clarify that, when the risk assessment concludes that the risk is high (or too high), there should be appropriate consequences:

(a) Refusal/avoidance of risk: either because of the high individual risk (at transaction or customer level) or because of the existence of a limit in terms of risk-level in the portfolio, the risk assessment might lead to a refusal of the transaction; only a few regulators mention this as an example, though;

[13] Bank Negara Malaysia. 2019. Value-based Intermediation Financing and Investment Impact Assessment Framework, 31. Available at: https://www.bnm.gov.my/-/value-based-intermediation-financing-and-investment-impact-assessment-framework-guidance-document.

(b) Risk classification and mitigation actions: the Nepalese regulator clearly states that transactions with E&S high and medium risks demand mitigation measures (see examples below in section "e" on risk mitigation); a clear definition of a trigger to risk mitigation measures looks very interesting;
(c) Decision-making process/escalation to higher level: many regulators (e.g., from Germany, the Netherlands, Austria, Bangladesh and Pakistan) mention the need of escalation to a higher decision-level in case of higher risks; however, this only makes sense if the FI does not have a previously defined risk appetite strategy at the portfolio-level; and
(d) Rating of the transaction (or other reflection in its conditions): Chinese, Georgian, Nigerian, Bangladeshi and Pakistani regulators recommend that the E&S risk level be integrated into rating; regulators who addressed the topic more recently, such as from Malaysia, Nepal, Australia and Singapore, clearly require that higher E&S risks can/should be reflected in the pricing of the transaction.

In terms of implementation, officers of the China Banking and Insurance Regulatory Commission reported in a research interview with this author in 2021 that, in China, "major banks use higher loan pricing for carbon intensive sectors (cement, iron and steel, refinery, etc) with interest rates 20–30% higher than the average."

3.5 *Risk Mitigation*

Most regulators mention the need of mitigating identified risks. For this purpose, a number of tools are usually referred:

3.5.1 E&S Covenants for Loan Agreements

Regulators from USA, Bangladesh, China and Peru were the first to mention them; the new Brazilian regulation (2021) also mentions them; regulations of Honduras and Pakistan go beyond and provide a list of very useful examples:

- Compliance with E&S regulations (national laws and treaties ratified by the country);
- Compliance with permits conditions/requirements;
- Reporting duties on specific E&S KPIs;
- Allow free access to physical facilities;
- Duties regarding supply chain E&S risk management;
- Duties regarding E&S governance structure;
- Duties of reporting any E&S investigation procedures or application of penalties against the borrower;
- Suspension of tranches or acceleration of the loan if there is violation of these duties.

3.5.2 Action Plans

Action plans with specific targets and timelines for critical E&S issues are mentioned implicitly or explicitly by regulators from China, Peru, Pakistan, Malaysia, Honduras, Nepal and the Netherlands.

An example from the Dutch regulator is that banks customers from CO_2 intensive sectors should be required to have an energy transition strategy in place.

3.5.3 Engagement with Customers

Regulators from UK, Germany, Georgia and Singapore, for example, refers to the need of engagement with customers to improve their E&S performance.

3.5.4 Offer of a Loan to Improve the E&S Compliance/Efficiency

The Nepalese regulation, for example, mentions the new business opportunities.

3.5.5 Environmental Insurance

Regulators from Ghana and the Netherlands mention it. The Dutch regulator does the same, exemplifying with customers whose production is highly dependent on weather conditions.

3.5.6 Restructuring the Size or Term of the Transaction

Again, regulatory guidelines from Ghana and the Netherlands refer to this mitigatory action. The Dutch regulator/supervisor exemplifies: loans to industries with higher climate transition risks might have lower term limits; clients whose real estate collaterals have higher climate physical or transition (energy efficiency) risks should have a lower credit limit.

It is useful to mention that the Georgian regulator recommends the disclosure of the **prioritisation** of risks and also the criteria to do so.

3.6 Risk Classification

A few regulators require the classification of E&S risks at transaction-level (Bangladesh, Brazil, China, Germany, Nigeria and Peru) sometimes already bringing the criteria, such as:

- industry;
- geography (Ghana's regulator gives two reasons why location is relevant, i.e. different E&S legislation and different levels of enforcement; however, the most relevant reason is the different levels of E&S sensitivity such as stress-level of environmental resources—biodiversity, water, soil, air—or the presence of vulnerable communities; Bangladeshi, Chinese, Nigerian, Pakistani and Peruvian regulators refer to the need of location consideration as well);
- compliance with E&S regulations;
- E&S risk management capacity/efficiency/performance (in this regard, it is important to consider the size—revenues/employees—of the enterprise/project); and
- transaction type (as exemplified by the Ghana regulator, the term of the financial relationship is a very relevant criterion; it also mentions the value, but these should actually be considered at portfolio level).

The Brazilian regulation allows each bank to have its own classification system, but already refers the criteria: industry, location, E&S compliance, E&S efficiency/risk management capacity. And it is worth to add that another specific regulation (Resolution BCB 151/2021) requires that the location of financed activities and projects, as well as of the operations of all issuers of bonds and equities, is shared with the Central Bank of Brazil, together with the economic sector and, if existent, any information concerning either environmental, social and climate risks or positive environmental, social or climate impact (including, but not limited to the emission, neutralization or capture of greenhouse gases). The last 2022 Philippines regulation refers to the need of considering the location of "client's business or sources of income, collaterals, or projects being financed" as it "may indicate potential increases in default probabilities and depreciation of the value of collateral" (2022b, p. 11).

The Pakistani regulator proposes a risk matrix of five levels that considers the severity (magnitude) and the probability of the E&S risks in order to classify them as extreme, hight, medium, low or negligible, but does not specify the criteria.

As a matter of fact, it would be interesting to see a combination of magnitude and probability of the risks, using all of the referred criteria to achieve a sound classification.

The Nigerian regulator recommends a classification that considers transaction type, size of customers activities (corporate or Small and Medium Enterprises—SMEs) and industry (a relevant criterion especially for SMEs).

The regulators from Paraguay and Honduras also mention the magnitude of impacts, that actually derives from industry/activity and levels of compliance and capacity/efficiency.

A few regulators (from Peru, Paraguay, Honduras and Nepal) already provide a risk classification into three categories (in general, inspired in the Equator Principles/IFC performance standards categorization), considering: the magnitude and the reversibility of the E&S adverse impacts, as well as the customer's ability/commitment to manage them.

Going beyond, a few regulators establish the **uses for the classification**, such as:

- frequency of risk monitoring;
- portfolio-level risk monitoring (and target-setting);
- rating of the transaction (reflecting on interest rates)—the Singaporean regulator does so.

The Honduras' regulation mentions very appropriately that risk monitoring can lead to the change of the classification of risk level.

It is important to emphasize that, if regulators create a classification system that should be applied by supervised entities, it will be possible for them to have a clear picture of systemic risks, because otherwise, in the current model (adopted for most jurisdictions), where FIs are free to define their own classifications, it is not possible to compare them to each other and it is not possible to see the "big picture" according to standardised criteria. Even for the financial institutions, it would be beneficial to have a clear comparison to their competitors.

Today, a systemic view of the risks is only possible (in a limited way) when and if there are platforms where at least industries and location of financed activities are registered (which is mostly not the case for locations, with the exception of Brazil, where the Central Bank requires this information from December 2022 on, as said above). But of course it is not very wise or even reasonable to consider that all the companies of the same industry and same location have the same E&S performance. It is more than necessary to consider their own compliance, performance and governance capacity, based in sound criteria and data sources.

3.7 Monitoring and Its Consequences

Although most regulators mention risk monitoring (whose tools and data sources are basically the same as those used for the identification of risks), only a few (Paraguay and Honduras, for example) mention the criteria/contents for its development such as:

- Compliance with action plans;
- Validity of environmental permits or other relevant authorizations;
- Compliance with new E&S regulations;
- Trackrecord in terms of E&S legal compliance;
- E&S efficiency according to relevant KPIs (see examples in section b) "criteria for identification/assessment of E&S risks" above) according to regular reporting;
- Media information on the customer project or activity;
- Complaints mechanism information (contents of stakeholders' complaints and response to them).

Another relevant issue that is mentioned by a few regulations (Honduras) is the potential consequences of E&S risk monitoring, including:

- Suspension of tranches (for long-term loans);
- Acceleration of the loan;
- Change of risk classification (for higher or lower risk-level); and
- Requirement of an action plan.

The suspension of tranches and acceleration of loans is also already mentioned by the Chinese regulator.

An additional issue that could be mentioned is the need of establishment of sound criteria to define the frequency of monitoring appropriate to the risk level (using criteria like the ones described in item 2.6 above).

3.8 Portfolio Risk Assessment: Tools and Methodologies

Regulations/guidance from Australia, Bangladesh, China, Pakistan, Malaysia, Nepal, European Union, Georgia, Brazil and Philippines (2022), among others, portfolio-level mention risk management. Moreover, the BIS' principles for climate risk management establish that banks should "*manage the concentrations within and between risk types associated with climate-related financial risks. For example, banks could use metrics or heatmaps to assess and monitor concentration of exposure to geographies and sectors with higher climate-related risk*" (Principle 8).

The Brazilian and Georgian regulations refer to the need of assessing significant *concentrations of credit risk exposure* in terms of ESG factors, especially climate risks. The Australian and Kenyan mention the same for climate risks.

The Pakistani and German regulators mention the definition of **limits in exposure to environmental risks** as a tool for that. Hong Kong also considers the definition of limits in exposure to climate/environmental risks and restrictions to certain sectors or activities at portfolio-level (the Kenyan does the same for climate risks). More sophisticated approaches refer to *limits to both sectors and geographies* (or a combination of them), as mentioned by Australian regulator.

The Australian and Malaysian regulators recommend the adoption of portfolio-level targets.

More recent regulations/guidance (from UK, Singapore, Germany, Hong Kong, Austria, Philippines, the Netherlands, European Union, Brazil, Australia and Kenya), inspired by the TCFD recommendations, mention that portfolio risk management should include **stress tests** and **scenario analysis**—tools that are also included under principles 5 and 12 of the BIS' principles for climate risk management. Principle 18 of the BIS' principles provides more specific guidelines regarding stress tests.

The Hong Kong regulator asks about the number of scenario analyses conducted in the previous three years, the scale (portfolios and asset classes), time horizons and the number and description of the scenarios used. It also asks about the size (values/percentages) of the FIs' exposure to relevant risks and methodologies used to measure them. It asks about criteria for monitoring (update) information, such as thresholds, concentration of risks and the frequency of monitoring.

The last Philippines guidelines recommend the "analysis of portfolios vis-à-vis the developments in the national government's policies and business environment" in order to get "indicators of the level of transition risk exposures of banks" (2022b, p. 12).

The Dutch regulator provides examples of stress tests using likely scenarios, one for physical risks (flood risk stress) in a cross-sectoral way (considering real estate collaterals' loss of value), and another for transition risks (replacement of fossil fuels per renewable energies), considering the industries across the fossil fuels value-chain (considering their stranded assets and loss of revenues).

The use of quantitative tools and metrics is recommended by the UK, Australia and Singapore regulators.

The Dutch regulator provides a few examples of metrics: concentration of CO_2 intensive assets; GHG emissions, avoided emissions and sequestration of emissions of the portfolio.

The Austrian regulator also provides several examples of tools for portfolio climate risk assessment, such as "heat maps" (with indication of sectors and geographies more exposed to climate physical and transition risks), percentage of companies that disclose CO_2 (should rather be GHG) emissions, sensitivity analysis, disclosure of CO_2 (GHG) emissions. The Dutch regulator also exemplifies with "heat maps", where different levels of transition and physical risks are assigned for different industries/sectors.

Regulators/supervisors from Brazil, UK, Austria, Netherlands and European Union mention the need to consider environmental (or social) risks in the **ICAAP (Internal Capital Adequacy Assessment Process)**. The Principles issued by the Bank for International Settlements (BIS)[14] and the guidances of the Australian prudential regulator, of the Bank of England and of the Central Bank of Kenya mention only climate risks for this purpose.

A potential tool that could be used by regulators would be a type of **taxonomy in terms of E&S risk level**, including the assignment of risks to specific industries and geographies according to their E&S sensitivity—this would also facilitate the comparison of the performance of different financial institutions, as well as systemic risks to the whole financial system, as mentioned in item 2.6.

3.9 Reporting/Disclosure and Relevant Indicators

As mentioned by the Malaysian regulator, "*appropriate and regular disclosures are necessary to communicate the progress and impact of the VBI strategy*" (p. 9), where VBI stands for Value-Based Intermediation financial activities.

[14] BIS, "Principles for the effective management and supervision of climate-related financial risks". Available at: https://www.bis.org/bcbs/publ/d532.htm.

There are three different target audiences of reporting for FIs on E&S risk management:

- Senior management;
- Regulator/supervisor; and
- External stakeholders (FIs customers, investors, and society).

Regulators do not always distinguish the three levels, but they have different purposes so, ideally, there should be definitions of minimal contents for each of them. The frequency of reporting should also be defined—although the most common is annual disclosure, a few regulators (Bangladesh and Vietnam) require quarterly disclosures for them. The BIS principles for climate risk management emphasize, under principle 7, the need of sound internal reporting systems with the aim to "produce timely information to ensure effective board and senior management decision-making".

Examples of indicators to be disclosed are:

(a) For external stakeholders:

   - Sustainability strategic objectives and risk appetite (Philippines);
   - Portfolio E&S risk/impact level (Nepal, Malaysia) with breakdown per industry (Philippines);
   - Reporting according to TCFD framework (Austria, Brazil, Germany, Hong Kong, the Netherlands and the United Kingdom);
   - Incorporation of ESG factors into business models and strategy; governance and due diligence processes; risk management; and KPIs to measure progress and trends, targets and outcomes (Georgia);
   - Monitoring and mitigatory actions (Australia);
   - Remuneration policies regarding sustainability risk management (Austria);
   - Financial products with positive E&S impacts (Philippines); and
   - Impact of applying the sustainable banking principles (Egypt);

(b) For regulator (examples from Ghana's regulation):

   - Implementation of the E&S risk management structure;
   - Identification of KPIs, baselines, target-setting;
   - Implementation of the targets;
   - Examples of KPIs: number/percentage of employees trained on ESG issues; number of hours of training; percentage of loan portfolio screened for E&S risks (note that this is misleading because portfolios might also include loans to natural persons and sectors that have no relevant E&S risks);

(c) For the regulator or senior management:

   - Capacity-building activities;
   - Team size/expertise;
   - Targets (and past achievements) in terms of reduction of risk exposure and increase of positive impact transactions;

- Percentage of transactions assessed with respect to E&S risks (the Vietnamese regulator requires this; the Nigerian requires disclosure of the percentage per financial product, per industry and per risk category);
- Consequences of E&S risk assessment (declined transactions; action plans; other engagement actions; etc)—the Vietnamese regulator requires the disclosure for itself of the percentage of declined transactions; and
- Tracking of loan defaults for E&S reasons (Bangladesh, Brazil, Pakistan), according to E&S risk level, or according to industry/geography/level of company ESG compliance/performance.

The Austrian and Georgian regulators mention that the risk management function must inform the management body both on a regular and on an *ad-hoc* basis about company-specific sustainability risks covering short and long-term perspectives.

The Egyptian 2022 regulation requires that banks report according to the standards of the Global Reporting Initiative (GRI).

3.10 Integration into Traditional Risk Categories

Many regulators (*e.g.*, from Australia, Brazil, Austria, Germany and Ghana) clearly state that E&S risks are transversal, rather than an independent type of risk. Hence, E&S factors might be translated/integrated into credit risk, market risk, operational/legal risks, liquidity risk and reputational risk management. The Austrian regulator also mentions systemic risks (actually, portfolio risk concentration, as well as contagion risks across sectors) and strategic risks, meaning the risks of the lack of consideration of sustainability factors in the business strategy (risk appetite). The BIS principles of climate risk management also include, under principle 6, all types of risk (credit, market, operational, reputational and liquidity risks), but goes beyond, highlighting **liability risks** (which are part of operational risks) in an unprecedented way, as the topic is not usually addressed by national regulators. Principle 11 mentions explicitly "*liability costs associated with climate-sensitive investments and businesses.*"—which makes a lot of sense considering the rising climate litigation trends, that will certainly reach financial institutions very soon. The European Central Bank had mentioned the topic in its guidance as well.

A few regulators require that E&S risk management is integrated in the risk management governance structure, while others state that, if a dedicated "sustainability unit" is created, it must interact with all relevant business units, especially risk management.

The Austrian and Kenyan regulators, for example, recommend that sustainability risks are also considered in terms of business continuity management when internal or outsourced operations might be threatened, for example, by extreme weather events arising from climate change.

3.11 E&S Risk Assessment of New Financial Products

The Brazilian regulation requires an assessment of E&S risks of new financial products. The Philippines' regulation mentions the assessment of E&S risks for banks products as well.

3.12 Specific Strategies for E&S Risk Management in Investment Activities

One of the new guidelines issued by the Central Bank of Philippines was apparently the first in the world to address the integration of E&S factors into investment management. It mentions the need of developing E&S due diligences also for investment portfolios, an exit strategy when appropriate, and also three strategies that are common in the market: (a) integration of E&S factors into decision-making (including, of course, the selection of investments); (b) exclusion of defined industries due to risks that are considered too high; (c) best-in-class approach, where companies are selected due to the fact that they are the best in their specific industry; (d) thematic approach where the focus is to generate a positive environmental or social impact.

The fact that this banking regulator adopted a specific approach for investments is quite interesting, but it is important to mention that most of the strategies of risk management already used for lending can and should be easily extended to investments, especially because, different from lending, companies that are part of investment portfolios are usually large ones, hence, should be able to provide much more E&S information than SMEs.

4 Positive Impacts

Ghana Central Bank addresses the identification of business opportunities involving E&S positive impacts, and gives examples, especially related to resources efficiency (from raw materials to energy and water) and improved waste management, recommending also that preferential interest rates are adopted. Another example strongly emphasized is the offer of loans for women-owned businesses (especially SMEs). German guidance recommends the adoption of "positive lists", where certain industries/geographies may be preferred based on certain compliance criteria.

Regulators of China, Nigeria, Pakistan, Bangladesh, Vietnam, Indonesia, Paraguay, Germany and Egypt, for example, also refer to the need to explore the "green" business opportunities and encourage the offer of financial products aiming to achieve environmental and/or social positive outcomes. A few (like the Nigerian and the Egyptian) also focus on financial inclusion.

In Brazil, there is a category of rural loans (available to all credit granting institutions) to finance specifically technologies of low carbon agriculture, many of them (such as the biological fixation of nitrogen, as a replacement for chemical fertilizers) also with positive impacts on biodiversity and natural capital. Moreover, recent regulations provide a definition of positive environmental, social and climate impacts that can be generated by financial activities—for positive environmental impact, the definition encompasses both conservation and restoration of nature; for positive social impact, the promotion, respect and protection of all human/basic rights are included; for positive climate impact, both mitigation and adaptation to climate change are included, whereas preservation of natural carbon sinks is explicitly mentioned for mitigation, as well as compensation of GHG emissions (together with GHG emissions reduction, of course); for adaptation, both strategies do deal with the increase in frequency and to tackle the intensity of extreme weather events and to tackle long-term changes are mentioned. The regulation also requires the disclosure of the list of financial products with positive environmental, social or climate impacts, but without any requirements on disclosure of the proportion of these products in the portfolio.

Ghana's principles require the disclosure of the amount of loans targeted at improving resource efficiency or to encourage improvement of E&S performance.

Another topic that is mentioned is the need of definition of appropriate processes to make sure that sustainable loans or bonds are used accordingly.

In terms of social aspects, it's important to mention that Ghana's and Nigeria's Central Banks included financial inclusion and women empowerment strategies in their Sustainable Banking Principles.

The Malaysian regulator raises a very important point, which is the higher financial risk level of many loans/investments on sectors/activities with positive social or environmental impacts, such as SMEs or new environmental technologies. In order to overcome this problem, it recommends to enhance internal capacity-building, collection of relevant datapoints and strategic technical partnerships, so that these underserved segments have access to capital.

Finally, it's important to mention that a few regulators (China, Bangladesh, Vietnam, Malaysia, Mongolia, Costa Rica, Sri Lanka) already established a framework to define green loans, which sometimes have a lot of common with the green taxonomies that have been created in a rising number of countries (with use not limited to loans, but must of the times prioritising investments and sometimes including insurance as well), such as Colombia, Mexico, South Africa, Rwanda, Indonesia, Singapore, and the European Union. Despite the concept of taxonomy (classification system) implies the reference to a pre-defined universe which is categorized according to certain criteria (in this case, environmental, climate and social risks and impacts), the model that has been adopted by the European Union and has been followed by other countries (including those who are currently elaborating their taxonomies) is a sort of certification system to label activities/projects of certain economic sectors as "green" (some countries, like Mexico, are including social positive impact too), provided that certain environmental (or social) requirements are achieved, and that some safeguards are respected.

It's worth mention the initiative of the Chinese regulator of tracking the default rate for green loans, whose outcome was to and realize that it was much lower than the default rate of traditional loans.[15]

The Vietnamese and Chinese regulators require the disclosure of values of green loans in the portfolio. The Bangladeshi one establishes minimal targets of percentage of green loans at portfolio-level.

The Bangladeshi definition of green loans was expanded in 2020 to include also social elements. There is a chapter on Sustainable Taxonomy (including environmental activities) and another one on Green Taxonomy (repeating mostly the environmental activities included in the Sustainable Taxonomy). The chapter on Sustainable Taxonomy comprises definitions for sustainable agriculture, sustainable activities of micro, small and medium enterprises, social finance (affordable housing, affordable healthcare, food security, employment generation through microfinance, working capital for a number of sectors (renewable energies, solid waste management, recycling and manufacturing of recyclable goods, energy efficiency, environmentally-friendly brick production, green buildings), "green products for trading sector" (renewable energies, energy efficiency, and a number of environmentally-friendly products). Following the example of the European green taxonomy, it refers to substantial contribution to the six environmental objectives set up in the European regulation (see below), as well as doing no significant harm to the other objectives and respecting minimum social safeguards. It adds also "governance safeguards", without a definition of what is meant for any of the safeguards. The chapters of the taxonomies bring a lot of requirements that have nothing to do with a taxonomy, referring actually to the Sustainability Policies of banks (including reporting), as well as a description of previous initiatives and future plans for the issuance of a green bonds standard. The most serious problem is the inclusion of palm oil production as "green agriculture" (in the green taxonomy), one of the three major deforestation drivers globally.[16]

The Malaysian green taxonomy (issued in April 2021) is inspired by the European green taxonomy for investments regarding the objectives of climate change mitigation and adaptation. Hence, it requires that there is a substantial contribution to one or both of these objectives while doing no significant harm to other environmental objectives, includes the avoidance or reduction of GHG emissions, as well as the strengthening of natural carbon sinks, and also enabling activities and transition activities. The main difference between this taxonomy and the European one for climate is that it is principles-based. Although the Malaysian regulator provides a number of examples of taxonomy-aligned activities for different

[15]The source of this information is a bilateral meeting between the Central Bank of Brazil and the China Banking Regulatory Commission (CBRC), in November 2015, when CBRC stated that, in the previous 2 years, while market default rate was around 2%, for green loans it was around only 0.4%.

[16]This database clearly shows the role of palm oil in deforestation, especially in Southeast Asia: https://ourworldindata.org/drivers-of-deforestation.

industries, it does not define minimal thresholds in terms of substantial contribution, as done by the European taxonomy.

5 Governance Structure/Measures (Both for Risk Management and Positive Impact Financial Products)

5.1 Definition of Roles and Responsibilities in the FI Structure

Many regulations (e.g., from Brazil, Honduras, Paraguay, Germany, Nepal, Singapore, Philippines, Pakistan) clearly define the roles of the Board of Directors/ Committee, senior management, and the credit risk management in the implementation of the policies. Internal auditing is usually assigned roles too. A few regulations even assign roles to the Legal Department (E&S covenants), relationship/ commercial managers/front office (usually: identification of risks), or to the compliance function (to keep updated with relevant E&S regulations). The Kenyan regulation mentions also that the climate policy should be formulated and approved by the board of Directors and senior management, who should effectively monitor its implementation through regular updates on risk exposure and the banks responses; it refers to the clear definition of roles and responsibilities as well. The Nigerian regulation mentions both internal and external audit reviews of the implementation of Sustainable Banking Principles as an indicator to be reported.

The Australian and Hong Kong regulators require oversight from Board/senior management regarding environmental/climate risks, with a clear definition of roles and responsibilities. The one of Hong Kong requests information on the frequency that the topic was addressed in Board meetings in the previous year. The Brazilian regulation, since 2014, requires that a Director is assigned the role to oversee the banks' Sustainability Policies implementation.

The Austrian regulator also mentions the need of clear definition of responsibilities (so that they are traceable), as well as ultimate responsibility for Sustainability Risk management relying on the ultimate management body. The European Central Bank guidance mentions the need to assign responsibility for management of climate-related and environmental risks in accordance with the three lines of defence model.

Philippines last 2022 regulation also mentions as supervisory expectations that Board of Directors and Senior Management shall oversee E&S risk management and that banks should define units or personnel specialized on the topic.

The Georgian regulator mentions **ESG expertise of high management bodies** as a topic to be disclosed, as well as the whole ESG governance structure, how the highest bodies oversee the implementation of ESG policies, and which are the KPIs for the monitoring of this implementation.

The Egyptian principles mention the need to assign tasks "to an officer of the bank's sector, provided that such tasks shall not fall under the umbrella of the corporate social responsibility (CSR)"—which is a very didactic remark, once many banks usually confuse integration of ESG factors into their activities with philanthropy. More recent binding regulation from the Central Bank of Egypt (2022) requires the establishment of an "independent department for Sustainability and Sustainable Finance that reports directly to the Chief Executive Officer".

5.2 *Staff Capacity and Budget*

This is a topic that started to appear explicitly in recent regulations, for example, the Hong Kong regulator mentions a "plan to enhance staff capacity" and actions taken to implement it. The Philippines' regulation mentions "adequate resources". The Austrian regulator also mentions "staffing provisions in the risk management function", and the German one mentions "appropriate resources and staff". The Georgian regulation mentions the need of disclosure of annual budgets of ESG strategies. The Kenyan regulator refers to "appropriate resources, processes, systems and controls to support the implementation of the [climate] strategy", clarifying these resources might be financial or non-financial.

It is very positive that regulators are really addressing the "how" in terms of implementation of sustainability strategies, as sufficient allocation of personnel and financial resources is also essential for embodying them.

5.3 *Capacity-Building*

Many regulators (e.g., from Australia, USA, Bangladesh, China, Nigeria, Peru, Paraguay, Indonesia, Singapore, Nepal, Honduras, Ghana and Kenya) include capacity-building in the recommendations/ requirements to regulated entities. A few mention also the recruiting of new staff members when there is no sufficient internal capacity. The Nigerian reporting template (2014) includes as an indicator the capacity-building activities on Sustainable Banking offered to Board, Senior Management, Risk Management unit, other employees, customers and service providers, as well as the number of employees participating.

The Hong Kong regulator asks about the trainings received by Board members on environmental and climate risks (with number or percentage of members) and their frequency. It also asks about the number and percentage of trainings to staff in general.

The Austrian regulator mentions that all employees conducting activities that are affected by sustainability risks (e.g., data collection) require knowledge that correspond to their profile.

The Australian one mentions appropriate training for board members as well (and it is the only one to do so, even if most regulators require that the Board define the institutions strategies—and of course some basic technical knowledge is required to do so properly.

Finally, it is important to point out that the BIS' principles for climate risk management, under principle 17, establishes that also "Supervisors should ensure that they have adequate resources and capacity to effectively assess banks' management of climate-related financial risks"—actually, capacity-building is not only a need from market side, there is a demand from regulatory side as well, otherwise they are not able to supervise financial institutions effectively.

5.4 Business Strategy

Hong Kong's regulation asks supervised entities about the integration into strategic planning, business plans (with examples), financial plans, and targets.

The business strategy might also include a "risk appetite" strategy, using, for example, exclusion lists (a possibility mentioned by many regulations) or industry/geographies limits of exposure.

The Austrian regulator mentions the need of integration of sustainability risks into the business strategy, and the one of Philippines (2020) mentions "strategic objectives". Philippines last 2022 guidelines mention their integration into banks' risk appetite.

The Nepalese regulation also requires the integration of environmental and social factors into the risk appetite and business strategy (including the offer of financial products that address E&S factors).

The Kenyan regulation is another example referring the integration of climate risks into the risk appetite statement (RAS), starting with qualitative indicators but evolving into quantitative metrics. The RAS should be reviewed annually with regards to climate risks. The Australian regulation also mentions the consideration of climate risks in the risk appeteiter framework, and in the business strategies and plans.

Many regulators mention the need of strategic goals. The idea is to make environmental and social considerations an integral part of the business model without harm to the expected financial results.

5.5 Target-Setting

Hong Kong refers to a methodology to measure performance (with defined indicators).

The Austrian regulator mentions goal-setting regarding sustainability risks.

Bangladeshi and Pakistani guidelines were the first to recommend target-setting for green financial products. Ghana recommends target-setting also on sustainable business opportunities.

This is a key strategy to assess progress over time.

5.6 *Integration into Compensation Schemes*

The Nigerian guidelines recommend the integration of green/social loans into remuneration policies. The Austrian guidance mentions that sustainability risks should be integrated within remuneration policies, "promote sound and effective risk management", and "be linked to risk-adjusted performance". The German guidance mentions the need to reflect E&S factors in remuneration policies too.

This topic is also crucial, as the financial system tends to think short-term, and this mindset is an enemy of sustainability objectives, making it necessary to create incentives to long-termism.

5.7 *Minimal Contents and Periodic Review of the Sustainability Policy*

Many regulators (e.g., Honduras, Singapore, Ghana) describe a minimal content for the E&S (or Sustainability) policy, usually referring to superior management commitments.

Although many mention the need of frequent update, the Brazilian regulator chose to define the periodicity of the review of the Policy (three years, in the new regulations).

A few regulations (such as the Kenyan, regarding climate risks) refer to the need of an Action Plan approved by the Board of Directors, followed by quarterly reporting on its implementation.

5.8 *Stakeholders' Involvement in the Elaboration of the Sustainability Policy*

Brazilian and Indonesian regulators require the participation of stakeholders in the elaboration of the policies. The Malaysian regulator also mentions the dialogue with stakeholders which is a useful tool in the implementation of a sustainability strategy as well. The Kenyan regulation refers to the involvement of relevant stakeholders too.

In all cases, there are advantages for understanding and addressing potential concerns. Sound stakeholders' engagement also potentially generates more buy-in and a smoother pathway in terms of the implementation of policies.

5.9 Transparency and Communication with Relevant Stakeholders

Many regulators (e.g., from Bangladesh, Brazil, Nigeria, Pakistan and Georgia) demand that supervised entities disclose their E&S policies. A few even mention disclosure of procedures, due diligence process or E&S risk management criteria. The Brazilian one mentions disclosure of actions towards its implementation; the mechanisms used to interact with stakeholders; as an option, they are also recommended to publish the assessment of the implementation of the Policy.

The Hong Kong regulator asks how the FIs communicate with stakeholders on their Environmental Policies, requesting specific information on events on the topic (and their format, audience and scale). The Egyptian Central Bank also mentions "involvement of the stakeholders" as a principle and the Georgian Central Bank recommends the disclosure of the stakeholder engagement policy.

5.10 Procedures to Be Followed on E&S Risk Management

Most regulators mention the need of definition and implementation of procedures for E&S risk management to be integrated in different stages of the business activities (usually reflected in manuals, for example).

5.11 Principle of Proportionality

With regards to the governance structure, a few regulators (e.g., Brazil, Germany, Austria, Philippines) refer, explicitly or implicitly, to the need to consider the principle of proportionality when assessing the supervised entities.

The Austrian regulator, for example, mentions the size and internal organization, the nature, scope, and complexity of the activities or transactions, as well as the risk structure of the supervised entity.

Of course, regulatory standards really need to consider the institutional capacity and nature of the activities of each financial institution.

5.12 Policies/Strategies Implementation Timeframe

Regarding the implementation of the E&S policies, some regulators (e.g., Bangladesh and Nigeria) adopted a general staged approach in which supervised entities would be required to implement different levels within different timeframes.

5.13 Effects of Voluntary Commitments

The Brazilian regulator requires that financial institutions disclose the list of self-regulations on environmental, social or climate matters to which the FI voluntarily adhered, which is interesting, but it is something that usually they already do, in order to enjoy the reputational benefits. The German guidance adds a relevant requirement on the topic, stating that, if the FI adheres to self-regulatory initiatives, their contents/standards should be reflected in its strategies and guidelines. That is a valuable example, in order to avoid greenwashing and the phenomenon of free-riding already mentioned.

5.14 Environmental and Social Impacts of Banks' Own Operations

A few regulators (from Nigeria, Pakistan, Indonesia, Ghana, Hong Kong, Egypt) consider that the environmental and social impacts from banks own operations should be addressed too, including suppliers management. The Brazilian regulation mentions only suppliers E&S risk management.

Regulators from Pakistan and Hong Kong also mention the need of indicators and targets to measure and improve the environmental performance of the financial institutions' own operations.

The Central Bank of Ghana provides examples of KPIs:

- Electricity consumption/GHG emissions per square meter of office;
- Paper/water consumption per full-time employee;
- Waste production per full-time employee;
- Labour health and safety hours of training per full-time employee;
- Workplace diversity data (especially on gender) in full workforce and senior management;
- Gender pay gap; and
- Number of health and safety incidents/sick days per full-time employee.

Ghana's regulator mentions the reduction of operational costs (including potential fines), motivation of workforce, and benefits to reputation as drivers to address these topics. The change of culture towards the integration of sustainability issues in every process could also be added.

6 Possible Supervisory Actions

Beyond specific recommendations for improvement in the E&S risk management of supervised entities, other possibilities are found in relevant regulations:

- Penalties for non-compliance (when they are actual regulations, not only non-binding guidance)—the Indonesian regulation includes them, for example;
- Ranking of banks (or awards)—regulators from Bangladesh, Indonesia and Ghana mention this possibility;
- Consideration for the authorization of new branches (Bangladesh and China) or in merger procedures;
- Assessment of E&S risk integration into capital requirements (e.g., regulators from Bangladesh, Brazil, UK and the Netherlands).

7 Final Remarks and Recommendations for Improvement

Considering the novelty of the topic in terms of mainstream banking activities (not as enunciation but as effective implementation) and the many open issues that still remain for market players, it is possible to conclude that, as a rule, the more detailed and clear banking regulations are on the integration of environmental and social considerations, the better.

Historical observation makes clear that principles-based approaches will actually have limited impact—and one of the reasons identified by market players is the uncertainties on how to implement a strategy on a topic that is not traditional at all. If it is clear that there is no "one size fits all" approach, it is also evident that regulatory guidance may set up the criteria for the definition of tailored approaches, and this will make it more feasible also the supervisory work in terms of assessment of their implementation.

In this paper, a description of all the topics that have already been covered by ESG banking regulations was made, but it also pointed out a few inconsistencies and remaining relevant gaps. To summarize, it is possible to consider that a sound banking regulation should include, at least:

(a) a clear definition of relevant environmental and social issues, both at compliance-level and at performance-level (considering the best international standards for the latter, and always including an industry-based approach);
(b) a clear definition of the universe of financial transactions, clients and collaterals to be assessed with regards to environmental and social risks—mentions to the principles of proportionality and relevance are too vague to create enough certainty;
(c) industry-specific KPIs and their respective weight;
(d) the need to consider the industry and the location of the financed activities to define the depth and comprehensiveness of the risk identification process;

(e) the specification of due diligences and which are the situations where they are appropriate, including consultation to public databases (especially data provided by environmental and social public bodies), site visits, questionnaires sent to companies, other public information disclosed by companies, external certifications, ESG ratings (if appropriate) and, in more relevant projects/activities, even on-site inspections and dialogue with stakeholders;
(f) consequences of the risk assessment in the decision-making process (either for lending or investing activities);
(g) clear examples of appropriate risk mitigation measures;
(h) sound criteria for risk classification, including location, industry, compliance-level, performance-level and size of the company/project;
(i) criteria to define the frequency, scope and consequences of risk monitoring;
(j) criteria and tools for portfolio risk management and its consequence;
(k) specific indicators for reporting disclosure on ESG performance to three different audiences: superior management, banking supervisor and external stakeholders;
(l) integration of environmental and social risks into traditional risk categories;
(m) environmental and social risk assessment of new financial products;
(n) definition of positive environmental or social impact activities/financial products and requirements on disclosure of the proportion of these products in the portfolio;
(o) minimal governance structure, including appropriate definition of roles, staff allocation and capacity, sufficient budget, minimal contents and periodic review of the Sustainability Policy;
(p) integration into business strategy and target-setting, reflecting on compensation schemes;
(q) stakeholders involvement in the elaboration and implementation of the Policy, complaint resolution mechanism and disclosure of information about stakeholders complaints and their consequences;
(r) integration of the Policy's principles into routine work procedures;
(s) effects of voluntary commitments;
(t) minimal information to be disclosed externally, including E&S portfolio governance, E&S diligences and risk management system and portfolio composition in terms of E&S risk level, including sector specific, location and categories of E&S risk for companies;
(u) penalties or other consequences for non-compliance.

Furthermore, regulators/supervisors must lead by example, integrating (when they are also Central Banks) environmental and social factors into their investment portfolio management, providing incentives to financial institutions with better ESG performance (rankings, awards, etc), considering this performance for other supervisory decisions (such as merging of financial institutions, authorization of new branches, etc) and, in appropriate cases and circumstances, applying corresponding penalties, because the regulatory role goes way beyond dialogue and education, comprising also discipline, in order to address market failures.

References

Haines F (2010) The paradox of regulation: what regulation can achieve and what it cannot. Edward Elgar

Lodge M, Wegrich K (2012) Managing regulation: regulatory analysis, politics and policy. Palgrave Macmillan

Wörsdörfer M (2013) 10 years "Equator Principles": a critical economic-ethical analysis. Comparative Research in Law & Political Economy, Research Paper No. 54/2013. York University, Osgoode Hall Law School. Available at: http://digitalcommons.osgoode.yorku.ca/clpe/296

Regulations References

Australian Prudential Regulation Authority [banking, insurance, pension and asset managers prudential regulator], Prudential Practice Guide (CPG 229) – Climate Change Financial Risks. 2021. Available at: https://www.apra.gov.au/sites/default/files/2021-11/Final%20Prudential%20Practice%20Guide%20CPG%20229%20Climate%20Change%20Financial%20Risks_0.pdf

Austria Financial Monetary Authority [banking, insurance, pension and asset managers supervisor]. Guide for Managing Sustainability Risks. 2020. Available at: https://www.fma.gv.at/en/fma/fma-guides/

Banco Central de Paraguay [country's Central Bank and banking regulator]. Guía para la gestión de riesgos ambientales y sociales para las entidades reguladas y supervisadas por el BCP. November 2018. Available at: https://www.bcp.gov.py/riesgos-ambientales-y-sociales-i657

Banco Central do Brasil [country's Central Bank and banking regulator]. Resolução do Conselho Monetário Nacional n. 3.545/2008 [creates environmental requirements for rural loans in Amazon]. Available at: http://www.bcb.gov.br/pre/normativos/res/2008/pdf/res_3545_v1_O.pdf

Banco Central do Brasil. Resolução do Conselho Monetário Nacional n. 3876/2010 [prohibits rural loans for employers included in the "dirty list" of forced labor]. Available at: https://www.bcb.gov.br/pre/normativos/res/2010/pdf/res_3876_v1_O.pdf

Banco Central do Brasil. Resolução do Conselho Monetário Nacional n. 4943/2021 [includes environmental and social risks in the structure for risk management, capital management and disclosure for financial institutions with larger structure]. Available at: https://www.bcb.gov.br/estabilidadefinanceira/exibenormativo?tipo=Resolu%C3%A7%C3%A3o%20CMN&numero=4943

Banco Central do Brasil. Resolução do Conselho Monetário Nacional n. 4944/2021 [includes a simplified version of environmental and social risks in the structure for risk management, capital management and disclosure for financial institutions with a smaller structure]. Available at: https://www.bcb.gov.br/estabilidadefinanceira/exibenormativo?tipo=Resolu%C3%A7%C3%A3o%20CMN&numero=4944

Banco Central do Brasil. Resolução do Conselho Monetário Nacional n. 4945/2021 [establishes the need for a Policy of Social, Environmental and Climate Responsibility for supervised institutions and the requirements for its implementation]. Available at: https://www.bcb.gov.br/estabilidadefinanceira/exibenormativo?tipo=Resolu%C3%A7%C3%A3o%20CMN&numero=4945

Banco Central do Brasil. Resolução BCB n. 139/2021 [establishes the Report of Social, Environmental and Climate Risks and Opportunities]. Available at: https://www.bcb.gov.br/estabilidadefinanceira/exibenormativo?tipo=Resolu%C3%A7%C3%A3o%20BCB&numero=139

Banco Central do Brasil. Instrução Normativa BCB n. 153/2021 [establishes the standardised tables for the reports of Social, Environmental and Climate Risks and Opportunities]. Available at: https://www.bcb.gov.br/estabilidadefinanceira/exibenormativo?tipo=Instru%C3%A7%C3%A3o%20Normativa%20BCB&numero=153

Banco Central do Brasil. Resolução n. 151/2021 [establishes information that financial institutions need to send to Central Bank of Brazil with regards to environmental, social and climate information of loans and investments]. Available at: https://www.bcb.gov.br/estabilidadefinanceira/exibenormativo?tipo=Resolu%C3%A7%C3%A3o%20BCB&numero=151

Banco Central do Brasil. Circular BCB n. 3.846/2017 [requires that banks that adopt the ICAAP regime consider environmental and social risks in their capital adequacy assessment]. Available at: https://www.bcb.gov.br/pre/normativos/busca/downloadNormativo.asp?arquivo=/Lists/Normativos/Attachments/50436/Circ_3846_v2_P.pdf

Bangladesh Bank [country's Central Bank and banking regulator], Environmental Risk Management (ERM) Guidelines for Banks and Financial Institutions in Bangladesh, January 2011. Available at: https://pt.scribd.com/document/100231398/BB-Guidelines-for-Environmental-Risk-Management-ERM

Bangladesh Bank. Policy Guidelines for Green Banking, February 2011, updated in 2013. Available at: https://www.bb.org.bd/mediaroom/circulars/brpd/feb272011brpd02e.pdf

Bangladesh Bank. Guidelines on Environmental and Social Risk Management for Banks and Financial Institutions, updated in February 2017. Available at: https://www.bb.org.bd/mediaroom/circulars/gbcrd/feb082017sfd02e.pdf

Bangladesh Bank. Sustainable Finance Policy for Banks and Financial Institutions, December 2020 (includes Sustainable Taxonomy): https://www.bb.org.bd/mediaroom/circulars/gbcrd/dec312020sfd05.pdf

Bangladesh Bank. Sustainability Rating of Banks and Financial Institutions. December 2020. Available at: https://www.bb.org.bd/mediaroom/circulars/gbcrd/dec312020sfd06.pdf

Bank Negara Malaysia [country's Central Bank and banking regulator]. Value-based Intermediation Financing and Investment Impact Assessment Framework. November 2019 [only for Islamic banks]. Available at: https://www.bnm.gov.my/-/value-based-intermediation-financing-and-investment-impact-assessment-framework-guidance-document

Bank Negara Malaysia. Implementation Guide for Value-based Intermediation. November 2019 [only for Islamic banks]. Available at: https://www.bnm.gov.my/documents/20124/761682/Implementation+Guide+for+Value-based+Intermediation.pdf

Bank Negara Malaysia. Value-based Intermediation Scorecard, Consultative Document. October 2018 [only for Islamic banks]. Available at: https://www.bnm.gov.my/documents/20124/759040/Value-based+Intermediation+Scorecard+%28Consultative+Document%29.pdf

Bank Negara Malaysia. Climate Change and Principle-based Taxonomy. April 2021 [for all banks and insurers]. Available at: https://www.bnm.gov.my/documents/20124/938039/Climate+Change+and+Principle-based+Taxonomy.pdf

Bank of England/Prudential Regulation Authority [country's Central Bank and one of the banking/insurance regulators]. Supervisory Statement SS3/19: Enhancing banks' and insurers' approaches to managing the financial risks from climate change. 2019. Available at: https://www.bankofengland.co.uk/-/media/boe/files/prudential-regulation/supervisory-statement/2019/ss319

Bank of Ghana [country's Central bank and banking regulator]. Sustainable Banking Principles. 2019. Available at: https://www.bog.gov.gh/wp-content/uploads/2019/12/Ghana-Sustainable-Banking-Principles-and-Guidelines-Book-1.pdf

Bank of International Settlements. Principles for the effective management and supervision of climate-related financial risks. June 2022. Available at: https://www.bis.org/bcbs/publ/d532.htm

Central Bank of Egypt [country's Central Bank and banking regulator]. Guiding Principles on Sustainable Finance. 2021. Available at: https://www.ifc.org/wps/wcm/connect/4a270ef4-2f91-

4c22-8bc9-465f978a0671/Central+Bank+of+Egypt+Sustainable+Finance+Principles+package_2021.pdf?MOD=AJPERES&CVID=nLPEKGg
Central Bank of Egypt. Sustainable Finance Binding Regulations. 2022. Available at: https://www.sbfnetwork.org/wp-content/assets/policy-library/688_Sustainable_Finance_Binding_Regulations_Egypt.pdf
Central Bank of Kenya [country's Central Bank and banking regulator]. Guidance on Climate-related Risk Management. 2021. Available at: https://www.centralbank.go.ke/wp-content/uploads/2021/10/Guidance-on-Climate-Related-Risk-Management.pdf
Central Bank of Nigeria [country's Central Bank and banking regulator]. Sustainable Banking Principles. 2012. Available at: https://www.cbn.gov.ng/out/2012/ccd/circular-nsbp.pdf
Central Bank of Philippines [country's Central Bank and banking regulator]. Sustainable Finance Framework. 2020. Available at: https://drive.google.com/file/d/1gXlU1PAbvFWHTzhMaLqpxghptWN4Nk4r/view?fbclid=IwAR1wjA3DcXxSpX6y6L4LovzJclIsPvso0OYAYr0gT2VyQd3P-5wS19e43W0
Central Bank of Philippines. Guidelines on the integration of Sustainability Principles in investment activities of Banks. 2022a. Available at: https://www.sbfnetwork.org/wp-content/assets/policy-library/1821_BSP_Circular_1149_for_banks_on_integrating_sustainability_principles_in_investment_activities_Oct2022_1.pdf~
Central Bank of Philippines. Guidelines on the integration of Sustainability Principles in investment activities of Banks. 2022b. Available at: https://www.sbfnetwork.org/wp-content/assets/policy-library/1822_BSP_guidance_on_implementing_ESRM_system_Oct2022_1.pdf
Central Bank of Sri Lanka [country's Central Bank and banking regulator]. Sri Lanka Green Finance Taxonomy. May 2022. Available at: https://www.cbsl.gov.lk/sites/default/files/cbslweb_documents/sl_green_finance_taxonomy.pdf
China Banking Regulatory Commission. Notice of the CBRC issuing the Green Credit Guidelines. 2012. Available at: https://www.cbirc.gov.cn/en/view/pages/ItemDetail.html?docId=68035&itemId=981
China Banking Regulatory Commission. Notice of the China Banking Regulatory Commission on Submission of Green Credit Statistics Form. 2013 (not available online anymore)
China Banking Regulatory Commission. General Office of the China Banking Regulatory Commission Opinions on Green Credit Implementation. 2014 (not available online anymore)
China Banking Regulatory Commission. Notice of the China Banking Regulatory Commission on Key Performance Indicators of Green Credit Implementation. 2014. Available at: https://www.cbirc.gov.cn/en/view/pages/ItemDetail.html?docId=68037&itemId=981
Costa Rica, Superintendencia General de Entidades Financeiras, (SUGEF). Guia de Monitoreo de Financiamiento Climático para Entidades Financieras de Costa Rica. [climate mitigation and adaptation taxonomy] 2019. Available at: https://www.sugef.fi.cr/informacion_relevante/manuales/manual_sicveca/crediticio/GUIA%20DE%20MONITOREO%20DE%20FINANCIAMIENTO%20CLIMATICO%20PARA%20ENTIDADES%20FINANCIERAS%20DE%20COSTA%20RICA.pdf
De Nederlandsche Bank [Netherland's Central Bank and banking regulator]. Good practice: integration of climate-related risk considerations into bank's risk management. 2020. Available at: https://www.dnb.nl/media/jwtjyvfn/definitieve-versie-gp-en-qa-klimaatrisico-s-banken.pdf
Germany, BaFin [banking, insurance, pensions and asset managers supervisor]. Guidance Notice on dealing with Sustainability Risks. 2020. Available at: https://www.bafin.de/SharedDocs/Downloads/EN/Merkblatt/dl_mb_Nachhaltigkeitsrisiken_en.html
Honduras, Comisión Nacional de Bancos Y Seguros [banking and insurance regulator]. Circular CNBS 28/2020, Guidelines for Environmental and Social Risk Management. 2020. Available at: https://www.cnbs.gob.hn/blog/circulares/circular-cnbs-no-028-2020/?fbclid=IwAR3JVrpyd07mjH2aC0vef4UnY8XjBt2Xd4njAtl-uoLWyIwR1oSOq0jm4zY

Hong Kong Monetary Authority. Common Assessment Framework on Green and Sustainable Banking. 2020. Available at: https://www.hkma.gov.hk/media/eng/doc/key-information/guidelines-and-circular/2020/20200513e1a1.pdf
Indonesia Financial Services Authority (OJK). Regulation on Application of Sustainable Finance to Financial Services Institutions, Issuer and Publicly Listed Companies. Jacarta, July 2017. Available at: https://www.ifc.org/wps/wcm/connect/bab66a7c-9dc2-412f-81f6-f83f94d79660/Indonesia+OJK+Sustainable+Finance+RegulationEnglish.pdf?MOD=AJPERES&CVID=lVXU.Oy
Indonesia Financial Services Authority (OJK). Technical Guidelines for Banks on the Implementation of the regulation. 2018. Available at: https://www.ifc.org/wps/wcm/connect/13d863ef-b8cf-4584-8602-14a63f9b9ede/Technical+Guideline+on+the+Implementation+of+POJK+51+2017+on+SF_English.pdf?MOD=AJPERES&CVID=mGmKSQ-
Monetary Authority of Singapore [country's Central Bank and banking regulator]. Guidelines on Environmental Risk Management for Banks. December 2020. Available at: https://www.mas.gov.sg/regulation/guidelines/guidelines-on-environmental-risk-management
National Bank of Georgia [country's Central Bank and banking regulator]. ESG Reporting and Disclosure Principles. 2020. Available at: https://www.sbfnetwork.org/wp-content/assets/policy-library/710_Georgia_ESG_Reporting_and_Disclosure_Principles_2020_NBG.pdf
Nepal Rastra Bank [country Central Bank and banking regulator]. Guideline on Environmental & Social Risk Management (ESRM) for Banks and Financial Institutions. May 2018. Available at: https://www.nrb.org.np/contents/uploads/2019/12/Guidelines-Guideline_on_Environmental__Social_Risk_Management_for_Banks_and_Financial_Institutions_2018-new.pdf
Peru, Superintendencia de Banca, Seguros Y Administradoras Privadas de Fondos de Pensiones (SBS). Regulation for Environmental and Social Risk Management 2015. Available at: https://www.ifc.org/wps/wcm/connect/ca2b24bc-1aa9-41a2-9eb3-abc3219ebcd2/SBN_Regulation+for+Social+and+Environmental+Risk+Management.pdf?MOD=AJPERES&CVID=kWtGcPU
State Bank of Pakistan [country's Central Bank and banking regulator]. Green Banking Guidelines. October 2017. Available at: http://www.sbp.org.pk/smefd/circulars/2017/C8-Annex.pdf
State Bank of Vietnam [country's Central Bank and banking regulator]. Directive on Promoting Green Credit Growth and Environmental – Social Risks Management in Credit Granting Activities. March 2015. Available at: https://www.ifc.org/wps/wcm/connect/758c9ed5-cf12-4f15-b0a5-952dcae9b0c4/Directive+on+Green+Credit+and+E%26S+Risk+management.pdf?MOD=AJPERES&CVID=kOkF7YL
State Bank of Vietnam. Circular n. 39/2016/TT-NHNN dated December 30, 2016 of the State Bank of Vietnam prescribing lending transactions of credit institutions and/or foreign bank branches with customers, article 4th. [requires compliance with environmental legislation]. Available at: https://www.ifc.org/wps/wcm/connect/e39a6557-4cad-49fc-b00c-c64708a5747b/Vietnam+Circular+Dec+2016.pdf?MOD=AJPERES&CVID=lJ4Edqf
United States of America, Federal Deposit Insurance Corporation (FDIC) [one of the country's banking regulators]. Guidelines for an Environmental Risk Program. 1993. Available at: https://www.fdic.gov/regulations/laws/rules/5000-4900.html

The Importance of Practicality: The Role of a Transition Green Asset Ratio for Banks

Sofia Santos

Abstract In Europe, the EU green taxonomy has been developed, and banks will have to start reporting their green asset ratio in 2024. Developments are also taking place so that capital requirements can be associated with the level of "green" loans that a bank has taken. Acknowledging the enlightenment that this approach could bring, it also incentivizes banks to lend money to green companies and potentially not to those that are still not green. Taking into account that a very small proportion of European companies are aligned with the EU green taxonomy, this could also be a very small market for banks. As such, this article argues for the importance of a transition green asset ratio that can be used by banks to actively promote the transition towards an economy aligned with decarbonization in 2050.

1 The Role of Banks

The main activity of banks as intermediaries between savers and investors is to allocate capital to promote investments.[1,2] Over the past few years, there has been an increase in lending for consumption that could be justified by the fact that financing by consumption banks were indirectly promoting further investment in companies. This is because it was assumed that more consumption implies greater economic activity and increased demand that leads to more investment.[3] Taking into account that any investment could have some level of environmental impact, then lending conceded by banks can have impacts on the existing and future availability of natural

[1] Boyd and Prescott (1985).
[2] Levine (2004).
[3] Levine (2004).

S. Santos (✉)
ISEG, Lisbon, Portugal
e-mail: sofia.santos@systemic.pt

R. Saraiva, P. A. Pardal (eds.), *Sustainable Finances and the Law*, Economic Analysis of Law in European Legal Scholarship 16,
https://doi.org/10.1007/978-3-031-49460-4_3

resources as discussed by some studies[4,5,6] and by some international organizations such as the United Nations Environmental Programme Finance Initiative (UNEP FI). In the 1980s, the United States developed legislation called the CERCLA—Comprehensive Environmental Response, Compensation, and Liability Act—for which banks could be considered liable for the environmental damage of a borrowing company under specific conditions. There were some court decisions in which the lending bank was found liable such as the *Fleet Factors Corporation* case in 1991 widely referred to in literature.[7,8]

Also, in the United Kingdom in 1995 and under the UK Environmental Act, banks could reach a second level of liability in relation with their borrowers' environmental damage. These legal frameworks brought strong controversy among the banking industry that started to develop position statements and lobbying the authorities[9] which has led to a softening in the legislation.

In Europe, it was from 2018 onwards that regulation linking finance and environmental performance started to be developed with the EU communication about the Action Plan: Financing Sustainable Growth.[10] This has led to several regulations and EU Directives that obligate banks to disclose the ratio of loans conceded that are aligned with carbon neutrality by 2050 using the EU green taxonomy definitions. These definitions, specific for several activities, indicate the science-based criteria that must be met so that such activity can be considered "green", i.e., aligned with decarbonization by 2050.

The demand for banks to disclose their green asset ratio comes from their structural power[11] related with the fact that banks can influence other sectors that depend on their lending to incorporate environmental concerns. These concerns can be incorporated when a borrowing company is defining a new product and when a borrowing consumer is purchasing goods such as housing, a car, and others. Moreover, due to their capacity in processing large amounts of information, banks have a greater level of efficiency than legislators, for instance, which allows banks to send information to outside investors about the creditworthiness of the borrowers.[12,13] Their structural power and their greater level of efficiency, as explained above, associated with the increasing pressure from society on companies to minimize their environmental impact has led to a worldwide recognition that banks have

[4] Sarokin and Schulkin (1991).

[5] Soppe (2004), pp. 213–224.

[6] Richardson (2005), pp. 280–290.

[7] Boyer and Laffont (1994), No. 94 s-22.

[8] Goldberg (1995).

[9] Coulson and Monks (1999), pp. 1–10.

[10] 2018 COM, Communication from the Commission, Action Plan: Financing Sustainable Growth. https://eur-lex.europa.eu/legal-content/EN/TXT/PDF/?uri=CELEX:52018DC0097.

[11] Schaper (2007).

[12] Diamond (1984), pp. 393–414.

[13] Diamond (1991), pp. 689–720.

a role to play in promoting sustainable development as Sarokin and Schulkin[14] had already recognized: "The business of moving money is inextricably linked to the movements of raw materials, finished goods, labour, and ultimately, to the quality of our environment ... If we are to achieve sustainable development, we must be prepared to finance it." This was the first time that the movement of money was associated with the use of natural resources via the investments that the banking sector decided to make and support. Therefore, during the 1990s, there was an emerging consensus that banks are linked via their lending in both investment and commercial areas to environmental degradation, nevertheless, the transposition from theory to regulation and practice only started in Europe in 2018.

2 The Financial Potential Losses From Climate

According with Mark Carney, former Governor of the Bank of England, "since the 1980s the number of registered weather-related loss events has tripled; and Inflation-adjusted insurance losses from these events have increased from an annual average of around $10bn in the 1980s to around $50bn over the past decade".[15] The European Commission has also stated:

> Between 2000 and 2016, annual weather-related disasters worldwide rose by 46%13 and between 2007 and 2016, economic losses from extreme weather worldwide rose by 86% (EUR 117 billion in 2016). This is a worrying trend, since close to 50% of the exposure of Euro area banks to risk is directly or indirectly linked to risks stemming from climate change. Other environmental issues are increasingly acknowledged to threaten current business models.[16]

The European Environmental Agency has also estimated that the EU Member States' (EU-28) disasters caused by weather and climate-related extremes accounted for some 83% of the monetary losses over the period 1980–2017 with these losses amounting to EUR 426 billion (at 2017 values). The most expensive climate extremes ***in** the EU Member States* include the 2002 flood in Central Europe (over EUR 21 billion), the 2003 drought and heat wave (almost EUR 15 billion), and the 1999 winter storm, Lothar, and October 2000 flood in Italy and France (both EUR 13 billion).[17]

---

[14]Sarokin and Schulkin (1991), p. 7.

[15]Mark Carney: Breaking the tragedy of the horizon – climate change and financial stability—Speech by Mr. Mark Carney, Governor of the Bank of England and Chairman of the Financial Stability Board, at Lloyd's of London, London, 29 September 2015. https://www.bis.org/review/r151009a.pdf.

[16]European Commission, 2018. Action plan to finance a sustainable growth. https://eur-lex.europa.eu/legal-content/EN/TXT/PDF/?uri=CELEX:52018DC0097&from=EN.

[17]https://www.eea.europa.eu/data-and-maps/indicators/direct-losses-from-weather-disasters-3/assessment-2.

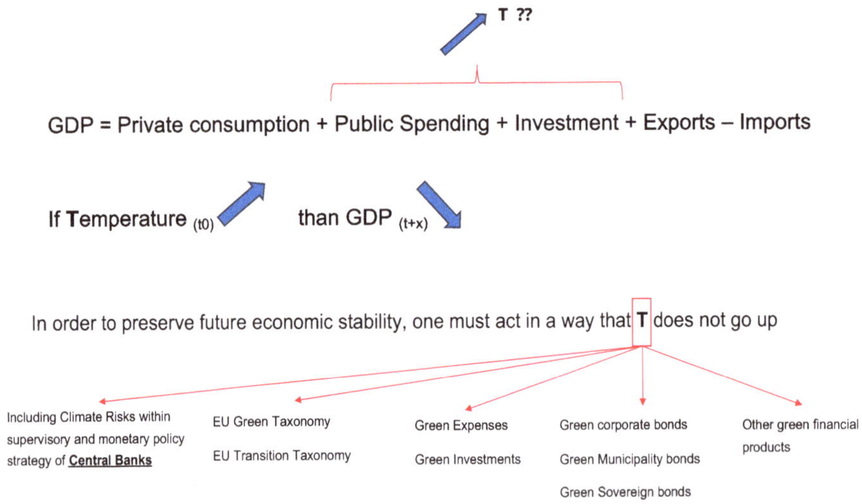

Fig. 1 Including Temperature in the GDP formula

A study by SwissRe[18] also concluded that global temperature rises will negatively impact GDP in all regions by mid-century; minus 4% if the Paris Agreement targets are met (a well-below 2 °C increase); minus 11% if further mitigating actions are taken (2 °C increase); minus 14% if some mitigating actions are taken (2.6 °C increase); and minus 18% if no mitigating actions are taken (3.2 °C increase).

This research raises a new relationship variable that should be included in the macroeconomic models, i.e., an increase in temperature today leads to a decrease in the GDP in the near future. This means that an increase in investment or public spending does not necessarily increase GDP in the future since it can be cancelled by the GDP drop due to a potential temperature increase (see Fig. 1).

Since temperature can have a significant negative impact in the GDP and is expected to grow, policy makers concerned about avoiding future recessions feel the pressure to define policies that will not contribute towards a temperature rise. For that, policy makers need to include temperature within the workings of the economic model. It is under this context that the EU has being regulating climate finance issues and that central banks have been working on developing knowledge and methodologies that can promote the inclusion of climate risks within the supervisory and monetary policy.

[18] Swiss Re Institute (2021). especially Table 1 in page 2.

3 Climate Risks and Transmission Channels

Despite all of the information available about the impacts of climate change, "climate risks" are probably the most poorly understood risks faced by banks today.[19] Climate risk has impacts across several industries and supply chains and creates damages to both private and public infrastructures under a context where the insurance gap regarding environmental risks is quite significant.

Nevertheless, it was only in 2018 that there was a recognition that climate-related risks are a source of financial risk. This acknowledgement came from the Network of Central Banks and Supervisors for Greening the Financial System (NGFS) launched in 2017. As this NGFS is a network of more than 100 central banks, such a statement provided by a milestone publication can be seen as a key moment for sustainable finance development. According to the NGFS[20] "... climate-related risks are a source of financial risk. It is therefore within the mandates of central banks and supervisors to ensure the financial system is resilient to these risks". This report also acknowledges that "there is a strong risk that climate related financial risks are not fully reflected in asset valuations. There is a need for collective leadership and globally coordinated action and, therefore, the role of international organisations and platforms is critical" that despite the

> prime responsibility for ensuring the success of the Paris Agreement rests with governments, it is up to central banks and supervisors to shape and deliver on their substantial role in addressing climate-related risks within the remit of their mandates. Understanding how structural changes affect the financial system and the economy is core to fulfilling these responsibilities.[21]

With this report, it became clear to the practitioners that climate risks can become more relevant for the economy since one of the paper recommendations was about the importance of integrating climate-related risks into financial stability monitoring and micro-supervision. In fact, further research by the NGFS has identified that climate change can lead to price changes which means that central banks should also have measures to minimize the climate change risk in the banks and in the economy.[22]

Recently, the European Central Bank published a "Guide on climate-related and environmental risks - Supervisory expectations relating to risk management and disclosure" where it states that "the European Central Bank (ECB) has identified climate-related risks as a key risk driver on the SSM Risk Map for the euro area banking system. The ECB is of the view that institutions should take a

---

[19] UNEP Finance Initiative Online Course - Climate Change & the TCFD: Risks and Opportunities for the Banking Industry.

[20] Network for Greening the Financial System – NGFS (2019a).

[21] Network for Greening the Financial System – NGFS (2019b).

[22] Network for Greening the Financial System – NGFS (2020).

forward-looking and comprehensive approach to considering climate-related and environmental risks."[23] This guide

> describes how the ECB expects institutions to consider climate-related and environmental risks – as drivers of established categories of prudential risks – when formulating and implementing their business strategy and governance and risk management frameworks. It further explains how the ECB expects institutions to become more transparent by enhancing their climate-related and environmental disclosures.[24]

It is now clear that climate related risks are a source of financial risk and are under the mandates of central banks and supervisors to guarantee the stability and resilience of the financial system.

4 Types of Climate Risk

In order to define the information that organizations, including financial institutions, should disclose to investors about how they assess and price climate-related risks and opportunities, in 2015, the G20 asked the Financial Stability Board (FSB) "to convene public- and private- sector participants to review how the financial sector can take account of climate-related issues[25]". As such, the FSB created the Task Force on Climate-related Financial Disclosures (TCFD) at COP21 in Paris in December 2015. This taskforce comprised 32 members selected by the Financial Stability Board from several organizations. In 2017, the TCDF published the "Final Report - Recommendations of the Task Force on Climate-related Financial Disclosures" in which it presents a set of definitions and also a framework about the information that all companies looking for investors, and financial institutions as well, should report about how they are incorporating climate risk in their strategy, processes, and targets. Despite the fact that this framework is voluntary, at the moment, the EU Non-Financial Reporting Directive is under revision, and it is expected that some of the TCFD disclosure recommendations can become mandatory. The TCFD 2017 report defines two types of climate-related risks that can affect companies, the economy, and the financial system: Transition risks that are related to the transition to a lower-carbon economy and physical risks related to the physical impacts of climate change.

The transition risks are related with the changes that will need to take place in order to achieve a lower-carbon economy that will happen:

- at policy and legal levels;
- in technology;

---

[23] European Central Bank - ECB (2020).

[24] European Central Bank - ECB (2020).

[25] Recommendations of the Task Force on Climate-related Financial Disclosures, June 2017. https://www.fsb-tcfd.org/wp-content/uploads/2017/06/FINAL-2017-TCFD-Report-11052018.pdf.

- in the market demand from consumers where there is a gradual increasing willingness to consume greener products; and
- in the reputational area since companies that are not aligned with societal expectations might lose their legitimacy, and thus their reputation can suffer.

The physical risks can be event driven (acute) or longer-term shifts (chronic) in climate patterns. Physical risks may have financial implications for organizations such as direct damage to assets and indirect impacts from supply chain disruption:

- the acute physical risks refer to those that are event-driven including increased severity of extreme weather events such as cyclones, hurricanes, or floods; and
- the chronic physical risks refer to longer-term shifts in climate patterns (e.g., sustained higher temperatures) that may cause sea levels to rise or chronic heat waves.

For each of the components of the transition and physical risks, the TCDF identifies the changes that can take place and their respective financial impact (page 10 of the TCFD 2017 Final Report) which provides with the structure needed to understand the indirect financial impacts that climate issues can have in the economy and financial system.

The TCFD methodology can be seen as a first step toward establishing some kind of transmission channels between climate risks and potential financial losses in companies. The TCFD can therefore help companies to understand why it is good for them to become aligned with the green management and technology practices since it provides them with the information about the risks they incur if they do not move towards a green approach.

5 Green Taxonomy of the EU

There is consensus among climate scientists that dramatic changes of the earth system will occur if the world temperature goes above 2 °C relative to preindustrial levels (1870). Some of those dramatic changes could be large rises in sea levels due to the melting of major ice sheets in Greenland and Antarctic, more frequent occurrences of climate-related extreme events, and massive species extinctions.[26] But, in 2005, the worldwide temperature already had increases of 1 °C above preindustrial levels, and the average temperatures in the Mediterranean have also risen by 1.5 °C and precipitation has fallen by 2.5%.[27]

As such, the scientists' concerns became focused on avoiding the world temperature increasing above 1.5 °C relative to preindustrial levels by the end of this

[26]Wang et al. (2017), 46,432.

[27]Worrying effects of accelerating climate change on the Mediterranean Basin, European Commission, Oct 2018.

century. According to the IPCC,[28] staying at or below 1.5 °C would see at least 420 million fewer people being frequently exposed to extreme heatwaves and at least 10.4 million fewer people exposed to the impacts of rising sea levels. It would also make it markedly easier to try to achieve the sustainable development goals.

Bearing all of this scientific information in mind, countries have agreed on the need to do whatever it takes to make sure the average worldwide temperature does not increase above 2 °C, ideally 1.5 °C, by signing the Paris Agreement. In order to reach a 1.5 °C temperature increase, countries will need to become carbon neutral by 2050. Achieving carbon neutrality implies promoting activities of mitigation in order to decrease CO_2 emissions and urge activities of adaptation allowing businesses to adapt to the fact that temperature will increase. For this to take place, investments and loans should be aligned with the decarbonization goal so that the temperature does not increase 1.5 °C.

Since Europe and its Member States are committed to the Paris Agreement and achieving decarbonization by 2050, the need became clear to use the capital flows in the economic activities that can lead us to carbon neutrality in 2050. In order to understand what those economic activities are that can lead the economy towards carbon neutrality in 2050, the European Commission together with several stakeholders and based on scientific criteria, elaborated the EU Green Taxonomy.[29] It expresses what sustainable environmental activities are and defines a list of technical screening criteria that specific activities should comply with in order to be catalogued as environmentally sustainable.

Therefore, the EU Green Taxonomy should be seen as a list of activities that can contribute to carbon neutrality and, as such, should be endorsed by the financial sector.

According with the EU Green Taxonomy, an environmentally sustainable activity is an activity that:

A) Must substantially contribute to one or more of the environmental objectives;

- mitigation of climate change;
- adaptation to climate change;
- use and protection of marine resources;
- transition to a circular economy, waste prevention, and recycling;
- pollution prevention and control; and
- protecting healthy sustainable ecosystems;

B) Cannot cause significant harm to any of the other objectives;

[28] IPCC SR15 2018.

[29] EU, 2020. Regulation (EU) 2020/852 of the European Parliament and of the Council, on the establishment of a framework to facilitate sustainable investment, and amending Regulation. https://eur-lex.europa.eu/legal-content/EN/TXT/PDF/?uri=CELEX:32020R0852.

C) Must comply with social minimum criteria (e.g., OECD Guidelines on Multinational Enterprises and the UN Guiding Principles on Business and Human Rights); and.
D) Comply with the technical criteria defined in the taxonomy.

The technical criteria are published via the EU Delegated Acts and identify the scientific minimum criteria for each significant activity that can make an activity identifiable as taxonomy aligned.

Since the goal of the taxonomy is to identify the activities that are aligned with the decarbonization path by 2050, organizations are obligated to disclose how aligned they are with such taxonomy. In 2023, large corporations (financial and non-financial) have to report the eligibility of their activities under the taxonomy regarding the mitigation and/or adaptation goal and, in 2024, for the remaining four goals. In 2024, they will be obligated to report—under the Directive for Corporate Sustainability Reporting—their alignment with the six environmental goals. The calculations for such alignment is well defined in the Article 8 delegated act[30] for companies, asset managers, credit institutions, investment firms, and insurance and reinsurance undertakings.

For nonfinancial organizations, such alignment will be provided by the percent of Turnover, Capex, and Opex that is aligned with the taxonomy. For banks, that alignment will be given by the Green Asset Ratio that aims to measure the percentage of loans that are aligned with the taxonomy.

So far, the literature does not provide the expected minimum level of alignment from companies, funds, or banks, but a lower alignment should be expected; otherwise, the current unbalanced planet would not exist.

6 The Real Meaning of the Green Asset Ratio of Banks

The precise formula to calculate the Green Asset Ratio (GAR) is provided in Annex V of the Article 8 delegated act.

According to Annex V:

> The GAR shall show the proportion of the of credit institution's assets financing and invested in taxonomy-aligned economic activities as a proportion of total covered assets in accordance with point 1.1.2 of this Annex.
>
> 1.1.2. Total covered Assets
>
> The calculation of the green asset ratio (GAR) for on-balance sheet exposures shall cover the following accounting categories of financial assets, including loans and advances, debt

[30]EU 2021. Commission Delegated Regulation (EU) 2021/2178 of 6 July 2021, supplementing Regulation (EU) 2020/852 of the European Parliament and of the Council by specifying the content and presentation of information to be disclosed by undertakings subject to Articles 19a or 29a of Directive 2013/34/EU concerning environmentally sustainable economic activities, and specifying the methodology to comply with that disclosure obligation. https://eur-lex.europa.eu/legal-content/EN/TXT/PDF/?uri=CELEX:32021R2178&from=EN.

> securities, equity holdings and repossessed collaterals: (a) financial assets at amortised cost; (b) financial assets at fair value through other comprehensive income; (c) investments in subsidiaries; (d) joint ventures and associates; (e) financial assets designated at fair value through profit or loss and non-trading financial assets mandatorily at fair value through profit or loss; (f) real estate collaterals obtained by credit institutions by taking possession in exchange for the cancellation of debts. The exposures referred to in Article 7(1) of this Regulation shall be excluded from the coverage of the GAR.
>
> The following assets shall be excluded from the numerator of the GAR: (a) financial assets held for trading; (b) on-demand interbank loans; (c) exposures to undertakings that are not obliged to publish non-financial information pursuant to Article 19a or 29a of Directive 2013/34/EU. The calculation of KPIs for off-balance sheet exposures shall consider financial guarantees granted by the credit institution and assets under management for guarantee and investee non-financial undertakings. Other off-balance sheet exposures such as commitments shall be excluded from that calculation.

Despite the formula to calculate the GAR, it is important to understand the real importance of this ratio. As referred to above, central banks consider climate risk as a financial risk. This means that, when banks have a high climate risk in their portfolios, they have greater risk and, as a consequence, could become in need of an increase in capital.

Even if the regulation about the relationship between climate risk and capital requirements does not yet exist, it is the market expectation that such requirements will exist soon. In fact, in 2022, the European Central Bank developed the first exercise on a climate risk stress test, concluding that:[31]

- Around 60% of banks do not have a climate risk stress testing framework;
- Most banks have not yet included climate risk in their credit risk models. Just 20% consider climate risk as a variable when granting loans;
- More than half of banks' income from nonfinancial corporate customers comes from greenhouse gas-intensive industries;
- Banks lack actual data regarding GHG emission availability. Around 70% of the reported S1, S2, and S3 emissions rely on proxies; and
- Banks do not have robust long-term strategies and show little differentiation between different possible long-term scenarios.

This study reinforced another done by the European Banking Authority in 2021.[32] This was *a first EU-wide pilot exercise on climate risk for which the main objective is to map banks' exposures to climate risk and provide insight into the green estimation efforts banks have carried out so far*. The sample included 29 volunteer banks from ten countries representing 50% of the EU banking sector's total assets that provided raw data on non-SME corporate exposures to EU domiciled obligors. *The study concluded that a first estimate of the starting point of their GAR currently stands at 7.9%. This lower GAR should not be a surprise. A low GAR means that few large companies in Europe have technology and business models aligned with*

[31] European Central Bank - ECB (2022).

[32] European Banking Authority - EBA (2021).

decarbonization by 2050. This is not a surprise, otherwise, the world would not have the existing climate risks.

If the ambition of the EU is to accelerate the transition towards decarbonization, than having a GAR as the only variable for banks could present real challenges for all of the EU banking system since it would indicate the future need to increase capital in a general way. Taking into account the economic situation in Europe, additional pressure on banks to raise capital probably would not bring the best results.

This is why a transition taxonomy is needed. Banks need to have an incentive to lend money to those companies that, having a high climate risk now, can present a substantive commitment towards achieving the green taxonomy requirements. That is why this contribution argues for the importance of having a Green Transition Asset Ratio (GTAR).

7 Green Transition Taxonomy

In order to have a *GTAR, there needs to be a Green Transition Taxonomy.*

In July 2023, the EU published a set of recommendations "on facilitating finance for the transition to a sustainable economy".[33] In this document are some important statements that reinforce the importance of a transition taxonomy and transition lending:

> Sustainable finance is about financing both what is already environment-friendly and what is transitioning to such performance levels over time. The level of sustainable investments is set to increase over time, as the transition progresses.
>
> Although the Union's legal framework does not define the concept of transition finance, transition finance should be understood as the financing of climate- and environmental performance improvements to transition towards a sustainable economy, at a pace that is compatible with the climate and environmental objectives of the EU.
>
> This Recommendation clarifies the concept of transition finance, acknowledging the significant role that market participants can play by voluntarily using tools from the Union sustainable finance framework, as needed, for transition finance.
>
> This Recommendation aims to support transition finance in a trusted environment for investors through encouraging the voluntary use of sustainable finance tools and disclosures in ways that can ensure the credibility of transition investment opportunities.
>
> The use of transition finance is voluntary. Not all undertakings, and not all economic sectors, have significant climate- or environmental transition finance needs. But where impacts can be reduced and are being reduced, that improvement should be recognised and financing for it should be facilitated.
>
> Small and medium-sized enterprises (SMEs) might need to finance their transition, and where this is the case, they could benefit from obtaining transition finance by providing key sustainability information. However, due to their size and more limited resources, this can be

[33] EU 2023. Commission Recommendation 2023/1425 of 27 June 2023 on facilitating finance for the transition to a sustainable economy. https://eur-lex.europa.eu/legal-content/EN/TXT/PDF/?uri=CELEX:32023H1425.

> difficult and costly. SMEs might need the support of their financing partners, suppliers and customers in their value chain when considering their transition finance needs and accessing transition finance in practice. Large corporate and financial intermediaries are encouraged to apply the principle of proportionality when engaging with SMEs and to exercise restraint when requesting information from SME value chain partners, suppliers and customers.
>
> Needs for transition finance can be determined by planning ahead and setting transition targets. This can be done, for instance, by setting out the company's short-, medium- and long-term targets and actions in line with the transition to a climate-neutral and sustainable economy, and investment and action plans that indicate the resources that have been allocated and the resources that are still needed, to ensure that the targets are reached and actions are planned and implemented in a transparent, credible and consistent way. This can be done at both company level and activity level, depending on where the need for transition finance arises.

This set of recommendations provides an opportunity for banks, large companies, and SMEs to continue to have access to loans. This is not because they are already fully aligned with the EU green taxonomy but because they have a solid transition plan to become aligned soon.

As such, these recommendations propose that companies looking for loans should have transition plans that can be substantiated on:

1. Having a materiality assessment. Undertakings can consider their transition finance needs based on their sustainability impacts, risks, and opportunities. These can be identified through a materiality assessment;
2. Having transition targets and defining individual transition pathways based on science-based scenarios and pathways;
3. Having the transition targets defined using the taxonomy or the EU climate benchmarks as well as credible transition plans;
4. Integrating transition targets and related transition finance needs in a credible transition plan;
5. Having plans to increase capital expenditures and, when appropriate, operating expenditures relating to achieving climate and environmental targets as well as current or targeted revenue related to the transition; and
6. Using green financial products to raise capital.

One relevant aspect is that this recommendation provides the openness for companies to set up a goal of 5 years (maximum 10) to reach the Green Taxonomy ambitions: "Undertakings are encouraged to use the Taxonomy to plan investments for meeting Taxonomy criteria for a given economic activity in 5 (exceptionally 10) years, as such investments are already recognised as fully Taxonomy aligned."

8 Green Transition Asset Ratio

As these recommendations are voluntary, banks have now the opportunity to tag their lendings as "green" or as "in transition". By having this opportunity, banks will also be able to voluntarily communicate their "Green Transition Asset Ratio" using the same logic as the GAR. By providing the market with these two ratios, banks are also sending a message to the market and regulators that they are much more exposed to transition companies which is beneficial to reach the 2050 goal of decarbonization. This implies that banks are using their structural power to induce companies to have transition plans based on science-based targets with a 5-year plan to achieve the green level as defined in the green taxonomy that will be achieved with green finance products.

9 Conclusions

The European Union has indirectly recognized the structural power of banks by proposing that a loan can be considered in transition if the undertakings have a substantive transition plan. This places pressure on banks to explain to companies the importance of having a transition towards decarbonized activity by 2050.

Despite the fact that no official document has referred to the existence of a GTAR and taking into account that central banks are working on methodologies that will lead to the incorporation of climate risks in the supervision and monetary policies of the central banks, it might make sense for banks to start producing the GTAR in a voluntary way. This variable can be of important use for central banks to analyse the exposure to climate risk in a loan portfolio. Those banks that also do not have clients with substantive transition plans are those with the highest climate risk which can become a pressing point for banks in raising their capital requirements with impacts on their performance.

References

Boyd J, Prescott E (1985) Financial intermediary-coalitions. Federal Reserve Bank of Minneapolis, Minneapolis

Boyer M, Laffont J (1994) Environmental risks and bank liabilities, Cirano, Scientific Series

Coulson A, Monks V (1999) Corporate environmental performance considerations within banking lending decisions, Eco-Management and Auditing Review

Diamond D (1984) Financial intermediation and delegated monitoring. Rev Econ Stud LI:393–414

Diamond D (1991) Monitoring and reputation: the choice between bank loans and directly placed debt. J Polit Econ 99:689–721

European Banking Authority - EBA (2021) Mapping climate risk. https://www.eba.europa.eu/sites/default/documents/files/document_library/Publications/Reports/2021/1001589/Mapping%20Climate%20Risk%20-%20Main%20findings%20from%20the%20EU-wide%20pilot%20exercise%20on%20climate%20risk.pdf

European Central Bank - ECB (2020) Guide on climate-related and environmental risks. Supervisory expectations relating to risk management and disclosure. https://www.bankingsupervision.europa.eu/legalframework/publiccons/pdf/climate-related_risks/ssm.202005_draft_guide_on_climate-related_and_environmental_risks.en.pdf

European Central Bank - ECB (2022) Climate Risk Stress Test 2022, Final Results. https://www.bankingsupervision.europa.eu/ecb/pub/pdf/annex/ssm.pr220708_annex2.en.pdf

Goldberg S (1995) Lender liability under CERCLA: shaping a new legal rule, vol 48. New York University Environmental Law Journal
Levine R. (2004) Finance and growth: theory and evidence
Network for Greening the Financial System – NGFS (2019a) A call for action Climate change as a source of financial risk. https://www.ngfs.net/sites/default/files/medias/documents/ngfs_first_comprehensive_report_-_17042019_0.pdf
Network for Greening the Financial System – NGFS (2019b) First comprehensive report- A call for action Climate change as a source of financial risk. https://www.ngfs.net/sites/default/files/medias/documents/ngfs_first_comprehensive_report_-_17042019_0.pdf
Network for Greening the Financial System – NGFS (2020) Climate Change and Monetary Policy Initial takeaways. https://www.ngfs.net/sites/default/files/medias/documents/climate_change_and_monetary_policy.pdf
Richardson B (2005) The equator principles: the voluntary approach to environmentally sustainable finance. Eur Environ Law Rev 14:280
Sarokin D, Schulkin J (1991) Environmental concerns and the business of banking. J Commercial Bank Lending
Schaper M (2007) Leveraging green power: environmental rules for project finance. Berkeley Electronic Press, Berkeley
Soppe A (2004) Sustainable corporate finance. J Bus Ethics 53:231–224
Swiss Re Institute (2021) The economics of climate change: no action not an option. swiss-re-institute-expertise-publication-economics-of-climate-change.pdf (swissre.com)
Wang Z, et al. (2017) Scenario dependence of future changes in climate extremes under 1.5 C and 2 C global warming, Scientific Reports, No. 7

EIB Group Climate Bank Roadmap 2021–2025

Miguel Morgado

Abstract The European Investment Bank is one of the world's main financiers of climate action and environmental sustainability.

The decade 2021–2030 is a critical timeframe for addressing our planet's climate and environment emergency. To achieve this, trillions of investment are required, as the world must:

- Limit global warming to 1.5 °C above preindustrial levels by the end of this century;
- Adapt to the unavoidable impacts of climate change;
- Combat environmental degradation;
- Halt biodiversity loss; and
- Stop widening inequalities.

The European Union is at the forefront of the global fight against climate change and environmental degradation. With the European Green Deal, the EU aims at making the European economy sustainable and inclusive. The EIB is an important partner in this new growth strategy while playing a leading role in the implementation of the Paris Agreement and the Sustainable Development Goals.

Sustainable development must be placed at the heart of all activities. All projects must meet Environmental and Social Standards with social development considerations increasingly mainstreamed in everything that is done.

This article follows a presentation from Miguel Morgado †, Former Head of the European Investment Bank (EIB) group representation in Lisbon, at a conference organized by the University of Lisbon School of Law on "Sustainable Finance: Between Public and Private solutions" that occurred on 4 July 2022 in Lisbon. It summarizes the document "EIB Group Climate Bank Roadmap 2021-2025" available at: https://www.eib.org/en/publications/the-eib-group-climate-bank-roadmap

R. Saraiva, P. A. Pardal (eds.), *Sustainable Finances and the Law*, Economic Analysis of Law in European Legal Scholarship 16,
https://doi.org/10.1007/978-3-031-49460-4_4

1 General Considerations

In November 2019 and in line with the political ambition behind the European Green Deal, the EIB Board of Directors decided to increase the level of climate and environmental commitment for the EIB Group. This increased ambition has far-reaching implications for the group, effectively transforming it from "an EU bank supporting climate" into "the EU climate bank".

The context behind this decision is alarming and clear. The combination of climate change and the destruction of ecosystems poses an increasing risk of environmental collapse with enormous human consequences. As illustrated by the Intergovernmental Panel on Climate Change's Special Report on Global Warming of 1.5 °C, the 2020s is the critical decade for meeting the long-term temperature and climate-resilience goals of the Paris Agreement and addressing the environmental crisis. Through the European Green Deal, the European Union (EU) has become the first region to endorse climate neutrality by 2050 and has committed to build Green Alliances with partner countries and regions worldwide. It works within the wider context of policies designed to enhance Europe's natural capital and eliminate pollution. The European Commission recently proposed to increase the level of ambition of greenhouse gas (GHG) emissions reduction by 2030—from the current 40% from the 1990 levels to at least 55%".

This is a global development challenge. Climate change and environmental degradation do not respect national borders. Their adverse impacts undermine the ability of all countries to achieve sustainable development. However, poor and developing countries, particularly least developed countries and small island developing states, will be among those most adversely affected and least able to cope with the anticipated shocks to their social, economic, and natural systems. Increasingly severe and more frequent droughts, rising sea levels, biodiversity loss, and other impacts create increasing risks to food and water security, coastal communities, and livelihoods. These challenges require internationally coordinated solutions and international cooperation to help developing countries move toward a low-carbon, climate-resilient, and sustainable economy. Meeting the United Nations (UN) Sustainable Development Goals also requires sustained long-term investment to decarbonize the physical capital stock and ensure it is resilient for a changing climate, to preserve and enhance natural capital, and to train and reskill people to work within a climate-neutral economy.

The coronavirus pandemic has made the challenge harder. It is currently placing an unprecedented burden on people, health systems, countries' economies, and government finances more generally. The EU has responded decisively to ensure recovery through an ambitious EUR 750 billion package known as Next Generation EU. Outside the EU, it has launched the "Team Europe" package which is part of its global response to the crisis and amounts to almost EUR 36 billion. Nevertheless, the recovery from COVID-19 is likely to dominate global public finances over the short to medium term and heed calls from many stakeholders for a green recovery.

The European Investment Bank Group—the European Investment Bank and Fund—can help support the EU to deliver on the long-term goals of the European Green Deal and UN Sustainable Development Goals more broadly. The EIB Group is one of the largest global financiers of sustainable development in general and climate action and environmental sustainability in particular. Through a wide spectrum of financial products and advisory services, it can work with partners to help support long-term green investment needs. Importantly, the EIB Group can support the entire spectrum of technological innovation from seed capital for very early-stage development to senior debt for mature technologies.

The EIB Board's decision has two broad elements. Firstly, the EIB will increase its level of support to climate action and environmental sustainability to exceed 50% of its overall lending activity by 2025 and beyond and thus help to leverage EUR 1 trillion of investment by the EIB Group over the critical decade ahead. This new level of commitment is designed to accelerate the transition to a climate-neutral, climate-resilient, and sustainable economy. Importantly, this includes a commitment for a proposal regarding a just transition.

The second core dimension of the EIB Board decision is to ensure that "all financing activities are aligned to the goals and principles of the Paris Agreement by the end of 2020". As the EU climate bank, the EIB Group cannot support the agreement with 50% of green finance if, at the same time, it undermines the goals with the remaining 50%. In line with the principles of sustainable finance, the EIB Group needs to ensure that all of its activities do no significant harm to the low-carbon and climate- resilient goals of the agreement.

Working within the joint MDB Paris alignment framework, the roadmap breaks down this commitment into four core work streams. The first concerns accelerating the green transition worldwide—increasing green investment and supporting long-term innovation and new business models. A second core work stream is focused on ensuring that the transition is just for all—working to support communities exposed to structural change or climate risks.

The EIB Group will continue to support a wide range of activities in line with its public policy goals. A third work stream is therefore directed at ensuring that none of these activities significantly harms the transition. In other words, all of its financing activities should be aligned with the goals of the Paris Agreement. Finally, the roadmap is rooted in a commitment to ensure that these different elements are embedded within a coherent policy approach towards supporting sustainable finance backed by the EIB Group's internal systems and building in the necessary accountability.

Before turning to the substance of this roadmap, it is important to stress its ambition. This next five- year period will undoubtedly be challenging, but it is also likely to be a defining period in which the European Green Deal becomes Europe's new growth strategy. It is a significant opportunity for the EIB Group to strengthen its dialogue with EU Member States to help deliver on long-term green investment needs.

This degree of ambition holds equally outside the EU. Meeting the goals of the Paris Agreement requires significant efforts to reduce greenhouse gas emissions and build climate resilience across the world. Building on its experience, the EIB will strengthen its support for EU external action through development financing, helping to ensure that this external action, environmental and social sustainability, and development cooperation are more than the sum of their parts. In close cooperation with all partners, it will seek to support countries adopting ambitious nationally determined contributions (NDCs) thereby ensuring access to long-term finance and advisory support.

2 Accelerating the Transition Through Green Finance

Progress overall in some aspects of the transition has already been extraordinary. This is most obviously the case with respect to electricity. Over the last decade, the cost of solar energy has fallen by more than an order of magnitude and continues to fall. As a result, it is the cheapest form of electricity generation in large parts of the world. Battery costs have undergone a similar cost reduction over the decade, helping ensure that electric vehicles are on the cusp of becoming competitive in many segments of the market. In addition, although less publicized, the technical performance of heat pumps has improved enormously over the decade, allowing electricity to replace carbon-intensive energy sources in heating homes or providing heat for industrial processes.

Faced with strong European political ambition backed up through a comprehensive legal framework, developing low-carbon technologies is increasingly a question of securing long-term global competitiveness. In other words, economic growth and green investment are increasingly interlinked.

In many other areas, however, the transition has barely begun. Global investment in natural capital—carbon sinks, biodiversity, and ecosystem preservation—remains insufficient. Significant innovation in low-carbon technologies is still required to cut emissions throughout the economy, notably in the “hard-to-abate” sectors. New business models are required to drive deployment and reduce the cost of the transition, and all of this needs to happen in a way that leaves no one behind, i.e., no people, no place.

The European Green Deal addresses these challenges. The EIB Group will seek to support this through its new level of commitment—gradually increasing its share of finance dedicated to green investment to over 50% by 2025 and beyond. The roadmap identifies several focus areas for EIB finance, including the just transition. This structure will help shape EIB Group business development including that with respect to financial and advisory product innovation.

In reviewing each of these focus areas, four general messages emerge as to the role of the EIB Group. The first is the need to substantially increase adaptation efforts with specific actions, prioritization, and initiatives that will be developed and enhanced in light of the forthcoming EU Adaptation Strategy. A second takeaway is the need to increase investment in innovative green technologies—from early-stage research to pilot demonstration of technologies complemented with support for new business models (battery storage, demand response, low- carbon hydrogen, e-charging). A third theme is the importance of driving down the long-term cost of capital in capital-intensive green infrastructure—urban public transport, rail and energy networks, waste and water networks, and carbon sinks. A fourth theme is the importance of aggregation, scalability, and replicability in ensuring investment at scale; this is particularly relevant for adaptation, energy efficiency, and sustainable agriculture. The EIB Group is active across all of these areas today in the EU and in developing countries. More can be done.

These focus areas help shape business development. In practice, local conditions are critical in shaping the way in which the EIB Group can most effectively support green investment. Within the EU, the EIB Group is therefore strengthening its dialogue with Member States by using national energy and climate plans, national adaptation strategies and plans, and recovery and resilience plans as a basis for reviewing how the EIB Group can fine-tune its support.

The EIB is equally committed outside the EU. There is an urgent need to strengthen resilience to climate change throughout some of the most vulnerable regions across the world. The EIB's business development activity will be anchored in the context of NDCs, national adaptation plans, and long-term strategies under the Paris Agreement and looking to engage particularly with countries with ambitious plans. Through this engagement, the EIB is ready to play a more active role in supporting countries' NDCs. This advisory service would need to be developed in close collaboration with the European Commission through EU delegations, the European External Action Service as well as partner multilateral development banks and international organizations.

The EIB Group has significant capability to support a broad range of green investment from large- scale infrastructure projects to development of innovative green technologies. Given the scale of the challenge and the extent of the investment needs identified, the EIB Group needs to build on its existing capability but also focus on product innovation. Work will continue to develop green loan and green debt products together with deployment of advisory services in order to support green investment through the provision of technical and financial expertise. Equity, funds, and other innovative financial products will be utilized to support development of higher-risk technologies and to address specific investment gaps and policy priorities.

3 Ensuring Just Transition for All

Supporting cohesion was one of the founding principles of the EIB when it was established in 1958. It continues to be a core priority—and, hence, the EIB Group will seek to ensure that no people or places are left behind along the transition pathway. This is of particular concern to regions that currently rely on carbon-intensive industries as a major source of local employment and income and to those sectors and livelihoods most at risk from climate change impacts.

The EIB has a solid track record in supporting the transition and economic restructuring of former coal and carbon-intensive regions through financing standalone environmental remediation projects as well as multi-sector investment programmes for modernization and integrated urban and regional development. Recent examples include projects to rehabilitate former open cast lignite mines, extensive restructuring of regional wastewater systems in industrial regions in order to restore environmental quality, and urban renewal in towns dependent on the mining industry.

The Just Transition Mechanism is the cornerstone of the EU response to this challenge. The EIB Group will play a central role within the mechanism by supporting each of its three main pillars in varying degrees. Most prominently, it will be the financing partner for the public-sector loan facility (or third pillar) and is expected to unlock investment of at least EUR 25 billion. However, it will also support the mechanism through InvestEU (and thus the second pillar designed to unlock private investment). Finally, it will look to support the Just Transition Fund itself (the first pillar) through structural programme loans. The EIB Group is also able to provide advisory services in support of all pillars of the mechanism as illustrated through the current activities of the Joint Assistance to Support Projects in European Regions (JASPERS).

The focus on a just transition has a wider interpretation worldwide in the context of social development. The EIB Group seeks to invest in projects that simultaneously support the transition and improve socio-economic development. This also entails focusing on building resilience of the people and employment sectors most vulnerable to climate change, both in Europe and worldwide, supplemented by advisory services to enhance the social impact of climate- and environment-eligible projects. For more than 40 years, the EIB has been functioning as the EU's development bank outside the European Union. The Climate Bank Roadmap forms a key component of the EIB Group's vision of how to achieve greater policy impact by focusing on the synergies between the EU climate and other priorities such as economic resilience; gender equality; and conflict, fragility, and migration.

4 Supporting Paris-Aligned Operations

The EIB Board has committed to "align all its financing activities with the principles and goals of the Paris Agreement by the end of 2020". Drawing from the agreement, this implies that financing activities need to be aligned with the Paris Agreement temperature and adaptation goals and "consistent with pathways towards low-carbon and climate-resilient development". This chapter presents an alignment framework to put this commitment into practice. It covers both dimensions – low-carbon and climate resilience. It first develops an approach in the context of new projects and then generalizes this across all EIB Group operations.

4.1 *Alignment to Low-Carbon Pathways*

The EU has committed to reduce greenhouse gas emissions significantly by 2030 and to achieve carbon neutrality by 2050. Despite the clarity of the overall pathway to climate neutrality, interpretation is required at the level of an individual operation. The purpose of the alignment framework is to provide an interpretation that is appropriate for the EIB Group as the EU climate bank and with its own particular public policy goals and business model.

In developing this framework, it builds upon key reference points. The EU Taxonomy is a natural starting point with the adoption of technical screening criteria to establish whether an activity "does no significant harm" to climate change mitigation or adaptation objectives. The Paris alignment methodological work of the multilateral development banks (MDBs) is also helpful in this regard.

In developing an approach to ensure alignment at a project level, the EIB has also looked to build on its economic assessment of investment projects, including the use of a shadow cost of carbon. The principles of this economic assessment are provided in the EIB Guide to Economic Appraisal. The test helps to ensure that EIB projects add net social benefits, i.e. that the benefit to society of a project outweighs the costs, including all externalities. This is equally the case along a transition pathway.

In the case of the energy sector, alignment is secured through the adoption of the recent EIB Energy Lending Policy.

A lack of clarity remains on the pathway to decarbonization for the aviation sector. The EIB Group will therefore focus on improving existing airport capacity including safety, security, rationalization, and resilience as well as decarbonization investment. Support will be withdrawn from investment in airport capacity expansion and conventionally fueled aircraft.

Road infrastructure: Given the relatively clear sectoral pathway towards decarbonization, the EIB will address concerns around capacity expansion through an adapted economic test for large projects. In particular, demand forecasts will be adapted in line with recognized long-term modelling studies with due attention to penetration rates of electric vehicles. Net emissions from the project will be valued at a shadow cost of carbon that is consistent with the path towards a 2050 climate neutrality target. This approach will screen out projects dependent on high short-term traffic growth (and hence emissions). The EIB will continue to support robust projects designed to improve existing traffic flows, rehabilitation projects, or projects with strong safety elements.

Road vehicles: In the first instance, the EIB Group will focus support on decarbonizing vehicle fleets and ensuring a substantial contribution where possible. In the current context of economic downturn and notably the difficulties experienced by many smaller companies, it is proposed to adopt the recommended values for "doing no significant harm" under the EU Taxonomy across multi-beneficiary intermediated loans (MBILs) and similar types of products.

Energy-Intensive Industry: The EIB does not support industry per se—but rather addresses the market failures associated with innovation, pollution, and carbon externalities. The EIB Group will therefore focus its support for innovation (research and development, pilot and demonstration projects) on low-carbon technologies. Support will be withdrawn from any new capacity based on traditional high-carbon processes (and without abatement technologies). In the case of existing conventional plants, the EIB Group will support energy efficiency, depollution, or circular economy projects that have an economic life expiring before 2035, i.e., well in advance of the 2050 date by which the sector should be operating on a net-zero emissions basis.

Research, development, and innovation (RDI): The EIB Group will continue to support research, development, and innovation in general. However, support will be withdrawn from activities that are no longer being supported under this framework (e.g. internal combustion engines or fossil fuel- based propulsion systems in the maritime and aviation sectors).

Agriculture and forestry: The EIB Group will ensure that activities do not expand into areas of high carbon stocks or high biodiversity value. Moreover, given the importance of livestock as a source of emissions, the EIB Group will focus support on meat and dairy industries adopting sustainable animal rearing methods that contribute to improved greenhouse gas emissions efficiency. In addition, given the approach adopted towards the aviation sector, it is proposed to no longer support export-orientated agribusiness models that focus on long-distance air transport for commercialization. This measure would exclude investments dependent on the international shipping of fresh, perishable agricultural goods through long-haul air cargo.

These principles are to be applied across EIB Group operations globally. However, in some cases, these principles have been interpreted with reference to EU regulations. In such instances, appropriate interpretation in the local context will be made for operations outside the EU. This is relevant to buildings, industry, agricultural practice, and roads.

As illustrated in the context of road infrastructure, the shadow cost of carbon is an integral part of the EIB Group alignment framework. It is a key technical parameter in the EIB economic assessment of projects. The current EIB carbon values are based on studies that predate the Paris Agreement and do not particularly reflect the net-zero emissions target by 2050 or 1.5 °C of global warming.

Based on a review of the latest modelling evidence, it is proposed to increase the EIB shadow cost of carbon to EUR 250 per tonne by 2030. By the time of net-zero emissions in 2050, this shadow cost rises to EUR 800 per tonne. These values are close to the recommendation of a recent study by France Stratégie that has subsequently been adopted to assess public sector projects in France. The shadow cost is a technical parameter used to estimate the full value to society from saving a tonne of carbon. The latest analysis on an appropriate shadow cost of carbon will be reviewed on an annual basis, and the cost will be adjusted accordingly (both up and down).

4.2 Alignment to Climate-Resilient Pathways

The second dimension of alignment concerns climate resilience. Climate change is already having profound consequences on all regions and across all sectors of the world. In order to manage this risk at the level of a project, the EIB has introduced a Climate Risk Assessment (CRA) system to provide a systematic assessment of the physical climate risk in direct lending. Drawing on robust climate data, the CRA system is a business process that helps the EIB and its clients to understand how climate change may affect their projects and to identify adaptation measures.

The CRA is the cornerstone of the EIB alignment framework. It focuses on the specific project and the client's operating environment. However, it is important to situate the project within the wider strategic context of climate resilience of the system. Over time, this wider aspect will need to be tackled systematically across all projects to ensure that EIB investments support broader resilience goals in line with clients' priorities.

4.3 Implementation Across New Operations

It is necessary to apply the approach set out above across a wide range of EIB Group operations. This raises two issues. The first is how to consider and then support the alignment of a counterparty rather than a project. The second is how to generalize application from a direct investment loan to the full range of EIB Group products. To address this, the EIB Group has developed counterparty alignment guidelines.

In terms of products, the full alignment framework will be applied in the case of direct investment loans, framework loans, infrastructure funds, and advisory assignments. The EIB Group also supports projects through intermediary financial institutions. In the case of intermediated products, low-carbon alignment will focus on three sectors: (i) energy through implementation of the EIB's Energy Lending Policy; (ii) mobile assets for transport services; and (iii) energy-intensive industries by excluding support for a limited number of industries. It should be noted that exclusions under points (ii) and (iii) would not apply to clearly defined investments in climate action or environmental sustainability activities, e.g. under dedicated climate action and environmental sustainability windows of intermediated loans. In terms of resilience, the EIB Group is developing an approach to systematically integrate climate resilience considerations into the due diligence process for financial intermediaries.

4.4 Climate-Related Risk Management

As a prudent financial institution, the EIB Group needs to be able to assess and mitigate risks to its balance sheet with respect to physical climate change risk and transition risk.

At the level of a project, risk assessment is based on the alignment framework set out above and underpinned by detailed climate-related due diligence. At the level of counterparties, climate risk screening tools have been developed for each of the EIB's main credit segments to assess climate risk and for the European Investment Fund's equity portfolio. Initially, the screening tool will be used for portfolio monitoring as well as internal reporting and disclosures. It will provide transparency on the EIB Group's exposure to climate risk and allow informed risk management decisions.

As of the end of 2019, the EIB managed a portfolio of approximately 7500 operations with more than 4000 counterparts with a total signed exposure of approximately EUR 560 billion, including EUR 65 billion in loans granted in 106 different countries outside the EU. Climate change risks in the portfolio have been assessed by approaching the portfolio as an aggregation of projects and as an aggregation of counterparts. The climate change risks for the credit portfolio will be assessed through aggregation of the results of the climate risk screening tools for counterparts.

5 Building Strategic Coherence and Accountability

To deliver on the actions laid out in the previous sections—to accelerate the transition through green finance, ensure a just transition for all, and align all operations to the goals of the Paris Agreement—these dimensions need to be placed into a coherent policy approach towards supporting sustainable finance. This approach must also ensure robust and timely delivery of all Paris alignment activities and allow for monitoring, learning, and improving. The EIB Group approach will be based on three crosscutting aspects: (1) policy to set out how climate-related activities fit within the wider context of sustainable finance and overall environmental and social sustainability; (2) transparency, accountability, and quality assurance; and (3) institutional support to the EIB Group's activities.

5.1 A Coherent Approach to Policy

The EIB Group's approach to support sustainable finance will mirror important parts of EU and international efforts in this field, particularly the European Commission's action plan for financing sustainable growth. Two elements of the European

Commission's action plan require particular attention: The EIB Group's use of the EU Taxonomy and a planned approach for climate and nature- related disclosures in line with EU guidelines.

The EIB Group will align its tracking methodology for climate action and environmental sustainability finance with the framework defined by the EU Taxonomy Regulation as this develops over time.

While aligning with the taxonomy both in its approach and technical criteria, the EIB Group will also remain within its externally audited tracking system for climate finance that is harmonized with other international financial institutions.

The EIB will remain active in supporting the emergence of a global sustainable finance sector through its active participation as a Member of the EU Sustainable Finance Platform and its involvement as an observer/partner in the International Platform on Sustainable Finance, the Network on Greening the Financial System, and the Coalition of Finance Ministers for Climate Action.

The update and consolidation process of the EIB Group's Environmental and Social Policy Framework will lead to a stronger and systematic integration of climate, environmental, and social actions into EIB Group policies and standards. As an important first step in the policy framework, the EIB Climate Strategy will be updated to bring its language in line with the Paris Agreement, the latest EU and international policy developments, and the latest scientific knowledge and to incorporate the new EIB Group climate action and environmental sustainability targets. Moreover, the EIB Group has further developed its Environmental and Social Policy Framework in order to address the new policy developments, emerging environmental and social issues, incorporating lessons learned, and meeting the changing needs of its clients and promoters.

5.2 *Transparency, Accountability, and Quality Assurance*

To further integrate climate change and environmental and social considerations into its financing activities, the EIB will enhance and develop additional risk management tools to assess physical, transition, and systemic risks at project, portfolio, and counterparty levels.

The EIB Group will also seek to generate the data necessary to track progress in meeting its commitments through further development of climate and environmental impact measurement and reporting systems, including allowing reporting on the climate impact of intermediated financing.

A coherent EIB Group approach must include a results framework that will allow the EIB Group to monitor progress and to assess and report on the outcomes of its activities related to the Climate Bank Roadmap both to its shareholders and to other stakeholders. This results framework must enable the EIB Group to continuously improve its practices and policies over time.

5.3 Institutional Elements

Several additional, “institutional” elements are designed to complete the EIB Group’s efforts to align financing activities with the goals of the Paris Agreement and to support the Climate Bank Roadmap from an institutional perspective. They encompass specific EIB Group initiatives to: (i) align internal operations to the goals of the Paris Agreement; (ii) share knowledge and experience with key stakeholders and develop strategic partnerships; (iii) communicate clearly and regularly on the progress, challenges, and lessons learned through the implementation of the Climate Bank Roadmap; and (iv) enhance the management of the human resources needed to achieve its ambitious goals.

6 Next Steps

The EIB will structure future work around new action plans that will build on the first five years of implementation of the EIB’s 2015 Climate Strategy and will revolve around the four main workstreams of the roadmap: (1) accelerating the transition through green finance; (2) ensuring a just transition for all; (3) supporting Paris-aligned operations; and (4) building strategic coherence and accountability. The EIB Group will prepare progress reports every year to update its governing bodies on the implementation of the Climate Bank Roadmap. The EIB Group will assess the Climate Bank Roadmap in 2024 with a view of informing revisions or modifications for subsequent implementation periods in accordance with the Paris Agreement’s five-year “ratchet mechanism” cycle.

Part II
Markets and Climate Change

Evaluating Additionality Analyses: California Cap and Trade and the Regional Greenhouse Gas Initiative

Ruthie Lazenby

Abstract This paper explores additionality analyses for offsets, a core theoretical requirement to ensure that emissions trading schemes reduce overall greenhouse gas emissions (GHGs). In the context of offsets, the additionality analysis evaluates whether an emission reduction would have occurred absent the incentive provided by the offset. The purpose is to determine whether reductions are caused by the policy intervention. The paper identifies a tension between adequate additionality analyses and the implementation costs they impose and evaluates these tensions in practice using two emissions trading programs in the United States, California Cap and Trade and the Regional Greenhouse Gas Initiative, as illustrative of the design challenges. The paper concludes that while holistic, project-specific quantifications of offset emissions relative to a counterfactual baseline scenario may not be necessary or practically feasible, evaluating one or two benchmarks may not be an adequate substitute to test such an important concept.

1 Introduction

This chapter examines the implementation of additionality analyses for offsets, a core theoretical requirement to ensure that emissions trading schemes actually reduce overall greenhouse gas emissions (GHGs). The stakes are high: Emissions trading schemes remain the dominant policy tool for reducing GHGs as global emissions are on course to reach the threshold for "catastrophic" climate change.[1]

[1] MIT CLIMATE. June 22, 2021. Why Did the IPCC Choose 2° C as the Goal for Limiting Global Warming?, https://climate.mit.edu/ask-mit/why-did-ipcc-choose-2deg-c-goal-limiting-global-warming. Emissions trading schemes are valued at approximately USD 277 million. Chestney, Nina. January 27, 2021. Global Carbon Markets Value Surged to Record $277 Billion Last Year, REUTERS, https://www.reuters.com/article/us-europe-carbon-idUSKBN29W1HR.

R. Lazenby (✉)
Shapiro Fellow in Environmental Law and Policy, UCLA Law Emmett Institute on Climate Change and the Environment, Los Angeles, CA, USA

R. Saraiva, P. A. Pardal (eds.), *Sustainable Finances and the Law*, Economic Analysis of Law in European Legal Scholarship 16,
https://doi.org/10.1007/978-3-031-49460-4_5

Offsets represent a significant portion of the reductions claimed by and revenue generated from these policy tools.[2] More pointedly, in mandatory emissions trading programs, offsets literally offset regulated parties' legal obligations to reduce emissions. Ensuring the integrity of the reductions claimed as offsets is, therefore, essential.

The premise of emissions trading schemes is based on the Coasian theories of property rules and tradeable allowances.[3] These schemes work by setting a limit on the total amount of pollution that can be emitted into the environment and issuing individual allowances to regulated parties designating how much they are allowed to emit. Regulated parties can then choose how to meet their allowance with options including selling or banking credits or buying credits or offsets to compensate for emissions above their allowance. In this system, credits represent GHGs that a regulated party had the right to emit but did not, and deficits represent GHGs above a regulated party's allowance. Offsets, on the other hand, represent activities that reduce overall GHGs by mitigating or avoiding anticipated emissions or by removing past emissions.[4] The function of offsets is to counterbalance the extra emissions (deficits) generated by regulated parties. Including offsets in emissions trading programs is intended to allow industry more flexibility while still ensuring an overall GHG reduction. While credits and deficits are generated by regulated parties, offsets generally come from voluntary entrants to the market.

Offsets allow and, in a sense, justify extra emissions from regulated industry, therefore, certifying that credited reductions actually counterbalance those emissions is crucial if the program is to reduce overall emissions. This requires comparing the quantity of extra emissions and extra reductions, but it also necessitates ensuring that credited reductions are, in fact, extra or "additional." This evaluation is called the additionality analysis.[5] Additionality is important for offsets from both mandatory and voluntary schemes, but because offsets applied to mandatory schemes are used directly to offset regulated parties' legal obligations to reduce emissions, their evaluation is especially significant. This chapter, therefore, focuses on offsets from

---

[2] Many emissions trading programs and "all extant GHG cap-and-trade systems" allow participants to purchase offsets in addition to credits. McNish (2012), p. 388. McNish points to EPA predictions from 2009 that 50% of emission reductions would come through offsetting "rather than inside-the-system reductions". *Id.* at 390.

[3] Wiener (1999), pp. 677, 679. Morag-Levine (2007), pp. 161, 199.

[4] McNish at 2 (explaining that "[u]nlike allowances, offsets are not created by government fiat, but are new rights created by additional emissions-reducing activities outside the system").

[5] One counter-intuitive outcome of this approach is that it rewards historically bad actors by paying them to change their behaviour. Historically good actors who had already, for example, accepted a cut in profits in order to reduce their emissions are not eligible to benefit because their reductions would have occurred despite the policy incentive. The additionality analysis only makes sense when the neoclassical economics assumption of autonomous, rational, and self-interested actors is embraced. This assumption is not always correct; therefore, it results in unfair outcomes to more responsible actors and arguably perverse long-term incentives for businesses not to act responsibly because the dominant approach to regulation is to pay off bad behavior rather than regulate it directly.

mandatory schemes, although many of the issues discussed apply to voluntary schemes as well.

Additionality evaluates whether a given emission reduction would have occurred absent the incentive provided by the offset credit.[6] The purpose of the analysis is not merely to guarantee that the reductions have taken place (or that they are "real") but to determine whether reductions are *caused by* the policy intervention.[7] If the reductions are not caused by the emissions trading program, it can be assumed that they are not additional, i.e., they would have occurred even in the absence of the policy. Non-additional reductions cannot compensate for additional emissions from regulated industry so should not be credited as offsets.[8]

There is tension between adequate additionality analyses, implementation costs, and the integrity of the emissions trading program. The primary purported benefits of emissions trading schemes over other policy interventions is the efficiency of such programs. Yet, additionality analyses generate substantial transaction costs. Offset programs can be expensive to implement relative to other policies because this calculation is complex, context-dependent, and can require information that is not readily available.[9]

This paper evaluates these tensions in practice using two of the major emissions trading programs in the United States, the California Cap and Trade and the Regional Greenhouse Gas Initiative, as illustrative of the design challenges. Additionality analyses are context-dependent,[10] therefore, the chapter specifically evaluates the tests for one kind of reduction project, i.e., the use of anaerobic digesters on animal agriculture operations. Anaerobic digester systems cap GHG-emitting manure lagoons to capture the GHGs that include large quantities of methane and use the gases for other purposes.[11] This paper concludes that, while holistic, project-specific quantifications of offset emissions relative to a counterfactual baseline scenario may

[6] In this paper, the author uses the term emission reduction to refer to the resulting overall reductions in emissions under the program as a result of offset eligible reductions but avoided/captured emissions and removal.

[7] Offsets are generally required to be "real, permanent, quantifiable, verifiable, and enforceable" in addition to additional. *See*, e.g., Cal. Health & Safety Code § 38562 (d)(1).

[8] Gillenwater, Michael. January 2012b. What is Additionality? Part 2: A Framework for More Precise Definitions and Standardized Approaches, Discussion Paper No. 002 Version 03, 3.

[9] Gillenwater, Michael. January 2012a. What is Additionality? Part 1: A Long Standing Problem, Discussion Paper No. 001, Version 02, 5 ("relative to other policies, have the potential to entail greater implementation costs associated with the assessment of additionality of and baselines for proposed activities.")

[10] For example, the additionality determination necessary for offset projects that remove $C0_2$ from the atmosphere requires a different kind of calculation than projects that purport to avoid projected future emissions. Even within the category of avoidance and mitigation projects, however, the method of calculation necessarily varies depending on the details of the project and the sector.

[11] *See, e.g.*, Roth, Sammy. April 9, 2020. Cow Poop Could Fuel California's Clean Energy Future. But Not Everyone's On Board, L. A. Times, https://www.latimes.com/environment/story/2020-04-09/cow-poop-california-clean-energy-future.

not be necessary or practically feasible, evaluating one or two benchmarks is not an adequate substitute for testing such an important concept.

2 Additionality Background

Academic and policy literature consistently refer to additionality as a determination of "what otherwise would have occurred". However, the literature frequently leaves out an important detail in the hypothetical: What otherwise would have occurred *except for what*?[12] This gap is sometimes implicitly filled with "if not for the offset project" and at others as "if not for the incentive provided by the policy intervention". Each interpretation begets a fundamentally different analysis. When evaluating reductions claimed for the capture of methane by an anaerobic digester, for example, asking whether the reduction would have occurred if not for the project only relates whether the anaerobic digester is, in fact, functioning as intended to capture methane emitted from the manure lagoon. As additionality scholar, Michael Gillenwater, has discussed, this approach "begets circular definitions of additionality and baseline", where a project is additional if it is different from what would have happened without the project.[13,14] On the other hand, asking whether the reduction would have occurred absent the incentive provided by the offset credit revenue forces regulators to grapple with whether the incentives actually result in additional reductions that can compensate for additional emissions.[15]

To determine whether a given emissions-reducing project would have occurred absent the incentive provided by the credits, regulators should theoretically calculate a counterfactual baseline scenario absent offset credits and compare the emissions associated with a given offset project to this baseline. Unfortunately, however, a holistic, rigorous, project-specific analysis is rarely feasible for emission reduction and avoidance projects.[16] Instead, most programs rely on benchmarks that approximate whether the offset project would have occurred absent the credits rather than comparing actual project emissions to a baseline.[17] To constitute a sound

[12] Gillenwater (2012a) Part 1, 9.

[13] Gillenwater (2012b) Part 2, 5.

[14] On circular and non-circular definitions of additionality, see Gillenwater (2012) Part 1, 14, Figure.

[15] Gillenwater (2012b) Part 2, 5.

[16] Removal (as opposed to reduction or avoidance) projects are eliminating existing GHGs, therefore, they do not require this kind of hypothetical projection.

[17] A World Bank report proposes that "Data availability whether on financial, technological, or social issues, should guide the choice of additionality testing approach", but shaping the analysis to available data presents worrisome implications for the soundness of the offsets. World Bank Group Partnership for Market Readiness. May 2016. Carbon Credits and Additionality: Past, Present, and Future, Technical Note 13, https://openknowledge.worldbank.org/bitstream/handle/10986/24295/K8835.pdf?sequence=2.

additionality analysis, benchmarks must approximate the mandates, barriers, and major incentives that shape project operators' actions.

The first emissions trading program to allow for offsets (certified emission reductions (CERs)) was the Clean Development Mechanism (CDM) created by the Kyoto Protocol.[18] More specifically, the CDM allowed industrialized nations to conduct offset projects in developing nations rather than reduce their emissions directly in order the meet their reduction targets under the agreement.[19] Concerns about the additionality requirement for CDM projects have been raised from the beginning. In 2012, "the most common reason for the rejection of proposed CDM emission reduction projects [had] been the inability of project proponents to demonstrate additionality using the CDM process for doing so".[20] At the same time, other emissions trading programs have borrowed heavily from the trailblazing structure and processes put in place by the CDM.

Academic and policy literature differentiates between multiple types of additionality including financial additionality, investment additionality, emissions additionality, barrier additionality, performance-based additionality, etc..[21] Unfortunately, these terms often lack consensus definitions. The two most conceptually important types of additionality are legal and financial additionality. The former is straightforward. It asks whether a given reduction is already mandated by law, policy, or judicial order. If a reduction is already required by law, it will not reduce total emissions below the baseline scenario and should not be eligible for an offset credit. The financial additionality analysis is more complex. It seeks to determine whether the existing financial incentives already provide adequate impetus to adopt a given emission-reducing practice. For example, in the context of anaerobic digester systems, the financial additionality analysis would evaluate whether the existing financial incentives to produce and sell biomethane are sufficient to motivate livestock operations to install digesters and other necessary infrastructure. If existing

[18]Clean Development Mechanism, United Nations Climate Change, https://unfccc.int/process-and-meetings/the-kyoto-protocol/mechanisms-under-the-kyoto-protocol/the-clean-development-mechanism.

[19]There are important environmental justice implications of offset programs' basic approach to fungibility of emissions, especially as offset projects are often created for developed countries in developing countries. After all, emission reducing projects do not necessarily minimize other environmental harms. Additionally, rapid increases in development due to offset markets can pose serious concerns around sovereignty and land justice. For an example of this critique, *see* Nyéléni Newsletter. November 2010. No. 1, available at https://nyeleni.org/DOWNLOADS/newsletters/Nyeleni_Newsletter_Num_1_EN.pdf ("[Offsets] allows rich countries to carry on polluting while funding controversial projects in developing countries (e.g. industrial gases projects, construction of big dams for hydroelectric power, or monoculture plantations for the biomass industry). Often these projects endanger local communities and their rights; serving only private businesses' profit and promoting land-grabbing.")

[20]Gillenwater (2012a) Part 1, 2.

[21]Gillenwater (2012a) Part 1, 18–19.

incentives are adequate, the resulting reductions would not be additional because they would not be motivated by offset revenue.[22]

The use of benchmarks often entails a sectoral or industry-wide analysis rather than a project-specific analysis.[23] For example, common practice tests, which are used as a standardized benchmark for financial additionality, can only be applied to sectoral- or industry-wide analyses because they ask whether the offset project is already common practice in the sector. This approach sacrifices detail about individual projects but may be necessary for offset programs to operate at scale.[24] However, sectoral analyses should also empower regulators to conduct deeper, more rigorous analyses of the sector since most emissions trading programs only review a handful of sectors as opposed to hundreds of unique projects.[25] At the same time, when additionality analyses are conducted for entire sectors, the stakes of false positives—determinations that a set of reductions are additional when, in fact, they are not—become much higher since they will apply to entire industries instead of just a single project.

3 Additionality Analysis Case Studies

This section surveys and analyses the requirements for additionality in California's cap-and-trade program and the Regional Greenhouse Gas Initiative. It focuses specifically on protocols for the use of anaerobic digester systems as one case study. Offset projects range from technologies that reduce active emissions to removal and sequestration, therefore, testing methodology must be designed with a nuanced understanding of the relevant industry. While the details vary across project types, the case of anaerobic digester systems illustrates some of the broader challenges in the implementation of additionality requirements.

[22] Note that financial additionality can include policy incentives as well as revenue from sales: Tax credits, grants, guaranteed loans, or other policy mechanisms fit into the financial additionality category because they provide financial incentives rather than legal mandates to shift behaviour. Note also that financial additionality is distinct from but closely related to the issue of double counting or credit stacking. Double counting occurs when parties claim multiple credits or other financial benefits for the same emission reductions. If double counting has occurred, the reduction is not additional. However, the underlying concern expressed is different in each case. With double counting, the project is the claiming of multiple benefits for the same action, and the concern is primarily fairness. With additionality, it is primarily the integrity of the program as a whole and ensuring that net emissions are reduced.

[23] Gillenwater (2012a) Part 1, 17.

[24] Gillenwater (2012a) Part 1, 17.

[25] There are exceptions, however. An offset project specifically mandated by a judicial decision, for example, to install GHG-reducing technology, would require project-specific research.

3.1 California Cap-and-Trade

California's cap-and-trade program allows regulated entities to use offsets to cover up to specified amounts of their compliance obligations (called the "quantitative usage limit").[26] The program allows regulated entities to cover up to 4% of their compliance obligation for emissions from 2021-2025."[27] The program allowed regulated entities to cover up to 8 percent of their obligations through 2020 and will allow up to 6 percent for emissions from 2026-2030.[28] Offset projects can be located anywhere in the United States,[29] however, as of 2021, no more than one half of a regulated party's quantitative usage limit may be sourced from projects that do not provide direct environmental benefits within the state of California.[30] The California Air Resources Board (CARB), which implements California Cap and Trade, has certified offset projects for anaerobic digester systems at over 100 livestock operations around the country and granted over three million livestock protocol offset credits.[31]

The California cap-and-trade regulation requires that offset credits represent additional GHG emission reductions.[32] The regulation's additionality requirement states: "The activities that result in GHG reductions and GHG removal enhancements are not required by law, regulation, or any legally binding mandate applicable in the offset project's jurisdiction, and would not otherwise occur in a conservative business-as-usual scenario...".[33] This provision articulates a legal additionality requirement and offers a description of CARB's baseline conservative business-as-usual scenario. "Business as Usual Scenario" is defined as "the set of conditions reasonably expected to occur within the offset project boundary in the absence of the financial incentives provided by offset credits, taking into account all current laws and regulations, as well as current economic and technological trends."[34] This language is precise as to the dependent variable: The baseline will reflect a world

[26] Cal. Air Resources Board, Direct Environmental Benefits (DEBS), https://ww2.arb.ca.gov/our-work/programs/compliance-offset-program/direct-environmental-benefits.

[27] Cal. Air Resources Board, Compliance Offset Program: About, https://ww2.arb.ca.gov/our-work/programs/compliance-offset-program/about.

[28] *Id.*

[29] Cal. Code Regs. tit. 17, § 95972 ("Geographic Applicability. A Compliance Offset Protocol must specify where the protocol is applicable. The geographic boundary must be within the United States or United States Territories.")

[30] Cal. Air Resources Board, ARBOCs Issuance Map, https://webmaps.arb.ca.gov/ARBOCIssuanceMap/; Cal. Air Resources Board, Direct Environmental Benefits (DEBS), https://ww2.arb.ca.gov/our-work/programs/compliance-offset-program/direct-environmental-benefits.

[31] The Carbon Offset Toolkit, The Livestock Offset Protocol, https://carbonoffsettoolkit.org/the-livestock-protocol/.

[32] Cal. Code Regs. tit. 17, § 95970.

[33] Cal. Code Regs. tit. 17, § 95973.

[34] Cal. Code Regs. tit. 17, § 95802 (a)(43).

in the absence of "the financial incentives provided by offset credits".[35] Meanwhile, the analysis proposed is broad, covering "the set of conditions" that would have otherwise occurred.[36]

The "compliance offset protocols" that CARB has issued to describe the methodologies for crediting specific types of offset projects refer back to these definitions and elaborate on the non-legal aspects of additionality.[37] The offset protocol for reductions from anaerobic digesters on livestock operations, for example, includes two parts, i.e., a legal additionality test and a "performance standard evaluation".[38] Performance standards evaluate the penetration of a given project in the relevant industry.[39] In subsection (a), the performance standard evaluation section states, in language that parallels the regulation, that reductions "must exceed those likely to occur in a business-as-usual scenario" but does not articulate any test or standard to evaluate this.[40] The performance standard evaluation then introduces two additional requirements in subsections (b) and (c).[41]

Subsection (b) requires that manure lagoons were anaerobic environments prior to the installation of the digester. This requirement is responsive to concerns that operations will create new manure lagoons in order to access the technology rewarded by offset credits. If facilities were to convert from dry manure management

---

[35] *Id.*

[36] Note that the qualifier "conservative" presents additional questions. By adding the conservative qualifier to the baseline – a business-as-usual scenario – CARB seems to be signaling a more generous metric to credit-seekers. If the business-as-usual baseline is interpreted more conservatively, a plain reading would suggest that it would be viewed as changing more slowly and therefore, facilities' emissions could decrease less and still generate larger credits in relationship to the baseline. However, the same regulation defines "conservative" as "in the context of offsets, utilizing project baseline assumptions, emission factors, and methodologies that are more likely than not to understate net GHG reductions or GHG removal enhancements for an offset project to address uncertainties affecting the calculation or measurement of GHG reductions or GHG removal enhancements". Cal. Code Regs. tit. 17, § 95802 (a)(77). This definition interprets the claimed *reductions* conservatively but not the baseline. However, the relationship between baseline and reductions is zero-sum. Given that the reduction only exists relative to a baseline, decreasing one value would necessarily decrease the other and vice versa. In an additionality analysis, clarity on whether a conservative scenario describes the set of conditions in the baseline or GHG reductions is essential.

[37] The offset protocols are for livestock projects, mine methane capture (MMC) projects, ozone depleting substances (ODS) projects, rice cultivation projects, US forest projects, and urban forest projects. Cal. Air Resources Board, Offset Protocols, https://ww2.arb.ca.gov/our-work/programs/compliance-offset-program/compliance-offset-protocols.

[38] Cal. Air Resources Board. November 14, 2014. Compliance Offset Protocol Livestock Projects: Capturing and Destroying Methane from Manure Management Systems at Ch. 3 *available at* https://ww2.arb.ca.gov/sites/default/files/barcu/regact/2014/capandtrade14/ctlivestockprotocol.pdf.

[39] *See, e.g.,* Cal. Air Resources Board. October 7, 2020. *Compliance Offsets Protocol Task Force Initial Draft Recommendations* at 34, https://ww2.arb.ca.gov/sites/default/files/2020-10/offsets_task_force_draft_report_100720.pdf.

[40] Compliance Offset Protocol Livestock Projects at Ch. 3.4.

[41] *Id.* at Ch. 3.4.1.

practices to the higher-emitting liquid manure management necessary for digesters in order to benefit from the credits, the program would be incentivizing an *increase* in baseline GHG emissions to only then pay operations for the capture of these new emissions. The requirement that anaerobic lagoons predate the project's commencement is important, but the test fails to address other, arguably more likely, ways that credits could perversely incentivize increased emissions. For example, increasing herd sizes to benefit from credit revenue would be much simpler that transitioning from dry to liquid manure management. Additionally, offset credits could incentivize operators who may have otherwise considered transitioning away from highly-emitting liquid systems to more sustainable dry manure management in order to maintain liquid systems despite their greater harms to climate, air, and water.

Subsection (c) requires that "uncontrolled anaerobic storage and/or treatment of manure is common practice in the industry and geographic region where the offset project is located".[42] Common practice is not defined in the protocol or in the cap-and-trade regulation, but this requirement is clearly intended to address financial additionality. The purpose of the test is to determine whether existing incentives are inadequate to promote the installation of digesters on a broad scale.

The inclusion of subsection (a) is puzzling. The language is broader than subsections (b) and (c). It reiterates a more specific version of the general regulatory language on additionality. Additionally, while (b) and (c) give specific tests, (a) simply states a standard that, as this chapter discusses, is challenging to calculate. However, the surplusage canon would give effect to every word, so (a) should not be simply written off. The inclusion of subsection (a) as a separate provision suggests that CARB does not view the legal test and performance standard subsections (b) and (c) as adequate to evaluate additionality on their own. It is not clear, however, whether and how CARB calculates a baseline to which it can compare quantified emission reductions from the digester projects in order to comply with subsection (a).

Regardless of how they structure their additionality analyses, all offset programs, including California's cap-and-trade program, must still quantify a baseline and reduction to ensure that offset reductions compensate for deficits and allocate credits.[43] Since credits compensate operators in proportion to the quantity of avoided emissions or additional reductions, that quantity must be determined. The cap-and-trade offset protocols provide detailed instructions on how reductions are calculated for these purposes. The livestock offset protocol calculates offset credits from reductions relatively to a baseline defined as "GHG emissions within the Offset Project Boundary that would have occurred if not for the installation of the [Biogas Control System]."[44] While these calculations are not exactly the same as those required for an additionality calculation, the data from these quantifications could help inform a more robust additionality analysis.

---

[42] *Id.*

[43] *Id.* at 3.1(3)(b) (project operators must "quantify GHG emission reductions...").

[44] *Id.* (Biogas control system refers to anaerobic digester.)

3.2 The Regional Greenhouse Gas Initiative

The Regional Greenhouse Gas Initiative (RGGI) is a collaboration among the states of Connecticut, Delaware, Maine, Maryland, Massachusetts, New Hampshire, New Jersey, New York, Pennsylvania, Rhode Island, Vermont, and Virginia. It is intended to reduce GHG emissions from the power sector and regulates "fossil-fuel-fired electric power generators with a capacity of 25 megawatts or greater".[45] The RGGI awards offset allowances from outside the power sector in the five project categories of landfill methane capture, sulfur hexafluoride, forestry or afforestation, end-use efficiency, and avoided agricultural methane (which refers to the use of anaerobic digester systems).[46]

While the RGGI itself issues model rules, the states issue their own regulations. States in the RGGI can promulgate regulations regarding additionality generally as well as sector-specific requirements.[47] Like the California cap-and-trade requirements, the RGGI's additionality analysis applies separate legal and financial additionality tests. Its model rules require legal additionality, prohibiting the inclusion of offset projects that are "required pursuant to any local, state, or federal law, regulation or administrative or judicial order".[48] The RGGI model rules address financial additionality generally by prohibiting projects that are "awarded credits or allowances under any other mandatory or voluntary greenhouse gas program" as well as projects that "receive funding or other incentives from any system benefit fund, or funds or other incentives provide through…" the consumer benefit fund conceived of by the RGGI model rules.[49]

Like California Cap and Trade, the RGGI also provides more detailed tests in provisions addressing specific offset categories. The model rules specific to anaerobic digestor projects put forth two additional financial additionality tests. Rather than use these metrics as direct benchmarks for financial additionality, however, offset projects are exempted from several of the general additionality criteria if project operators meet the tests' criteria. The first test evaluates the market penetration rate in the state where the offset project is located. If the market penetration rate is "5% or less", the general additionality requirements do not apply.[50] The second test exempts offsets projects from the general additionality requirements if the

[45] Regional Greenhouse Gas Initiative, Elements of RGGI, https://www.rggi.org/program-overview-and-design/elements.

[46] Regional Greenhouse Gas Initiative, Offsets, https://www.rggi.org/allowance-tracking/offsets.

[47] Regional Greenhouse Gas Initiative, Offset Requirements, https://www.rggi.org/allowance-tracking/offsets/requirements.

[48] Regional Greenhouse Gas Initiative, 2017 Model Rules at XX-10.3(c)(1), available at https://www.rggi.org/program-overview-and-design/design-archive/mou-model-rule.

[49] *Id.* at XX-10.3(c)(3)-(4).

[50] *Id.* at XX-10.5(c)(1)(iii)(a). Importantly, the provision requires that the "most recent market data available at the time of submission of the consistency determination" must be used. This is especially important in the case of a technology like biogas where overlapping incentives are quickly changing the market.

"project is located at a farm with 4,000 or less head of dairy cows, or a farm with equivalent animal units...".[51] This test is likely responsive to the fact that existing research suggests that anaerobic digesters are not currently financially viable on dairy farms with fewer than several thousand cows.

The RGGI's approach of exempting operations from general additionality requirements is smart. The two tests for exemption are relatively stringent and precisely target the kind of livestock operations where digesters would be unlikely without the incentives that the RGGI provides. However, the general additionality requirements are not adequate to conduct rigorous analyses for the offset projects that are not exempted. The RGGI's requirement that offset projects do not receive funding from other emission reduction programs is important but fails to account for market incentives or public funding sources beyond emission reduction programs.

4 Conclusions

The California Cap and Trade tests provide useful but far from comprehensive estimations of whether credited reductions would have occurred absent the policy incentive. The tests for anaerobic digester projects include two important benchmarks but leave significant gaps that are highly relevant to the sector. The RGGI's two-tiered approach of exempting projects for which emissions are highly likely to be financially additional is elegant and efficient, but the general analyses applied to the remaining projects fall short. To ensure more robust additionality analyses, regulators should dig more deeply into the limited sectors they evaluate and explicitly address how frequently baseline scenarios should be reevaluated.

Regulators' responsibility to ensure adequate analyses is made all the more important by the fact that the hyper-technical nature of additionality creates barriers to meaningful public participation on this issue. The concepts are ambiguous and poorly defined in the academic literature. There are no consensus approaches to standardized tests, and the tests themselves require technical knowledge of both sectors and calculation methods. This can make it especially challenging for community members to participate in public comment processes and public hearings to influence the details of offset programs.

The theoretical basis of emissions trading schemes that the optimal allocation of property rights can be achieved through the market "only holds if transaction costs are zero".[52] However, transaction costs are not zero in the context of offsets and the multiple requirements to ensure their integrity, including the additionality analysis. While emissions trading programs reduce compliance costs for the industry, they create substantial implementation costs for regulators. Additionality analyses have "[elicited] frustration, disagreement, and even despair" because they represent a

[51] *Id.* at XX-10.5(c)(1)(iii)(b).

[52] McNish at 393.

crucial and resource-intensive implementation point in a policy mechanism supported primarily due to its purported efficiency and low-cost implementation. The inclusion of offsets in emissions trading schemes requires rigorous additionality analyses in order to prevent offsets from endangering the integrity of the programs. If regulators cannot conduct sound additionality analyses with available resources, they should reevaluate the inclusion of offsets in these programs altogether as they are not necessary to reduce emissions. Inexpensive implementation cannot come at the expense of the integrity of the overall programs if emission trading schemes are to play a constructive role in climate response.

References

Gillenwater M (2012a) What is Additionality? Part 1: A long standing problem, Discussion Paper No. 001, Version 03

Gillenwater M (2012b) What is Additionality? Part 2: A Framework for More Precise Definitions and Standardized Approaches, Discussion Paper No. 002, Version 03

McNish T (2012) Carbon offsets are a bridge too far in the tradable property rights revolution. Harv Environ Law Rev 36

Morag-Levine N (2007) The problem of pollution hotspots: pollution markets, Coase, and common law. Cornell J Law Public Policy 17

Wiener JB (1999) Global environmental regulation: instrument choice in legal context. Yale Law J 108

World Bank Group Partnership for Market Readiness, Carbon Credits and Additionality: Past, Present, and Future

Paying the Piper: On the Legal Qualification of Carbon Prices

Tatiana Falcão

Abstract This chapter borrows from the economic and legal interpretation of carbon pricing approaches to identify what types of instruments could, in fact, be characterized as carbon pricing measures meaning an instrument that is capable of capturing the external costs of emitting an additional tonne of carbon by shifting the cost burden from the public to the private consumer. It looks into this topic from two different perspectives, i.e. national and international. The national perspective converses with the essence of the Paris Agreement. These would be the carbon pricing instruments a country could resort to in order to meet its nationally determined contributions (NDCs). At the international level, is the consideration for instruments that are capable not just of conferring a price on carbon but of finding price correspondence with other instruments that might have been administered by other countries. This paper ultimately brings to light the different dimensions of pricing carbon from national and international perspectives. It is expected that the classification and organization of the different instruments according to their ability to price carbon as an externality will assist policy makers not just in meeting their Paris Agreement commitments but also understanding the different instruments that are available to them when devising national mitigation strategies or undergoing environmental fiscal reforms.

T. Falcão (✉)
Member of the Subcommittee on Environmental Taxation, Rio de Janeiro, Brazil

R. Saraiva, P. A. Pardal (eds.), *Sustainable Finances and the Law*, Economic Analysis of Law in European Legal Scholarship 16,
https://doi.org/10.1007/978-3-031-49460-4_6

1 Introduction: Carbon Pricing Within the Context of the Paris Agreement and the NDCs

Carbon pricing is not mentioned anywhere in the Paris Agreement.[1] However, carbon pricing is known to be one of the most powerful mitigation instruments[2] to foster the main long-term goal of the Paris Agreement, namely to hold the increase in the global average temperature to well below 2 °C above pre-industrial levels and pursue efforts to limit the temperature increase to 1.5 °C above pre-industrial levels.[3] Rather than informing countries as to how they are to achieve the long-term goal set out in Article 2, the Paris Agreement determines[4] that parties ought to prepare, communicate, and maintain successive nationally determined contributions that they intend to achieve in a true bottom-up approach.

There is no definition in the Paris Agreement nor in the rulebook that accompanies it over the way in which parties ought to frame their nationally determined contribution (NDC) targets. Issues considered to be key in defining the effectiveness of a climate target, such as the base year, the point of reference of the planned reduction (i.e., whether based on a business-as-usual scenario or on different criteria), how ambitious the targets are, or how detailed the plans are all issues that are up for each party to decide. Therefore, one of the biggest criticisms concerning the reporting of NDCs to date has been about making sure that the NDCs proposed by countries are, in fact, ambitious enough. For example, it is possible for a country that has experienced an extended period of growth and therefore high emissions patterns to choose that period as a baseline to compute subsequent emissions reductions. Likewise, a country with an expected GDP increase could base its emissions reduction target in comparison to the national GDP and, as a result, produce a very low ambition mitigation outcome. The lack of clarity of the text allows parties to therefore use artifices in order to obtain the minimum level of emissions reduction and still meet the self-imposed NDC target. The text of the Paris Agreement is vague,[5] contending only that, starting in 2020, countries ought to

[1]The UNFCCC argues that carbon pricing would be referenced in Articles 6.2 (allowing for the linking of carbon pricing approaches across countries, Article 6.4 (foreseeing the creation of a voluntary carbon market that would allow the offsetting of emissions through the trading of emissions reduction units), and Article 6.5 (foreseeing accounting measures to avoid double counting emissions reduction). This author contends that these instruments would not per se qualify as carbon pricing instruments in this article even if they are capable of affecting the price (i.e., reducing or increasing the national carbon price). See in this respect, UNFCCC, About carbon pricing, available at: https://unfccc.int/about-us/regional-collaboration-centres/the-ciaca/about-carbon-pricing#What-is-the-current-status-of-carbon-pricing-in-the.

[2]Parry et al. (2021).

[3]Article 2.1 (a) of the Paris Agreement.

[4]Article 4.2 of the Paris Agreement.

[5]Decision 4/CMA.1, annex I contains the rules for the reporting of the information. According to Annex I the parties must identify reference years, base years, reference periods, or other starting points to measure the baseline. Further, quantifiable information on the reference indicators for

participate in 5-year updates of its NDC with a view of increasing ambition each time.

In spite of those criticisms, it is contended that at least two-thirds of all submitted NDCs under the Paris Agreement consider the use of carbon pricing to achieve their emission reduction targets. This means 100 countries are looking into carbon pricing to achieve their NDCs.[6] However the term "carbon pricing" itself is still very vague. Intergovernmental organizations are still working to define what is meant by carbon pricing, and most of the literature referring to pricing methodologies only really mean carbon taxation and emissions trading schemes that are the two instruments capable of conferring an explicit price on carbon when using the term carbon pricing.

That begs the question of what is, in fact, carbon pricing. Broadly speaking, carbon pricing is any instrument that is capable of capturing the external costs of emitting an additional tonne of carbon by shifting the cost burden from the public to the private consumer. The question that then follows is to define what instruments are capable of, in fact, costing the externality or a proxy of it. This is exactly the object of the present article which looks into this topic from two different perspectives, i.e., a national and an international perspective.

The national perspective converses with the essence of the Paris Agreement as outlined above. These would be the carbon pricing instruments a country could resort to in order meet its NDCs. At the international level, this is the consideration for instruments that are capable not just of conferring a price on carbon but of finding correspondence with other instruments that might have been administered by other countries. The computation of an equivalent carbon price in this case is not destitute of political considerations as the equivalent carbon price might require an assessment of different types of technologies and their contribution in leading to a "greener" process.

This topic is timely as nations are working to obtain consensus in the administration of carbon prices internationally even if they work towards the implementation of national carbon pricing approaches. There are many recent examples to illustrate this.

The European Union's proposal for a Carbon Border Adjustment Mechanism (CBAM),[7] for example, was designed to create a common and uniform framework to

---

comparison with the base year must be included. The target must likewise be expressed numerically, for example, as a percentage or amount of reduction. Parties are requested to include time frames and/or periods for implementation with start and end dates. The information must include a general description of the target (which could be a single-year target or a multi-year target), sectors, gases, categories, and pools. As Minnerop (2019).

[6]UNFCCC, About carbon pricing, available at: https://unfccc.int/about-us/regional-collaboration-centres/the-ciaca/about-carbon-pricing#What-is-the-current-status-of-carbon-pricing-in-th.

[7]Information based on: European Commission, *Proposal for a Regulation of the European Parliament and of the Council Establishing a carbon border adjustment mechanism*, COM (2021) 564 final, Brussels, 14.7.2021; and Council of the European Union, CBAM: Commission Proposal/Council General Approach/Position of the EP, 13063/22, available at: https://data.consilium.europa.eu/doc/document/ST-13063-2022-INIT/en/pdf.

ensure an equivalence between the carbon pricing policy applied in the EU's internal market and the carbon pricing policy applied on imports. As such, it contains a provision allowing importers to reduce the CBAM price applied at the border by the amount equivalent to the carbon price already paid in the country of origin. The CBAM rules only accept a corresponding adjustment in respect of the application of a carbon tax or emissions trading scheme (ETS) that is not rebated or compensated in any other way upon export.

At the close of lights in 2002, the German presidency of the G7 approved the terms of reference for the creation of a climate club. A Climate Club Task Force launched the work on the governance structure of the climate club and is expected to be formalized by the COP28. The informal group will be hosted by the secretariat of the OECD and the IEA. The objective of the club is to contribute to raising climate action globally by facilitating a near zero emission industrial production transition by providing a high-level intergovernmental forum for discussion of key climate issues. The framework endorsed by the G7 is built on top of three pillars aiming to (1) advance ambitious and transparent climate change mitigation policies (2) transform industries by enabling conditions for substantial sectoral industry decarbonization by discussing and aiming to align, as far as possible, methodologies, standards, sectoral strategies, and milestones and expanding markets for green industrial products, and (3) boost international climate cooperation and partnerships by enhancing multi- and bilateral cooperation between members in the areas of cooperation identified under pillars one and two. The climate club is open for participation by all climate-ambitious countries.[8]

Both of these initiatives will require the creation of a common definitional standard to compare approaches and levels of ambition if they are to be inclusive towards participating partners. Right now, what is seen in practice at the international level[9] is the narrowing down of approaches to two instruments—carbon taxes and ETSs—due to the lack of political agreement on the mathematical computation applied in deriving proxies from the pricing of carbon.

Moreover, under the procedure of the Paris Agreement, a global stocktake[10] is expected to take place 2 years before the next round of NDC submissions therefore

---

[8] G7, Terms of Reference for the Climate Club, 12 December 2022.

[9] At the international level, countries are required to compare their pricing approaches to other countries' approaches and find emissions equivalents for the computation of carbon imbedded in the production of foreign derived products.

[10] The global stocktake is a process whereby "every five years, countries assess collective progress toward the agreement's long-term goals, considering mitigation, adaptation and finance, as well as equity and the best available science. Each country, informed by this periodic stocktake, is then to submit an updated NDC reflecting a 'progression' beyond its current NDC and 'its highest possible ambition'". This combination of the GST and NDC updating is known as the 'ambition cycle.' Properly executed, the GST process can provide the critical foundation for a regular series of high-level political moments that progressively ratchet up climate ambition." UNFCCC, Center for Climate and Energy Solutions and Energy Defense Fund (2022).

starting in 2023.[11] The global stocktake is an opportunity for countries to engage with each other and not just assess the success of the methodologies employed under the Paris Agreement to date but also discuss how these may be improved in order to meet the climate long-term goals.[12] The stocktake could therefore be a moment to convene and define how carbon pricing policies employed by the members will be most efficiently computed towards national NDCs and find international correspondence through coordinated mechanisms.

In light of all of these commitments, international organizations are working to establish a framework to define what is a carbon price. The sections that follow analyse the constitutive elements of a carbon price from a legal and regulatory perspective considering what types of measures would fulfill the purpose of pricing externalities either positively or negatively in a manner that leads to a behavioral incentive to shift consumption patterns and stimulate the greening of the economy.

2 Carbon Pricing in a Nutshell: What to Consider

Prior to discussing the instruments that could come to constitute a carbon price, it should be highlighted that there is no common consensus at the intergovernmental level as to what the term carbon pricing stands for. This is an ongoing and ever-changing debate. However, there are certain instruments that are generally perceived to price carbon either because they are capable of conferring a positive price on carbon or because they detract from the overall carbon price. There are four instruments capable of conferring an explicit or implicit price on carbon. Those are carbon taxes, emissions trading schemes, energy excise taxes or taxes based on energy use, and fossil fuel taxes. Carbon taxes and ETSs[13] are the only two instruments capable of conferring an explicit price on carbon because the operation of the instrument is, in itself, capable of conferring a clear price indicator. Excises on energy and on fossil fuel products confer only an implicit price because these do not tend to be introduced having in mind the pricing of carbon as a main consideration. To start with, they are levied on the retail, ad valorem price meaning they are not specific and, therefore, they depend on a mathematical computation to be able to draw the inbuilt carbon price.

In addition to the above, there are instruments that detract from the price. These are fossil fuel subsidies, any type of exemption or tax rate reduction that might be conferred nationally, state subventions, incentives, and other reductive measures.

---

[11] UNFCCC, Technical Dialogues of the first Global Stocktake, available at: https://unfccc.int/topics/global-stocktake/components-of-the-gst/technical-dialogues-of-the-first-global-stocktake.

[12] Decision 19/CMA.1 FCCC/PA/CMA/2018/3/Add.2, para. 3 establishes the methodology to conduct the technical assessment required to take stock of the implementation of the Paris Agreement as well as opportunities for enhanced action and support to achieve its goals.

[13] ETSs will derive an explicit carbon price provided the original allowance is auctioned rather than grandfathered. Please refer to Sect. 3.1.2 for further information.

Finally, an array of instruments could be brought to the table whose roles are considered to be questionable when it comes to the computation of the carbon price. These are instruments that can have the effect of either inflicting a positive price on carbon, equalizing a domestic price, or impacting a national price positively or negatively. These would include regulatory measures, tariffs, and other border measures as well as the role that a credit or offset created from the operation of a voluntary market has to play in adding or detracting from the price.

The two subsections that follow will explore how these instruments may interact when it comes to the consideration of a carbon price from a national and an international perspective.

2.1 The National Framework in the Context of NDCs

Both the United Nations Framework Convention on Climate Change (UNFCCC) and the Kyoto Protocol (and the Intergovernmental Panel on Climate Change (IPCC) as a result of it) require a territorial approach to the apportioning of greenhouse gas emissions. This creates a presumption that is in favour of states adopting only instruments that are capable of computing emissions released within their territory within the scope of their domestic climate change laws.[14] This is a fact that is, in fact, consubstantiated in countries' NDC commitments as over 90% of countries' NDCs cover carbon dioxide emissions when it comes to the reporting of the greenhouse gas emissions (GHGs).[15]

As a result, if considering the role that the carbon price has to play in devising only national climate strategies, attention would be centered on those instruments capable of informing a national carbon price that is apt to meet the country's NDCs. Figure 1 illustrates how these instruments might be organized systematically.

Figure 1 is to be analysed mathematically. In green are the instruments capable of conferring a positive price on carbon. Meaning, they are capable of pricing carbon directly either as a result of the operation of the instrument itself or of a derivation by using the ad valorem price of the commercialized energy or fuel product as a starting point to derive the carbon price.[16] In red are the instruments that would have the effect of detracting from the carbon price. These are instruments that are also imposed on the ad valorem price of final products (fuels or energy items). Therefore, achieving price equivalence to the instruments imposing a positive price would likewise require a previously agreed mathematical formula to equate the cost of

[14] Scott (2015), pp. 92, 93 & 100–102.

[15] UNFCCC, Nationally determined contributions under the Paris Agreement, Synthesis Report by the Secretariat, FCCC/PA/CMA/2021/8, 4, available at: https://unfccc.int/sites/default/files/resource/cma2021_08_adv_1.pdf, (last accessed 4 Jan 2023).

[16] Section 4.2 will cover this latter point more extensively.

Equating the domestic carbon price	
(+) Instruments capable of generating a clear price indicator either explicitly or implicitly	Carbon Taxes
	Emissions Trading System
	Energy Excise Taxes/Taxes based on energy use
	Fossil fuel Taxes and otherpollution taxes
(-) Instruments that will have the effect of reducing the price	Fossil fuel subsidies
	Exemptions and tax rate reduction
	State subvention and special regimes
(+/-) Questionable Instrument Assimilations (non-price based instruments)	Regulatory policies that result in an implicit marginal price on carbon
	Tariffs and other border measures
	Offsets/credits derived from voluntary carbon markets

Fig. 1 Equating the carbon price for the purposes of accounting for Nationally Determined Contributions (NDCs)

carbon. This author is unaware of any ongoing economic study in this area; however, it is known that this would be a feasible exercise.

In orange are the instruments marked as questionable in the sense that it is still unclear whether these could, in fact, come to be linked to the attribution of a carbon price. The difficulties are practical and political in nature. For example, recognizing a regulatory measure such as an energy efficiency standard as equivalent to a carbon price would require (1) an agreement on the mathematical computation to derive the carbon economy resulting in the price; (2) oversight and potential equalization of the technologies employed to obtain the higher efficiency standard; and (3) a transboundary recognition of the equalization measures employed by different countries. The literature is still split on this topic. For example, the OECD has

(+) Instruments capable of generating a clear price indicator explicitly	Carbon Taxes
	Emissions Trading System
(+) Questionable Instrument Assimilations	Energy Excise Taxes/Taxes based onenergy use
	Fossil fuel Taxes
	Regulatory policies which result in an implicit marginal price on carbon

Fig. 2 Instruments subject to carbon price equivalence transnationally

recently qualified these as non-price-based instruments for which the main policy motivation is to reduce GHG emissions.[17]

These are instruments that would certainly have an impact—be it positive or negative—on a country's carbon price, but it is unclear whether the operation of the instruments themselves could qualify as a price for the purposes of computing a country's NDCs.

2.2 International Aspects: Computing and Finding Equivalence in a Carbon Price

In theory, all of the instruments mentioned in Fig. 1 above, when applied by one state, should find a transnational correspondence in another state. In other words, the application of a carbon tax in State A should be relatable and equivalent to the carbon tax employed in State B with all things being equal (tax rate, tax base, and taxpayer[18]).

In practice, however, that is a much more difficult exercise because of the lack of political agreement in finding uniformity on the computation of a carbon proxy based on an ad valorem price. Included in this section are therefore: (1) only positive instruments aiming at pricing carbon explicitly; (2) instruments that may find parity in other instruments employed overseas; and (3) could therefore be subjected to a corresponding adjustment on a transactional basis.

A comparison of Figs. 1 and 2 delineates the problem arising from the application of unilateral measures with a global impact. When it comes to the assimilation of

[17] OECD (2022). (last accessed 3/1/2023).

[18] Meaning at what stage of the supply chain the tax is levied.

policies on a transboundary basis, the lack of international agreement on the premises for computation of a carbon price become ever more evident, and only explicit carbon pricing instruments are acknowledged as equivalent.

That is the case, for example, under the European Commission Proposal for a Carbon Border Adjustment Measure (CBAM).[19] The EU-wide CBAM is designed to create a common and uniform framework to ensure an equivalence between the carbon pricing policy applied in the EU's internal market and the carbon pricing policy applied on imports. As such, it is required to obey the rules imposed by the World Trade Organization (WTO) General Agreement on Trade and Tariffs. One such rule is that, to be admissible under Article XX (g) exception of the GATT,[20] the EU has to (1) provide compensatory measures towards countries already employing a domestic carbon price; and (2) allow trading partners the opportunity to prove (or demonstrate) that they run a comparable program (aimed at fulfilling the same environmental objectives) and provide a credit or exemption that is proportionate to the tax or price previously employed in the country of origin.

In line with the above, under the latest circulated version of the CBAM proposal, the declarant is entitled to claim in the CBAM declaration a reduction in the number of CBAM certificates to be surrendered in order to take into account the explicit carbon price paid in the country of origin.[21] This means that, in assessing corresponding measures in the country of origin, the EU shall (1) only accept carbon taxes and prices subjected via ETSs for purposes of deduction from the CBAM price, and (2) it is doubtful that the EU will be able to deduct any subsidies or reductions granted on fossil fuel products. This is because there is no institutional framework to assess the domestic carbon price in the country of origin (as there is none to infer the impact of subsidies and other reductions in the EU as well). The international correspondence mechanism is therefore an approximation at its best.

[19]Council of the European Union, CBAM: Commission Proposal/Council General Approach/ Position of the EP, 13063/22, available at: https://data.consilium.europa.eu/doc/document/ST-13063-2022-INIT/en/pdf.

[20]Marrakesh Agreement, Appendix, General Agreement on Tariffs and Trade 1947, art. XX, in WTO (1999), p. 455.

[21]There are currently three versions of the CBAM proposal, i.e., the original version as proposed by the commission, the council position, and the European Parliament position. The original proposal refers loosely to the corresponding adjustment based on the carbon price employed at the country of origin. The council proposal talks about adjustment based on the price effectively paid in the country of origin. Finally, the parliament proposal refers to an adjustment in respect of the explicit carbon price employed in the country of origin. The latter option is likely to be the one adopted as it is consistent with the messaging delivered by the commission in meetings and open consultation processes. The language used in this provision will have important impacts on third states trading with the EU. The commission has yet to adopt implementing acts establishing the methodology to calculate the reduction in the number of CBAM certificates to be surrendered. Council of the European Union, CBAM: Commission Proposal/Council General Approach/Position of the EP, 13063/22, available at: https://data.consilium.europa.eu/doc/document/ST-13063-2022-INIT/en/pdf.

(+) Instruments capable of generating a clear price indicator either explicitly or implicitly	Carbon Taxes
	Emissions Trading System
	Energy Excise Taxes/Taxe s based on energy use
	Fossil fuel Taxes and other pollution taxes
(-) Instruments that will have the effect of reducing the price	Fossil fuel subsidies
	Exemptions and tax rate reduction
	State subvention and special regimes

Fig. 3 International carbon price correspondence

Figure 3 reflects current practice rather than the optimal theoretical answer from a pricing perspective. In theory, countries should be able to assess the domestic carbon price applied by the country of origin by taking into account both positive[22] and negative[23] pricing approaches. In the absence of a political agreement concerning the real complex questions that derive from the application of non-pricing instruments, the ideal table for an international comparative assessment of pricing instruments should look closer like Fig. 3.

The intergovernmental organizations have started working on this issue, deriving complex indicators that would be based on all or some of the instruments identified above. However, it is contended that much of the data needed to make global generalizations is still lacking as is agreement at the intergovernmental level as to which mathematical assimilation to employ.

For example, a recent OECD study presents a new indicator called the net effective rate which consists of three components: (1) explicit carbon pricing, (2) fuel excise taxes, and (3) fossil fuel subsidies that reduce the price on carbon.[24] This is the first time an intergovernmental organization has tried to make a comprehensive assessment of a carbon price, although the results would have been impacted by the methodology employed to compute the implicit price and subsidy components.

---

[22] As per Sect. 3.

[23] As per Sect. 4.

[24] OECD (2022).

In the same vein, the IMF has recently commanded policy equivalence at the national level in terms of pricing. For that purpose, the IMF has devised the economywide carbon price equivalent (ECPE) that would assess the emissions abatement of a policy by comparing it to a carbon price equivalent measure and thereby deriving a corresponding value for the measure.[25]

Going forward, there will be high demand for more uniformity in the computation of international price equivalents, especially in light of the Climate Club Task Force launched by the G7 to formalize a climate club by COP28. In addition, other countries such as Canada, Japan, Taiwan, and the United States are looking into the development of national border carbon adjustment measures. These international initiatives will need to correspond with each other.

3 The Constitutive Elements: Pricing Instruments

3.1 The Unequivocal Components: Explicit Carbon Prices

Explicit carbon pricing instruments are among the most efficient and effective mitigation instruments. Carbon taxes and emissions trading schemes are generally referred to as explicit carbon pricing instruments because they are both capable of internalizing the environmental damage caused by the release of emissions.[26] This means that the price so applied is directly inflicted on the pollution itself and not on the ad valorem price as is the case with other taxes known to only result in an implicit carbon price. Carbon taxes and ETSs fulfill the same aim, namely, to reduce carbon dioxide emissions. However, they do so in different ways.

In a carbon tax system, the price is fixed, but the emissions reduction achieved is uncertain. On the other hand, under an ETS, the number of emissions reductions is fixed, but the price is uncertain. The sections that follow provide a more detailed overview of the pricing system when employing one of these instruments.

3.1.1 Carbon Taxes

Carbon taxes are among some of the most efficient policies in pricing carbon, particularly if employed at "choke points" at the upstream level, because of their ability to reach the whole of the economy without the need to focus on certain industries or sectors. An upstream carbon tax is simple to administer and is capable

---

[25] Black et al. (2022), p. 4. Available at https://www.imf.org/en/Publications/WP/Issues/2022/12/16/A-Framework-for-Comparing-Climate-Mitigation-Policies-Across-Countries-527049.

[26] In the case of ETSs, the internalization only occurs provided the permits are sold or auctioned by the country in question. If the permits are grandfathered in or distributed for free, the price effect of an ETS might only be implicit.

of impacting both the formal and the informal economies, a point that is particularly relevant for middle- and low-income countries.[27]

A carbon tax is a specific excise tax — a price per tonne of carbon that is usually applied by weight or volume. A carbon tax is relatively easy to administer, and the revenue-generating potential can be determined even before the tax is applied. If it is known how much fossil fuel is employed in a process, then both the taxpayer and the tax administration can predict the amount of carbon tax revenue that will be generated as a result of the combustion of that product. The law can apply precalculated tax rates without verifying actual emissions because the correlation between a volume of product and the carbon content is mathematical. The tax is expressed in terms of weight or volume and is based on the average carbon content of the relevant fuel.[28]

Proponents assert that a carbon tax can encourage positive change in consumer behaviour to the extent it provides an incentive for the consumer to acquire the least carbon-intensive product. That is because the tax would apply to a greater or lesser extent depending on the carbon intensity of the product, resulting in a higher tax burden on more carbon-intensive products and a lower tax burden for products that generate less carbon. A carbon tax on fossil fuels would automatically create a price differentiation between diesel, gasoline, and natural gas because diesel is more carbon-intensive than gasoline which, in turn, is more carbon-intensive than natural gas. Therefore, a carbon tax employed per tonne of carbon would automatically affect diesel more than it would natural gas, creating an incentive for consumers to purchase products that use natural gas rather than diesel.[29] Likewise, it would encourage both consumers and businesses to use natural-gas-based vehicles and machinery because they would be cheaper to operate than a diesel-based vehicle.

3.1.2 Emissions Trading Schemes

The ETSs are the second type of explicit pricing mechanism. ETS schemes set a ceiling on the number of emissions released by certain sectors. Emissions permits are distributed to producers, either for free (grandfathering of permits tends to occur at the initial stages of operation of an ETS) or through the auctioning of permits. Polluters will be bound by the cap set for them in the regulatory process. If they pollute more than the cap, they are required to buy additional permits in a secondary

[27] There is extensive literature on the mechanics of a carbon tax. See, for example: Metcalf (2019); IMF (2019b); IMF (2019a), p. 3, available at https://www.imf.org/en/Publications/FM/Issues/2019/10/16/Fiscal-Monitor-October-2019-How-to-Mitigate-Climate-Change-47027 (accessed 03 Jan. 2023); Ramseur and Parker (2009), p. 2.

[28] United Nations (2021), Chap. 4, available at: https://www.un.org/development/desa/financing/document/un-handbook-carbon-taxation-developing-countries-2021. (last accessed 4 January 2023).

[29] Falcão (2021c), p. 775.

market. If they produce less pollution than the cap, they are given the opportunity to trade their surplus permits in a secondary market as if it were a capital asset.

Permits are usually grandfathered in during the initial phases of an ETM as a trial period in order to identify the number of allowances that are subject to negotiation and forestall a potential competitive disadvantage for industries trading products that are negotiated in international markets.[30] The free allowance period gives the regulator time to identify which sectors would be subject to carbon leakage.[31] Carbon leakage refers to a situation of increased production costs due to the implementation of climate policies, leading to the relocation of production to other countries with laxer emissions constraints, raising emissions abroad. The increased cost of doing business caused by a carbon price could likewise affect the competitiveness of industries subjected to a carbon price, particularly if they compete in international markets (i.e., industry relocation as a result of the increase in energy cost).

As a matter of fact, even though ETS systems are said to be able to confer an explicit price on carbon, they only do so if the permits are auctioned rather than distributed for free. That is because the only revenue raising opportunity available for countries grandfathering in permits is to tax the gain attributed to a permit when negotiated in the secondary market through the capital gains tax system. Absent the negotiation in the secondary market, there is no other opportunity to, in fact, price the permit, and hence the externality and, as a result, the government is, in fact, merely giving away a new negotiable asset for industries to speculate on for free. Since most of the ETS schemes in force across the globe grandfather in emissions permits in order to address the leakage concern, most ETS systems fail to, in fact, allocate an explicit price on carbon. This is one of the main disadvantages with the choice of this instrument over a carbon tax.

Another disadvantage concerns the time that is required to introduce a fully functioning ETS into a legal system. ETS markets take, on average, 5–10 years to be on a full working status and requires extensive monitoring, review, and verification processes (MRV)[32] to assess the level of pollution being emitted by the selected industries and set the cap under that threshold. Through the operational life of the ETS, MRV functions are also key to make sure the covered industries are compliant.

[30] See, in this respect, Kasa (2000).

[31] The grandfathering in of permits is, in fact, one of the biggest obstacles to the effectiveness of an ETS. The European Union, responsible for hosting the longest running ETS scheme in the world, has historically had difficulties in taking the EU ETS through to the next step in which there would be the auctioning off of permits. The market is only a regional one, therefore, the fear is that the full auctioning of permits might impose competitive disadvantages on the European-based industries trading on a worldwide scale. The EU is currently in its Phase 4 of the EU ETS system in which the auctioning of permits is now the default rule, however, the estimate is that only approximately 57% of allowances are, in effect, auctioned. The Fit for 55 plan intends to substitute the grandfathering of permits under the EU ETS for a Carbon Border Adjustment Mechanism, hence substituting the instrument used to protect the internal market against carbon leakage.

[32] Based on the practical experience from Chile, China, and the EU.

Therefore, this instrument requires much more time and human resources from governments than the administration of a single tax applied at the upstream level.

Finally, the ETSs usually operate at the downstream level of the value chain. Meaning it is a burden that is usually imposed on select carbon intensive industries. It is not a system that is geared towards obtaining a whole of economy carbon price. It aims to only price the externality of certain industries. Therefore, it is less effective at meeting a country's climate objectives. On the other hand, it can be used in combination with the administration of carbon taxes as is the case in many countries across the globe.[33]

3.2 *Implicit Carbon Prices*

Implicit carbon prices are instruments that change the price of products associated with carbon emissions in ways that are not directly proportional to those emissions. These instruments may be capable of providing a carbon price signal even though they might be (primarily) adopted for other socioeconomic objectives such as raising revenues or addressing air pollution.[34] Implicit carbon prices require "calculating the equivalent monetary value per tonne of carbon associated with a given policy instrument". An example of implicit carbon prices includes all excise taxes that are levied on fuels, energy, electricity, or pollution that are not carbon taxes.

Work is still under way for deriving a consensual approach to compute what would be the inbuilt carbon price in energy and fossil fuel taxes employed by countries traditionally known not to promote an explicit carbon price, such as a carbon tax. The recognition of an implicit carbon price in other environmental taxes, like energy taxes, could be beneficial over time to low-income countries in meeting their NDC commitments under the Paris Agreement. This is because it might provide evidence that countries are already on track to meeting their climate commitments through the employment of indirect measures, provided these fuels are not subject to any subsidies.[35] That is because high- and middle-income countries are known to make more use of explicit pricing instrument whereas low-income countries tend to resort to implicit pricing instruments more often.

In considering environmental taxes such as energy and fossil fuel taxes as integral parts of a carbon price approach, intergovernmental organizations such as the World Bank, the IMF, and the OECD have suggested methodologies to derive a shadow carbon price from the application of these taxes. These organizations have been

---

[33] That is the case, for example, in, Germany, Indonesia, the Netherlands, and the United Kingdom (when it administered the carbon price floor), and others.

[34] World Bank (2022), p. 13.

[35] OECD (2021). accessed 1 Jan. 2023; OECD (2019). (accessed 25 Jul. 2021); Parry et al. (2014), p. 8, available at https://www.elibrary.imf.org/view/books/071/21171-9781484388570-en/21171-9781484388570-en-book.xml (accessed 25 Jul. 2021).

deriving economic models to compute what would be the inbuilt carbon price in energy and fossil fuel taxes employed by countries traditionally known not to promote an explicit carbon price. There is still no agreement as to the mathematical formula that is to be used in computing the shadow carbon price. Several different methodologies[36] have been suggested in the recent literature. For example, the IMF and the OECD have discussed the value of deriving a carbon price equivalent[37] measure from implicit pricing techniques to the G7 in December 2022 using both economy-wide[38] and sector-wide carbon prices.[39]

One approach proposed by the IMF to ensure comparability between implicit and explicit carbon prices employed by countries was to use the "effective" carbon prices that can be calculated by (1) expressing existing fuel taxes on a carbon dioxide (CO_2)-equivalent basis (i.e. dividing them by the fuel's CO_2 emission factor); and (2) weighting CO_2-equivalent fuel taxes and any direct carbon pricing by their relative effectiveness at reducing CO_2 emissions compared with a comprehensive carbon price and then aggregating across these tax and pricing systems.[40] This would allow intergovernmental organizations to effectively compare the carbon price utilized by countries applying different price measures and derive a carbon price equivalent. Such an approach would be important (1) for comparing policies between countries that have an explicit carbon price and those that do not; and (2) for verifying whether the carbon price is in accordance with each fuel or product's polluting potential.

The literature on this topic is not straightforward, and the classification of instruments, how they are priced, and whether they are considered to be pricing or non-pricing instruments progresses at the same rate as our increased as the knowledge of climate related policies. For example, there is literature that defends the inclusion of regulatory measures within the classification of implicit pricing policies. This author prefers to distinguish both and to include those as the non-price-based policies discussed in Sect. 5.[41] Likewise, feed-in-tariffs are, at times, qualified as

[36]For example, Black et al. (2022), p. 4.

[37]The carbon price equivalent measure is the carbon price that would be needed to trigger the same amount of emission reductions of a given policy.

[38]Recent research from the IMF has derived an average corresponding price for fuel taxes of $5–40 per tonne in most cases (and moderately negative in cases where fuels are subsidized) under an economy carbon price equivalent assessment for G20 countries. Black et al. (2022), p. 4.

[39]The IMF and OECD have discussed methodologies for assessing carbon price equivalence of alternative mitigation policies (IMF, OECD (2022), p. 48. Available at: https://www.oecd-ilibrary.org/docserver/20179e63-en.pdf?expires=1672949219&id=id&accname=guest&checksum=9D92699C50108E7FD039F083D4627896, last accessed 5 Jan 2023) and for further discussion of the challenges involved see Stern and Lankes (2022).

[40]IMF (2019a) Box 1.3, Operationalizing International Carbon Price Floors.

[41]For example, OECD (2013), p. 23.

pricing[42] and others as non-pricing approaches. Please refer to Sect. 5.1.1 for the reasons why this author considers them to be non-pricing approaches.

3.2.1 Feebates

A feebate is a system of charges and rebates whereby energy-efficient or environmentally friendly practices are rewarded while failure to adhere to certain practices are penalized. For example, the IMF notes that there would be a fee that would payable (or a receivable rebate) for a power generator in proportion to its output times the difference between its emission rate per kilowatt-hour (averaged across the plants) and the industry average emission rate. The structure of fees and rebates would usually be set to make the system revenue-neutral. Feebates have so far mostly been employed to improve vehicle efficiency in domestic fleets. When using it towards car efficiency standards, it is simply employed when inefficient vehicles receive a surcharge, and efficient vehicles are granted a rebate. The fees on the inefficient vehicles finance the rebate on efficient vehicles, making the system self-sufficient and revenue neutral. Although the stimulus is a price stimulus, the policy is akin to an implicit price where there is a retail price stimulus for acquisition of more efficient cars.

4 Negative Carbon Pricing Approaches

Carbon pricing tools can be expressed in the form of positive, affirmative actions, envisaging the establishment of an effective price on carbon, for example, through the employment of a carbon tax or an emissions trading scheme. However, they can also be implemented through negative action, for example, through the elimination of fossil fuel subsidies and other price reducing measures that have the effect of emptying the carbon price base. Fiscal reforms geared towards the achievement of a net zero target are based on both positive and negative integrative measures because only through the full implementation of such measures are governments capable of deriving an environmental cost from the cost of doing business.

[42] See, in this respect, OECD (2022) Table 1.1. A tentative Typology of selected mitigation policies, where feed in tariffs are classified as "other price-based instruments.

4.1 Subsidies

In 2021, an important agreement was reached in COP26 and incorporated into the Glasgow Climate Pact[43] in order to phase down inefficient fossil fuel subsidies. This agreement alone could contribute to the implementation of a global carbon pricing agreement through the diminution of negative carbon pricing approaches such as fossil fuel subsidies and other reductive measures.[44]

Subsidies are considered to be negative carbon pricing approaches because they have a diametrically opposite effect to the imposition of carbon taxes even if subsidies are usually granted taking into account the ad valorem price of fuel, rather than the specific cost of the pollutant, as is the case under a carbon tax system. In other words, subsidies are usually applied in relation to implicit carbon prices such as fossil fuel taxes and other indirect taxes on fuels like fuel-based VATs or GSTs.

A subsidy, by definition, aims to stimulate a behaviour (in this case, consumption of the carbon-intensive product such as coal, diesel, and gasoline). Economically, subsidies can distort otherwise efficient markets, or they can correct existing market failures in order to enhance efficiency. Environmentally, subsidies can encourage the overuse of scarce environmental resources, or they can provide incentives for environmentally sound behaviour.[45] Reducing subsidies means putting fossil fuels on an equal footing, from a pricing perspective, with all other similar energy products.[46]

Subsidizing energy use and consumption is still a widespread approach that is employed by many countries, including those enacting successful carbon taxes.[47] According to the OECD, government support for the production and consumption of fossil fuels totalled USD 468 billion in 2019[48]; this amounts to more than 20% of the value of internationally traded fossil fuels. It is estimated that the complete removal of fossil fuel subsidies would lead to an estimated 12% of the total abatement needed by 2020 from energy sector emissions.

Urgent reform is needed to gradually eliminate fossil fuel subsidies that encourage the consumption of carbon rich fuels. The Glasgow climate pact agreement is important, but it is not the first of its kind. At the WTO Ministerial Conference in

[43] UNFCCC, Glasgow Climate Pact, 13 November 2021, available at: https://unfccc.int/documents/310475, last accessed 5 Jan 2023.

[44] World Bank (2022), p. 14.

[45] *See* Stillwell and Bohanes (2005), ch. 58, 548–549.

[46] IEA (2006). (accessed 25 Jul. 2021).

[47] Countries will typically subsidize diesel over gasoline even though diesel is more carbon intensive or subsidize coal over other sources of energy because coal reserves are abundant in the country. Although such measures may be justifiable from a public policy and energy security perspective, they are contradictory to a robust and well-developed environmental policy.

[48] OECD (2019).

December 2017 in Buenos Aires,[49] twelve[50] WTO member countries adopted a Ministerial Statement on Fossil Fuel Subsidy Reform.[51] It urged the WTO to consider fossil fuel subsidy reform in ongoing discussions and called for, among others, enhanced WTO transparency and reporting to enable evaluation of the trade and resource effects of fossil fuel subsidies.[52]

One of the main problems associated with the imposition and tracking of fossil fuel subsidies is the lack of a common understanding as to what constitutes a fossil fuel subsidy. Countries have different interpretations of the concept which makes it difficult to identify, track, and eliminate nationally based subsidies. A framework to identify this instrument will need to be developed at the international level if countries are to succeed at achieving this important target.[53]

Work on the establishment of a common framework has started, but agreement on the constitutive elements is still meagre. At the intergovernmental level in 2019, the United Nations Environment Program[54] together with the OECD, IISD, and GSI developed a methodology to measure fossil fuel subsidies at the national, regional, and global levels. The methodology relies on the WTO's subsidies definition that is contained in the Agreement on Subsidies and Countervailing Measures (ASCM) and on certain sub-classifications expressed in the IEA Statistical Manual.[55]

As the methodology does not make the commitment to uniformize the definition of FFSs binding, it relies on three sub-indicators for reporting on the FFS indicator: (1) direct transfer of government funds; (2) induced transfers (price support); and, as an optional sub-indicator, (3) tax expenditure, other revenue foregone, and under-pricing of goods and services. The lack of a common definition in which to qualify FFSs hampers further unified international action to curb the widespread application of such policy.

Countries have also dedicated themselves to classifying subsidies at the national level. This exercise, initiated as a result of a workplan hosted by the G20, comprises

---

[49] WTO, *Fossil Fuel Subsidies Reform Ministerial Statement,* WT/MIN(17)/54, (12 Dec. 2017), available at https://docs.wto.org/dol2fe/Pages/SS/directdoc.aspx?filename=q:/WT/MIN17/54.pdf&Open=True (accessed 25 Jul. 2021).

[50] Chile; Costa Rica; Iceland; Liechtenstein; Mexico; the Republic of Moldova; New Zealand; Norway; Samoa; Switzerland; the Separate Customs Territory of Taiwan, Penghu, Kinmen and Matsu; and Uruguay.

[51] WTO, *Fossil Fuel Subsidies Reform Ministerial Statement* (11 Dec. 2017), available at https://docs.wto.org/dol2fe/Pages/FE_Search/FE_S_S009-DP.aspx?language=E&CatalogueIdList=240841,240845,240847,240848,240824,240821,240788,240773,240787,240774&CurrentCatalogueIdIndex=2&FullTextHash=371857150&HasEnglishRecord=True&HasFrenchRecord=False&HasSpanishRecord=False (accessed 25 Jul. 2021).

[52] The statement was led by the Friends of Fossil Fuel subsidy Reform which is an informal group of non-G20 countries established in 2010 to build political consensus on the importance of fossil fuel subsidy reform. See, in this respect: FFFsR, *What is the Friends of Fossil Fuel Subsidy Reform,* available at http://fffsr.org/ (accessed 25 Jul. 2021).

[53] Falcão (2021b), pp. 897–914.

[54] UNEP, IISD, OECD (2019). (accessed 2 Aug 2021).

[55] IEA (2004). (accessed 25 Jul. 2021).

the identification and quantification of the fossil fuel subsidies employed at the national level.[56] Germany, Italy, and the Netherlands are some of the countries that are known to have undertaken that exercise either as part of the G20 process or at their own initiative.[57]

4.2 Incentives and Other Reductive Tax Measures

There are many other tax measures with the effect of reducing the effectiveness of excise taxes employed on fossil fuels and other energy products. The more evident example would be the application of a reduced tax rate towards the most carbon intensive fuels or government indexation of fuel prices to create a fictitiously low price towards the more carbon intensive products.

This section could also include certain tax measures that indirectly deter the implementation of a robust, positive carbon pricing policy. These are measures for which the primary aim is to foster economic activity or incentivize a particular sector but that, in fact, lead to negative environmental results or are in conflict with an environmental measure. It could include, for example, certain expenditures that have the effect of undermining the positive environmental effect achieved via a carbon pricing approach.

Direct measures might include, for example, the application of a lower excise tax on the most polluting types of fuels to subsidize a specific industry or economic category. For example, in Latin America, many countries impose a very low or no excise on diesel because it is the fuel used for long-haul transport.

Indirect measures could include (1) the application of VAT or GST rate reductions or exemptions that lead to a distortionary effect from an environmental tax perspective; or (2) corporate income tax deductions granted to producers or manufacturers for the purchase of fossil fuels.

These measures are more difficult to identify and quantify and would also depend on a specific internationally agreed methodology to derive the equivalent price.

[56] The G20 has produced a number of reports on the use and removal of harmful and inefficient fossil fuel subsidies covering countries that employ a carbon tax or price domestically. See, for example: G20 (2017a), A report on the G20 peer-review of inefficient fossil-fuel subsidies that encourage wasteful consumption in Mexico, available at https://www.oecd.org/fossil-fuels/Mexico-Peer-Review.pdf (accessed 25 Jul. 2021); G20 (2017b), A report on the G20 peer-review of inefficient fossil-fuel subsidies that encourage wasteful consumption in Germany, available at http://www.oecd.org/site/tadffss/Germany-Peer-Review.pdf (accessed 25 Jul. 2021); and G20 (2016), A report on the G20 peer review of inefficient fossil-fuel subsidies that encourage wasteful consumption in China, available at https://www.oecd.org/fossil-fuels/publication/G20%20China%20Peer%20Review_G20_FFS_Review_final_of_20160902.pdf (accessed 25 Jul. 2021).

[57] The Netherlands has run a national campaign to create a methodology to qualify subsidies with the intent to eliminate them. See, in this respect, The Coalition of Finance Ministers for Climate Action, HP3 workshop on The Conceptualization and Quantification of Fossil Fuel Subsidies in the Netherlands, 28 October 2021 (author's files).

Achieving agreement might require the development of a taxonomy[58] for the (positive and negative) pricing of carbon. Climate based taxonomies are under discussion but have so far not included carbon pricing approaches.[59] This could be the next area of work.[60]

Indeed, many countries[61] are already adopting green taxonomies as a type of classification framework to serve as a blueprint for the greening of the economy. However, to date, these have not included carbon pricing initiatives. Rather, they concentrate on developing a classification system to determine which economic activities are deemed as sustainable or green and is linked to the private sector. Governments could likewise use taxonomy-based instruments to locate budgetary entries within a government's expenditure system that are considered to contribute to a negative pricing approach and, in that way, work towards eliminating them as part of a whole of the economy's green transition process.

5 Non-pricing Instruments

Non-price-based instruments differ from price-based instruments to the extent that these do not have the impact of changing the price of goods and services. Non-price-based instruments merely provide a regulatory or economic incentive for consumers and producers to only pursue certain activities or invest in certain assets that are aligned with the climate objectives intended by the national state. From an economic perspective, they are fewer effective instruments because they do not achieve a direct

[58] A taxonomy is a classification system establishing a list of environmentally sustainable economic activities. The EU was the first region to consider an EU wide taxonomy to meet the targets of the European Green Deal. One of the objectives of the EU taxonomy is to address climate mitigation, although pricing approaches have not yet been contended as part of the framework. See, in this respect, Regulation (EU) 2020/852 of 18 June 2020, on the establishment of a framework to facilitate sustainable investment, available at: https://eur-lex.europa.eu/legal-content/EN/TXT/PDF/?uri=CELEX:32020R0852&from=EN (last accessed 6 Jan 2023).

[59] For a discussion of other approaches at EU level, see. Ezcurra et al. (2021), pp. 198–213.

[60] Wolff (2021), pp. 184–197.

[61] For example, In May 2021, Chile published its *Taxonomy Roadmap for Chile* that will guide the country's development of a green taxonomy – a multifunctional classification system for financial and nonfinancial sectors that will serve as a blueprint for the greening of Chile's economy. In Mexico in 2020, the Financial System Stability Council (CESF) created the Sustainable Finance Committee (CFS). The committee's role was to promote the dialogue toward defining a national taxonomy for sustainable investments that would be aligned with the country's NDCs and sustainable development goals. Examples taken from Coalition of Finance Ministers for Climate Action, Ministries of Finance and Nationally Determined Contributions: Raising Ambitions and Accelerating Climate Action, HP6 Workstream, 29–30, November 2022, available at: https://www.financeministersforclimate.org/sites/cape/files/inline-files/MoFs%20and%20NDCs%20-%20Raising%20Ambition%20and%20Accelerating%20Climate%20Action.pdf (last accessed 6 Jan 2023).

price incentive for consumers and producers to change behaviour. Instead, they can be complementary to other mitigation strategies.[62]

It is this author's understanding that non-price-based instruments would include (1) regulatory measures such as energy efficiency standards and vehicle emission rate standards, (2) voluntary carbon markets capable of producing credits that can be offset against a country's or private entity's carbon price, and (3) equalization measures such as tariffs and other border measures. This is a list that is by no means exhaustive nor destitute of controversy. As further explored in the sections that follow, there is expressive political interest from one of the biggest emitters in the world to derive a carbon price from some types of regulatory measures. Likewise, the UNFCCC is adamant in qualifying voluntary carbon markets regulated by Article 6 of the Paris Agreement as carbon pricing approaches.

This is a topic that is likely to undergo substantive changes in the coming years, especially as countries position themselves politically in the annual conference of the parties climate negotiations. The three sections that follow aim to explain why it is this author's understanding that these three classes of action should not be considered to be equivalent to a pricing approach.

5.1 Regulatory Measures

An open question is whether regulatory measures, such as tradeable performance standards, energy economy standards, coal phaseouts, fuel efficiency standards, emissions rate regulation and others are capable of conferring an implicit price signal. This is an open debate, and an agreement has not been reached under the Paris Agreement negotiation rounds.[63]

The issue, as noted, is that estimating the emissions reduction obtained via a regulatory measure would require either the development of a model (using a top bottom approach that is not akin to the Paris Agreement process), to capture economy-wide features that can be applied to different countries after being parametrized, or a thorough an assessment of the sectoral and technological specificities of the regulatory measures in a country (under the bottom-up approach). The latter would entail acquiring detailed sectoral knowledge, benchmarking the technology employed in the country in question (to measure the emissions reduction in light of the level of technology available in the country), and eventually the calculation of the carbon price equivalent in comparison to the methodologies employed in other countries.

If considering the implementation of these policies on a step-by-step basis, it might be imagined that countries would start by implementing a bottom-up approach, deriving a carbon price equivalent, and then leaving it for the international

[62] IMF, OECD (2022), p. 9.

[63] IMF, OECD (2022), p. 17.

organizations and political negotiations to derive a universal parameter under the top bottom approach.[64] The problem, as might be imagined, is that countries are subject to different levels of development and, as a result, their industries are subject to different types of (more or less efficient) technology. One of the main challenges in deriving a carbon price equivalent would therefore be in equating those different technologies in a manner that would be fair to all countries and not just some.

In addition to that, whatever equivalence measure is derived for non-price based regulatory measures would need to be compared against price-based policies. In 2022, the OECD updated its Environmental Policy Stringency (EPS) index that was originally developed in 2013 to measure price and non-price-based policies. It is an index that is still at its infancy, only covering and rating 13 policies across 40 countries over three decades from 1990 to 2020. The indicator does not measure the emission coverage and includes a restricted set of key mitigation policies.[65]

Historically, at least in the literature, there has been some consideration for the thought that regulatory measures might be capable of deriving a carbon price – if not now, then when there is agreement on a consensual carbon price equivalency methodology. For example, the Explanatory Notes to the Helsinki Principles of the Coalition of Finance Ministers for Climate Action note that carbon pricing policies could include "regulatory policies which result in an implicit marginal price on carbon, such as tradable performance standards."[66]

Despite the above understanding, the standing majority opinion to date is that these should really be qualified as non-pricing instruments.[67] This means that these are instruments that can complement and reinforce a robust carbon mitigation policy but do not necessarily contribute to the establishment of a carbon price nationally (for the purposes of NDC computation) or internationally when comparing policies under international approaches.

Why would there then be so much attention paid to the derivation of a price via a regulatory approach? For one, it is because countries lacking a national carbon price policy, the United States being included among them, are looking towards regulatory measures in order to be able to "claim" a national carbon price that would make viable the application of a border carbon adjustment (BCA) measure capable of protecting national producers against carbon leakage.

A border carbon adjustment works by taxing (or pricing) an import in order to ensure that these are taxed or priced at the same level as a domestically produced equivalent and/or by providing a credit (or exemption) on carbon-pricing paid on exports to avoid imposing an undue burden on the domestic product when the foreign equivalent is not burdened by a similar price or tax.

[64] IMF, OECD (2022), p. 18.

[65] IMF, OECD (2022), p. 9.

[66] Coalition of Finance Ministers for Climate Action (2019). Explanatory Notes to the Helsinki Principles, 4, available at: https://www.financeministersforclimate.org/sites/cape/files/inline-files/Explanatory%20Note%20designed%20copy.pdf (last accessed 10 Jan 2023).

[67] IMF (2019a, b), p. 5.

For a border adjustment to be permissible under the WTO's General Agreement on Tariffs and Trade (GATT), whether it is applied at the border on import or credited on export, the price or tax must impose an equivalent burden on both products that are produced domestically and those imported from abroad. The charge cannot impose an undue burden on the foreign-derived product, or it will be classified as a discriminatory measure under the GATT.[68] This means that the BCA cannot impose a higher price on the emissions embodied in products from third states compared to the *price* employed at the national level. Likewise, the BCA should correspond to the national carbon price. As a result, countries lacking a country-wide carbon price policy would not be permitted to apply a BCA as it would be in breach of the GATT.[69]

Specific to this point is the first ever policy proposal to introduce a BCA in respect of a regulatory approach, advanced by the United States in the Fair, Affordable, Innovative, and Resilient Transition and Competition Act of 2021 (act of 2021).[70] This act proposes the establishment of a BCA in proportion to the "price" derived from the application of a national benchmarked measure to reduce carbon emissions.[71]

---

[68] A unilateral measure with the potential to impose a restriction on trade must be nondiscriminatory for it to comply with the GATT and other WTO rules. A measure is considered nondiscriminatory if it is consistent with the main provisions of the GATT—namely, the most-favoured- nation clause in Article I, the national treatment provision in Article III, and quantitative restrictions in Article XI—or is justifiable under one of the Article XX exceptions. If the policy is consistent with Articles I, III, and XI or is justifiable under Article XX, there is no margin for dispute. An explicit carbon price would fall under the Article XX (g) exception of the GATT and would therefore probably be admissible (there is a stronger argument for the acceptability of carbon taxes than there is for the admissibility of ETSs, although they can be considered to be largely comparable provided there is no grandfathering in of permits under the ETS scheme). Equivalence requires that the price employed on the national product and the imported product are similar so that there is no undue burden on the foreign-derived product that might hinder trade.

[69] Falcão (2015), p. 571.

[70] US Senate, *Fair, Affordable, Innovative, and Resilient Transition and Competition Act,* GAI21718 59G, available at: https://www.coons.senate.gov/imo/media/doc/GAI21718.pdf. The proposal suggests that by 1 July 2023, the treasury department would determine the average cost to producers of steel, aluminum, cement, iron, and covered fuels of complying with federal or sub-federal climate policy in effect at the time. In computing the relative baseline environmental cost incurred for each sector, the proposed law foresees that it shall take into account (1) cap and trade and tax measures as well as (2) greenhouse gas emissions standards for passenger cars and light trucks. The question that would arise would thus be whether the computation of efficiency standards would be compatible with WTO law. For the purposes of this proposed act, domestic environmental cost means the sum of the ETS, tax, and GHG emissions efficiency standards for the transport vehicles mentioned above.

[71] Some states in the United States are covered by a carbon price. For example, the American northeast states are covered by the Regional Greenhouse Gas Initiative (GGGI), an ETS program covering 11 states (Connecticut, Delaware, Maine, Maryland, Massachusetts, New Hampshire, New Jersey, New York, Rhode Island, Vermont, and Virginia); California has a cap-and-trade system while California and Washington; and the Canadian provinces of Nova Scotia and Quebec are united by the Western Climate Initiative, also an ETS regime.

Under the terms of this law, the BCA for covered fuels—entering into force on 1 January 2024—will correspond to an amount equal to the product of (1) the domestic environmental cost incurred in the production of the fuel multiplied by (2) the upstream GHG emissions of the fuel. In the case of production of covered products, the BCA will likewise correspond to (1) the domestic environmental cost incurred in the production of the product multiplied by (2) the GHG emissions produced during the production process or, in the absence of reliable data on the GHG released during the production process, the benchmark emissions for the sector.

Commentators argue that the BCA proposal put forward under the act of 2021 is unlikely to pass congress. However, a more recent legislative piece has been issued as part of the US Inflation Reduction Act of 2022[72] devising rules to promote clean investment and electrification of the national grid. The legislation foresees a long list of activities that qualify for a tax credit when private parties invest in renewables, new technologies, and carbon capture and storage that is conditional on satisfying certain labour requirements. This being a regulation of national coverage, new attempts could be made to derive a BCA from the implementation of the national standard.

In assessing the compatibility of such a BCA with WTO rules, a number of questions would surface: (1) how to compute efficiency standards in a manner that is apt to effectively input an effective cost on carbon; (2) absent a federal carbon pricing approach, how to compute the environmental cost in the states where neither an ETS nor a carbon tax are in place[73]; (3) in the absence of available data, how to establish benchmark emissions per sector in a manner that does not lead to the imposition of US based standards on third states; and finally (4) how to take account of carbon pricing or regulations already imposed in the exporting country.

5.1.1 Feed-in-Tariffs

A feed in tariff is a policy tool designed to promote investment in renewable resources. Through it, governments support (or subsidize) small scale producers of renewable resources by offering them above the market prices for the energy they deliver to the grid. This allows producers to invest in renewables even when it is more costly than the equivalent brown, fossil-based energy source. Likewise, it provides scalability and consumption certainty in the use of the renewable resource.

[72] IRS, Inflation Reduction Act of 2022, available at: https://www.irs.gov/inflation-reduction-act-of-2022 (last accessed 16 Jan 2023).

[73] Some states in the United States are covered by pricing regimes. These are the initiatives in force in the United States: The Regional Greenhouse Gas Initiative, the California cap and trade system, and the Western Climate Initiative. All of these initiatives are limited to sectoral coverage of emissions.

The OECD qualifies feed in tariffs as equivalent to a pricing measure.[74] This author understands that, although feed in tariffs can be complementary to a carbon pricing policy, they do not, in fact, price carbon, nor do they discourage the use of fossil resources.[75] The United States National Renewable Energy Laboratory notes that feed-in-tariffs are the most widely used policy in the world for accelerating renewable energy deployment, exceeding the shares attributable to tax incentives or renewable portfolio standard policies.[76] Therefore, these are important measures, albeit of a more regulatory nature. It has an important role to play in complementing other pricing policies and providing an incentive towards the generation and use of renewable energy resources. In that sense, it could be comparable to a regulatory measure aiming to mainstream the use of certain technologies.

5.2 Voluntary Carbon Markets

Voluntary Carbon Markets (VCMs) are seen as a prime instrument to attract the foreign investment needed to help poorer countries transition to renewables and stave off disastrous climate impacts while, at the same time, foster local job creation and general economic development. Voluntary markets have been in existence since the Kyoto Protocol through the operation of the Clean Development Mechanism (CDM) and Joint Implementation (JI) framework. However, the role of VCMs in climate mitigation has been formalized more recently in the Paris Agreement (Article 6.4). While many governments have started preparing to attract climate finance through the international state-state cooperation mechanisms under Article 6 of the Paris Agreement, how governments can engage with VCMs to meet their Paris Agreement commitments and Nationally Determined Contributions is yet to be decided. The Glasgow Pact determined that negotiations of Article 6 would start in 2018 and end in 2030. In the meantime, countries are undergoing a pre-negotiation phase of Article 6 which occurs every year during the COP. Understanding what the negotiations of Article 6 will entail and how it can impact the revenue generation potential of climate projects in Africa will be of utmost significance for countries entering into negotiations in 2018.

Voluntary carbon market schemes are privately run certification programs under which a voluntary demand for carbon offset credits is generated by individuals or companies who purchase offsets to mitigate their greenhouse gas emissions in order to meet self-imposed emission reduction goals. The carbon offset credits are created and sold by the developers of offset projects that reduce emissions of greenhouse gases. Common offset type projects are related to renewable energy, energy

[74] OECD (2022) Table 1.1. A tentative Typology of selected mitigation policies where feed in tariffs are classified as "other price-based instruments".

[75] OECD (2022).

[76] Couture et al (2010). See also, Klein et al (2010).

efficiency, carbon sequestration through forest preservation, methane waste reduction, and others. Credits generated as a result of the operation of a VCM can have the effect of positively or negatively impacting a country's carbon price but, in this author's view, should not be mistaken for a price.

Credits acquired as a result of the execution of a voluntary project can play an important role in allowing countries to meet their net zero targets.[77] Achieving net zero means that, for every emission released by a country or party, there will be a compensation measure (credit) to offset those emissions. Therefore, net zero does not mean zero emissions; it means 100% compensation of emissions. Likewise, producing offsets from voluntary projects means that the parties involved are merely transferring the burden of reducing emissions to future generations. It is a timing issue. The net-zero target will be met in the short-term via the offset (acquired or produced), but the emissions will not have been reduced as a result of that process.

An offset can hence affect a country's carbon price because it can be used to reduce an explicit carbon price (offsetting it against the carbon tax rate as is the case in South Africa or against the permit price as used to be the case under the EU ETS during the Kyoto Protocol).

The UNFCCC argues[78] that carbon pricing would be referenced in Articles 6.2 (allowing the linking of carbon pricing approaches across countries), Article 6.4 (foreseeing the creation of a voluntary carbon market that would allow the offsetting of emissions through the trading of emissions reduction units), and Article 6.5 (foreseeing accounting measures to avoid double counting emissions reduction).[79]

---

[77] Achieving net zero means that, for every emission released by a country or party, there will be a compensation measure (credit) to offset those emissions. Therefore, net zero does not mean zero emissions as it needs 100% compensation of emissions.

[78] Because the UNFCCC classifies voluntary markets as being equivalent to carbon pricing approaches, it also monitors the use and application of voluntary approaches by the parties of the Paris Agreement. In the UNFCCC, nationally determined contributions under the Paris Agreement, Synthesis Report by the Secretariat, FCCC/PA/CMA/2021/8, pg. 5, available at: https://unfccc.int/sites/default/files/resource/cma2021_08_adv_1.pdf, (last accessed 4 Jan 2023), the following is reported:

> 8. Most Parties provided information on voluntary cooperation under Article 6 of the Paris Agreement. Almost all of them stated that they plan to or will possibly use at least one type of voluntary cooperation. At the same time, some Parties have set qualitative limits on their use of voluntary cooperation for achieving their mitigation targets.
>
> 9. Of the Parties that communicated new or updated NDCs, the share that indicated planned or possible use of at least one type of voluntary cooperation has nearly doubled (from 44 to 87 per cent) since their previous NDCs. Similarly, the share of those Parties that have set qualitative limits on their use of voluntary cooperation has doubled (from 19 to 39 per cent) since their previous NDCs.

The widespread adoption of the instrument by the Parties of the Paris Agreement heightens the need for the conceptual delimitation of the carbon pricing terminology and deeper assessment of the effect of the application of Article 6 of the Paris Agreement.

[79] UNFCCC, About carbon pricing, available at: https://unfccc.int/about-us/regional-collaboration-centres/the-ciaca/about-carbon-pricing#What-is-the-current-status-of-carbon-pricing-in-the.

This author contends that this is a mistaken interpretation of the term "carbon price" that does not reflect the progression of the topic through the years and the different international agreements.[80]

Under the Kyoto Protocol, developing countries were not required to reduce emissions and could use the credits generated from the trading of permits in the international compliance market—regulated by the Clean Development Mechanism—towards domestic compliance markets. The CDMs were therefore used as an instrument to provide concessional finance to developing countries not listed under Annex I.

Under the Paris Agreement, this mechanism has been substituted by Article 6.4 establishing a multilateral mechanism to effectively replace the Clean Development Mechanism of the Kyoto Protocol. Trading will be run by a central body with agreed methodologies and a registration system for activities to be traded. The supervisory body that will help to put the centralized mechanism in place for Article 6.4 has now been established, but it is expected to take 2 years before it will be fully operational. Further regulation is expected on issues such as the application of corresponding adjustments in order to avoid double counting for transactions involving counterparts who may wish to use the mitigation outcomes nationally or wish to record them only for purposes like results-based financing.

In addition to that, the Paris Agreement brings about a new mechanism for the inter-state bilateral trade of permits. Under the procedure of Article 6.2, parties can form a cooperative approach where they can agree on the terms, the criteria of trade, standards used, and methodology to trade offsets generated from voluntary markets. The credits, denominated Internationally Transferred Mitigation Outcomes, should comply with the basic requirements of Article 6 requiring that they are permanent, are above and beyond business as usual, and are not double counted.[81]

This process is important for assisting countries in meeting their NDCs as the acquisition of an ITMO might allow the acquiring country a higher emissions benchmark and still allow it to meet its NDC target by compensating the surplus emissions release with the credit (emissions reduction activity) occurring in a different state. Both of these mechanisms therefore operate as deferral schemes that protract the obligation to reduce emissions to a later time.

Not surprisingly, the VCMs proved to be controversial in the past with critics pointing out that voluntary carbon offsetting is little more than a bookkeeping trick that allows polluters to keep polluting while polishing their green reputation instead of reducing greenhouse gas emissions which scientists agree is the only way to curtail global heating. The VCMs furthermore often involve forests and agricultural

---

[80] Against, World Bank (2022), p. 13. The World Bank argues that carbon crediting mechanisms there included the system where tradable credits (typically representing a metric tonne of carbon dioxide equivalent) are generated through voluntarily implemented emission reduction or removal activities and are another form of carbon pricing.

[81] Based on Coalition of Finance Ministers for Climate Action, HP3 seminar on Carbon Markets, Organized in cooperation with Global Green Growth Initiative (GGGI), 31 October 2022, author's files.

land where local communities live and have lived sustainably with carbon markets putting pressure on ground and food prices thereby potentially undermining human rights.

5.3 *Tariffs and Other Border Measures*

5.3.1 Tariffs

According to the WTO, tariffs are customs duties imposed on merchandise when transported across international borders. The purpose of a customs duty or tariff is to protect the country's economy by controlling the flow of goods into the country, particularly if they are subject to restrictions or are prohibited. If the tariff is higher than the corresponding domestic tax, it may provide a price advantage to locally produced goods over similar goods that are imported and, in that sense, raise revenues for governments.[82] Tariffs may be imposed on a specific tax base or an ad valorem basis.[83]

Tariffs are regulated by Article II.1 of the GATT. This article requires parties not to grant treatment that is less favourable than that provided for in the schedule of concessions attached to the GATT 94. The schedule of concessions provides the maximum customs duties applicable to foreign product upon import into a national territory. The WTO acts to reduce customs tariffs as much as possible, therefore, the scheduled concessions provide the maximum negotiated rate that a country is willing to apply. The objective, in the interest of free trade, is that all commerce would ultimately be exempt from customs duties.

In line with that thought, during the Uruguay round of negotiation of tariff agreements, many countries agreed to cut and "bind" their customs duties rates on the import of goods. Many cut customs rates to close to zero. For example, in developed countries, 50% of industrial products are duty free. Tariff binding means that a country commits not to increase a rate of duty beyond the agreed level. If a bound rate is raised, the country must provide compensation to the affected parties.[84] According to the WTO, during the Uruguay round, developed countries increased the number of imports for which tariff rates are "bound", meaning committed and difficult to increase, to 99%. For developing countries, the increase

[82] WTO, Tariffs, available at: https://www.wto.org/english/tratop_e/tariffs_e/tariffs_e.htm#:~:text=Customs%20duties%20on%20merchandise%20imports,they%20raise%20revenues%20for%20governments. (last accessed 12.01.2023).

[83] WTO, Jargon Buster, available at: https://www.wto.org/english/tratop_e/dda_e/status_e/jargon_e.htm#:~:text=non%2Dad%2Dvalorem%20tariff%20A,mixed%E2%80%9D%20or%20some%20other%20form, (last accessed 13 Jan 2023).

[84] WTO, Jargon Buster, available at: https://www.wto.org/english/tratop_e/dda_e/status_e/jargon_e.htm#:~:text=non%2Dad%2Dvalorem%20tariff%20A,mixed%E2%80%9D%20or%20some%20other%20form, (last accessed 13 Jan 2023).

was in the line of 73%. Economies in transition from central planning increased their bindings to 98%.[85]

Tariffs differ from import duties or taxes from both a legal perspective (taxes and duties are regulated under Article II.2 of the GATT) and from a regulatory perspective—taxes and duties tend to be applied unilaterally and not subject to negotiation.

The recent economic literature has contended that a tariff could be assimilated to a carbon price in terms of the price effects it produces. According to Shapirro, "import tariffs and non-tariff barriers are substantially lower on dirty than on clean industries, where an industry's 'dirtiness' is defined as its carbon dioxide (CO_2) emissions per dollar of output. This difference in trade policy creates a global implicit subsidy to CO_2 emissions in internationally traded goods and so contributes to climate change."[86] Shapiro demonstrated that countries impose higher tariffs on clean than on dirty industries with one possible explanation being the lobbying of the dirtier industries. The global implicit subsidy (through the application of tariffs) is estimated to be at the level of USD 85 to USD 120 per tonne of CO_2 emissions, higher than the optimal tax of CO_2 which is often estimated at USD 40 per tonne of CO_2.[87] The author thus suggests that policy makers consider a reform that considers CO_2 intensity of an industry when negotiating tariff concessions in order not to neutralize the price incentive granted for other pricing policies such as carbon taxation.[88]

To make a tariff concession equivalent to a carbon price, the possibility would have to be considered that a trade reform might be executed having in mind the carbon intensity of certain products—there considering both the products one aims to employ a high tariff in order to hinder free trade, and those one wishes to stimulate for being "clean". In theory, at least, tariffs for which the basis is calculated on a specific basis would be assimilable to an explicit price, and tariffs for which the basis are established on an ad valorem basis would be similar to an implicit price. However, the practice is much more complicated than that.

As previously noted, many tariffs are already bound through the extensive WTO negotiation process and, therefore, changing them to a higher ground taking into account the high polluting content of a carbon intensive product would be difficult, if not impossible. In the EU, for example, the maximum tariffs (the "bound rates") that the EU has conceded are very low, e.g., regarding two carbon intensive fuels, cement and steel, the rates are 1,7% and zero, respectively. The option would be to introduce

---

[85] WTO, Tariffs: more bindings and closer to zero, available at: https://www.wto.org/english/thewto_e/whatis_e/tif_e/agrm2_e.htm#con, (last accessed 13 Jan 2023).

[86] Shapiro (2020).

[87] Shapiro (2020), p. 3.

[88] Tarr (2000).

new carbon customs duties in excess of WTO tariff concessions; but that would contravene Article II:1(b) GATT.[89,90]

It should be noted for completion purposes that WTO members are already engaged in negotiations of an Environmental Goods Agreement to eliminate tariffs on a number of products considered to be important for environmental purposes. Environmentally important products are cited by the WTO as being those that "can help achieve environmental and climate protection goals, such as generating clean and renewable energy, improving energy and resource efficiency, controlling air pollution, managing waste, treating wastewater, monitoring the quality of the environment, and combatting noise pollution".[91]

In conclusion, even if it might be theoretically possible to compare tariffs to explicit and implicit carbon taxes because of their bases for computation, in practice, the legal regime to which the negotiation of a new tariff or the renegotiation of an old one is subjected means that having a rate distinction on account of the level of pollution of the product is nearly impossible. For this reason, it is understood that a tariff cannot be interpreted to be within the definition of a carbon price.

5.3.2 Border Adjustment Measures

A border adjustment can be characterized as

> any fiscal measures which puts into effect, in whole or in part, the destination principle (i.e. which enable exported products to be relieved of some or all of the tax charged in the exporting country in respect of similar domestic products sold to consumers on the home market and which enable imported products sold to consumers to be charged with some or all of the tax charged in the importing country in respect of similar domestic products).[92]

In a nutshell, a BCA is a charge on embodied carbon in products imported into a jurisdiction with carbon pricing that is potentially matched by rebates for embodied carbon in exports.[93] Following this principle, "border carbon adjustments convert origin-based carbon prices to destination-based prices"[94], although some BCAs under consideration would not meet this definition (notably by not rebating carbon taxes paid on exports).

---

[89] Wiers (2008), p. 22 ss; Quick 2008, p. 164; Pauwelyn (2017), p. 466; see also Moore (2017), p. 49.

[90] For further information on the relationship between Articles II.1 and II.2 of the GATT, see Tatiana and Joachim (2021), 51, 10857, (part 1).

[91] WTO, Environmental Goods Agreement, available at: https://www.wto.org/english/tratop_e/envir_e/ega_e.htm (last accessed 16 Jan 2023).

[92] WTO/GATT, *Border Tax Adjustments, Report of the Working Party adopted on 2 December 1970*, (Doc. L/3464), available at http://www.worldtradelaw.net/reports/gattpanels/bordertax.pdf.

[93] Parry, et al. (2021).

[94] McLure (2011), p. 456.

Without entering into the merits of why a border adjustment measure would be introduced, what the definition above portrays is that a BCA is an equalization measure. The aim is thus to equalize the price of the imported good to the carbon price employed domestically by using the carbon embodied into the product in the country of production as a parameter to infer the carbon intensity of the good.

In this fact lies one of the biggest stalemates in the assessment of legality of a BCA measure.[95] That is because the Paris Agreement privileges the country of production as the default rule for accounting the emissions attributed to a good, service, or activity.[96] On the other hand, the GATT assesses the legality of a BCA in respect of its proportionality to the measures employed in the country of consumption. In fact, when defining border adjustment measures, the WTO authorities reference the application of the destination principle, which is the principle that is privileged under the GATT, through the use of the concepts of equivalence, proportionality, and fairness in the application of border measures (there included the application of tariffs). According to the working party, a border adjustment can be characterized as:

> any fiscal measures which puts into effect, in whole or in part, the destination principle (i.e. which enable exported products to be relieved of some or all of the tax charged in the exporting country in respect of similar domestic products sold to consumers on the home market and which enable imported products sold to consumers to be charged with some or all of the tax charged in the importing country in respect of similar domestic products).[97]

Equating inbuilt emissions on production to emissions priced in a consumption country is a possible exercise only when the expectation is that the production process will be more carbon intensive (and any carbon prices employed in the country where the product originates from are lower) than those applicable in the country of consumption/destination. That is, in fact, what is expected to occur under the EU proposal for a CBAM[98] since the price adopted at the EU level is significantly higher than any other price employed at the level of its trading partners. As a result, the expectation is that there will be an outstanding positive amount to charge at the border. One question not yet catered for in the proposal is whether the EU

---

[95] For a complete exposé on the legality of a BCA under WTO rules, see Falcão (2021a, b, c).

[96] *See* Intergovernmental Panel on Climate Change (IPCC), *Revised 1996 IPCC Guidelines for National Greenhouse Gas Inventories* (1996), available at https://www.ipcc-nggip.iges.or.jp/public/gl/invs4.html; Intergovernmental Panel on Climate Change (IPCC), *2006 IPCC Guidelines for National Greenhouse Gas Inventories* (2006), *available at* https://www.ipcc-nggip.iges.or.jp/public/2006gl/vol1.html.

[97] WTO/GATT, Border Tax Adjustments, Report of the Working Party adopted on 2 December 1970, (Doc. L/3464).

[98] The final language of the proposal is not yet available. This is a compilation by the commission comparing the three versions of the CBAM proposal put forward by the commission, the council and the parliament. The final text is expected to be a compromise of these versions. Council of the European Union, CBAM: Commission Proposal/Council General Approach/Position of the EP, 13063/22, available at: https://data.consilium.europa.eu/doc/document/ST-13063-2022-INIT/en/pdf.

would be willing to provide a credit (or pay back) to countries if it comes to the point that carbon prices employed in the country of production are higher or the corresponding emissions intensity of the products produced in the country of origin is lower than the corresponding price/carbon intensity observed in the EU territory.

This being an equalizing measure on imports, it can be employed in respect of several different carbon pricing instruments including carbon taxes, emissions trading schemes, implicit pricing instruments and, some would argue, even regulatory measures. There are open proposals for the adoption of BCAs in respect of each of these instruments across the world. Taiwan[99] has recently proposed a BCA in respect of a carbon tax, the EU has the CBAM proposal which is in respect of an ETS, and the United States has a proposal for a BCA in respect of a regulatory measure built into the Fair, Affordable, Innovative, and Resilient Transition and Competition Act of 2021 mentioned previously. The legality of each of these measures under WTO law and their consistency with the GATT is the subject of extensive literature but will not be the object of further discussion in this chapter.[100]

As a measure of equalization employed at the border to avoid carbon leakage, BCAs have the effect of complementing a national carbon price. That is particularly the case under the CBAM proposal (the most advanced proposal to date) as the objective there is to bring carbon prices at par with the regional price employed within the EU under the EU ETS program. For this reason, the proposal only allows compensation for explicit carbon prices employed by other countries trading with the EU. However, as noted, BCAs tend to be employed in order to address carbon leakage.

Carbon leakage is characterized by the relocation of domestic industry to a country offering a lower carbon price. This means that it intends to avoid a race to the bottom in a scenario where industry might relocate to carbon free jurisdictions or to a jurisdiction offering a lower cost of doing business because of no or very low carbon price. Although BCAs have been widely discussed recently, they are not the only instruments aiming to protect energy intensive industry from international competitiveness. Other approaches include adopting a very low carbon price or tax rate (or granting a tax rate reduction/exemption), allocating free permits under an ETS context, or providing for an export BCA where the BCA measure could be matched by rebates for embodied carbon in exports. Except for the last item, all of these would fall into the categories of implicit or negative carbon pricing approaches. Hence, it demonstrates the level of complexity the subject gains when deriving coordinated or multilateral approaches from the application of unilateral measures that have not been properly defined and categorized, even if only for statistical purposes.

[99] See Taiwan, Climate Change Responses Act, October 21, 2021, Articles 26 and 27. See also Lexology, Carbon Fees and Carbon Tariffs – What Businesses Must Know (Formosan Brothers), April 6, 2022 (author's files).

[100] For a full account of the legality of BCAs in their different forms, see: Falcão and Englisch (2021); Falcão (2021a), p. 485; Falcão 2020, 1047 (specifically on the CBAM).

6 Conclusion

It is clear from the text above that a clear conceptual approach to define the term "carbon pricing" as well as a methodology to determine equivalency of different carbon pricing approaches is key for countries to be able to (1) establish their NDCs and reform national tax systems in light of the assigned goals; and (2) derive policy equivalents when searching for coordinated or multilateral approaches to pricing carbon on a cross-border basis.

It is clear that this is a live debate, and it is likely that the terminology will change over time and adapt to the concessions granted by countries during the negotiation processes occurring through the UNFCCC process (as part of the annual conference of the parties meeting) but also through the stocktake process of the Paris Agreement.

In spite of all of the progress made on this subject, these are still early days in the carbon pricing debate. A principled conceptual approach to carbon pricing will require a reform of national systems to derive a wholesome carbon price that will be based not just on explicit and implicit pricing but also take into account all sorts of expenditures employed directly on pollutants and indirectly via concessions granted by other taxes (such as low VATs on carbon intensive fuels, land tax exemptions for agricultural products, and others). It will also require a strong methodology of equivalency at the international level to be able to compare policies and their environmental effects.[101]

The application so far is somewhat restricted as the debate is centred only around the application of border carbon adjustment measures (with an emphasis on the application of the EU CBAM proposal in particular) and climate clubs. These are stirred by the German proposal for the creation of a climate club and consequent creation of a climate club intergovernmental body managed by the OECD secretariat following the mandate of the G7.

However, it is likely to become even more complex as (1) BCA proposals proliferate, (2) other regional coalitions are formed with diverse interests, and (3) the deadline (currently scheduled for 2030) for achieving consensual agreements on complex issues such as the administration of voluntary carbon markets approaches. It would be desirable if it was not imperative for experts in the field to agree on a single conceptual approach shared by the international community, as represented by the four intergovernmental institutions active in this area—United Nations, OECD, IMF, and World Bank. Not doing so risks not just a legal stalemate but also collective failure in achieving the climate commitments humanity has set for itself via the Paris Agreement.

[101] World Bank (2022), p. 30.

References

Black D et al (2022) A framework for comparing climate mitigation policies across countries, IMF Working Papers. https://www.imf.org/en/Publications/WP/Issues/2022/12/16/A-Framework-for-Comparing-Climate-Mitigation-Policies-Across-Countries-527049

Couture T et al (2010) A policymaker's guide to feed-in-tariff policy design, United States National Renewable Energy Laboratory, Technical Report NREL/TP-6A2–44849

Ezcurra MV, Grau Ruiz MA (2021) Assessing public aid for true green digital recovery: a matter of good tax governance in the European Union. In: Ashiabor H et al (eds) Critical issues of environmental taxation: environmental taxation in the pandemic era: opportunities and challenges. Edward Elgar, Cheltenham

Falcão T (2015) Is a carbon tax compatible with the WTO treaties? Intertax 43(10):571

Falcão T (2020) Toward carbon tax internationalism: the EU border carbon adjustment proposal, tax notes international, emerging economies segment

Falcão T (2021a) Updating carbon tax policy is crucial to the EU green deal, tax notes international

Falcão T (2021b) Highlights of the United Nations handbook on carbon taxation. Intertax 49(11): 897–914

Falcão T (2021c) A multilateral approach to carbon taxation, tax notes international

Falcão T, Englisch J (2021) EU carbon border adjustments for imported products and WTO law, environmental law reporter

Kasa S (2000) Explaining emissions tax exemptions for heavy industries: a comparison of Norway, Denmark and the Netherlands, Center for International Climate and Environmental Research (Cicero), Policy Note 2000

Klein A et al (2010) Evaluation of different feed-in tariff design options – best practice paper for the international feed-in cooperation, 3rd edn. Energy Economic Group & Fraunhofer ISI, Karlsruhe

McLure C (2011) A primer on the legality of border adjustments for carbon prices: through a GATT darkly. Carbon Climate Law Rev 5(4):456

Metcalf GE (2019) On the economics of a carbon tax for the United States, Brookings papers on economic activity

Minnerop P (2019) The legal effect of the Paris rulebook under the doctrine of treaty interpretation. In: Cameron P et al (eds) Global energy in transition. Towards rules-based multilateral governance of generation, markets and investment. Hart publishing, Oxford. https://papers.ssrn.com/sol3/papers.cfm?abstract_id=3491775

Moore M (2017) Carbon safeguard? Managing the friction between trade rules and climate policy. J World Trade 51(1)

Parry I et al (2014) Getting energy prices right: from principle to practice, IMF. https://www.elibrary.imf.org/view/books/071/21171-9781484388570-en/21171-9781484388570-en-book.xml

Parry I et al (2021) Carbon pricing: what role for border carbon adjustments?, IMF Staff Climate Note 2021/004

Pauwelyn J (2017) Carbon leakage measures and border tax adjustments under WTO law. In: Van Calster G, Prévost D (eds) Research handbook on environment, health and the WTO. Edward Elgar, Cheltenham

Quick R (2008) Border tax adjustment' in the context of emission trading: climate protection or 'naked' protectionism? Global Trade Customs J 3(5):164

Ramseur J, Parker L (2009) Carbon tax and greenhouse gas control: Options and considerations for Congress, CRS Report for Congress

Scott J (2015) The geographical scope of the EU's climate responsibilities, Cambridge Yearbook European Legal Studies, No. 17

Shapiro J (2020) The environmental bias of trade policy, Working Paper 26845

Stern N, Lankes HP (2022) Collaborating and delivering on climate action through a climate club: an independent report to the G7, LSE

Stillwell M, Bohanes J (2005) Trade and the environment. In: Macrory PFJ et al (eds) The World Trade Organization: legal, economic and political analysis. Springer, Cham
Tarr DG (2000) On the design of tariff policy: a practical guide to the arguments for and against uniform tariffs
Wiers J (2008) French ideas on climate and trade policies. Carbon Climate Law Rev 2(1)
Wolff S (2021) A taxonomy of environmentally sustainable activities to orient covid-19 tax measures to environmental objectives. In: Ashiabor H et al (eds) Critical issues of environmental taxation: environmental taxation in the pandemic era: opportunities and challenges. Edward Elgar, Cheltenham

Institutional References

Coalition of Finance Ministers for Climate Action (2019) Explanatory Notes to the Helsinki Principles. https://www.financeministersforclimate.org/sites/cape/files/inline-files/Explanatory%20Note%20designed%20copy.pdf
G20 (2016) China's efforts to phase out and rationalise its inefficient fossil-fuel subsidies. https://www.oecd.org/fossil-fuels/publication/G20%20China%20Peer%20Review_G20_FFS_Review_final_of_20160902.pdf
G20 (2017a) Mexico's efforts to phase out and rationalise its fossil - fuel subsidies. https://www.oecd.org/fossil-fuels/Mexico-Peer-Review.pdf
G20 (2017b) Germany's effort to phase out and rationalise its fossil -fuel subsidies. http://www.oecd.org/site/tadffss/Germany-Peer-Review.pdf
IEA (2004) Energy statistics–manual, international energy agency. OECD Publishing, Paris. https://www.oecd-ilibrary.org/energy/energy-statistics-manual_9789264033986-en
IEA (2006) Carrots and sticks: taxing and subsidising energy. https://www.iea.org/reports/carrots-and-sticks-taxing-and-subsidising-energy
IMF (2019a) Fiscal Monitor, How to Mitigate Climate Change
IMF (2019b) Fiscal Policies for Paris Climate Strategies – from Principle to Practice, IMF Policy Papers
IMF, OECD (2022) Delivering Climate-Change Mitigation under Diverse National Policy Approaches, joint report. https://www.oecd-ilibrary.org/docserver/20179e63-en.pdf?expires=1672949219&id=id&accname=guest&checksum=9D92699C50108E7FD039F083D4627896
OECD (2013) Climate and Carbon: Aligning Prices and Polices, OECD environment Policy Paper No. 1
OECD (2019) Taxing Energy Use 2019: Using Taxes for Climate Action. https://doi.org/10.1787/058ca239-en
OECD (2021) Taxing Energy Use for Sustainable Development. https://www.oecd.org/tax/tax-policy/taxing-energy-use-for-sustainable-development.pdf
OECD (2022) Pricing greenhouse gas emissions: turning climate targes into climate action. https://www.oecd-ilibrary.org/sites/e9778969-en/1/3/1/index.html?itemId=/content/publication/e9778969-en&_csp_=52c8137b50988e25208d117dee9bbae3&itemIGO=oecd&itemContentType=book
UNEP, IISD, OECD (2019) Measuring fossil fuel subsidies in the context of the sustainable development goals. https://www.unep.org/resources/report/measuring-fossil-fuel-subsidies-context-sustainable-development-goals
UNFCCC, Center for Climate and Energy Solutions and Energy Defense Fund (2022) The global stocktake: an opportunity for ambition. Available at: https://www4.unfccc.int/sites/SubmissionsStaging/Documents/202202281810%2D%2D-C2ES_EDF%20Climate%20Finance%20Landscape%20Analysis%20Themes%20and%20Trends.pdf

United Nations (2021) Handbook on Carbon Taxation for Developing Countries. https://www.un.org/development/desa/financing/document/un-handbook-carbon-taxation-developing-countries-2021

World Bank (2022) State and trends of carbon pricing. https://openknowledge.worldbank.org/handle/10986/37455

WTO (1999) The legal texts: the results of the Uruguay round of multilateral trade negotiations. Cambridge University Press, Cambridge

The Economics of Adaptation to Climate Change and Its Main Challenges

Miguel Patrício

Abstract The economics of adaptation to climate change is a relatively new area of research that aims to contribute to the selection of efficient adaptations or to assess whether adaptation actions that are already being implemented are efficient or not. However, the economics of adaptation is also confronted with several challenges and some of them are analysed in this text.

The first part of the text briefly describes the origins of climate change awareness in the scientific community and shows the recent (and very fast) progression of global adaptation planning. A basic definition of adaptation is given and related (and unrelated but, in this context, relevant) concepts are also mentioned. The basic criteria underlying the economics of adaptation to climate change are presented, as well as the main economic methods used to evaluate adaptation measures.

The second part of the text analyses some of the most important challenges to the economics of adaptation to climate change, which have been divided into three main categories: (1) methodological challenges; (2) challenges posed by the interactions between adaptation and relevant variables; and (3) challenges that stem from cognitive biases and behavioural issues.

An emphasis is given to cognitive bias and behavioural issues because the environmental challenges that the world is currently facing stem, to a large extend, from the fact that many didn't see (and many still seem to not see) the urgent need to counteract (through adaptation or mitigation actions) the adverse effects of climate change.

M. Patrício (✉)
CIDEEFF, University of Lisbon, School of Law, Lisbon, Portugal
e-mail: miguelpatricio@fd.ulisboa.pt

R. Saraiva, P. A. Pardal (eds.), *Sustainable Finances and the Law*, Economic Analysis of Law in European Legal Scholarship 16,
https://doi.org/10.1007/978-3-031-49460-4_7

1 Adaptation to Climate Change: Definition and (un)Related Concepts

It is well known that an international scientific consensus has been established, particularly in the last decades, on the existence of a significant climate change on this planet as a result of human action. It has now become clear to almost all countries and also to international institutions that it is imperative (more than ever before) to find effective and innovative tools to fight climate change, its causes. and consequences.

According to Diego Lindoso and Joana Araújo Maria,[1] the scientific research on climate change started slowly around the end of the nineteenth century (Arrhenius 1986[2]). It re-emerged in the 1940s (the first theories of anthropogenic global warming came to light at the end of the previous decade: see Guy Stewart Callendar 1938[3]) and established itself with the prominence known today between the 1950s and 1970s.

By that time—as D. Lindoso and J. Maria say—it became an indisputable fact in the scientific community that carbon dioxide (CO_2) is one of the main greenhouse gases: The commissioning of the first systematic monitoring stations of carbon dioxide concentrations in the atmosphere (Keeling 1960[4]), the advances in computing that gave us the first weather forecasting models (Phillips 1956[5]), and the first artificial satellites orbiting the Earth and bringing unprecedented images that illustrated climate dynamics, and (other) scientific advances of the time all contributed to the prominence mentioned previously. On the other end, between the 1950s and the 1970s, a better understanding of Earth's distant past was being better understood which allowed realizing (with the help of paleoclimatology and paleoceanography)

[1] See Lindoso and Araújo (2013), pp. 107–123. See also, for example: Page (2006), p. 23.

[2] Arrhenius (1986), pp. 237–276. Arrhenius's paper is the first to quantify the contribution of carbon dioxide ("carbonic acid") to the greenhouse effect and to speculate about whether variations in the atmospheric concentration of carbon dioxide have contributed to long-term variations in climate. Even before (in 1856), Eunice N. Foote was the first to hypothesize that changing amounts of CO_2 in the atmosphere would alter the climate: "An atmosphere of that ['carbonic acid'] gas would give to our earth a high temperature": see Foote (1856), p. 383.

[3] Callendar (1938), pp. 223–240. Although Callendar attributed the rise in average air temperature to the buildup of carbon dioxide from the burning of fossil fuels, he thought this warming would be beneficial: "In conclusion it may be said that the combustion of fossil fuel [...] is likely to prove beneficial to mankind in several ways, besides the provision of heat and power. In any case, the return of the deadly glaciers should be delayed indefinitely." (236).

[4] Keeling (1960), pp. 200–203.

[5] Phillips (1956), pp. 123–164. According to Edwards, Paul N.. 2011. History of climate modeling, WIREs Climate Change, No. 2, 131, "The first person to attempt a computerized GCM [General Circulation Model] was Norman Phillips at Princeton's Institute for Advanced Study. Phillips applied nascent NWP [Numerical Weather Prediction] techniques, completing a 2-layer hemispheric, quasi-geostrophic computer model in mid-1955."

the dangers of (past and actual) severe climatic instability and the perils of climate feedback loops.[6]

It is natural to emphasize the effects of CO_2 (as already said, CO_2 is one of the main GHGs), but the very negative impact that other greenhouse gases emissions can also have should not be forgotten. In this regard, the table (and especially the last column that shows the negative impact ratio that other harmful gases released into the atmosphere can have in comparison with the reference that is $CO_2 = 1$) in E. Page is illustrative.[7]

It is also worth mentioning that it was in the 1970s when neo-Malthusian ideas (re-)emerged warning that there are limits to economic growth that are imposed by global environmental limits (Ehrlich 1968[8]; Georgescu-Roegen 1971[9]; Club of Rome, 1972[10]). It also raised awareness that, before it is too late, the industrialized countries need to start making the transition to an economic nongrowth or even an economic degrowth.

This growing concern about the impact of anthropogenic climate change would eventually become part of the international political agenda. After several meetings promoted by the UN and the World Meteorological Organization (WMO) in the 1980s and 1990s, the first major result is seen with the creation during the 1992 Rio Summit of the United Nations Framework Convention on Climate Change (or UNFCCC). This is the moment (and the framework convention) from which the climate change subject starts to be seen as a relevant one in the international negotiations. Additionally, it is also when two environmental policies to counter the impact of climate changes are outlined: (i) on the one hand, mitigation, through which there is an attempt to find ways to slow down (or even prevent) the advance of climate change and its consequences; and (ii) on the other hand, adaptation[11] by which current climate changes are acknowledged and national, regional, and local economies are sought to respond (or adapt) to them, even if only partially.

Some examples that are frequently given of these two options are, on the one hand, mitigation by limiting or reducing the anthropogenic emissions of greenhouse gases; on the other hand, adaptation through the use of air conditioning to withstand

---

[6]See, for example: Emiliani (1955), pp. 538–578; also Emiliani (1972), p. 400: "[...] man's interference with climate through deforestation, urban development, and pollution must be viewed with alarm. If the present climatic balance is not maintained, we may soon be confronted with either a runaway glaciation or a runaway deglaciation, both of which would generate unacceptable environmental stresses."

[7]See Page (2006), p. 25, table 2.1.

[8]Ehrlich (1968). The Population Bomb, Ballantine Books. The words for the title were first used on the cover of a pamphlet issued by the Hugh Moore Fund in 1954. Not surprisingly, this book was inspired by two 1948 neo-Malthusian books: Osborn (1948); Vogt (1948).

[9]Georgescu-Roegen (1971). According to N. Georgescu-Roegen (1986), the essay for his 1966 *Analytical Economics*, "which by way of a second edition turned into the 1971 volume", had one main idea: "that the economic process is entropic in all its material fibers".

[10]Meadows et al. (1972).

[11]About the concept (and its origins), see: Simonet (2009), pp. 392–401.

the rise in air temperature or the construction of sea or flood barrier systems to cope with floods or the rising of sea water levels.[12]

It should also be noted that, in the context of the framework convention mentioned before, the parties are divided into three main groups (Annex I, Annex II, and Non-Annex I) according to differing commitments. Annex I parties include the industrialized countries that were members of the OECD in 1992 plus the countries with *economies in transition* (EIT Parties); they all should undertake and communicate mitigation efforts.[13] Annex II parties are a subgroup of Annex I (the OECD members of Annex I), being committed not only to the mitigation efforts but also to providing new and additional financing and promoting the development and transfer of environmentally friendly technologies to EIT Parties and developing countries.[14] Finally, there are the so-called Non-Annex I Parties (154 countries)—mostly developing countries that are only required to report emissions (even though Non-Annex I Parties like China and India are among some of the largest contributors to greenhouse gas emissions).

Later, the challenges that conciliation between these two options (mitigation and adaptation) poses will be briefly analysed. This is because a global and effective strategy to fight climate change must try to achieve a balance between mitigation and adaptation options with a view to minimizing the costs (and the so-called *residual damages*) that inevitably arise from climate change. According to Astrid Dannenberg et al.,[15] economist William Dawbney Nordhaus (in a 1991 article[16])

> derives two conditions for such a cost minimum: First, the marginal costs of emissions reduction should be equal to the marginal benefits of emission reduction, i.e. the avoided marginal residual costs of climate change. Second, adaptation should be realized up to the point where the marginal benefits of adaptation are equal to the marginal costs of adaptation.

---

[12] Other examples—referred by de Murieta et al. (2015), p. 20—are: "Efficient cooling systems, desalination technologies or increasingly advanced weather forecasts that anticipate extreme events are examples of how technology can enhance adaptive capacity." To understand the importance of this last example ("advanced weather forecasts"), the 2004 Indian Ocean earthquake and tsunami or, even before that, in 1999, the cyclone *Lothar*, with its virtually undetectable superfast approach to Europe must be remembered. *Extreme events* like these, quite hard to anticipate, are a big challenge for those who wish to integrate them into an economic model regarding their potential impacts, although some methodologies can be applied. For example, according to de Murieta et al. (2015), p. 21, "Okuyama offers an exhaustive review of methodologies for disaster impact analysis, such as input-output (IO), social accounting matrix (SAM), computable general equilibrium (CGE) and econometric models, each method showing strong and weak features (e.g., IO and SAM tend to overestimate economic impacts while CGE may lead to underestimations)."

[13] *Vide* Article 4, paragraph 2, subparagraphs (a) and (b).

[14] *Vide* Article 4, paragraph 3. The "developed Parties included in annex II shall also assist the developing country Parties that are particularly vulnerable to the adverse effects of climate change in meeting costs of adaptation to those adverse effects." (Paragraph 4). However, it is debatable which developing country parties are "particularly vulnerable"; in this regard, *vide* Klein (2009), pp. 284–291.

[15] See Dannenberg et al. (2009), p. 1.

[16] See Nordhaus (1991), pp. 920–937.

> There is a trade-off between both policy options at the global level: More emissions reduction makes less adaptation necessary and vice versa.[17]

The very close relationship between adaptation and mitigation can be illustrated with the chart presented in Burton et al.[18]

The awareness of the importance of adaptation began for two main reasons: (i) on the one hand, because it was perceived that, even without an increase in global average temperatures above the objectives outlined (previously 2 °C and now 1.5° above the values registered in pre-industrial times), adaptation to the current undeniable impacts of climate change is still needed to decrease systems' vulnerability; (ii) on the other hand, the recognition that the uncertainty about the speed or scale of the climate change and the continuing inability to build a global consensus on mitigation (probably the result of a free-riding problem in international negotiations[19]) requires, as an alternative, increased adaptation efforts. To these two reasons, Nobuo Mimura[20] adds two more: (iii) "First, adaptation is particularly important for the next 30 years because the effects of mitigation efforts will not be realized for a few decades. [iv)] Second, mitigation is of fundamental importance to stabilize global warming in the long run."

Until now, there has not been an elaborate definition of adaptation. However, the one that was presented by the Intergovernmental Panel on Climate Change (IPCC)[21] is a very good starting point: Adaptation consists of an "[a]djustment in natural or human systems in response to actual or expected climatic stimuli or their effects, which moderates harm or exploits beneficial opportunities".

So, adaptation is apparently a quite broad concept that encompasses all types of responses that aim at reducing vulnerability to climate change,[22] i.e., that aim to reduce the potential risk of suffering loss or damage (taking into account the ability of systems to absorb the impact of climate change or to recover from that impact). Additionally, according to the IPCC definition, adaptation also includes actions aimed at taking advantage of new beneficial opportunities that may arise as a result of climate change.[23] Nevertheless, and as Barry Smit et al. have pointed out, there

---

[17]About the trade-off between mitigation and adaptation, see infra (III.2.3.) and also: Grasso (2010), p. 13.

[18]Burton et al. (2001), p. 881. See also: Berry (2009), p. 282.

[19]In this regard, see, e.g.: Nordhaus (2019), p. 2006.

[20]Mimura (2010), p. 132.

[21]Parry et al. (2007), p. 27. Other definitions of adaptation can be found, e.g., in Agrawal (2018), p. 152.

[22]"*Adaptation* is adjustment in ecological, social, or economic systems in response to actual or expected climatic stimuli and their effects or impacts. This term refers to changes in processes, practices, or structures to moderate or offset potential damages or to take advantage of opportunities associated with changes in climate. It involves adjustments to reduce the vulnerability of communities, regions, or activities to climatic change and variability.": Burton et al. (2001), p. 881.

[23]That is why some invoke a so-called triple dividend of adaptation "avoiding future human, natural and material losses; generating economic benefits by reducing risks, increasing productivity, and

are also other aspects of adaptation not directly mentioned in that definition, though they can be found in other definitions. For example,

> [r]eferring only to societal adaptation to climate, Burton (1992) defines it as 'the process through which people reduce the adverse effects of climate on their health and well-being, and take advantage of the opportunities that their climatic environment provides'. [And to] Stakhiv (1993), the term adaptation [also] means 'any adjustment, whether passive, reactive or anticipatory, that is proposed as a means for ameliorating the anticipated adverse consequences associated with climate change'.[24]

Furthermore, there is also a peculiarity with adaptation that should be noted. The absence of adaptation measures does not necessarily mean the absence of a *cost-benefit analysis* on adaptation measures (because, in some cases, it may be considered—with or without a good reason—that the costs of the potential adaptive responses were higher than the risks that climate change will impose if nothing is done).

Besides loss and damage,[25] there are also other (un)related concepts that cannot be ignored when defining adaptation. One of them is maladaptations,[26] i.e. human actions that fail to adjust adequately to the environment (or to the impact of climate change), increasing vulnerability,[27] whether those actions are triggered by climate change (e.g. the Republic of Kiribati bought, in 2014, 20km^2 from Vanua Levu, the second largest island of Fiji, an island that is almost 2000 km away from Kiribati; and Tuvalu and the Maldives already tried to do the same[28]) or not (e.g. Germany reactivated, in 2022, mothballed coal-fired power stations in response to the energy crisis fuelled by Russia's war on Ukraine). Not unexpectedly, all maladaptations (climate-related or not) increase vulnerability and raise the costs of future adaptations to them.

Another (un)related concept relevant to understand the scope of adaptation is the concept of restoration. Some consider it a type of adaptation[29] but being that adaptation is a process of continuous learning and a response to an ever-changing

stimulating innovation; and the social, environmental and cultural benefits". (Communication from the Commission COM (2021) 82 final, 24.2.2021).

[24] See Smit et al. (1999), p. 203.

[25] Recognized as a separate concept from adaptation in 2008. About the concept of loss and damage, see, e.g.: Mathew and Akter (2017), pp. 17–45.

[26] About these and their impact, see, e.g.: Lisa and Schipper (2020), pp. 409–414.

[27] About this concept, see, for example: Eakin and Luers (2006), pp. 365–394.

[28] On the other hand, the creation of the artificial island of Hulhumalé by the Maldives (in the 1990s) was (and, it seems, still is) a good adaptation to the sea level rise, at least until the end of this century: see Brown et al. (2020), p. e12567.

[29] See Parry and Martens (1999), p. 233: "*Restoration* [is a type of adaptation that] aims to restore a system to its original condition following damage or modification due to climate [though] [t]his is not strictly an adaptation to climate".

natural environment, actions intended to go back to the *status quo ante* (and not to increase the environmental resilience) should not be seen as true adaptation.[30]

2 A Brief Introduction to the Economics of Adaptation to Climate Change

According to Elisa Sainz de Murieta et al.,[31] it wasn't until the Nairobi Work Programme (NWP), formally approved at the COP 12 in Nairobi (Kenya) in 2006, that the international community acknowledged adaptation policy as a cornerstone of the effort to fight climate change. The NWP was agreed on to support all countries, especially developing countries, to: (1) improve their understanding and assessment of impacts, vulnerability and adaptation to climate change and [also to] (2) decide on specific adaptation actions and measures taking, as a basis, the sound scientific, technical and socioeconomic information. The constitution of the *Adaptation Fund* (AF) was another decisive issue on the adaptation agenda in Nairobi, [a *Fund*] which aims at financing specific adaptation projects and programmes in developing countries that are Parties to the Kyoto Protocol. [Despite] these efforts, it was not until 2010, at the Cancun Summit (COP 16), that the Cancun Accords stated that adaptation 'must be addressed with the same priority as mitigation'.

Proof of that was the invitation then addressed to all parties to prepare and implement their National Adaptation Plans (or NAP) (see Decision 1/ COP 16, § 14a 2011).

The increase in the number of NAPs from 2010 onwards (even though the growing curves also include mere strategies, laws, or policies of the first, second, or third generations) is notorious.[32]

The Portuguese NAP (called *Estratégia Nacional de Adaptação às Alterações Climáticas* or ENAAC), for example, was first adopted in 2010. In 2020, the most recent ENAAC (ENAAC 2020, approved in 2015) was extended until the end of 2025.[33] So, given the growing importance of adaptation, the growing interest in the Economics of Adaptation to Climate Change will come as no surprise.

[30] *Restoration* should only mean, as in the recent *Proposal for a Nature Restoration Law* by the European Commission, the adoption of measures to *repair* and *rehabilitate* current habitats in a poor condition.

[31] de Murieta et al. (2015), p. 6.

[32] United Nations Environment Programme (2021), p. 17, Figure 3.2. Progression of global adaptation planning since 2020.

[33] In the last 5 years, a number of subnational adaptation plans have also emerged in Portugal: *Planos Metropolitanos de Adaptação às Alterações Climáticas* – PMAAC-AML / PMAAC-AMP (Lisbon and Oporto metropolitan areas), *Planos Municipais de Adaptação às Alterações Climáticas* (municipalities), and *Planos Locais de Adaptação às Alterações Climáticas* – PLAAC (for example, PLAAC-Arrábida).

The Economics of Adaptation tries to identify and test the most efficient and effective measures (taking into account the costs incurred and also the targets pursued) for the implementation of climate change adaptation actions or strategies. Another way of putting it is to say that the Economics of Adaptation seeks, through the use of economic tools (scientific method, graphs, and economic models), to carry out climate change adaptation assessments, i.e., the identification of the available options to carry out adaptation and their evaluation based on criteria such as, e.g., "availability, benefits, costs, effectiveness, efficiency and feasibility".[34]

To carry out the climate change adaptation assessments mentioned before, the method plays, as expected, an important role. However, stating "method" also indicates multiple methods. These will not be analysed one by one in detail, but it should be noted that, in all of them, the purpose is to evaluate how different actions, practices, or technologies allow better dealing with climate change by either by preventing or minimizing its negative impacts, by allowing fast and efficient recovery when possible, or by taking the advantages of positive impacts of climate change.

Some of the most used or proposed methods for evaluating adaptation measures or strategies are, e.g.: (1) forecasting by analogy[35]; (2) cost-benefit analysis (CBA)[36]; (3) cost-effectiveness analysis (CEA)[37]; (4) multi-criteria decision analysis (MCDA)[38]; and (5) BASE [Bottom-up climate Adaptation Strategies towards a Sustainable Europe] Evaluation Criteria for Climate Adaptation (BECCA).[39]

Regardless of the method chosen, a total of seven steps must be met (according to the IPCC)[40]: (1) Define the objectives (of adaptation); (2) specify the climatic impacts of importance; (3) identify the adaptation options; (4) examine the constraints (namely, social and legal constraints); (5) quantify measures and formulate alternative strategies; (6) weight objectives and evaluate trade-offs; and (7) recommend adaptation measures.

---

[34] See NWP. 2021, Assessing the Costs and Benefits of Adaptation Options. An Overview of Approaches. Bonn, United Nations Climate Change Secretariat, 45.

[35] See Burton et al. (1998), pp. 5–12.

[36] A CBA is often used to assess adaptation options when efficiency is the only decision-making criteria. A CBA involves calculating and comparing all of the costs and benefits that are expressed in monetary terms (this can mean that non-market costs and benefits are excluded).

[37] The CEA is often used to find the least costly adaptation option for meeting selected targets. The CEA is usually applied in assessing adaptation options in areas where benefits are difficult to express in monetary terms.

[38] The MCDA allows assessment of different adaptation options against a number of criteria. Each criterion is given a weighting. Using this weighting, an overall score for each adaptation option is obtained, and the adaptation option with the highest score is selected.

[39] The *BECCA* are subdivided into outcome and process-criteria (and each one is subdivided into several subcategories or criteria *stricto sensu*). The seven outcome criteria categories are: Effectiveness, efficiency, equity, side effects, acceptability, coherence (external and internal) and robustness. The process criteria categories are: Adaptive capacity, dependencies, deliverability and feasibility, flexibility, participation and lessons learnt. See, e.g.: Campos et al. (2018), p. 147.

[40] See Carter et al. (1994).

Although there are specific issues related to the assessment of costs and benefits of environmental impacts or adaptation measures, the choice of a method will depend on its response to the following four conditions: (i) whether the method is able to build (social and political) consensus or not; or if is compatible with existing decision making (for example, if public policy options are usually assessed using a CBA, assessing the adaptation options using a CEA may be less acceptable); (ii) its ability to deal with uncertainties (e.g., uncertainties regarding the scale of impacts; the area and time period covered by the impacts; or the effectiveness of proposed measures); (iii) the availability of information to carry out the assessment (for example, if the benefits cannot be quantified in monetary terms, it is not advisable to undertake a CBA); and (iv) the availability of resources to carry out the evaluation on time (or present the results on time or even if there are specialists to properly carry out the evaluation).

3 Main Challenges to the Economics of Adaptation

Three main categories will be analysed here: 3.1. Methodological challenges; 3.2. Challenges posed by the interactions between adaptation and relevant variables; and 3.3. Challenges that stem from cognitive biases and behavioural issues.

3.1 Methodological Challenges

If the aim of the Economics of Adaptation to Climate Change is, as has been seen, to contribute to the selection of efficient adaptations (that is to say, adaptations in which the gains are or will be greater than the costs[41]) or to assess whether adaptation actions that are already being implemented are efficient, it is essential to take into account the challenges posed by the method.

One of the main challenges that every method faces is uncertainty. First and foremost is the uncertainty as to the timing, speed, or size of the climate change that is thought to take place.[42] This is a very difficult challenge to overcome because it will inevitably affect the calculation of costs and benefits, and it will also have an impact on the evaluation of relevant items to the adaptation assessment such as susceptibility (which means the fragility of a system to climate change), resilience/adaptability (i.e. the ability to resist and adapt to climate change), or vulnerability (i.e., the overall balance on damages caused to a system due to climate change).[43]

[41] See Mendelsohn (2000), p. 585.
[42] On this particular uncertainty, see, for example: Markandya (2015), p. 99.
[43] See Watson et al. (1995), p. 23.

Moreover, since adaptation measures are usually designed for local or regional contexts, it must be kept in mind that climate prediction models may not be able to fine-tune their predictions for these smaller scales – which, in turn, will mean that adaptations will have to be reactive rather than anticipatory (probably only including the so-called no-regret measures that are able to cope with current risks but are/were not specifically adjusted to the changes that will actually take place on those smaller scales or adjusted to the risks that are expected to happen in the near future on those scales).

If adaptations planned collectively and supported or led by public entities are more capable of gathering the necessary information to counteract, as far as possible, the uncertainty about the expected climate change (and about other uncertainties), it is also true that they tend to be decided and implemented more slowly (than the so-called autonomous or private adaptations) and, also because of that, they tend to be reactive rather than anticipatory.

This is not in the least because anticipatory measures also have their own issues. For example, knowing when such a measure should be taken and what will be the cost of anticipation (compared to the cost of not taking such a measure) requires complex economic calculations (for instance, the selection and evaluation of several scenarios for phased anticipatory measures in order to avoid "*one-time actions*" that may entail the risk of total losses in the case of failure of long-term forecasting or the analysis of intermediate losses and devaluations in capital assets or natural resources due to the absence of those anticipatory adaptation measures).

As previously mentioned, uncertainty can be present in any area relevant to the calculation, for example, uncertainty over the amount of economic losses involved in the *status quo* scenario or uncertainty about the amount of economic benefits generated by adaptation against that business-as-usual scenario (or baseline scenario).[44]

Additionally, as Elisa Sainz de Murieta et al.[45] say, "we should also be aware that each step (input data, climate modelling, impacts and adaptation...) adds uncertainty to the previous one, so cumulative uncertainties should also be addressed when measuring the impacts of adaptation".

The cost-benefit analysis (CBA), the cost-effectiveness analysis (CEA), and the multi-criteria decision analysis (MCDA) are among some of the most widely used methods, but Jenny Tröltzsch et al.[46] also suggest, when conducting a risk assessment, three other alternative methods,[47] especially when there is *deep uncertainty*:

i) When the risk of maladaptations (i.e. adaptations harmful to the environment) is high and there is also deep uncertainty, they propose the so-called Robust Decision Making (RDM)—a method based on three key premises:

[44] See Callaway et al. (2016), p. 2.

[45] de Murieta et al. (2015), p. 7.

[46] Tröltzsch et al. (2016), pp. 27–33 and 37 ss.

[47] Additional alternatives can be found, e.g., in Markandya (2015), p. 110.

(1) uncertainty is treated as containing multiple views of the future, each one associated with plausible probabilistic information; (2) the use of robustness (or satisfaction) instead of optimality when assessing the criteria; and (3) instead of a traditional "predict-then-act approach", the use of a "vulnerability-and-response-option approach" (which means that uncertainty over the future is determined in the context of a specific action and not in abstract terms).

ii) When there is *deep uncertainty* about the right combination of adaptation actions that are perceived as being potentially complementary, they propose the so-called portfolio analysis (PA)—in which the evaluation of risk and returns provided by each potential action is not individually made but always in combination with others in order to determine the global impact on the portfolio of adaptation measures.

iii) When there is *deep uncertainty* about the future value of the adaptation options (taking into account their life cycles), they propose the Real-Option Analysis (ROA) method. In this method, a risk analysis makes use of some technical concepts taken from the field of financial risk measurement, such as the Value-at-Risk (VaR) (that answers the question, "How bad can things get?". For example, what is the risk or loss probability of an option within the next 50 years?) or the expected shortfall (ES) (that answers the question, "What is the expected loss value of the tail beyond the VaR?").

3.2 *Challenges Posed by the Interactions Between Adaptation and Relevant Variables*

There are several interactions (only four of them will be selected here) that should be taken into account when doing an impact assessment of adaptation measures or projects.

3.2.1 The Interaction Between Adaptation and Equity

When implementing adaptation measures at the international level, the distributional impacts between rich and poor countries should be taken into account, namely because the latter ones generally pollute less than the former ones but, on the other hand, need more economic growth than developed countries. Additionally, despite the positive externalities that could be generated by increased solidarity and fairness in the international financing of adaptation, there is still a lack of support from the more developed countries.

The distributional impacts within national or local communities should also be taken into account (because the fight against inter-regional inequalities and poverty areas will reduce *vulnerability* and the *adaptation deficit*, and that will also help to reduce tensions between social groups or between regions).[48] Nonetheless, and at least at the international level, it must be kept in mind that solidarity can be based on different principles of distributive justice and that those differences will lead to very different outcomes in terms of international equity, as shown in the table 6.2 of Hunt and Ferguson.[49]

3.2.2 The Interaction Between Adaptation and Its Funding

This is an interaction that is more complex than one might think. As Nobuo Mimura et al.[50] say, although there are several sources and mechanisms for financing adaptation—"[a]daptation financing broadly refers to resources that are deployed to support climate-resilient development (World Bank Group, 2011)"—at multiple levels (international and national, public and private[51]), the fact is that, "[i]n both the public and private arenas, financing for adaptation is currently substantially less than financing for mitigation".

There are a number of reasons to why that happens. For example:

i) "Adaptation is often most needed in non-market sectors or is focused on public goods that benefit many stakeholders, which makes it challenging to mobilize private finance"[52];
ii) Secondly, public financing for adaptation also faces a number of challenges because, despite the progress that has been made in recent years, it is still not as transparent or effective as it could be. According to a recent technical report prepared for the UNFCCC Standing Committee on Finance (or SCF),[53]

[48] Regarding these distributive impacts, see in more depth, for example: Hunt and Fergunson (2014), pp. 120–37.

[49] See Hunt and Fergunson (2014), p. 127, Table 6.2.

[50] See Mimura et al. (2014), p. 880. See, also, e.g.: Huq (2011), p. 293 ss.

[51] See, again, Mimura et al. (2014), p. 880: "Sources of public financing for adaptation include contributions from national budgets, multilateral and bilateral development funds, and UNFCCC operational funds – the Adaptation Fund, the Least Developed Countries Fund, and the Special Climate Change Fund [...]. A potentially key source of future public financing for adaptation is the Green Climate Fund that was officially designated at the 17th Conference of the Parties to the UNFCCC in Durban [in 2018, this fund already represented, according to the UNFCCC, 67% of total funding through multilateral climate funds]. [...]. Private financing for adaptation is primarily of two types: debt and equity. Debt-based financing typically consists of loans (e.g., bank loans) or bonds that must be paid back over time with interest. Equity-based financing generally involves a transfer of ownership rights through stocks or other assets. Export credits and foreign direct investment are two additional potential forms of private financing for adaptation. [...] Foreign direct investment is seen as having only limited potential for adaptation financing because it is highly concentrated in a few sectors and in a limited number of countries."

[52] *Vide* United Nations Environment Programme (2021), p. 24.

[53] SCF (2021), p. 107.

> the MDBs [Multilateral Development Banks] and IDFC [International Development Finance Club] do not include information on mitigation and adaptation outcomes in their joint reports and bilateral contributors have variable approaches to reporting on impacts. However, the multilateral climate funds have continued making progress on impact reporting [...]. [And] [t]he results reported from the funds provide useful insight into climate finance effectiveness.

Nonetheless, when looking at the reported results, there must be a conclusion that (with regard, specifically, to adaptation strategies or cross-cutting ones, like the recent Green Climate Fund) they fall short of expectations.[54]

iii) Thirdly, it is also important to note that, as mentioned in the same recent technical report,[55]

> [t]here is no singularly accepted impact metric for adaptation-focused climate finance. This, in part, reflects the broad suite of sectors and approaches that are part of adaptation efforts. [For example,] [c]onventional development interventions, including those supporting sustainable livelihoods or social protection, can [also] strengthen resilience and adaptive capacity, [therefore] making it difficult to distinguish between good development and adaptation activities. [About 'growth with the environment taken into account', see *infra*, III.2.4.] [On the other hand,] the timescale and frequency over which the multiple impacts of climate change will materialize, further complicate the creation of common impact metrics for adaptation.

It is needless to say that all of these issues have a negative impact on obtaining more funding for adaptation.

3.2.3 The Interaction Between (Aggregate) Adaptation and Mitigation

Regarding, specifically, this potential trade-off, it is important to note that it is particularly relevant at the international level since, though adaptation is usually local or regional based, its (aggregate) success depends, to some extent, on international cooperation (and funding).

Indeed, as Elisa Sainz de Murieta et al.[56] say,

> an efficient and fair adaptation policy may need a certain level of international cooperation. [...] [That] international cooperation on adaptation may also have positive side effects, [like] contributing to a climate of trust among developing countries with respect to developed countries, which in turn could contribute to global mitigation efforts. And the other way around: developing countries have asked for adaptation reinforcement as a previous requirement for getting involved in a global compromise for emissions reduction. Therefore, a lack of clear international support for adaptation could also obstruct an international agreement on mitigation.

---

[54] For example, the expected results for the Green Climate Fund were 111 million direct beneficiaries, but the reported results were instead only ten million direct and indirect beneficiaries: see SCF (2021), p. 108. On the other hand, the 2021 EIB [European Investment Bank] Adaptation Plan pledges to increase the share of adaptation support to 15% of the bank's overall finance for climate action by 2025 (an almost threefold increase compared to the 2012–2019 period).

[55] SCF (2021), p. 109.

[56] de Murieta et al. (2015), p. 18.

It can thus be concluded that increasing support for adaptation does not undermine the targets set for mitigation – it can help to achieve those targets.[57]

In this context, Paul Watkiss et al.,[58] when analysing the interaction between mitigation and aggregate adaptation, concluded that such interaction is a function of the increase in the global mean temperature. However, they also concluded that it has its limits because, if the temperature increase is too high (over 4 °C), adaptation must, at that point, simply be discarded as a viable strategy (because the response it can provide falls short of the consequences of such a catastrophic scenario).

On the other hand, it is also important to bear in mind that, as Clemens Heuson et al.[59] say, "from a dynamic perspective, [mitigation and adaptation] strategies may be complements in the sense that mitigation slows down climate change. Consequently, societies gain time and are likely to face lower future costs of adaptation".

However, as they also point out,[60]

> [d]espite the strategic complementarity, there is a trade-off between adaptation and mitigation, since both compete for scarce resources (Hof et al., 2009). Furthermore, expansion of adaptation diminishes the marginal utility of mitigation, and vice versa (Fankhauser, 2010). The reciprocal crowding-out of both strategies is, however, characterized by asymmetry: adaptation displaces mitigation to a greater degree than in the reverse situation because, in the medium to long term, the extent of the damage avoided by mitigation is too small to reduce the need for adaptation.

It is needless to say that this advantage of adaptation in the medium to long term does not make it particularly appealing to those (individuals, firms, or countries) that tend to give priority to the short-term perspective.

This is all the more so since the costs involved in adaptation can be very high. Giving some examples, notably of the aggregate adaptation costs for Europe, Stéphane Isoard[61] notes (although with due caution because of the uncertainty of these estimates) that

> [e]stimates, in global aggregated studies, of adaptation costs for Europe include the UNFCCC (2007 [...]) review with an indicative assessment of USD 3–19 billion/year by 2030 (EUR 2.5-16 billion/year) [just] for the infrastructure and coastal zones, while estimates given in the Stern Review (2006) [...] imply adaptation costs for infrastructure for Europe of EUR 4-60 billion/year.

---

[57] In more depth, see, e.g.: Pickering and Rübbelke (2014), p. 56 ss.

[58] Watkiss et al. (2015), p. 545.

[59] Heuson et al. (2014), p. 32.

[60] Heuson et al. (2014), p. 37.

[61] Isoard (2011), p. 64.

3.2.4 The Interaction Between Economic Growth and (Aggregate) Adaptation and Mitigation

To analyse this interaction, the heated debate over the impact on economic growth and human development of adopting measures for environmental sustainability, especially in developing countries must be taken into consideration. This is because, as stated by Thomas Schelling in 1992,[62]

> [w]hat is desired is to optimize development by investing in greenhouse-gas abatement only when that appears, subject to all the uncertainties, to contribute more to their development in the future than the alternative direct investment in development. It is not economic growth versus environment; it is growth with the environment taken into account.

(Richard Tol revisits and adapts this argument to demonstrate the "double trade-off" between adaptation and mitigation.[63])

Although, nowadays, it is almost consensual that climate change can significantly harm economic growth (and human well-being[64]), particularly in the most vulnerable countries, some simply reject the conflict between economic growth and environmental sustainability.[65] This kind of economic rationale (based on the idea that the trade-off is false or, at least, that it is impossible to overcome it without damaging the economic and living standards) is still used by some countries to avoid adaptation and mitigation.

For those who accept the trade-off mentioned previously (and share an environmental rationale), if economic growth reduces environmental sustainability, then the former one must cease (nongrowth) or even be inverted (degrowth).[66] Therefore, to save the planet and the economy, economic growth should come to an end, making the transition to a "steady-state economy".[67] Alternatively, assuming that the tipping

---

[62] See Schelling (1992), p. 7.

[63] See Tol (2007), p. 742: "If we would mitigate more, climate change and its impacts are lower and we would have to adapt less. [...]. However, if we would mitigate more, we would have less resources left for adaptation, and climate change impacts may be higher. This argument [...] [was] eloquently made by Schelling (1992)".

[64] Despite the so-called "environmentalist's paradox": Raudsepp-Hearne et al. 2010, pp. 576–589.

[65] See, e.g.: Grossman and Krueger (1995), p. 370: "Contrary to the alarmist cries of some environmental groups, we find no evidence that economic growth does unavoidable harm to the natural habitat."; Byrne (1997), p. 278: "A policy which restricts economic growth to zero, presumably in hopes of preventing environmental degradation, may actually increase the growth rate of pollution."

[66] See: Meadows et al. (1972), p. 24 (proposing "the transition from growth to global equilibrium") and *maxime* 170 ff.; Marín-Beltran et al. (2022), p. 9 (proposing "that industrialized countries should follow a degrowth strategy to face immediate challenges, at least until an eventual decoupling between economic growth and material extraction is achieved").

[67] See, for example: Daly (1973a), pp. 945–954; Daly (1973b); Daly (1993), pp. 811–816.

point in the climate system has already been surpassed, current (industry-based) economic growth should be reversed.[68]

Innovation and technology can counteract these two gloomy rationales, allowing adaptation to be successful worldwide (and showing that there can be economic growth[69] *and* environmental sustainability[70])—but, for that to happen, it is also crucial to inform and persuade with reliable information that is relevant to the recipients. However, even in those countries where access to trustworthy knowledge does not seem to be a problem, *cognitive biases* and behavioural issues are also faced that can hinder adaptation efforts.

3.3 Challenges That Stem from Cognitive Biases and Behavioural Issues

As Robert Mendelsohn says,[71] "[e]ven with government intervention, it is not clear whether joint adaptation will be efficient. People will disagree about how much adaptation is desirable, they will argue about who should pay for it, and they may try to manipulate the process for private gain".

To avoid some of these problems, more should be done to engage the communities[72]—even knowing that the benefits of mitigation are easier to perceive than the benefits of adaptation. Indeed, as Clemens Heuson et al. say,

> the benefits of mitigation are certain because mitigation combats climate change-related problems directly at the source. In contrast, the effectiveness of (proactive) adaptation frequently depends on predictions about the regional vulnerability situation and the related, typically highly uncertain, climate change impacts. [...] [Furthermore, it is also] much more difficult to measure the effectiveness of adaptation since, due to its heterogeneity, no universal measure of success exists.[73]

[68] See, e.g.: Georgescu-Roegen (1971); Georgescu-Roegen (1975), pp. 66–69; Georgescu-Roegen (1979).

[69] About measuring growth with indexes that *correct* (or do not use) the GDP, see Constanza et al. (2009).

[70] "[T]he transition to the low-carbon economy can be full of innovation, creativity and rising living standards on all relevant dimensions": Stern (2015), p. 20150820.

[71] See Mendelsohn (2000), p. 598.

[72] Niggol Seo considers that, "[a]t the personal level, there is no need for a government to intervene to force an individual to take adaptation measures. An individual will compare the costs and benefits of multiple options that are available to him/her in the current and altered conditions [...]. The individual will make a transition from one enterprise to another, relocate from one location to another, and take up one task against another, considering relevant costs and benefits involved" (Seo Niggol 2017, p. 186). In autonomous adaptation, this is only true if it is presumed that individuals are (entirely) rational and have access to all relevant information.

[73] Heuson et al. (2014), p. 32.

So, winning over public opinion is very important for the success of adaptation strategies[74] because the *vox populi*, particularly in less developed countries (but also in more developed countries), tend to be less able to impose the fight against the adaptation deficit on the political agenda,

Knowing that almost all of the "controlling factors of adaptability"[75] (such as technology, information management, human resources, or knowledge and awareness) are, more or less, related to the access, production, or diffusion of scientific knowledge and information, it is important to see what kind of problems may arise in this context.

For Behavioural Economics, some of the most relevant causes of those problems are related to the so-called cognitive biases (that were first studied by psychologist and economist Daniel Kahneman and psychologist Amos Tversky in 1972[76]).[77]

Some of these biases can be listed to show how they can hinder the adoption of needed actions or strategies of adaptation (and mitigation): i) the so-called optimism bias[78] according to which people have a tendency to unrealistically underestimate the likelihood of experiencing negative events (like, e.g. climate change); ii) the so-called framing effect[79] according to which choices are influenced by the way they are framed through different wording, settings, or situations; and iii) the so-called confirmation bias,[80] a tendency to search for, interpret, favour, or recall information (reliable or not) that supports prior beliefs or values (and ignores or distorts data contradicting them).

The way individuals tend to apply discount rates is also relevant:

> Adaptation to climate change is an intertemporal decision. [...]. In contrast to the constant discounting assumption of the DU [Discounting Utility] model [see Paul Samuelson 1937[81]], some empirical evidence suggests that discount rates are not constant over time. People instead apply discount rates that decline over time «as the discounted event is moved further away in time»" [Laibson, 1997]. This form of discounting is known in the literature as hyperbolic discounting. [...]. A declining discount rate also implies that intertemporal preferences are time-inconsistent and people exhibit preference reversals. People who discount hyperbolically do not fulfill the plans they make today because when the time to commit arrives present consumption seems more valuable than the future profits of the new endeavor. Such time inconsistency has clear implications for adaptation to climate change: individuals will delay investing in adaptation.[82]

[74]Also because, as Agrawala and Fankhauser (2008), say, being "adaptation [...] a decentralised process, there is the question whether, and if so how, economic agents need to be incentivised to adapt."

[75]See Mimura et al. (2014), p. 136.

[76]See Kahneman and Tversky (1972), pp. 430–454.

[77]On the relevance of some of these behavioural factors, see also, for example: Domingos et al. (2018), p. 49 ss.

[78]See Weinstein (1980), pp. 806–820.

[79]Tversky and Kahneman (1981), pp. 453–458.

[80]Wason (1960), pp. 129–140.

[81]Samuelson (1937), pp. 155–161.

[82]See Bernedo and Ferraro (2016), p. 165.

Additionally, the impact of the internet and social media cannot be forgotten, particularly when they do not block out anti-scientific political agendas—thus making it much more difficult to inform the communities and engage them in new adaptive strategies.[83]

Another behavioural problem (that social psychologists John Darley and Bibb Latané were the first to emphasize[84]) is the so-called "diffusion of responsibility" (or bystander effect/apathy), according to which individuals are less likely to offer help to a victim when there are other people present. Similarly, in the context of adaptation to climate change, when we are not alone in the presence of a climate change—because there are many other bystanders—the majority will tend to wait and see what others do (if they do anything at all) and will simply replicate their behaviour (apathy).

Finally, the (social) issue of consumer habits is also a relevant one, particularly in wealthier economies. To discourage excessive (or even what economists usually call conspicuous[85]) consumptions, nudging techniques[86] (that aim to reduce the discrepancy known as the value-action gap) can also help to engage communities in the adoption of new adaptation measures or strategies. This can occur, for instance, through the use of new digital devices able to give users real-time feedback[87] on the environmental impacts of their everyday consumption (e.g., hot water consumption or power consumption).[88]

[83] On the impact of mass media in climate change mitigation, see: Swain (2017), pp. 167–220. On the impact of the so-called echo chamber effect, see: Cinelli, Matteo, et al. 2021. The echo chamber effect on social media, PNAS, Vol. 118, No. 9.

[84] Darley and Latané (1968), pp. 377–383.

[85] A concept coined by Veblen (1899).

[86] The nudge concept was popularized by behavioural economist Richard Thaler and legal scholar Cass Sunstein with their famous book called Nudge (Thaler and Sunstein 2008). About green nudges, see, for example: Wee et al. (2021), p. 100364; Kind and Savelsberg (2016), pp. 253–273; Enste, Dominik, Potthoff, Jennifer. 2021. Behavioral Economics and Climate Protection: Better Regulation and Green Nudges for More Sustainability, IW-Analysen, No. 146. Considering that green nudges are "insufficient to address environmental issues that are deeply politically and structurally embedded", see: Petel (2020), pp. 223–247.

[87] About the importance of real-time feedback, see: Tiefenbeck, Verena, et al. 2014. On the effectiveness of real-time feedback: the influence of demographics, attitudes, and personality traits, Final report to the Swiss Federal Office of Energy. One example of these new real-time feedback digital devices has emerged thanks to a scientific study carried out by the ETH Zürich and the UNIL that helped to design the world's first smart meter incorporated in the hand shower (made by a Swiss company called *Amphiro*, a cleantech spinoff from the ETH Zürich, created in 2009) through which users can get real-time feedback on their water and energy consumption. The main goal is to persuade users to reduce their environmental footprint thus saving ice floes for polar bears (in the climate animation on the screen).

[88] On the impact of technology and how it contributes to adaptation, see: Callaway, John M. 2014. The role of technology in adaptation, in A. Markandya, et al. (eds.) 395–416.

References

Agrawal N (2018) Natural disasters and risk Management in Canada. Springer, Cham
Agrawala S, Fankhauser SS (2008) Putting climate change adaptation in an economic context. In: Agrawala S, Fankhauser S (eds) Economic aspects of adaptation to climate change. Costs, benefits and policy instruments. OECD Publishing, Paris
Arrhenius S (1986) On the influence of carbonic acid in the air upon the temperature of the ground. Philos Magazine J Sci 41:237–276
Bernedo M, Ferraro PJ (2016) Behavioral economics and climate change adaptation: insights from experimental economics on the role of risk and time preferences. In: Botelho A (ed) The WSPC reference on natural resources and environmental policy in the era of global change. World Scientific, Singapore
Berry P (2009) Synthesis of interactions between mitigation, adaptation and biodiversity. In: Berry P (ed) Biodiversity in the balance – mitigation and adaptation conflicts and synergies. Pensoft Publishers, Sofia
Brown S et al (2020) Land raising as a solution to sea-level rise: an analysis of coastal flooding on an artificial Island in the Maldives. J Flood Risk Manag 13(1):e12567
Burton I et al (1998) Adaptation to climate change: theory and assessment. In: Feenstra J et al (eds) Handbook on methods for climate change impact assessment and adaptation strategies. Vrije Universiteit Amsterdam, Institute for Environmental Studies, Amsterdam
Burton I et al (2001) Adaptation to climate change in the context of sustainable development and equity. In: McCarthy JJ et al (eds) Climate change 2001: impacts, adaptation, and vulnerability. Cambridge University Press, Cambridge
Byrne MM (1997) Is growth a dirty word? Pollution, abatement and endogenous growth. J Dev Econ 54(2):261–284
Callaway JM et al (2016) The economics of adaptation: concepts, methods and examples. UNEP DTU Partnership, Nairobi
Callendar GS (1938) The artificial production of carbon dioxide and its influence on temperature. Q J R Meteorol Soc 64:223–240
Campos I et al (2018) The diversity of adaptation in a multilevel governance setting. In: Sanderson H et al (eds) Adapting to climate change in Europe. Elsevier, Amsterdam
Carter TR et al (1994) IPCC Technical Guidelines for Assessing Climate Change Impacts and Adaptations. University College and Center for Global Environmental Research
Constanza R et al (2009) Beyond GDP: The Need for New Measures of Progress, The Pardee Papers, No. 4
Daly HE (1973a) In defense of a steady-state economy. AJAE 54(5):945–954
Daly HE (ed) (1973b) Toward a steady-state economy. W. H. Freeman, New York
Daly HE (1993) Steady-state economics: a new paradigm. New Literary History 24(4):811–816
Dannenberg A et al (2009) The economics of adaptation to climate change - the case of Germany, ZEW Discussion Paper No. 09–057
Darley JM, Latané B (1968) Bystander intervention in emergencies: diffusion of responsibility. J Pers Soc Psychol 8(4, Pt. 1):377–383
de Murieta ES et al (2015) An introduction to the economics of adaptation to climate change. In: de Murieta ES et al (eds) Routledge handbook of the economics of climate change adaptation. Routledge, Milton Park
Domingos S et al (2018) Understanding climate change adaptation: the role of citizens' perceptions and appraisals about extreme weather events. In: Fátima FA et al (eds) Theory and practice of climate adaptation. Springer, Cham
Eakin H, Luers AL (2006) Assessing the vulnerability of social-environmental systems. Annu Rev Environ Resour 31(1):365–394
Ehrlich PR (1968) The population bomb. Ballantine Books, New York City
Emiliani C (1955) Pleistocene temperatures. J Geol 63(6):538

Emiliani, Cesare. 1972. Quaternary paleotemperatures and the duration of the high-temperature intervals, Science178, 4059, pp. 398–401

Foote E (1856) Circumstances affecting the heat of the sun's bays. Am J Sci Arts XXII(1):382–383

Georgescu-Roegen N (1971) The entropy law and the economic process. Harvard University Press, Cambridge

Georgescu-Roegen N (1975) Energy and economic myths. SEJ 41(3):347–381

Georgescu-Roegen N (1979) Demain La Décroissance. P.-M. Favre, Paris

Georgescu-Roegen N (1986) The entropy law and the economic process in retrospect. East Econ J 12(1):3–25

Grasso M (2010) Justice in funding adaptation. Springer, Cham

Grossman GM, Krueger AB (1995) Economic growth and the environment. Q J Econ 110(2): 353–377

Heuson C et al (2014) State of the art on the economics of adaptation. In: Markandya A et al (eds) Routledge handbook of the economics of climate change adaptation. Routledge, Milton Park

Hunt A, Fergunson J (2014) Distributional impacts. Intra-national, international and inter-temporal aspects of equity in adaptation. In: Markandya A et al (eds) Intra-national, international and inter-temporal aspects of equity in adaptation. Routledge, Milton Park, pp 120–137

Huq N (2011) Financing adaptation: for whom, by whom, and how. In: Filho WL (ed) The economic, social and political elements of climate change. Springer, Berlin

Isoard S (2011) Perspectives on adaptation to climate change in Europe. In: Ford JD, Berrang-Ford L (eds) Climate change adaptation in developed nations. Springer, Cham

Kahneman D, Tversky A (1972) Subjective probability: a judgment of representativeness. Cogn Psychol 3(3):430–454

Keeling CD (1960) The concentration and isotopic abundances of carbon dioxide in the atmosphere. Tellus 12(2):200–203

Kind C, Savelsberg J (2016) Implications of Behavioral economics for designing adaptation policies. In: Beckenbach F, Kahlenborn W (eds) New perspectives for environmental policies through Behavioral economics. Springer, Cham

Klein RJT (2009) Identifying countries that are particularly vulnerable to the adverse effects of climate change: an academic or a political challenge? Carbon & Climate Law Review 3(3)

Lindoso D, Araújo MJ (2013) Evolução da adaptação à mudança climática na agenda da ONU: vinte anos de avanços e descaminhos. Revista Colombiana de Geografía 22(2)

Lisa E, Schipper F (2020) Maladaptation: when adaptation to climate change goes very wrong. One Earth 3(4)

Marín-Beltran I et al (2022) Scientists' warning against the society of waste. Sci Total Environ 811: 151359

Markandya A (2015) Incorporating climate change into adaptation programmes and project appraisal. In: Markandya A et al (eds)

Mathew LM, Akter S (2017) Loss and damage associated with climate change impacts. In: Chen W-Y et al (eds) Handbook of climate change mitigation and adaptation, 2nd edn. Springer, Cham

Meadows DH et al (1972) The limits to growth. A report for the Club of Rome's project on the predicament of mankind. Universe Books, Bloomington

Mendelsohn R (2000) Efficient adaptation to climate change. Clim Chang 45

Mimura N (2010) Scope and roles of adaptation to climate change. In: Sumi A et al (eds) Adaptation and mitigation strategies for climate change. Springer, Cham

Mimura N et al (2014) Adaptation planning and implementation. In: Field CB et al (eds) Climate change 2014: impacts, adaptation, and vulnerability. Part a: global and sectoral aspects. Cambridge University Press, Cambridge

Nordhaus W (1991) To slow or not to slow: the economics of the greenhouse effect. Econ J 101: 920–937

Nordhaus W (2019) Climate change: the ultimate challenge for economics. Am Econ Rev 109: 1991–2011

Osborn F (1948) Our Plundered Planet. Faber and Faber, London
Page EA (2006) Climate change, justice and future generations. Edward Elgar, Cheltenham
Parry ML, Martens P (1999) Impact assessment of climate change. In: Martens P, Rotmans J (eds) Climate change. An integrated perspective. Kluwer Academic Publishers, Dordrecht
Parry ML et al (eds) (2007) Contribution of working group II to the fourth assessment report of the intergovernmental panel on climate change. Cambridge University Press, Cambridge
Petel M (2020) Nudging towards sustainability? A critical perspective on Behavioral economics. Environ Forensic 43(2)
Phillips NA (1956) The general circulation of the atmosphere: a numerical experiment. Q J R Meteorol Soc 82:123–164
Pickering J, Rübbelke D (2014) International cooperation on adaptation to climate change. In: Markandya A et al (eds) Routledge Handbook of the Economics of Climate Change Adaptation. Routledge, Milton Park, p 56 ss
Raudsepp-Hearne C et al (2010) Untangling the environmentalist's paradox: why is human Well-being increasing as ecosystem services degrade? Bioscience 60:576–589
Samuelson PA (1937) A note on measurement of utility. Rev Econ Stud 4(2):155–161
SCF (2021) Fourth (2020) Biennial Assessment and Overview of Climate Finance Flows, vol 107. UNFCCC, Bonn
Schelling TC (1992) Some economics of global warming. Am Econ Rev 82:1–14
Seo Niggol S (2017) The Behavioral Economics of Climate Change. Elsevier, Amsterdam, p 186
Simonet G (2009) Le concept d'adaptation: polysémie interdisciplinaire et implication pour les changements climatiques. Natures Sciences Sociétés 17:392
Smit B et al (1999) The science of adaptation: a framework for assessment. In: Mitigation and adaptation strategies for global change, vol 4. Springer, Cham, pp 199–213
Stern N (2015) Economic development, climate and values: making policy. Proc R Soc B 282: 20150820
Swain KA (2017) Mass media roles in climate change mitigation. In: Chen WY et al (eds) Handbook of climate change mitigation and adaptation, 2nd edn. Springer, Cham
Thaler RH, Sunstein C (2008) Nudge. Yale University Press, New Haven
Tol RSJ (2007) The double trade-off between adaptation and mitigation for sea level rise: an application of FUND, in mitigation and adaptation strategies for global change. In: Mitigation and Adaptation Strategies for Global Change. Springer, Cham
Tröltzsch J et al (2016) The Economics of Climate Change Adaptation: Insights into Economic Assessment Methods, ECONADAPT Deliverable 10.2 (Research project led by the University of Bath)
Tversky A, Kahneman D (1981) The framing of decisions and the psychology of choice. Science 211:453–458
United Nations Environment Programme (2021) Adaptation Gap Report 2020. UNEP, Nairobi, p 24
Veblen T (1899) The theory of the leisure class. Macmillan, London
Vogt W (1948) Road to survival. William Sloane Associates, Winchester
Wason PC (1960) On the failure to eliminate hypotheses in a conceptual task. Q J Exp Psychol 12(3):129–140
Watkiss P, Benzie M, Klein RJT (2015) The complementarity and comparability of climate change adaptation and mitigation. WIREs Climate Change 6:541–557
Watson RT et al (eds) (1995) Impacts, adaptations and mitigation of climate change: scientific-technical analyses. Cambridge University Press, Cambridge
Wee S-C et al (2021) Can «nudging» play a role to promote pro-environmental behaviour? Environ Challenges
Weinstein ND (1980) Unrealistic optimism about future life events. J Pers Soc Psychol

Part III
Green Public Finance, Budgeting and Procurement

When Climate Change Knocks on the Finance Minister's Door

Paulo Alves Pardal

Abstract Traditionally, the management of climate change issues has been the responsibility of environment ministers. However, due to its cross-cutting nature to international commitments and its growing impact on the economy and fiscal governance, finance ministers are called upon to play a key role in this matter. Indeed, finance ministers can no longer ignore the dangers that climate change poses to the real economy, financial stability, and public finance.

Climate-related risks—both physical climate risks and climate transition risks—can affect public finance through both microeconomic and macroeconomic transmission channels. Indeed, climate-related risks could cause direct and indirect fiscal impacts thereby deteriorating public finance.

Due to the effects of climate change, the government, and in particular the finance minister, may be called upon to play a kind of "lender of last resort" or, more precisely, the role of "insurer or bailout provider of last resort" for families, companies or even financial institutions.

Despite some uncertainties, geographical heterogeneity, and different legal systems, there is a strong likelihood that, to a greater or lesser extent, climate change will increasingly pose a challenge to public finance in the various jurisdictions.

1 Introduction

The Intergovernmental Panel on Climate Change (IPCC) has played an important role in the scientific approach to climate change.[1] Scientists bluntly state that human activities have led to the warming of our planet and that recent climate change is

[1]The Intergovernmental Panel on Climate Change (IPCC) was created in 1988 by the World Meteorological Organization (WMO) and the United Nations Environment Program (UNEP)

P. A. Pardal (✉)
CIDEEFF, University of Lisbon, Law School, Lisbon, Portugal
e-mail: alvespardal@fd.ulisboa.pt

R. Saraiva, P. A. Pardal (eds.), *Sustainable Finances and the Law*, Economic Analysis of Law in European Legal Scholarship 16,
https://doi.org/10.1007/978-3-031-49460-4_8

rapid and unprecedented in human history.[2] The burning of fossil fuels (such as coal, oil, and gas) and other human activities of the industrial age has led to an increase in greenhouse gases (GHGs). The main GHGs are carbon dioxide (CO_2), methane (CH_4), and nitrous oxide (N_2O), and it turns out that these continue to rise.[3] As a matter of fact, the increase in GHGs causes the planet to overheat which translates into an increase in the average temperature thereby accelerating climate change. Scientists insist that climate change is a threat to human well-being and our planet, creating difficulties in many domains including with regard to efforts to achieve the Sustainable Development Goals.[4]

Although some climate change can be attributed to natural phenomena (e.g., volcanic eruptions, variations in solar radiation, tectonic changes), what is certain is that the greatest concern today is related to climate change caused by human action.[5] In this context, it is worth invoking the contribution of a scientific analysis on the Anthropocene. For instance, Paul Crutzen (Nobel Prize in Chemistry) stated that humanity had left the Holocene and entered the Anthropocene (a new geological epoch).[6] Although there may be discussions about the moment of the beginning of the Anthropocene, namely at the beginning of the industrial revolution or other, what matters is to underline that the great change took place after the second world war, more precisely in the 1950s, known as the "Great Acceleration" with an acceleration of human activity on the planet.[7] As Roka[8] in 2019 pointed out, the Anthropocene can be seen as a good force for humans but also as a bad force. In this dichotomy, climate change is part of the bad part of the Anthropocene. The climate change that is currently taking place on the planet is that which results from GHG emissions that have been taking place in the Anthropocene. Human activity is a climate driver on a planetary scale, especially through the emission of GHGs.[9] In brief, it has been human action mainly since the 1950s that has caused global warming (so-called anthropogenic origin) which, in turn, triggers climate change that has negative impacts. By the way, a distinction can be made between climate and weather. Both weather and climate describe the state of the atmosphere but under different time scales; that is, while weather refers to the state of the atmosphere at a given

having been endorsed by United Nations General Assembly as outlined in UN General Assembly Resolution 43/53 of 6 December 1988.

[2] IPCC - Intergovernmental Panel on Climate Change (2021), e.g., Summary for Policymakers and Chap. 5

[3] WMO - World Meteorological Organization (2022).

[4] IPCC (2021) e.g., Chap. 1.

[5] IPCC (2021) e.g., Summary for Policymakers, Chapters 1 and 3.

[6] Zalasiewicz et al. (2008).

[7] Summerhayes and Zalasiewicz (2018), pp. 194–200; Roka (2019).

[8] Roka (2019).

[9] Summerhayes and Zalasiewicz (2018).

location over the short term, climate refers to the average weather patterns at a location over a longer period of time, usually 30 years or more[10,11]).

The impact of climate change on finance cannot be ignored. However, as Chenet in 2019 pointed out,[12] despite the first IPCC warnings, at an early stage, the financial system seemed absent from the debate on the effects of climate change, but the approach changed mainly during the last years. Awareness was raised of the impact that climate change could also have on the financial world. There have been articles, analyses, studies, and reports related to the effects of climate change at the financial level both in terms of banks and insurance. The issue of climate-related financial risks has become a topic of enormous importance. Even the time horizon issue is relevant. Indeed, financial actors may tend to view climate-related risks only as long-term risks, but short-term impacts are increasingly evident, as shown, for example, from the aggravation of extreme weather events and associated economic losses.[13] The macroeconomic and public finance impact has also seen increasing interest from international organizations and agencies, central banks, supervisory institutions, government bodies, think tanks, and researchers.

To analyse the impact that climate risks may have on public finance, this author is going to use some concepts and methodologies that have been developed in connection with the various studies on the impact of climate risks on the financial sector. This will start with climate-related risks, then the issue of transmission channels will be addressed and, finally, the impact on public finance and the range of measures to be adopted by finance ministries will be examined.

2 Climate-Related Risks and Environment-Related Risks

Before addressing only climate-related risks, it should be noted that there are still other risks arising from human action. Indeed, in the relations between human beings and planet earth, climate change is not the only threat. Therefore, in this context and from a broader point of view, the main threats to our planet are climate change, loss of biodiversity, pollution, and environmental degradation.[14] Cases are known in which the quality of the air and water are not the best and, on the other hand, the

---

[10] ISDR – International Strategy for Disaster Reduction (2008) and NOAA - National Oceanic and Atmospheric Administration (2016).

[11] The National Oceanic and Atmospheric Administration (NOAA) is an American Agency created in 1970 but with antecedents that go back to 1870 (when the agencies dedicated to the physical and atmospheric sciences were founded by President Jefferson, namely the Weather Bureau and the Survey of the Coast office). The NOAA's mission is to provide daily weather forecasts, severe storm warnings, climate monitoring for fisheries management, coastal restoration, and support for maritime trade https://www.noaa.gov/.

[12] Chenet (2019).

[13] UNEP-FI - United Nations Environment Programme Finance Initiative (2022).

[14] Battersby et al. (2021).

pressures that, in many parts of the world, are exerted on the land and other natural resources are also known (e.g., the case of pressure on the fish stocks in the oceans).[15] However, in this analysis, it is appropriate to focus on climate risks rather than on environmental risks overall. Indeed, a distinction can be made between climate risks and environmental risks in general. Thus, following the Network for Greening the Financial System[16] approach[17] while environment-related risks refer to risks potentially or actually caused by environmental degradation (e.g., air pollution, water pollution and freshwater scarcity, soil contamination, reduction of biodiversity and deforestation), climate-related risks refer to risks related to climate change (e.g., damage caused by extreme weather events). As such, this analysis remains primarily focused on climate-related risks.

3 Climate-Related Risk Categories

Several studies and reports distinguish two main categories of climate-related risks, i.e., climate physical risks, on the one hand, and climate transition risks on the other. For example, the Task Force on Climate Related Financial Disclosures (TCFD)[18] is one of the entities that contributed to the debate around the distinction between these two categories of risks. Thus, this distinction was already included in a draft report presented in December 2016.[19] Subsequently, this distinction was enshrined in the TCFD Final Report on Recommendations of the Task Force on Climate Related Financial Disclosures dated June 2017.[20]

In the debate on climate hazards, the concept of climate tipping points is also sometimes addressed. Crossing these tipping points can lead to large, non-linear

[15] UNEP, Green Economy (2010).

[16] The Network for Greening the Financial System (NGFS) is a network of central banks and financial supervisors that was created in 2017 and has more than one hundred members. According to its charter (Article 1). The Central Banks and Supervisors Network for Greening the Financial System (NGFS) is a group of Central Banks and prudential supervisory authorities willing, on a voluntary basis, to exchange experiences, share best practices, contribute to the development of environment and climate risk management in the financial sector, and to mobilise mainstream finance to support the transition toward a sustainable economy. Its purpose is to define, promote and contribute to the development of best practices to be implemented within and outside of the Membership of the NGFS and to conduct or commission analytical work on green finance (https://www.ngfs.net/en/).

[17] NGFS - Network for Greening the Financial System (2019).

[18] The Task Force on Climate-related Financial Disclosures (TCFD) was created by the Financial Stability Board (FSB) in December 2015 in order to develop voluntary and consistent disclosures of climate-related financial risks for use by companies in providing information to creditors, insurers, investors, and other stakeholders https://assets.bbhub.io/company/sites/60/2015/12/12-4-2015-Climate-change-task-force-press-release.pdf.

[19] TCFD - Task Force on Climate-Related Financial Disclosures (2016).

[20] TCFD - Task Force on Climate-Related Financial Disclosures (2017).

changes in the climate system. An example is the eventual collapse of the Atlantic Meridional Circulation (AMOC) that could cause changes and disruptions at the global level.[21] This issue is quite worrying and seems to lead to truly disastrous scenarios. However, given its greater materialization, this author will address only the two categories mentioned above in this chapter.

First, the focus will be on the category of physical climate risk, that is, on risks strictly linked to the physical effects of climate change and within these the subcategories of acute risks and chronic risks. Next, the focus will be on climate transition risks. Finally, the high and rising costs derived from climate physical risks will be discussed.

3.1 Climate Physical Risk Category

Climate physical risks are already being felt by a number of countries and regions, varying in significance between geographies and time horizon.[22] Despite their economic and financial difficulties, many of the countries and communities have already suffered severe loss and damage and, as climate change intensifies, the impacts will worsen.[23]

For instance, like many other countries and regions in the world, Portugal is affected by climate change. Thus, a report by the Portuguese authorities acknowledges that, notably due to sea level rise and storm surges, the Portuguese coast is particularly vulnerable to coastal erosion (Portugal's Adaptation Communication to the United Nations Framework Convention on Climate Change 2021).

In turn, the category of climate physical risks is divided into two subcategories of acute risks, on the one hand, and chronic risks, on the other. So, while some of the climate physical risks are caused by disruptive events (e.g., cyclones, hurricanes, and floods), others are caused by a long-term change in weather patterns (e.g., higher temperatures).[24]

3.2 Climate Physical Acute Risk

Acute physical risks are related to extreme weather events. These include cyclones, hurricanes and typhoons, heavy rainfall and (often) subsequent flooding, as well as heat waves, wildfires, and droughts.[25] They are usually sudden phenomena with

[21] Lenton et al. (2019), pp. 592–595.

[22] Connell et al. (2020).

[23] Åberg and Jeffs (2022).

[24] Spinaci (2021).

[25] BCBS - Basel Committee on Banking Supervision (2021a); OECD (2021), Chap. 3.

high severity and immediate repercussions. They can cause high material damage, damaging and sometimes destroying assets such as housing, public buildings, infrastructure, and communication networks. However, in addition to the damage caused immediately, the harmful effects often last for a long time. Just look at the example of Hurricane Katrina that occurred in 2005 but with negative effects over several years.[26]

Climate change contributes to increasing the severity, diversity, and frequency of many extreme weather events.[27] In fact, more and more countries and regions around the world are being affected by extreme weather events. Thus, acute physical risks have been increasingly manifested. However, its impact varies between different regions of the globe and even between different industry sectors as well as time horizons.[28]

3.3 Climate Physical Chronic Risk

Chronic physical risks are related to slow onset changes. These include rising sea levels, increasing temperatures, ocean acidification, glacial retreat and related impacts, salinization, land and forest degradation, loss of biodiversity, and desertification.[29] Often, these risks are interconnected with each other. Thus, a rising sea level is essentially due to the increase in temperature of the oceans and the progressive decrease of the cryosphere, that is, the melting of ice in the frozen regions of the Earth system.[30] In addition, taking into account that coastal areas have advantages but are also exposed to dangers such as storms, it cannot be overemphasized that rising sea levels caused by climate change is a risk multiplier of the hazards that already affect coastal zones.[31] Its effects will be felt in different areas of the planet, affecting the way of life of the populations.

3.4 Climate Transition Risks

Transition risks are those arising from the transition to lower-carbon economies. In view of the dangers of climate change, decarbonization and the greener economy have become important issues.[32] However, a question that arises is whether

---

[26] OECD (2021), Chap. 1.

[27] OECD (2021), Chap. 1.

[28] Connell et al. (2020).

[29] BCBS - Basel Committee on Banking Supervision (2021a, 2021b); OECD (2021), Chap. 3.

[30] OECD (2021) Chap. 1.

[31] Schäfer et al. (2021).

[32] UNEP, Green Economy (2010).

decarbonization will be carried out in a timely manner or, on the contrary, will be postponed, ending up being done in a delayed and disorderly manner.[33] If the transition occurs in an orderly manner, the transition risks are likely to be more moderate but, if the transition occurs disorderly, the transition risks will certainly be higher.[34] What is certain is that transition entails risks that are so-called climate transition risks. These risks can have an impact on the supply side or the demand side. Generally speaking, these risks may arise from policy or regulatory changes (e.g., tighter restrictions on CO_2 emissions) or technological development (e.g., production of electric vehicles) and, on the demand side, the possibility cannot be ruled out of changes in the behaviour of consumers who start to prefer greener products which ends up having financial implications for businesses.[35] Transition risks must be duly considered as they not only affect companies directly linked to fossil fuels but also other areas of the economy.[36] A sudden and disorderly transition can lead to the abrupt exit of sectors of economic activity with negative implications for the real economy and public budgets.[37] The earlier that action to reduce carbon emissions is taken, the more it will avoid a delayed, disorderly, or disruptive transition.[38]

4 Climate-Related Risks and Disaster Risks

Before proceeding with the analysis of climate-related risks, this author will briefly refer to the topic of risks arising from disasters. From a broader point of view, it is possible to analyse climate-related risks in the context of the disasters risks that can have high impacts. There has been a growing international concern about the occurrence of disasters or catastrophes and their impacts at the human, social, financial, economic, and environmental levels.[39] While some of those disasters are natural (e.g., violent storms), others are man-made (e.g., terrorism and industrial accidents).[40] Many of those disasters have caused enormous damage. In addition to the loss of human lives, those disasters have caused damage to public and private assets as well as to infrastructure which can translate into relevant fiscal impacts.[41] Hence, this results in the growing importance that has been given to the mitigation and financing of risks arising from disasters. Several studies, reports, and normative

[33] Rudebusch (2021).
[34] NGFS - Network for Greening the Financial System (2022a).
[35] Spinaci (2021).
[36] NGFS (2019).
[37] Dunz and Power (2021).
[38] NGFS (2022a).
[39] OECD - Organisation for Economic Co-operation and Development (2015).
[40] OECD (2015).
[41] OECD (2015).

texts have been published on the mitigation and/or financing of disaster risks. The OECD, for example, has adopted recommendations on this matter, namely the "OECD Recommendation on Disaster Risk Financing Strategies" that was adopted by the OECD Council on 23 February 2017.[42] This recommendation replaces a previous one that had been adopted in 2010 under the title "Good Practices for Mitigating and Financing Catastrophic Risks".[43]

The 2017 "OECD Recommendation on Disaster Risk Financing Strategies" mentioned previously recognizes

> (...) the significant social, economic and financial impact of disasters, both natural and man-made, and the potential for climate change to increase the frequency and intensity of extreme events, which combined with increases in the value of assets in locations exposed to hazards can be expected to lead to larger impacts in the future

On the other hand, it is noted "(...) that the effective financial management of disaster risks is critical for achieving the objectives of the Sendai Framework for Disaster Risk Reduction (2015) and the goals related to loss and damage included in the Paris Agreement on Climate Change (2015)".

In fact, the relationship between risks arising from disasters and climate change is also highlighted in the 2015 Sendai Framework for Disaster Risk Reduction.[44] Among the various references to climate change, it suffices to mention two passages in the preamble of this document, namely that the "disasters, many of which are exacerbated by climate change and which are increasing in frequency and intensity, significantly impede progress towards sustainable development" (preamble, pt. 4) and that "addressing climate change as one of the drivers of disaster risk, while respecting the mandate of the United Nations Framework Convention on Climate Change, represents an opportunity to reduce disaster risk in a meaningful and coherent manner throughout the interrelated intergovernmental processes" (preamble, pt. 13).[45] Climate change is expected to have significant impacts on the frequency and intensity of disaster events and to therefore have important financial and economic implications.[46] It seems that climate change can be seen as a kind of ignition and accelerator of a wide range of disasters that cause enormous human and material damage.

Concerned with the financial management of these impacts, G20 Finance Ministers and Central Bank Governors and Asia-Pacific Economic Co-operation Finance Ministers have recognized the importance and priority for disaster risk management strategies and, in particular, of respective components, namely disaster risk assessment and risk financing.[47] Among other papers, documents, and/or reports in which the OECD participated can be highlighted the "G20/OECD Methodological

[42] OECD - Organisation for Economic Co-operation and Development (2017).

[43] OECD (2017).

[44] UNDRR - United Nations Office for Disaster Risk Reduction (2015).

[45] UNDRR (2015).

[46] Wolfrom and Yokoi-Arai (2016).

[47] OECD (2015).

Framework for Disaster Risk Assessment and Risk Financing"[48] as well as the "Disaster Risk Financing – a global survey of practices and challenges".[49] While the former highlights the important role played by financial policymakers in disaster risk management, the latter provides practical illustrations of what has been done in different economies.[50]

Taking into account the high economic damages and losses caused by disasters and the expectation of their potential increase, financial resilience is considered a key policy objective underlining the importance of finance ministers in the adoption and implementation of disaster risk management that includes two components, namely disaster risk assessment and risk financing.[51] In sum, disaster risks and their implications concern both developed and developing countries.[52]

The European Union and its Member States are no exception to these concerns. Indeed, several European regions have been plagued by climate-related disasters, although their economic impact varies considerably across countries.[53] In any case, fiscal costs cannot be neglected especially when "the State acts as a disaster insurer of last resort", as Radu points out.[54]

Other international organizations and/or agencies have worked with programs related to disaster risk management as well as disaster risk financing and insurance. It is enough to see the performance of the World Bank Group for this subject, including the concern to smooth out the impact of disasters on public finance.[55]

Although integrated into the broader theme of disasters and their respective impacts, what is certain is that this is yet another example of how climate change cannot go unnoticed by the ministers of finance. However, without prejudice to addressing the broader topic of disasters whenever necessary, this author will continue to focus the analysis on the topic of climate-related risks.

5 The High and Rising Costs Derived From Climate-Related Risks

In general, the occurrence of adverse climate impacts entails costs, many of them quite high. In fact, physical risks can lead to health effects, changes in work, destruction of productive capacity, changes to ecosystems, and displacement of

48 G20/OECD (2012).
49 OECD (2015).
50 OECD (2015).
51 OECD (2015).
52 OECD (2015).
53 Radu (2022).
54 Radu (2022).
55 World Bank, GFDRR (2013).

people.[56] For instance, rising sea levels and more destructive storms may endanger coastal real estate and low-lying public infrastructure.[57] Furthermore, the fact must not be overlooked that, in the international context, some countries are more affected than others. Just look at the cases of least developed countries and small island developing states that have been hit by the harmful effects of climate change.[58] On the other hand, rising temperatures tend to affect colder regions differently from warmer regions. For instance, Kalkuhl and Wenz,[59] using a new dataset of subnational economic production, estimate that rising temperatures tend to affect colder regions differently from warmer regions, leading to a decrease in economic output in the latter. The banking and financial system cannot fail to be aware of these and other issues even though it is difficult to predict and quantify future climate physical risks.[60] *Mutatis mutandis* for the insurance industry.[61,62]

Moreover, physical climate risks, whether acute or chronic, can have cascading effects on the economy with implications for both private and public finance.[63] However, in addition to material losses and damages, intangible losses and damages must also be taken into account (e.g., psychological problems, feelings of loss of sense of identity and security), although these are difficult to quantify.[64] Besides the costs arising from climate physical risks, account must also be taken of possible costs arising from climate transition risks. Furthermore, as the NGFS draws attention, it is also necessary to consider the combination of both risks.[65] In summary, in addition to other impacts, both physical climate risks and climate transition risks or even the combination of these two types of risks have economic, financial, and fiscal implications. Another issue, however, is to assess, measure, or seek to ascertain the impact of both physical climate risks and climate transition risks that can prove to be extremely challenging.[66]

[56] OECD - Organisation for Economic Co-operation and Development (2021).

[57] Rudebusch (2021).

[58] OECD (2021), Chap. 1.

[59] Kalkuhl and Wenz (2020).

[60] UNEP-FI (2022).

[61] IAIS - International Association of Insurance Supervisors (2021).

[62] The International Association of Insurance Supervisors (IAIS) was established in 1994 and is an international organization of insurance supervisors and regulators. https://www.iaisweb.org/.

[63] Dunz and Power (2021).

[64] OECD (2021), Chap. 1.

[65] NGFS - Network for Greening the Financial System (2020b).

[66] NGFS (2020b).

6 The Conceptualization of Climate-Related Risk Transmission Channels

Climate-related risks can impact the economy and financial systems through various transmission channels. In that regard, several institutions and organizations have been concerned with identifying these transmission channels. For instance, the NGFS highlights the importance of mapping the transmission channels of physical and transition risks in the financial system.[67] In turn, as early as 2020, the Financial Stability Board (FSB)[68] was seeking to investigate the channels through which climate-related risks could affect the financial system as well as their amplification.[69] For its part, the Basel Committee on Banking Supervision (BCBS) analyses and explores the various transmission channels of climate risks that may affect banks and the banking system as well as their geographical heterogeneity, amplifiers, and mitigants.[70]

These analyses and reports also aim at contributing to the understanding of the transmission channels of climate-related risks and their impacts, including on the economy and on finance. For instance, the main objective of the BCBS is to analyse how financial risks related to the climate can arise and impact banks and the banking system and, in this sense, it defines the transmission channels as being "the causal chains linking climate risk drivers to the financial risks faced by banks and the banking sector".[71] Furthermore, the BCBS recognizes that banks and the banking system are exposed to climate change through micro and macroeconomic transmission channels and may suffer economic costs and financial losses arising from physical climate risks and climate transition risks.[72] However, the BCBS considers, that the impacts of these risks can be reflected and, therefore, observed through the traditional risk categories, namely: credit risk; market risk; liquidity risk; operational risk; and reputational risk.[73]

In other words, climate-related risks (whether physical or climate transition) may increase risks that banks and the banking system already know and face, i.e., the traditional risk categories (as noted below).

Other papers and/or reports seek to identify and analyse climate risk transmission channels more from a public finance perspective. This is the case, for example, with

[67] NGFS - Network for Greening the Financial System (2019, 2020a, 2022a, b).

[68] The Financial Stability Board (FSB) is an international body that was established in 2009 and performs the functions of monitoring and making recommendations about the global financial system. With regard to climate risks, the FSB plays a coordinating role in dealing with climate-related financial risks. https://www.fsb.org/work-of-the-fsb/financial-innovation-and-structural-change/climate-related-risks/.

[69] FSB - Financial Stability Board (2022).

[70] BCBS - Basel Committee on Banking Supervision (2021a, b).

[71] BCBS - Basel Committee on Banking Supervision (2021a), p. 10.

[72] BCBS - Basel Committee on Banking Supervision (2021a).

[73] BCBS - Basel Committee on Banking Supervision (2021a).

the analysis undertaken within the Coalition of Finance Ministers for Climate Action[74] which examines how climate-related risks may manifest themselves in different sectors of the economy and alter macroeconomic conditions thereby affecting the responsibilities of finance ministries.[75] Other analyses focus more on the nexus between climate change and sovereign risk.[76] Other examples of the importance of analysing transmission channels of climate-related risks are provided by other studies and reports like Fiscal Policies for Development and Climate Action.[77]

However, contrary to what happens with the categorization of climate-related risks where, in general, the conceptual distinction between physical climate risks and climate transition risks seems to be stabilized, the categorization, identification, and distinction of the various channels of transmission of climate-related risks appear to be open to discussion. Despite the research and analysis that has already been carried out, it is necessary to further deepen the understanding of the transmission channels of climate risks and assess their impact. For example, with regard to the financial system, some difficulties can be identified. Indeed, the breadth and complexity of transmission channels must not be neglected.[78] Although there is a high degree of certainty regarding the materialization of climate-related risks, the truth is that there are still many uncertainties regarding the exact results of the impacts of climate change regarding the time horizon and the future pathway.[79] Besides, there may be both direct and indirect transmission channels.[80] Furthermore, the challenge of measuring risks in a systematic, consistent, and repeatable manner remains.[81] However, it seems that these difficulties do not exist only in relation to the financial system. They also arise with regard to other domains of analyses. In this sense, it is necessary to take into account the nature and specificities of the matter or area to be analysed. Thus, the transmission channels may be different or contain specificities depending on the area or domain that may be affected (e.g., banking, insurance, financial stability, public finance, or others). So, it seems that the identification of transmission channels depends on the matter or area to be analysed. For example, if the analysis focuses on banks and the banking system, then it is important to investigate the transmission channels that lead to climate-related risks (both physical and transitional) having an impact on banks and the banking system (e.g., the analysis of the Basel Committee on Banking Supervision in the field of banks and

[74] The Coalition of Finance Ministers for Climate Action has existed since 2019 and brings together fiscal and economic policymakers from several dozen countries to lead the global climate response and ensure a just transition to low-carbon resilient development- The Coalition of Finance Ministers for Climate Action (2022).

[75] Dunz and Power (2021).

[76] Volz et al. (2020).

[77] Pigato et al. (2019).

[78] NGFS - Network for Greening the Financial System (2020b).

[79] NGFS - Network for Greening the Financial System (2020b).

[80] NGFS - Network for Greening the Financial System (2020a).

[81] NGFS - Network for Greening the Financial System (2020b).

the banking system).[82] However, if the analysis focuses on public finance, then it is important to investigate the transmission channels that lead to climate-related risks (both physical and transitional) having an impact on public finance.[83] Regarding the latter, it is enough to recall the first major financial crisis of the twenty-first century in which the serious problems suffered by banks and the banking system forced public intervention (e.g., nationalizations, bailouts, public guarantees), thus implying greater public expenditures. Therefore, in the former, an attempt is made to determine how banks and the banking system can be affected by climate change, through various transmission channels. Instead, in the latter, an attempt is made to determine how public finance could be directly or indirectly affected by climate change, whereby, in this case, banks and the banking system are also being part of one of the transmission channels that may affect public finance.

Despite the difficulties mentioned above, this author thinks it is worth theoretically illustrating the transmission channels through which climate-related risks can impact public finance for the following reasons. First, it is relevant to try to find out how climate-related risks could impact public finance, i.e., seeking to trace the path from climate-related risks to the impact on public finance. Second, the importance of transmission channels cannot be overlooked as they can amplify but also mitigate the negative effects of climate change. Third, action can certainly be taken on the transmission channels to prevent, adapt, mitigate, or react to the negative effects of climate change, notably in economic and public finance terms.

This author will therefore focus on the public finance perspective but using many of the tools used by analyses of the impacts of climate risks on the banking and financial systems. In this regard, what is important to highlight is that, currently or potentially, climate-related risks will have an impact on public finance. From this point of view, what matters is to identify the climate-related risk transmission channels that, in some way, can reduce public revenues, increase public expenditures, increase governments' financing costs, or hinder access to financial markets, among others. Put another way, it is a set of circumstances that may create additional difficulties for finance ministers. In this context and taking advantage of the analytical contribution of the BCBS,[84] it seems that, from the point of view of public finance, the transmission channels are the causal chains through which climate risks can impact public finance.

[82]BCBS - Basel Committee on Banking Supervision (2021a, b).

[83]Dunz and Power (2021).

[84]BCBS (2021a).

7 Climate-Related Risk Transmission Channels From a Public Finance Point of View

What are the transmission channels through which climate-related risks that, directly or indirectly, could affect public finance? There are already analyses of how climate change could directly or indirectly affect public finance. Some are more comprehensive while others are more sectorial or more directed to a certain matter. For instance, in an approach more focused on the complex nexus between climate change and sovereign risk, Volz et al.[85] identify six risk transmission channels, namely: (1) Fiscal impacts of climate-related natural disasters; (2) Fiscal consequences of adaptation and mitigation policies; (3) Macroeconomic impacts of climate change; (4) Climate-related risks and financial sector stability; (5) Impacts on international trade and capital flows; and (6) Impacts on political stability. On the other hand, following the NGFS conceptualization, Dunz and Power identify the following transmission channels:[86] Households, businesses, finance, government, and macroeconomic impacts that may interact with each other and potentiate feedback effects.

It may be added that, in other domains, similar approaches are used. For example, in the broader analysis on the impacts of disasters (as noted above), efforts are made to highlight the major segments of the economy that may be affected, that is, households, the corporate sector, the financial sector, and government (central and local).[87] Therefore, with regard to the transmission channels through which physical and transitional risks or a combination of both can affect public finance and taking into account the various analyses already carried out, this author will follow the following order: Households, businesses, financial system, government (both central and local) and, lastly, the macroeconomic impact.

7.1 *The Climate-Related Risks and the Impact on Households*

Climate-related risks currently or potentially affect households in various ways including health, labour, income, wealth, and livelihoods. As for health issues, a World Health Organisation publication points out that climate change and associated extreme events cause a substantial increase in health problems, including ill health and even premature death as well as mental health and psychosocial problems.[88] It also draws attention to contributing to the deepening of health inequalities.[89] The

[85] Volz et al. (2020).

[86] Dunz and Power (2021).

[87] OECD - Organisation for Economic Co-operation and Development (2015), Chap. 2.

[88] WHO - World Health Organization (2022).

[89] WHO - World Health Organization (2022).

impact of climate-related risks in the world of work should not be overlooked either. As highlighted in a study published by several international organizations, including the United Nations Development Programme,[90] excessive heat causes health problems and impairs productivity. Indeed, it affects outdoor workers (for example, in sectors such as agriculture and construction) as well as other workplaces, causing health problems that can be quite serious (for instance, exhaustion or even death itself). Furthermore, losses are expected to increase, especially in the most vulnerable economies.[91] Increased unemployment and worse working conditions due to climate change are also a matter of concern. Thus, a 2011 working paper by the International Labour Office[92] already highlighted the concerns that climate change could have in terms of wage losses and worse working conditions, affecting the most vulnerable even more due to their exposure and lower capacity to adapt. On the other hand, there may be, for example, job losses as a result of a climate-related disaster that may lead to increased expenditures on mechanisms such as unemployment insurance.[93]

Due to climate-related risks, households could see their wealth and income seriously affected. Houses and private buildings may be damaged by, among other things, extreme weather events (e.g., storms, floods, droughts, wildfires, heatwaves, cold, and frost) which can result in economic losses that are, in some cases, quite substantial.[94] Furthermore, the market value of houses or their value as collateral may be affected if, for example, they are in areas where flooding occurs or areas that may be affected by rising sea levels.[95] Extreme weather events can reduce household income and wealth.[96] Moreover, if commodity prices increase (e.g., due to disruptions or difficulties in global supply chains caused by climate change) or job loss occurs because the employer or business has suffered serious climate change-related damage, this may also result in loss of income. As far as livelihoods are concerned, it must be seen that many of them are very dependent on the climate.[97]

Certainly, the harmful effects of climate change are heterogeneous, weighing more on the most disadvantaged households and those who stay in more sensitive areas. For example, to support a household, children may quit school even temporarily, or there may be a need to sell assets.[98] In order to avoid these and other cases, it will be very important to implement social protection measures (as noted below) which implies more public expenditures, but this is certainly necessary to support

[90] UNDP et al. (2016).

[91] UNDP, et al. (2016).

[92] ILO - International Labour Office. (2011).

[93] OECD (2022).

[94] OECD - Organisation for Economic Co-operation and Development (2021), Chap. 3.

[95] BCBS - Basel Committee on Banking Supervision (2021a).

[96] Volz et al. (2020).

[97] ISDR (2008).

[98] Feyen et al. (2020).

households and even allow for recovery in the event of the negative impact of climate-related risks.[99]

On the other hand, the shift to lower-carbon economies may also imply changes and more costs, namely in terms of labour (e.g., unemployment of workers in high carbon sectors) or the adaptation of houses (e.g., insulation). The combination of different elements such as lower household income, less wealth, and higher product prices can generate a demand shock.[100]

In the face of adversities such as those mentioned above, there is a strong likelihood that, on the one hand, there will be lower tax revenues and, on the other, an increase in public expenditures on, for example, social benefits. In short, through this transmission channel, public finance could deteriorate substantially, requiring difficult measures to be taken (as noted below).

7.2 The Climate-Related Risks and the Impact on Businesses

Businesses are also exposed to climate-related risks, both physical and transition risks. Physical climate-related risks can cause damage and losses to business activity.[101] In that regard, some economic activities are particularly exposed to climate-related physical risks such as agriculture, fisheries, construction, and tourism. Just see, for example, the case of crops that can be decimated or how tourist destinations may be affected by extreme weather disasters. Like other economic activities, fisheries and aquaculture are also affected by climate change. Due to the changes that have taken place in the ocean currents, river flows, lake levels, thermal structure, and others, the communities that depend on fisheries and aquaculture are significantly impacted.[102] However, the greater or lesser exposure of these and other sectors depends on several factors such as, for instance, the respective geographic location. In this context, the most vulnerable industries are closely linked to climate-sensitive resources or are, for example, located in coastal areas or in river floodplains.[103] Where extreme weather events become more intense or more frequent, the economic and social costs of these events will increase.[104] In addition, climate-related transition risks can also entail significant damage, especially for businesses linked to the carbon economy as the transition to lower-carbon economies can lead to high stranded assets.[105] The legal responsibilities faced by companies in the context of climate change must not be overlooked. Just remember the case of the

[99] OECD - Organisation for Economic Co-operation and Development (2021).
[100] Dunz and Power (2021).
[101] BCBS - Basel Committee on Banking Supervision (2021a).
[102] FAO - Food and Agriculture Organization of the United Nations (2021).
[103] ISDR (2008).
[104] ISDR (2008).
[105] BCBS - Basel Committee on Banking Supervision (2021a) and Dunz and Power (2021).

Pacific Electric & Gas that went bankrupt.[106] Transport and supply chains can also be severely impacted which can cause delays and hamper international trade.[107]

For instance, due to bankruptcies and/or disruptions in supply chains, this will most likely imply a slowdown in economic activity thus implying less tax revenue or even the adoption of other types of measures such as tax relief, resulting, after all, in greater tightening of public finance (as noted below).

7.3 The Climate-Related Risks and the Impact on Financial System

The financial sector plays a crucial role in economies and societies. In this theme, the main question it seems the follow is how do climate-related risks add up to traditional financial risks? Indeed, climate-related risks can pose enormous challenges to both financial institutions and financial stability. These issues are of concern to several jurisdictions. For instance, as the European Central Bank (ECB) pointed out, "climate risk may adversely affect the balance sheets of financial institutions and therefore may be relevant for financial stability, in particular if markets are not pricing the related risks correctly".[108] Taking into account the importance of financial stability, Darvas et al.[109] for instance, even called for more attention to be paid to the impact of climate-related risks on financial stability. Several institutions and/or agencies continue to pay attention to the impact of climate change, including on financial stability. For example, the ECB continues to focus on this issue. Indeed, according to this European Institution, "the ECB is continuing its work on incorporating climate-related risks into assessments of financial stability. This includes a new analysis of disclosure, pricing and greenwashing risks in financial markets, as well as continued monitoring of financial institutions' exposure to transition and physical risks".[110]

In addition to financial stability, it is also relevant to pay attention to financial institutions. This includes banks, insurance companies, and institutional investors.[111] Like households and businesses, banks and the banking system are also exposed to climate-related risks, both physical and transition and therewith may suffer economic costs and financial losses.[112] Due to climate-related risks, banks may be affected by activities stemming from other transmission channels. Just look at some cases linked to households and businesses. Thus, as previously mentioned,

[106] Gundlach (2020), pp. 94–97; BCBS - Basel Committee on Banking Supervision (2021a).

[107] Volz et al. (2020).

[108] ECB – European Central Bank (2019), p. 132.

[109] Darvas et al. (2020).

[110] ECB – European Central Bank (2022).

[111] Feyen et al. (2020).

[112] BCBS - Basel Committee on Banking Supervision (2021a).

the market value of houses and/or their value as collateral may be affected which could bring added problems to banks given the importance of mortgage loans on their balance sheets.[113] Likewise, as mentioned above, businesses can also be a source of concern for banks, both for climate-related physical risks and climate-related transition risks. Some economic sectors such as agriculture, fisheries, construction and tourism are particularly exposed to climate-related physical risks. With regard to climate transition risks, it must be remembered that carbon-intensive sectors and/or assets may be particularly exposed, hence material transition risks may arise for banks.[114] In terms of geographical location, coastal areas, for instance, may be more vulnerable to violent storms like hurricanes, and/or rising sea levels.[115]

As noted above, according to the BCBS, the impacts of climate-related risks on banks can be observed through the following traditional risk categories, i.e., credit risk, market risk, liquidity risks, operational risks, and reputational risk.[116] In this context, banks may experience more difficulties if climate-related risks manage to trigger or increase these traditional risks. Based on the expert literature, the BCBS[117] has provided notions and examples; the author will try to summarize the main ideas below.

Credit risk can impact households, corporations, or sovereigns through two effects, namely the income effect and the wealth effect. Thus, climate-related risks can reduce the ability of borrowers to repay their debts (income effect) or can reduce the ability of banks to fully recover the value of a loan in a case of default (wealth effect). Market risk relates to the impact of climate-related risks on the value of real or financial assets, thereby increasing market volatility in traded assets. Banks may also face an increase in liquidity risk. Thus, in the event of a disaster, depositors may try to quickly withdraw their deposits or apply for loans which can put banks in serious liquidity shortages. Operational risk occurs, for instance, if banks' operational capacity is reduced due to physical climate hazards that disrupt transport facilities and/or telecommunications infrastructures. In turn, reputational risks can arise if, for example, banks provide finance to corporations or for activities that are considered to be responsible for negative climate impacts.[118]

Insurance companies can suffer from climate-related risks both as investors and as underwriters.[119] On the other hand, they can also play a very important role in terms of financial resilience. Risk coverage by insurers reduces the economic repercussions of the adverse effects of climate change.[120] It is therefore very important to have strong and resilient insurance and reinsurance companies in

[113] Feyen et al. (2020).
[114] Feyen et al. (2020).
[115] Feyen et al. (2020).
[116] BCBS - Basel Committee on Banking Supervision (2021a).
[117] BCBS - Basel Committee on Banking Supervision (2021a).
[118] BCBS - Basel Committee on Banking Supervision (2021a).
[119] Feyen et al. (2020).
[120] OECD - Organisation for Economic Co-operation and Development (2022), Chap. 5.

place. Where insurance coverage is non-existent or where insurance penetration levels are lower, the burden is likely to fall more heavily on public authorities, potentially resulting in further constraints on public finances.

Climate-related risks are also a challenge for institutional investors such as pension funds and life insurance companies. This type of investor is guided by long-term horizons and so, in addition to financial stability issues, they are still faced with the second-tier impacts from climate change (e.g., food security and social and political unrest) that are unlikely to be linear.[121]

7.4 *The Climate-Related Risks and the Impact on Governments*

The public sector could directly suffer the impact of the climate-related risks, which certainly implies an increase in public spending. In the case of physical climate hazards, it is more likely that there will be an increase in public spending in the face of the need to adopt some urgent measures such as rescue operations, disaster relief, and actions to address the damage caused by climate hazards. On the other hand, natural disasters could damage or even destroy government physical assets as well as public infrastructure.[122] This puts greater pressure on public finance and may involve a multilevel governance dimension.[123] Indeed, the negative impact could affect central governments as well as infra-national authorities. In the case of violent storms such as cyclones or hurricanes, infrastructure and utilities could be heavily affected. In terms of infrastructure, there may be roads that become impassable, damaged railway lines, and bridges destroyed or temporarily unusable. As for utilities, there may be breakdowns in the energy supply network or in the water supply. In addition to violent storms, other physical climatic hazards can be cited such as floods or heat waves and wildfires.[124] In these and other cases, subnational authorities and central governments are often obligated to intervene and as quickly as possible which involves operational means and, consequently, public expenditures. In fact, central governments could bear the loss and damage to public assets owned or managed at subnational levels as local governments in affected areas generally request support from the central government to compensate for their losses, namely for damage to things such as roads, bridges, or other infrastructure.[125]

Moreover, damage to infrastructure networks can in turn lead to high losses for infrastructure users. According to calculations carried out by the OECD, the occurrence of floods in a large city such as Paris would mean that companies operating

[121] Feyen et al. (2020).

[122] Volz et al. (2020), Chap. 3.

[123] OECD - Organisation for Economic Co-operation and Development (2022), Chap. 3.

[124] OECD - Organisation for Economic Co-operation and Development (2023).

[125] OECD - Organisation for Economic Co-operation and Development (2022), Chap. 3.

there could suffer more losses due to the interruption of energy supply and interruption of transport than due to the flood itself.[126] In these cases, there are impacts between the different transmission channels. So, for example, an impact on the public sector leads to an impact on the business sector which, in turn, will have a negative effect on public finance through, namely, less tax revenue (e.g., firms have more losses and perhaps less taxable profits) and more public expenditure (e.g., subsidies to help firms recover). This is one of many examples of how there can be impacts across transmission channels which makes it challenging to accurately understand how each of the transmission channels works and to measure or estimate how these transmission channels may currently or potentially affect public finance.

More worrying is that, due to global warming, physical hazards are expected to increase in frequency and intensity which will result, among others, in more and greater damage to infrastructure and public assets and consequently an increase in public spending. The costs that climate change could cause to infrastructure and public buildings is a matter of growing concern. For example, in a study of the Financial Accountability Office of Ontario (2021)[127] it is underlined that, for the Province of Ontario in Canada, adapting public buildings to withstand climate-related risks will require significant.

Another example of how climate change could have a direct impact on public spending concerns programs undertaken by governments to support certain economic or social activities. For example, see the cases of programs supported by the US Federal Budget. Thus, a report entitled "Climate Change: The fiscal risks facing the Federal Government – A Preliminary Assessment"[128] refers to the fiscal risks that may arise from five programs that are directly influenced by climate change, namely crop insurance, health care, wildfire suppression, hurricane-related disaster relief, and federal facility flood risk. According to this report, each of the five evaluations of these programs unequivocally points out that climate change will bring an increase in public spending.[129]

It should also not be overlooked that, given international commitments, namely the 2015 Paris Agreement on Climate Change, it is very likely that mitigation and adaptation policies will involve more public expenditure. While climate mitigation policies aim to reduce greenhouse gas emissions, adaptation policies aim to build resilience (such as investing in more resilient infrastructure) and reduce vulnerabilities to climate risks.[130] Therefore, it is not only due to international commitments that finance ministers should be concerned with the issue of climate change. It is also due to the impact that the climate-related risks will have on the public sector causing an increase in public expenditure.

---

[126] OECD - Organisation for Economic Co-operation and Development (2014) and OECD - Organisation for Economic Co-operation and Development (2018).

[127] Financial Accountability Office of Ontario (2021).

[128] OMB - Office of Management and Budget (2016).

[129] OMB - Office of Management and Budget (2016).

[130] Gonguet et al. (2021).

Another example of the negative impact that climate change could induce concerns state-owned enterprises (SOE) that may not only have less profit but even greater losses which may imply government assistance, probably translating into greater public spending. However, the potential increase in public expenditure does not just stem from the materialization of climate-related physical risks, whether acute or chronic. Even transition risks can lead to an increase in public expenditures as could be the case, for example, of losses incurred by SOE with carbon-dependent assets that could present not only less profit but even greater losses which may imply government assistance probably translating into higher public expenses.

7.5 *Climate Change's Macroeconomic Impacts and Other Issues*

Climate-related risks can also alter macroeconomic conditions, including, inter alia, to economic shocks, structural changes, and/or impacts on economic growth. Just look at a few cases to see how climate-related risks can be transmitted through altered macroeconomic conditions.

The occurrence of extreme weather events, for instance, could trigger economic shocks seen as "as unpredictable events that produce a significant change within an economy".[131] These shocks can be demand-side or supply-side. As Batten points out, while the former affect the components of aggregate demand (e.g. private and public consumption and investment, business investment, and international trade), the latter affects the productive capacity of the economy (e.g. labour, physical capital, and technology).[132] As noted above, a demand shock can be generated by the combination of different elements such as lower household income, less wealth, and higher product prices. Instead, a supply-side shock can occur if, for example, food shortages occur as well as volatility in prices due to shortages.[133] Inflationary pressures may arise.[134] These matters are also relevant for central banks both in the context of monetary policy and financial stability. From a monetary policy perspective, supply shocks are generally more challenging than demand shocks as the former imply, as NGFS stresses, "a trade-off for central banks between stabilising inflation and stabilising output fluctuations".[135]

Climate change can bring structural changes to many economies in the medium and long term. According to Feyen et al.,[136] these structural changes can be seen through four channels, namely "productive changes due to physical risks, crowding

[131] Batten (2018).

[132] Batten (2018).

[133] Batten (2018).

[134] Batten (2018).

[135] NGFS - Network for Greening the Financial System (2020b).

[136] Feyen et al. (2020).

out of productive investments by investments in adaptation and mitigation measures, transition to a low carbo economy, and, finally, innovation and the emergence of green sectors".[137] In this regard, climate-related physical risks have the potential to affect the productivity of some economic sectors (e.g., agriculture) or regions (e.g., low-lying coastal areas) which can trigger a whole range of effects, including changes in crops, intensification of particular crops, shifts in labour supply, voluntary or forced displacement of populations, and internal and international migration (ibid.). Certainly, this whole situation is linked to socio-economic changes. In fact, if the resources of certain regions are severely affected (e.g., extreme weather, desertification, rising sea levels), this could lead to a relocation of households or even to phenomena of strong migrations or violent conflicts.[138] On the other hand, disruption of production in one or several sectors may have a rebound effect, affecting, for example, trade, foreign earnings, and exchange rates.[139]

The issue of economic growth in the context of climate change also raises heated debates, particularly regarding its economic costs. The Integrated Assessment Model (IAM) is one of the main tools used to assess the economic costs of climate change, but it has been criticized for not capturing the full implications of climate change, notably not taking into account the negative impacts on children, their cognitive development and education process as well as the fact that they may drop out of school following a disaster to help their families economically.[140] Thus, despite the attempts that have been made to estimate the expected economic impacts of climate change, considerable uncertainties still remain.[141] Apart from these controversies, what is certain is that the issue of losses in terms of GDP is taken seriously. In summary, both from the point of view of the physical impact of climate change and of mitigation and adaptation policies, it is very likely that macroeconomic conditions will be altered which will have repercussions at the level of public finance.

8 The Financing and Management of the Risks of Losses and Damages

As noted above, climate-related risks, both physical and transitional, cause losses and damages.[142] With regard to economic losses and damages, they can affect property (public and private) and/or income and livelihoods. Losses and damages

[137] Feyen et al. (2020).

[138] BCBS - Basel Committee on Banking Supervision (2021a).

[139] OECD - Organisation for Economic Co-operation and Development (2021), Chap. 5.

[140] Feyen et al. (2020).

[141] Andersson et al. (2020). Climate change and the macro economy, ECB Occasional Paper Series No 243/June 2020. https://www.ecb.europa.eu/pub/pdf/scpops/ecb.op243~2ce3c7c4e1.en.pdf.

[142] According to the OECD report, under the title Building Financial Resilience to Climate Impacts – a Framework for Governments to manage the risks of losses and damages, it is important to

can be substantial and have been increasing due to the greater frequency and intensity of events resulting from climate change. It is in this context that organizations such as the OECD address the issue of "risk management strategy" as well as the different approaches of governments to access funds to reduce and manage the risks of losses and damages.[143] This may entail blended funding and other measures such as regulatory measures. Indeed, finance may be public or private as well domestic or international. Thus, according to the OECD, a "comprehensive risk finance strategy" can be adopted by national and subnational governments based on three key functions, namely "risk reduction", "risk retention", and "risk transfer".[144]

The risk reduction approach is essentially preventive seeking to reduce the risk of loss and damage to assets (both public and private) and/or income and livelihoods. With regard to private property, the aim is, for example, to improve the physical durability of buildings to better cope with the impacts of climate change. Similarly, public buildings and infrastructure (e.g., schools, hospitals, and roads) should also be targeted for improvement. Thus, through this approach, the role of financing in reducing and managing economic losses is emphasized. Therefore, regarding property, funding should be provided for the improvement of buildings (private and public) and infrastructure to better cope with the adverse effects of climate change. With regard to income and livelihoods, due attention should be paid to strengthening the resilience of vulnerable and marginalized population groups through, for example, social protection mechanisms. This is especially important in cases when the population or part of it is unable to contract with an insurer. According to the OECD report[145] "regular cash transfers to segments of the population based on a set of criteria such as age, income or disability can ensure alternative sources of income", thus reducing pressure on families and preventing them from having to, for example, withdraw children from schools or sell assets that ensure their livelihoods in the event of climatic hazards. However, a moral hazard problem may arise.[146] On the other hand, in addition to investment in adaptation strengthening resilience and reducing exposure to adverse climate events, governments can provide an environment for the private sector to manage its own risks, taking into account that periods of high regulatory uncertainty are dissuasive from investments.

---

distinguish between economic losses and damages whereby it is emphasized in this report that, while damages refer to the physical assets that are totally or partially destroyed in the affected areas that are measured in physical units (e.g., the number of damaged houses, roads, crops, and land) and assigned monetary values based on replacement costs according to prices prevailing just before the event, losses refer to changes in economic flows arising from an event from the date of its occurrence until full economic recovery and reconstruction (including the decline in output in productive sectors such as agriculture, industry, and services) OECD - Organisation for Economic Co-operation and Development (2022).

[143] OECD - Organisation for Economic Co-operation and Development (2021), Chap. 5.

[144] OECD - Organisation for Economic Co-operation and Development (2021).

[145] OECD - Organisation for Economic Co-operation and Development (2021), Chap. 5.

[146] OECD - Organisation for Economic Co-operation and Development (2021).

In turn, since the risks can be reduced (risk reduction), but it is certainly not possible to eliminate them completely, this means that such risks materialize through losses and damages. This is how the risk retention approach comes about.[147] Thus, governments are exposed to these losses and damages due to the damage caused to public assets and their role as "insurer of last resort".[148] Despite the many difficulties, in order to face climate or weather events, governments must certainly carry out an "assessment of the potential explicit and implicit contingent liabilities".[149] This will be especially difficult for implicit liabilities that are not secured in advance and/or savings are not sufficient to cover losses. This may imply that costs have to be shifted, for example, from subnational entities to national governments or from the private sector to the public sector. From a financing point of view, the risk retention approach implies using savings and current funds to deal with frequent but less severe climatic hazards (e.g., annual flooding) or the use of borrowing to deal with the phenomena of medium frequency and medium severity events (e.g., widespread flooding).

However, as this OECD report points out, the inconveniences that resorting to borrowing may present and an increase in the level of taxation to respond to financing needs arising from an adverse climate event cannot be overlooked. For instance, in the case of borrowing, this could create more difficulties and concerns in terms of fiscal sustainability, and, in the case of increased tax burden, this means more taxes levied on households and businesses thereby making economic recovery more difficult.[150]

Lastly, this OECD report addresses risk transfer in that the risk or part of it can be transferred to a third party (e.g., insurer) for a price (insurance premium) which also allows risk sharing. As a rule, insurance enables households, businesses, and even public bodies themselves to be compensated in the event of adverse climate or weather events. The situation differs depending on whether there is a large, small, or almost non-existent insurance coverage. The higher levels of insurance coverage enable more quick economic recovery. However, this is a challenging task even for developed economies with strong insurance markets. This OECD report points out three factors that may explain low levels of insurance coverage of climate-related hazards, namely "severity of hazards", "consumer behaviour", and "lack of financial literacy".[151] With regard to the first, it is noted that less frequent and highly impacting adverse climate or weather events are difficult and costly to insure. With regard to the second factor, consumers may be less inclined to pay insurance for less frequent adverse climate or weather events, all the more so as they expect that, in these cases, there will be some kind of compensation from the government. Additionally, as for the third factor, this concerns the lack of understanding of

[147] OECD - Organisation for Economic Co-operation and Development (2021), Chap. 5.

[148] OECD - Organisation for Economic Co-operation and Development (2021).

[149] OECD - Organisation for Economic Co-operation and Development (2021).

[150] OECD - Organisation for Economic Co-operation and Development (2021).

[151] OECD - Organisation for Economic Co-operation and Development (2021).

insurance products and markets. In addition to the insurance mechanisms, the risk transfer approach also includes other mechanisms such as pooling risks and/or catastrophe bonds. It is relevant in all of these cases that there is access to solid reinsurance companies and international capital markets.[152]

Governments have a special responsibility in designing, adopting, and implementing a comprehensive risk finance strategy that encompasses, in a complementary way, the three approaches mentioned above, namely risk reduction, risk retention, and risk transfer. In fact, the risk management strategy must be in line with fiscal and public finance mechanisms, taking into account even the fiscal impact that risks of losses and damages may have directly or indirectly.[153] It should also be added that, in a context of risk reduction, public procurement can better be used to minimize ex ante expenses.[154]

In brief, in the context of a risk management strategy, and more precisely a risk financing strategy, governments are called upon to play relevant roles, namely with regard to the adoption of regulations, acting at the level of preparation and execution of the budget, with regard to measures aimed at framing and encouraging private operators (e.g., insurance companies), and even eventually establishing various forms of public-private partnerships to support the coverage of risks arising from disasters.[155] All of this certainly presupposes risk assessment management.[156] Taking into account their functions, finance ministers cannot fail to be at the epicentre of these issues and measures.

9 More Challenges for Public Finances

The occurrence of adverse climate or weather events may imply a deterioration in public finance conditions, notably through a decrease in tax revenues and an increase in public expenditures.[157] The decrease in tax revenues is mainly due to the slowdown or even disruption of economic activity. On the other hand, tax relief measures can also be adopted to promote and stimulate economic activity which also translates into lower tax revenues. The increase in public expenditures can result from several factors. Indeed, in addition to direct impacts, climate-related risks could trigger explicit and implicit contingent liabilities that, if realized, could generate substantial costs for governments.[158] Explicit contingent liabilities arise, for

[152] OECD - Organisation for Economic Co-operation and Development (2021).

[153] OECD - Organisation for Economic Co-operation and Development (2021).

[154] OECD - Organisation for Economic Co-operation and Development (2022), Chap. 4.

[155] OECD - Organisation for Economic Co-operation and Development (2015).

[156] OECD - Organisation for Economic Co-operation and Development (2015).

[157] Dunz and Power (2021).

[158] Dunz and Power (2021).

example, from legislation or contracts.[159] Instead, implicit contingent liabilities are not directly provided in legislation or contractual instruments but result from a kind of moral or political obligation, i.e., in the face of a major natural disaster, for example, the government is expected to act by providing subsidies or other types of measures.[160]

Following a disaster, for example, emergency (short-term) measures as well as recovery and reconstruction measures may be adopted which certainly entails more public expenditures. Depending on the instruments that are used, such expenditures may lead to an increase in the budget deficit, an increase in public debt, or imply a reduction in other types of investments.[161] For some countries, it may be more difficult to borrow following a disaster, and the costs may be higher.[162] In addition, the debt ratio can increase enormously which can put some countries in a situation of over-indebtedness, making debt repayment even more difficult.[163] Moreover, a vicious circle can occur between, inter alia, high levels of debt and the difficulty of borrowing more to meet further expenditures arising from climate change impacts.[164]

When it comes to managing disaster-related costs, governments may have a range of instruments at their disposal such as budgetary instruments, public guarantees, financial instruments, and investments in risk prevention.[165] Budgetary instruments can consist of budget reallocations, contingency funds, and reserve funds. Budgetary reallocations can take various forms such as transferring between lines in the budget itself, adopting a supplementary budget, or changing priorities in budgets in the years following a disaster. In addition to budgetary reallocations, contingency funds and reserve funds are also part of budgetary instruments of which both can be used as fiscal buffers to mitigate climate-related risks.[166] Through public guarantees, governments can contribute to strengthening the resilience and soundness of certain financial institutions, including reinsurers, which reduces public expenditure in the event of a disaster but does not completely remove fiscal risks as guarantees can be called upon in a case of need. As for financial instruments, these basically refer to financing through debt issuance or risk transfer to a third party, usually an insurer or reinsurer, as noted above.[167] Finally, investments in risk prevention aim to reduce social and/or economic exposure to potential losses and damages from climate change and can translate into structural investments in public infrastructure to make it more resilient. In addition, non-structural measures can also be adopted as

[159] Dunz and Power (2021).

[160] OECD - Organisation for Economic Co-operation and Development (2015), Chapters 1 and 4.

[161] OECD - Organisation for Economic Co-operation and Development (2021), Chap. 5.

[162] OECD - Organisation for Economic Co-operation and Development (2021).

[163] OECD - Organisation for Economic Co-operation and Development (2021).

[164] OECD - Organisation for Economic Co-operation and Development (2021).

[165] OECD - Organisation for Economic Co-operation and Development (2022), Chapters 4 and 5.

[166] OECD - Organisation for Economic Co-operation and Development (2022).

[167] OECD - Organisation for Economic Co-operation and Development (2022).

part of prevention involving policies and regulations to incentivize private investments to adapt to climate change.[168] In the event of a disaster, the best use must be made of the various instruments to achieve "a government's optimal post-disaster response".[169]

However, the fact that pressures on public finances can result in fiscal risks should not be disregarded.[170] In this context, it is convenient to emphasize that, according to the International Monetary Fund (IMF), fiscal risks "are factors that may cause fiscal outcomes to deviate from expectations or forecasts"[171] where these factors "comprise potential shocks to government revenues, expenditures, assets, or liabilities, which are not reflected in the government's fiscal forecasts or reports".[172] Thus, climate-related risks can impact fiscal risks, translating into deviations in fiscal outcomes from what was expected at the time of budget approval or other forecasting. Therefore, in order to strengthen the financial management of climate-related risks and anticipate the implications that may result for public finances and governments, such fiscal risks should be identified, assessed, and mitigated, and sufficient financing should be secured to better respond to the occurrence of adverse climate or weather events in the context of public financial management. Moreover, the materialization of fiscal risks due to climate change certainly requires rapid and significant adjustments to both the level and composition of government revenues and expenditures.[173]

10 Final Remarks

Climate change adds up to the demographic, economic, technological, political, and social challenges.[174] In fact, the negative effects of climate change can occur at the same time as other disruptions such as the floods that occurred in East Africa in 2020 at the same time as the Covid-19 pandemic.

In addition to many other negative effects, anthropocentric climate change leads to increasingly significant losses and damages. Due to the occurrence of climate-related risks, both physical (acute and chronic) and transitional, these losses and damages put increasing pressure on public finances. This pressure stems both from impacts on governments (central and/or local) and through other transmission channels such as households, businesses, and the financial sector in addition to impacts through altering macroeconomic conditions. Given these transmission

[168] OECD - Organisation for Economic Co-operation and Development (2022).

[169] OECD - Organisation for Economic Co-operation and Development (2022).

[170] OECD - Organisation for Economic Co-operation and Development (2022), Chap. 5.

[171] IMF - International Monetary Fund (2016) and IMF - International Monetary Fund (2018).

[172] IMF - International Monetary Fund (2018), Chap. 4.

[173] OECD - Organisation for Economic Co-operation and Development (2022), Chapters 4 and 5.

[174] OECD - Organisation for Economic Co-operation and Development (2021), Chapters 1 and 4.

channels, the impact on public finance could be even more substantial despite the uncertainties as to the timing and amounts involved.

Due to the cross-cutting nature of climate change, its impacts, and the scale of the challenges, this matter does not only concern the ministers of the environment or ecology. It concerns the entire government, and finance ministers cannot fail to be prepared not only for long-term actions but also to adopt immediate measures under penalty of jeopardizing, among other things, fiscal sustainability.

References

Åberg A, Jeffs N (2022) Loss and damage finance in the climate negotiations: key challenges and next steps, Research Paper, Royal Institute of International Affairs. https://doi.org/10.55317/9781784135461

Andersson M et al (2020) Climate change and the macro economy, ECB Occasional Paper Series No 243/June 2020. https://www.ecb.europa.eu/pub/pdf/scpops/ecb.op243~2ce3c7c4e1.en.pdf

Batten S (2018) Climate change and the macro-economy: a critical review. Bank of England, Working Paper No. 706. https://www.bankofengland.co.uk/-/media/boe/files/working-paper/2018/climate-change-and-the-macro-economy-a-critical-review.pdf

Battersby B et al (2021) Green Budgetting: towards common principles. OECD, European Commission, IMF, Geneva. https://economy-finance.ec.europa.eu/system/files/2021-11/cop26_en.pdf

Chenet H (2019) Climate change and financial risk. Available at SSRN: https://ssrn.com/abstract=3407940 or https://doi.org/10.2139/ssrn.3407940

Connell R et al (2020) Charting a new climate. Loughborough University - Acclimatise - UNEP FI. https://www.unepfi.org/wordpress/wp-content/uploads/2020/09/Charting-a-New-Climate-UNEP-FI-TCFD-Banking-Physical-Risk.pdf

Darvas ZM et al (2020) From climate change to cyber-attacks: Incipient financial-stability risks for the euro area, Bruegel Policy Contribution, No. 2020/02, Bruegel. https://www.econstor.eu/bitstream/10419/237640/1/1694819124.pdf

Dunz N, Power S (2021) Climate-related risks for ministries of finance – an overview. Coalition of Finance Ministers for Climate Action, Coalition of Finance Ministers for Climate Action. https://www.financeministersforclimate.org/sites/cape/files/inline-files/Climate-Related%20Risks%20for%20Ministries%20of%20Finance%20-%20An%20Overview%20%28CFMCA%29_1.pdf

Feyen E et al (2020) Macro-financial aspects of climate change, World Bank policy research working paper No. 9109. http://hdl.handle.net/10986/33193

Gonguet F et al (2021) Climate-Sensitive Management of Public Finances — Green PFM, IMF Staff Climate Note 2021/002, International Monetary Fund. https://www.imf.org/en/Publications/staff-climate-notes/Issues/2021/08/10/Climate-Sensitive-Management-of-Public-Finances-Green-PFM-460635

Gundlach J (2020) Climate risks are becoming legal liabilities for the energy sector. Nat Energy 5: 94–97. https://doi.org/10.1038/s41560-019-0540-x

Kalkuhl M, Wenz L (2020) The impact of climate conditions on economic production. Evidence from a global panel of regions. J Environ Econ Manag. https://doi.org/10.1016/j.jeem.2020.102360

Lenton T et al (2019) Climate tipping points – too risky to bet against. Nature 575:592–595. https://doi.org/10.1038/d41586-019-03595-0

Pigato MA (ed) (2019) Fiscal policies for development and climate action. International development in focus. World Bank, Washington D.C. https://doi.org/10.1596/978-1-4648-1358-0

Radu D (2022) Disaster risk financing: limiting the fiscal cost of climate-related disasters. European Commission, Brussels. https://economy-finance.ec.europa.eu/system/files/2022-11/dp174_en.pdf
Roka K (2019) Anthropocene and climate change. In: Leal Filho W et al (eds) Climate action. Encyclopedia of the UN sustainable development goals. Springer, Cham. https://doi.org/10.1007/978-3-319-71063-1_26-1
Rudebusch G (2021) Climate change is a source of financial risk, Federal Reserve Bank of San Francisco Economic Letter. https://www.frbsf.org/economic-research/wp-content/uploads/sites/4/el2021-03.pdf
Schäfer L et al (2021) Slow-onset processes and resulting loss and damage–an introduction. https://www.germanwatch.org/sites/default/files/FINAL_Slow-onset%20paper%20Teil%201_20.01.pdf
Spinaci S (2021) Green and sustainable finance, European Parliamentary Research Service. https://www.europarl.europa.eu/RegData/etudes/BRIE/2021/679081/EPRS_BRI(2021)679081_EN.pdf
Summerhayes CP, Zalasiewicz J (2018) Global warming and the Anthropocene. Geol Today (34): 194–200. https://doi.org/10.1111/gto.12247
Volz U et al (2020) Climate Change and Sovereign Risk, SOAS University of London, Asian Development Bank Institute, Worldwide Fund for Nature Singapore, and Four Twenty Seven. https://doi.org/10.25501/SOAS.00033524
Zalasiewicz et al (2008) Are we now living in the Anthropocene? GSA Today 18(2). https://doi.org/10.1130/GSAT01802A.1

Institutional References

BCBS - Basel Committee on Banking Supervision (2021a) Climate-related risk drivers and their transmission channels, Bank for International Settlements. https://www.bis.org/bcbs/publ/d517.pdf
BCBS - Basel Committee on Banking Supervision (2021b) Climate-related financial risks - measurement methodologies, Bank for International Settlements. https://www.bis.org/bcbs/publ/d518.pdf
ECB – European Central Bank (2019) Financial stability review, May. https://www.ecb.europa.eu/pub/pdf/fsr/ecb.fsr201905~266e856634.en.pdf
ECB – European Central Bank (2022) Financial stability review, May. https://www.ecb.europa.eu/pub/pdf/fsr/ecb.fsr202205~f207f46ea0.en.pdf
FAO - Food and Agriculture Organization of the United Nations (2021) FAO's work on climate change – Fisheries and aquaculture 2020. https://doi.org/10.4060/cb3414en
Financial Accountability Office of Ontario (2021) Costing climate change impacts to public infrastructure. https://www.fao-on.org/web/default/files/publications/EC2105%20CIPI%20Buildings/CIPI%20Buildings-EN.pdf
FSB - Financial Stability Board (2022) Supervisory and regulatory approaches to climate-related risks – final report. https://www.fsb.org/wp-content/uploads/P131022-1.pdf
G20/OECD (2012) G20/OECD Methodological framework on disaster risk assessment and risk financing http://www.oecd.org/gov/riskmanagement/g20oecdframeworkfordisasterriskmanagement.htm
IAIS - International Association of Insurance Supervisors (2021) Global Insurance Market Report – The impact of climate change on the financial stability of the insurance sector. https://www.iaisweb.org/uploads/2022/01/210930-GIMAR-special-topic-edition-climate-change.pdf

ILO - International Labour Office (2011) Towards an ILO approach to climate change adaptation. https://www.ilo.org/wcmsp5/groups/public/%2D%2D-ed_emp/%2D%2D-emp_policy/%2D%2D-invest/documents/publication/wcms_174612.pdf
IMF - International Monetary Fund (2016) Analyzing and managing fiscal risks — best practices. International Monetary Fund, Washington, D.C. https://www.imf.org/external/np/pp/eng/2016/050416.pdf
IMF - International Monetary Fund (2018) Fiscal transparency handbook. International Monetary Fund, Washington, D.C. https://doi.org/10.5089/9781484331859.069
IPCC - Intergovernmental Panel on Climate Change (2021) The physical science basis. Contribution of working group I to the sixth assessment report of the intergovernmental panel on climate change. Cambridge University Press, Cambridge. https://doi.org/10.1017/9781009157896
ISDR – International Strategy for Disaster Reduction (2008) Climate change and disaster risk reduction – briefing note 01. https://eird.org/publicaciones/Climate-Change-DRR.pdf
NGFS - Network for Greening the Financial System (2019) A call for action climate change as a source of financial risk. https://www.ngfs.net/sites/default/files/medias/documents/ngfs_first_comprehensive_report_-_17042019_0.pdf
NGFS - Network for Greening the Financial System (2020a) NGFS scenarios for central banks and supervisors. https://www.ngfs.net/sites/default/files/medias/documents/820184_ngfs_scenarios_final_version_v6_0.pdf
NGFS - Network for Greening the Financial System (2020b) The macroeconomic and financial stability impacts of climate change – research priorities. https://www.ngfs.net/sites/default/files/medias/documents/ngfs_research_priorities_final.pdf
NGFS - Network for Greening the Financial System (2022a) NGFS scenarios for central banks and supervisors. https://www.ngfs.net/sites/default/files/medias/documents/ngfs_climate_scenarios_for_central_banks_and_supervisors_.pdf.pdf
NGFS - Network for Greening the Financial System (2022b) Not too late – confronting the growing odds of a late and disorderly transition. https://www.ngfs.net/sites/default/files/media/2022/09/07/not_too_late_-_confronting_the_growing_odds_of_a_late_and_disorderly_transition.pdf
NOAA - National Oceanic and Atmospheric Administration (2016) What is the difference between weather and climate? (Last updated March 9, 2016). https://www.noaa.gov/explainers/what-s-difference-between-climate-and-weather
OECD - Organisation for Economic Co-operation and Development (2014) Seine Basin, Île-de-France, 2014: resilience to major floods. OECD Publishing, Paris. https://doi.org/10.1787/9789264208728-en
OECD - Organisation for Economic Co-operation and Development (2015) Disaster risk financing. A global survey of practices and challenges. OECD Publishing, Paris. https://doi.org/10.1787/9789264234246-en
OECD - Organisation for Economic Co-operation and Development (2017) Recommendation on disaster risk financing strategies. https://www.oecd.org/daf/fin/insurance/OECD-Recommendation-Disaster-Risk-Financing-Strategies.pdf
OECD - Organisation for Economic Co-operation and Development (2018) Climate-resilient infrastructure, OECD Environment Policy Paper No. 14. https://www.oecd.org/environment/cc/policy-perspectives-climate-resilient-infrastructure.pdf
OECD - Organisation for Economic Co-operation and Development (2021) Managing climate risks, facing up to losses and damages. OECD Publishing, Paris. https://read.oecd.org/10.1787/55ea1cc9-en?format=pdf
OECD - Organisation for Economic Co-operation and Development (2022) Building financial resilience to climate impacts: a framework for governments to manage the risks of losses and damages. OECD Publishing, Paris. https://read.oecd.org/10.1787/9e2e1412-en?format=pdf
OECD - Organisation for Economic Co-operation and Development (2023) Taming wildfires in the context of climate change. OECD Publishing, Paris. https://read.oecd.org/10.1787/dd00c367-en?format=pdf

OMB - Office of Management and Budget (2016) Climate Change: The fiscal risks facing the Federal Government – A Preliminary Assessment. https://obamawhitehouse.archives.gov/sites/default/files/omb/reports/omb_climate_change_fiscal_risk_report.pdf
Portugal's Adaptation Communication to the United Nations Framework Convention on Climate Change (2021). https://www.ohchr.org/sites/default/files/2022-03/portugal-nhri-annex-IV.pdf
TCFD - Task Force on Climate-Related Financial Disclosures (2016) Draft report recommendations of the task force on climate-related financial disclosures. https://assets.bbhub.io/company/sites/60/2020/10/16_1221_TCFD_Report_Letter.pdf
TCFD - Task Force on Climate-Related Financial Disclosures (2017) Final report recommendations of the task force on climate-related financial disclosures. https://assets.bbhub.io/company/sites/60/2021/10/FINAL-2017-TCFD-Report.pdf
The Coalition of Finance Ministers for Climate Action (2022) Climate change adaptation and role of the coalition of finance ministers for climate action. https://www.financeministersforclimate.org/sites/cape/files/inline-files/Climate%20Change%20Adaptation%20and%20Role%20of%20CFMCA.pdf
UNDRR - United Nations Office for Disaster Risk Reduction (2015) Sendai framework for disaster risk reduction 2015-2030. https://www.undrr.org/publication/sendai-framework-disaster-risk-reduction-2015-2030
UNEP - United Nations Development Programme (2016) Climate change and labour: impacts of heat in the workplace. http://www.undp.org/sites/g/files/zskgke326/files/publications/Climate%20and%20Labour%20Issue%20Paper_28%20April%202016_v1_lowres.pdf
UNEP, Green Economy (2010) Driving a green economy through public finance and fiscal policy reform. https://d1bf23g64f8xve.cloudfront.net/sites/default/files/downloads/resource//Driving_a_GE_through_public_finance_and_fiscal_policy_reform_UNEP.pdf
UNEP-FI - United Nations Environment Programme Finance Initiative (2022) Adapting to a new climate. https://www.unepfi.org/industries/banking/adapting-to-a-new-climate/
WHO - World Health Organization (2022) Review of IPCC Evidence 2022 climate change, health, and well-being. https://cdn.who.int/media/docs/default-source/climate-change/who-review-of-ipcc-evidence-2022-adv-version.pdf?sfvrsn=cce71a2c_3&download=true
WMO - World Meteorological Organization (2022) United in Science: A multi-organization high-level compilation of the most recent science related to climate change, impacts and responses. https://library.wmo.int/doc_num.php?explnum_id=11308
Wolfrom L, Yokoi-Arai M (2016) Financial instruments for managing disaster risks related to climate change. OECD J Financ Market Trends 2015(1). https://doi.org/10.1787/fmt-2015-5jrqdkpxk5d5
World Bank, GFDRR (2013) Building resilience: integrating climate and disaster risk into development - the World Bank Group experience. http://documents1.worldbank.org/curated/en/762871468148506173/pdf/826480WP0v10Bu0130Box37986200OUO090.pdf

The Climate Dimension of Fiscal Policy Sustainability: Best Practices in Green Budgeting and Lessons for Portugal

Carlos Fonseca Marinheiro, Amílcar do Rosário e Sousa, and Ana Pinheiro

Abstract The green budgeting technique is being adopted by an increasing number of countries and has the potential to align fiscal policy objectives with climate and environmental goals. Given that the (financial) sustainability of public finances and environmental sustainability are intrinsically interconnected with each other, this section argues that the traditional public debt sustainability analysis should be expanded to encompass climate and environmental sustainability considerations. Other key elements of a proper budgetary framework, such as fiscal transparency, should also be broadened to include the disclosure of the environmental and climate impacts of fiscal policy. The Green budgeting technique is increasingly used to expand the scope of such usual fiscal concepts. One of the main tools for its adoption is green tagging that enables citizens to assess the environmental and climate impacts of fiscal policy on both the revenue and spending sides of the state budget. It enables capturing both the positive and negative impacts of fiscal policy. Additionally, it provides more visibility to the amount financial resources countries allocate to climate and environment goals and to mitigation and adaptation policies while allowing the assessment of whether such goals are attained. A proper working fiscal framework, including the adoption of accrual accounting and performance programme budgeting, seems to be instrumental in this domain along with strong political commitment. Portugal has already taken a few steps such as the recently enacted Climate Law but still has a long way to go in terms of green budgeting. This section proposes a roadmap for its adoption. To start with, both the completion of the public accounts reform and the full adoption of programme budgeting foreseen in the

---

The opinions expressed here are those of the authors and not necessarily those of the CFP.

C. F. Marinheiro (✉)
Conselho das Finanças Públicas -Portuguese Public Finance Council (CFP), Lisboa and University of Coimbra, Faculty of Economics, Coimbra, Portugal
e-mail: carlos.marinheiro@cfp.pt

A. do Rosário e Sousa · A. Pinheiro
Conselho das Finanças Públicas -Portuguese Public Finance Council (CFP), Lisbon, Portugal
e-mail: amilcar.sousa@cfp.pt; ana.pinheiro@cfp.pt

R. Saraiva, P. A. Pardal (eds.), *Sustainable Finances and the Law*, Economic Analysis of Law in European Legal Scholarship 16,
https://doi.org/10.1007/978-3-031-49460-4_9

2015 Budgetary Framework Law should be attained. The meeting of such two pre-conditions will then lay the foundations for the implementation of green budgeting and disclose the climate and environmental impacts of policy measures following the international best practices. The adoption of green budgeting might also pave the way to the emission of green bonds to finance specific environmental and climate related projects. Such bonds might be a cost-effective way to finance the substantial green investment needs in a highly indebted country while contributing to the decrease of global risk.

1 Introduction

The sustainability of public finances is a central issue in recent economic policy debate.[1] Although, at first glance, the economic intuition points to a simple definition of sustainability considering that a sustainable policy must ultimately avoid government bankruptcy, in practice as pointed out by,[2] despite such clear economic intuition, there are serious difficulties in both the analytical and operational definition of fiscal sustainability. Besides the usual discussion regarding the limits to the public debt accumulation,[3] in the present juncture characterized by a climate and environment emergency,[4] the assessment of sustainability must also include the climate and environment dimensions. As a matter of fact, if fiscal policy should contribute to achieving sustainable development of the economy, such climate and environment dimensions must be taken into account. This is clear when the Brundtland Commission definition of sustainable development is retained as "development that meets the needs of the present without compromising the ability of future generations to meet their own needs".[5,6] A sustainable policy should try to reconcile economic development with the protection of social and environmental balance. As a central part of public policies, fiscal policy should contribute toward the goal of sustainable development.

---

[1] Marinheiro (2006), pp. 155–179.

[2] Balassone and Franco (2000), pp. 21–60.

[3] Hamilton and Flavin (1986), pp. 808–819.

[4] European Parliament (2019).

[5] United Nations General Assembly – UN (1987).

[6] This widely used definition is the one retained in the glossary of summaries of the European Union's law, EUR-Lex (https://eur-lex.europa.eu/legal content/EN/TXT/?uri=LEGISSUM:sustain able_development), and sustainable development has formally became one of the European Union's long-term goals under Article 3(3) of the Treaty on European Union. It states that "The Union shall establish an internal market. It shall work for the sustainable development of Europe based on balanced economic growth and price stability, a highly competitive social market economy, aiming at full employment and social progress, and a high level of protection and improvement of the quality of the environment. It shall promote scientific and technological advance."

In the authors' opinion there is a clear and direct relationship between the "traditional" sustainability of public finances and environmental sustainability. Only financially sustainable public finances can provide the resources needed for counteracting the adverse effects of climate change, and only a sustainable environment can preserve the sustainability of the public finances. A degraded environment would likely increase the frequency and dimension of natural catastrophes[7] which would imperil the health of public finances. According to this study, "conservative estimates show that the current trend in global warming could result in an additional annual loss of at least € 170 billion (1.36% of EU GDP)." The consequent damage to public infrastructures and the role of the government as a sort of insurer of last resort can take a heavy toll on public finances.

In what directly concerns climate action and fiscal policy, there are two interconnected dimensions. On one hand, fiscal policy should provide the financial resources needed to tackle mitigation and adaptation policies and, on the other hand, the environmental impact of the remaining fiscal policy decisions, of the tax system, and of the public expenditure should be assessed. This is exactly where green budgeting fits in. It is in the light of the role that fiscal policy should have in the achievement of the broader goal of sustainable development that green budgeting stands out as a powerful tool.

Besides summarizing the state of the art on this domain, this section adds the view to the literature that the new "green dimension" to fiscal policy can be seen as an extension to the existing principles of fiscal sustainability and fiscal transparency and its main instrument of "green tagging" as a required addition to a proper public financial management (PFM). It also outlines what needs to be done for Portugal to catch up with the best practices.

The remainder of the section is organized as follows. Section 2 describes the concept of green budgeting, its context, and the most common tools used to implement this practice (with special emphasis on green tagging) and also includes a brief description of green bonds. In Sect. 3, the case study of the adoption of green budgeting by France is analysed. In Sect. 4, the attention is shifted to Portugal, describing the steps that were already taken and the lessons to be learned from those best practices. The main conclusions of this paper are presented in Sect. 5.

[7] Radu (2021).

2 Green Budgeting

2.1 Definition, Context and Tools

There is no universal definition of green budgeting. According to the European Commission,[8] "Green budgeting means using the tools of budgetary policymaking to help achieve climate and environmental goals." In a more extended version, the European Commission also states that "Green budgeting is a process whereby the environmental contributions of budgetary items and policies are identified and assessed with respect to specific performance indicators, with the objective of better aligning budgetary policies with environmental goals". In the opinion of the OECD,

> Green budgeting is a practice which uses the tools of budgetary policy-making to help achieve 'green' objectives, i.e., those relating to the climate and environmental dimensions such as biodiversity, air quality and water. (...) While by itself green budgeting does not change existing policies, it provides decision-makers with a clearer understanding of the overall environmental and climate impacts of budgeting choices. It brings evidence together in a systematic and co-ordinated manner to allow more informed decision-making on how to optimise revenue-raising and resource allocation in order to fulfil national and international commitments.[9]

In the authors' view, green budgeting can be seen as another layer of budget transparency. Budget transparency is mainly related to the full disclosure of all relevant fiscal information in a timely and systematic manner in order to enable the public to understand the fiscal policy decisions or simply meaning "being fully open with people about how public money is raised and used".[10] Green budgeting practice adds to this financial dimension yet another layer disclosing the impact of the budget on the environment, reinforcing the accountability of decision makers in relation to the achievement of climate goals and therefore contributing to an informed, evidence-based *debate* on *sustainable growth.*

As mentioned by Petrie,[11] the concept of a green budget has been evolving over time, having its roots in the 1987 Brundtland Commission Report[12] that called for "an annual report and an audit of changes in environmental quality and in the stock of the nation's environmental resource assets are needed to complement the traditional annual fiscal budget and economic development plans". The boost to the adoption of what now is known as "green budgeting" was driven by key international commitments on climate change and on inclusive development, particularly the 2015 Paris Agreement that commits countries to keep the average rise in global temperature below 2 degrees Celsius this century, preferably to limit it to 1.5 °C

---

[8] See https://economy-finance.ec.europa.eu/economic-and-fiscal-governance/green-budgeting-eu_en.

[9] OECD (2021c).

[10] OECD (2017).

[11] Petrie (2021).

[12] United Nations General Assembly - UN (1987), Sect. 12, paragraph 27.

above pre-industrial levels, and the adoption of the United Nations Sustainable Development Goals (SDG) also in 2015. In December of 2019, the European Union Green Deal presented by the European Commission[13] included an explicit commitment to foster green budgeting practices in the EU:

> A greater use of green budgeting tools will help to redirect public investment, consumption and taxation to green priorities and away from harmful subsidies. The Commission will work with the Member States to screen and benchmark green budgeting practices. This will make it easier to assess to what extent annual budgets and medium-term fiscal plans take environmental considerations and risks into account, and learn from best practices.[14]

There are some international platforms that currently provide technical support to countries in the process of green transition, including the implementation of green budgeting practices:

(i) The OECD Paris Collaborative on Green Budgeting[15] was launched in 2017 to help countries develop budgetary tools to progress towards national commitments on climate change and the environment. This platform provides technical support to align national policy frameworks towards lower greenhouse gas emissions and environmentally sustainable development.
(ii) The EU Technical Assistance Instrument[16] is a program managed by DG-REFORM which provides training to help Member States acquire technical capacity to develop a green budget framework at a national level, seeking to align national green budget practices with national recommendations of the European Commission in this matter. In 2021, an online training course on the green budget was started for 23 EU Member States, including Portugal, in which the perceptions of experts from the European Commission and from green budget professionals from the OECD were presented.
(iii) The Coalition of Finance Ministers for Climate Action,[17] created in 2019, brings together finance ministers and policymakers from over 70 countries, including Portugal. The work of this coalition is built around the Helsinki Principles that underpin the commitment of finance ministers to align policy actions with the Paris Agreement; promote capacity building, and mutual exchange of knowledge and expertise; integrate climate change in macroeconomic management and public finance; mobilize private climate finance; and develop a financial sector that recognizes mitigation and adaptation.
(iv) The IMF and Climate Change[18] supports its members in addressing the challenges of climate change for which fiscal and macroeconomic policies are an

[13] European Commission (2019).

[14] There are also additional resources on the European Green Deal in a dedicated part of the Europa portal: https://ec.europa.eu/info/strategy/priorities-2019-2024/european-green-deal_en.

[15] https://www.oecd.org/environment/green-budgeting/.

[16] https://commission.europa.eu/overview-funding-programmes/technical-support-instrument-tsi_en#aboutthesrsp.

[17] https://www.financeministersforclimate.org/.

[18] https://www.imf.org/en/Topics/climate-change.

important component of the appropriate policy response. The IMF also publishes research on the economic implications of climate change and provides policy advice on mitigation, adaptation, and transition strategies to help them capture the opportunities of low-carbon, resilient growth.

Although there is no common methodology yet for the implementation of a green budget, several countries initiated this process through differentiated methods with distinct priorities using several instruments. A recently published joint work by the EC, IMF, and OECD[19] describes several tools currently used to implement the green budget, namely: (i) the inclusion of a green perspective in medium-term plans, integrating climate forecasts in macro-fiscal government forecasts; (ii) introducing climate change and environmental degradation in the assessment of fiscal risks to the sustainability of public finances, using a sensitivity analysis to quantify the impacts of unanticipated environmental shocks as well as of gradual transformation environmental shocks; (iii) ex-ante and ex-post evaluation of the impact of environmental policies and systematic use of this information for budget decision making; (iv) adoption of a green perspective in the spending review exercise, ensuring its alignment with environmental and climate policies; (v) green accounting balances through the standardization of definitions and classifications, producing reports that facilitate international comparisons; (vi) institutional design based on a legislated green budgeting process, providing a basis for defining the responsibilities and requirements of the government and other intervening entities focusing on: the role of the ministry of finance, the inclusion of the state-owned enterprises, and the need for evaluation by independent entities, and; (vii) budget tagging of "green" and "brown" elements (discussed below).

Recognizing the need to integrate the challenges to fiscal sustainability posed by climate change, some Independent fiscal institutions already incorporated some work on such risks in their latest sustainability reports. In a non-exhaustive way, it was the case of the United Kingdom,[20] and Portugal.[21]

2.2 *Green Tagging*

Originally, budget classification methodologies were developed with the support of the United Nations Development Program and the World Bank based on the experience acquired in the areas of poverty, gender equality, international development goals, and climate (World Bank 2020). The standardization of the green budget classification was significantly accelerated by the creation of the Rio Markers in 1998 by the OECD Development Assistance Committee. The Rio Markers

[19] Battersby et al (2021).

[20] Office for Budget Responsibility (2021).

[21] Conselho das Finanças Públicas (2021).

constitute a system for evaluating budgetary policies that allow the statistical monitorization and reporting of the development of financial flows on topics covered in the Rio Conventions, namely biodiversity, desertification, climate change mitigation, and adaptation to climate change. There are three possible values for the Rio markers[22] assigned according to the context, objectives and results, and activities analysed: Zero indicates not targeted; One for a significant objective; and Two for a principal objective of fiscal policy. Depending on the value attributed, fixed percentages of the overall budget are considered relevant for the respective themes. The EU has decided to use 0%, 40%, and 100%, respectively.

In recent years, various countries have adopted some degree of green budget tagging in a heterogeneous process. In many cases, this process is adaptive and takes a restricted form at an early stage covering a limited number of budget activities and sectors determined by each country. Thus, with the goal of facilitating the comparison of progress made and finding the means to progressively move towards tagging the budget as comprehensively as possible, a joint effort has been made by the main international institutions in defining the different stages of the budget tagging process.

In the joint EC, IMF, and OECD document,[23] these institutions present two lists that serve as basis for the budget classification at the national level, defining the budget elements that should be classified as "green" (with a favourable impact on the climate or in the environment) or "brown" (adverse impact on climate or environment).[24] These lists are updated on an annual basis on the EC platform for green budgets. There are also other entities that apply some degree of climate or environmental classification with special emphasis for the United Nations that developed the System of Environmental-Economic Accounting (SEEA). It applies the principles of national accounting to the classification and reporting of activities, products, expenses, and other environmental transactions. It is compatible with most national budget systems, facilitating its application by all national authorities in the future. In what regards the procedural steps, the OECD summarizes the green budget tagging implementation methodologies in four phases[25]:

i) Definition of relevant climate and environmental expenditure (what is green?): Use of international or national definitions taking into account national climate and environmental change policy documents;
ii) Definition of the scope of the analysis (which sectors? which elements to rank?): Several countries have started by implementing an adaptive strategy in which the

[22]https://capacity4dev.europa.eu/groups/public-environment-climate/info/short-guide-use-rio-markers_en.

[23]Battersby et al. (2021).

[24]Lists available at: http://www.oecd.org/environment/indicators-modelling-outlooks/policy-instrument-database/, https://ec.europa.eu/eurostat/documents/1798247/6191549/EGSS+list+of+env+products.xlsx, https://ec.europa.eu/eurostat/statistics-explained/images/0/0e/National_tax_lists_20210203.xlsx, http://www.oecd.org/fossil-fuels/.

[25]OECD (2021a).

ranking is applied to few budget elements. After this first phase, the number of elements analysed increases along with the capacity for analysis and training of the human resources involved. In particular, the process generally involves the central government and some key institutions and may, at an early stage and due to the lack of sufficient resources, exclude some sectors, such as the SOE. It is also common to start by classifying only the activities related to climate change and later to extend this classification to other environmental areas as is already practiced in France (more detail in Sect. 3);

iii) Development of a classification system: On projects that indicate climate and environmental change as an objective (binary system), classifying their entire budget, or on activities with climate and environmental relevance, assigning a "climate or environmental weight" to the fraction of that activity that will be related to the climate or the environment (scale system);

iv) Identification of information needs: Countries that adopt the binary system do not need as detailed information as those that adopt the scale system. In the former system, countries tag items according to their favourable or unfavourable contribution to green objectives while, in the latter system, budgetary appropriations are tagged according to the extent to which they promote green objectives.

The biggest advantage of the green budget tagging lies in the transparency and transmission of relevant information that it provides. Indeed, this method promotes discussion and knowledge sharing among civil society, instilling greater responsibility and commitment on the government and agencies involved in the process as well as greater visibility of their actions. In this sense, the effectiveness of the budget classification could also benefit from an alignment with other tools that are still minimally used such as the addition of a green dimension to the assessment of budgetary performance,[26] namely in the debt sustainability analysis exercise. A study by Pizarro et al.[27] argues that any climate and environmental classification methodology is strengthened if connected to the broad existing statistical framework. This is namely to public sector financial accounts and the System of Environmental-Economic Accounting, being consistent with statistical standards currently in use such as the Government Finance Statistics Framework and the System of National Accounts. Otherwise, the methodology may identify climate actions and their expenditures adequately but may not be consistent or comparable or may be of limited use for analytical purposes.

Despite the progress made so far, there is still significant challenges to green budgeting regarding:

- *Ex-ante impact:* In what concerns resource allocation and project design, the impact of tagging does not yet seem to be of great importance since it is usually assigned only after the project approval. However, the existence of the classification *per se* could motivate greater environmental and climate awareness on the

[26] OECD (2021a).

[27] Pizarro et al. (2021).

investment decision making process, providing access to the information allowing the alignment of new projects with climate and environmental objectives. There are still some aspects to be improved in the implementation of this system which may be overcome after the initial implementation phase, such as (i) the significant omissions of the sectors covered (in several cases, public companies, tax expenditure, or external financing); (ii) the need to tag not only activities with a favourable impact on the climate or environment but also those with an unfavourable impact, which is still minimally used; (iii) functional limitations and costs related to the budget process itself (limited resources and technical capacity); and (iv) a greater focus on expenditure than on revenue (taxes on carbon, on fossil fuels, permits on resource exploitation, etc.) for which funds could be channelled towards climate and environmental expenditure, demonstrating a link that is generally of simple communication to civil society and; (v) greater granularity in the classification of budget elements could promote a more accurate calculation of the respective impacts;
- *Ex-post impact:* It is difficult to quantify the impact of budget tagging in part due to the inability of this system to simultaneously and adequately consider the three dimensions of the evaluation of results, namely the (i) political alignment; (ii) efficiency; and (iii) the effectiveness of climate and environmental policy measures. The simple classification of this methodology does not allow a global consideration of the macro-fiscal impact of climate and environmental policies in all its aspects, focusing only on the analysis that is easier to quantify – the allocation of resources through budget expenditure. According to the World Bank, countries rarely do systematic post-monitoring of budgeted climate and environment-related expenditures. The lack of assessment of the results achieved by policies adopted makes it difficult to use this information later in the preparation of future budgets.[28]

However, a word of caution should be added when an unfavourable expenditure is found as a result of the tagging process. As duly noted by the French Government, which is systematically applying green tagging, finding a "brown" expenditure does not necessarily mean that it should be eradicated:

> Tagging an expenditure as unfavourable is not enough to conclude it needs to be eliminated; it may respond to the requirements of another policy deemed to be a priority, such as public safety, balanced local development, equitable access to public services, or the availability of basic necessities. The value of green budget tagging is that it highlights such priorities, raises questions about the right policy tools and, if environmentally unfavourable expenditures need to be maintained, it may lead to efforts to mitigate their impact. In most cases, mixed expenditures are investment expenditures that have a favourable impact in the medium term with regard to climate goals, even though construction may harm the environment in the short term. This is the case for major mass transport infrastructure projects, for example.[29]

[28] OECD (2021a).

[29] France Gouvernement (2021).

2.3 Green Bonds

Green bonds are defined as debt securities issued by an entity that is committed to earmarking the invested funds to projects focused on climate and environmental sustainability (energy efficiency, pollution prevention, non-polluting transports, water management). The first principles[30] for a Green Bond were defined by the International Capital Markets Association (ICMA),[31] focusing on the eligibility of the projects to which the funds are allocated and in the reporting transparency. At the same time, the Climate Bonds Initiative developed more restrictive criteria[32] that were less disseminated. These criteria included a taxonomy defining green activities along with a certification and approval by green bonds external auditors. Afterwards, the need for uniformization and regulation in the green bond market was recognized. In 2019, the EC made a recommendation for the adoption of the EU Green Bond Standard[33] and, in 2020, two lists of activities considered sustainable in the EU were approved by the EC in the delegated acts published in December 2021[34] and February 2022.[35] In June 2020, the EU Taxonomy Regulation (Regulation (EU) 2020/852 of 18 June 2020) was published in the Official Journal of the European Union, entering into force in the following month, with the goals of "creating security for investors, protect private investors from greenwashing, help companies to become more climate-friendly, mitigate market fragmentation and help shift investments where they are most needed",[36] according to the EC.

The first green bond—a climate awareness bond—was issued by the European Investment Bank (EIB) in 2007. It was followed by the World Bank in 2008 in an operation with the participation of Scandinavian pension funds looking to finance the transition to lower carbon emissions. Other entities such as investment banks, public enterprises, financial institutions, and sovereigns started issuing green bonds; according to the OECD,[37] more than USD 130 billion of green bonds were issued by 19 different sovereigns until the end of 2020.

Particularly since 2017, there is evidence of a fast growth of the green bond market explained by the larger demand by socially and environmentally committed investors. In some sense, green bonds changed the investors rationale, offering them

[30] See https://www.icmagroup.org/sustainable-finance/the-principles-guidelines-and-handbooks/green-bond-principles-gbp.

[31] ICMA (2018).

[32] See https://www.climatebonds.net/climate-bonds-standard-v3.

[33] See https://finance.ec.europa.eu/sustainable-finance/tools-and-standards/european-green-bond-standard_en#recommendations.

[34] See https://finance.ec.europa.eu/publications/sustainable-finance-package_en#taxonomy.

[35] See https://finance.ec.europa.eu/publications/eu-taxonomy-complementary-climate-delegated-act-accelerate-decarbonisation_en.

[36] https://ec.europa.eu/info/business-economy-euro/banking-and-finance/sustainable-finance/eu-taxonomy-sustainable-activities_en.

[37] OECD (2021b).

the possibility to choose to what type of projects their funds are allocated.[38] Traditional debt management goals – access to budget efficient financing and building of a liquid yield curve – seem to have been adapted to accommodate green bonds programmes. In an enquiry to sovereign issuers conducted by the Climate Bonds Initiative (CBI) on the motivation for issuing a green bond over a traditional one, the respondents referred the attainment of new objectives such as reputational benefits, investors demand, and mitigation of climate change related to green bonds.[39] Additionally, issuers state that the international commitments assumed under the scope of fighting climate change have contributed favourably to the decision of issuing green bonds. Until the end of March 2021, 10 European countries had issued green bonds with a total amount of EUR 82 billion.[40]

Recently, the Next Generation EU contributed largely to green bonds dynamism: From the global envelope of EUR 750 billion available in response to the pandemic crisis, 30% (roughly EUR 250 billion) will be financed thought this type of security (to be issued by the European Commission). In October 2021, the EC, representing the EU, performed the largest green bonds issuance so far and the first under the scope of Next Generation EU amounting to EUR 12 billion with redemption in 2037. Additionally, all SURE bonds were issued as "social" bonds. Those qualify, respectively, under the Green Bond Principles and Social Bond Principles established by the ICMA.

Growth in the green bond market reflects the main advantage of this type of security, i.e., the signalling of the associated commitment with climate and environmental objectives. Hence, given the extent of the maturities and end-loaded payment structure of typical infrastructure projects, these instruments are expected to be crucial for financing the energy transition process.[41] However, some relevant limitations to this market persist. Due to the absence of a group of rules and directives, these debt instruments (i) can have a negative impact in the process of compliance with sovereign debt management principles[42] since they are not issued efficiently, implying a time and resource-consuming report, and (ii) the impact of the green investment is difficult to quantify. More information and transparency are still needed, ensuring that green investments are correctly directed to new sustainable projects and not to other ongoing expenditures – greenwashing – due to the fungibility of financial resources (see Fig. 1).

The issuance of green bonds implies additional costs vis-à-vis a traditional sovereign bond issuance due to the need of identifying the project(s) to be financed, the need of elaborating regular reports providing performance indicators of the objectives to be attained by such project(s), and a less liquid and less deep market.

[38] Reichelt and Keenan (2017).

[39] Harrison and Muething (2021).

[40] On green bond issuance in European countries by the end of March 2021, see Domínguez-Jiménez and Lehmann (2021).

[41] Lehmann (2021).

[42] Domínguez-Jiménez and Lehmann (2021).

Fig. 1 Global green bonds issuance 2014–2021 (USD billion). *Source*: Climate Bonds Initiative database (available at www.climatebonds.net/market/data)

	Total	Supranational
2014	37	9
2015	46	8,3
2016	85	10,2
2017	160	9,5
2018	173	12,7
2019	269	14,4
2020	298	13,5
2021	509	13,3

Therefore, it is relevant to know whether such kinds of bonds have or do not have a negative spread versus traditional ones. In recent years, several authors studied the presence of a green bond premium. The green bond premium (greenium) can be defined as the difference in yield between thematic bonds and regular bonds of a similar maturity based on the rationale that investors are willing to pay a superior amount for a bond with a sustainable impact.[43] According to the same United Nations blog post, there are several technical arguments that support the existence of a greenium: (i) the sustainability factor associated with a green bond is credit positive since it implies lower global risk, resulting in a lower yield relatively to a vanilla bond and therefore at a higher price for investors; (ii) excess demand for (sustainable) bonds results in higher prices for investors, and (iii) the sustainable features result in a willingness from investors to accept a lower return for a thematic bond.

While, in the past, some studies suggested mixed evidence on the existence and signal of the greenium,[44] the most recent data supports a positive green bond premium.[45] In general, there is an agreement on the existence of a greenium mainly driven by the simple fact that demand outpaces supply. The CBI found that the premium on green bonds is evident globally and is particularly strong for US dollar denominated debt with savings for borrowers ranging between 1 basis point and 10 basis points on a global basis.[46] Moreover, the finding that green bonds including external evaluations can contribute to increasing the premium on green bonds[47] supports the recognition of the value that the bond sustainable features have for socially responsible investors. In fact, investors accept larger premiums (up to 5 basis points) in cases when there is a substantial environmental agenda, externally validated, reducing information search costs and uncertainty.[48] This recognition by investors of the need to implement green perspectives in public financial

[43] D'Incau et al (2022).

[44] Bachelet et al. (2019) and Harrison and Filkova (2019).

[45] Baker et al. (2018), D'Incau, et al. (2022) and Harrison (2022).

[46] Harrison (2022).

[47] Gutsche and Zwergel (2020), pp. 111–157.

[48] Dorfleitner et al. (2022), pp. 797–834.

management, given that the achievement of climate and environmental goals contribute to the decrease in global risk, supports the case for the inclusion of such tools into a debt sustainability analysis.

3 The Case Study of the Adoption of Green Budgeting by France

Although, to this date, only very few countries have some form of green budgeting in place, some of them have already made considerable advances in green budgeting. In a recent paper, Bova[49] makes a first review of green budgeting practices in the EU. Petrie[50] also presents experiences from developing economies that are not part of the OECD. For the sake of brevity, in this section, the focus will be on France that can be seen as one of the best practices in Europe.

France presented its first green budget report in 2020 included within the global fiscal process and an appendix to the budget bill published in the first week of October. Article 179 of the 2020 Budget Act 2019–1479 of 28 December 2019 stipulates that the government submits to Parliament, as an appendix to the budget bill, a report on the environmental impact of the budget. It resulted from the OECD initiative, the "Paris Collaborative on Green Budgeting" launched at the One Planet Summit in December 2017. The report, called "Rapport sur l'Impact Environnemental du Budget de L'État", presents the tagging of budgeat appropriations, earmarked-revenue, and some tax expenditures as favourable, neutral, or unfavourable for the environment and their share of total central government expenditure. The more recent edition introduced methodological refinements including a finer tagging of certain expenditures and clearer differentiation between expenditures tagged as neutral and the year's expenditures that have not been tagged because of methodological difficulties.[51] Besides the report, there is also an open data website that represents the data in an interactive way, showing the aggregate figures and a break down by mission.[52]

The classification identifies the impact of expenditures on six environmental objectives that were inspired by the European taxonomy of activities: Fighting climate change; adapting to climate change and preventing natural risks; water management; transition to the circular economy, waste management, and man-made risk prevention; fighting water, air, and soil pollution; and conservation of biodiversity as well as protection of natural, agricultural, and forest areas. A score of −1 to +3 is given to each expenditure for each of the environmental objectives according to the environmental impact of the expenditure. To facilitate

[49] Bova (2021).

[50] Petrie (2021).

[51] France Gouvernement (2021).

[52] https://datavision.economie.gouv.fr/budget-vert/.

Table 1 Tags for expenditure at the more disaggregated level in the French case

Colour	Designation	Scores
Green	Favourable expenditures	*Score 3*: Environmentally targeted expenditures or expenditures contributing directly to the production of an environmental good or service (green activity) *Score 2*: Expenditures with no explicit environmental target, but with an indirect positive impact *Score 1*: Favourable but controversial expenditures with favourable short-term effects but a potential technology lock-in risk in the long term
Grey	Neutral expenditures	*Score 0*: Expenditures with no significant impact on the environment
Brown	Unfavourable expenditures	*Score−1*: Expenditures causing direct harm to the environment or creating incentives for environmentally harmful behaviour

Source: France Gouvernement (2021)

communication, the green budget report aggregates the scores into the colours green for favourable expenditures, grey for neutral ones, and brown for unfavourable expenditures. The report retains only the aggregated colour as the detailed numerical scores are only available on the mentioned website (Table 1).

This classification is applied to the expenditures disaggregated by action or sub-action, and an overall tag is then calculated depending on the total scores for all of the six objectives. Therefore, an expenditure may be tagged as:

- favourable overall: if impacts are favourable or favourable and neutral for all objectives;
- unfavourable overall: if impacts are unfavourable or unfavourable and neutral for all objectives;
- mixed overall: if impacts are simultaneously favourable and unfavourable and even neutral for different objectives; and
- neutral overall: if impacts are neutral for all objectives.

In the latest edition of the report, neutral expenditures are distinguished from untagged expenditures which are "expenditures where environmental impacts cannot be assessed reliably or no consensus can be reached, given the current state of scientific knowledge or a lack of available data". The 2022 report gives examples of neutral and untagged expenditures. Social transfers to households, most expenditures on central government payrolls and retirement pensions, and sovereign expenditures were tagged as neutral. Untagged expenditures were represented by a grey and white striped area in the budget mission ring charts and comprised "digital technology expenditures, the levy on revenue paid to the European Union, most of the financial support given to local governments, support for electricity-intensive industries exposed to international competition, some operating expenditure (see Table 2), some property expenditures and some of the expenditures for the 'Invest for the Future' mission."

As documented in Table 2, the bulk of the French Central Government expenditures, including tax expenditures, were found to have a neutral impact on the

Table 2 Summary of Green Tagging of the expenditures covered by the Total Central Government Expenditures Target (ODETE) in France, 2022 budget (EUR bn)

	Expenditures	Tax expenditures	Total with tax expenditures	Weight on total
Environmental impact, of which:	42.0	11.4	53.4	9%
- Favourable	34.8	3.4	38.2	7%
- Mixed	4.0	0.4	4.5	1%
- Unfavourable	3.2	7.6	10.8	2%
Neutral impact	354.7	78.4	433.1	74%
Not tagged	98.5	1.6	100.1	17%
Total	495.1	91.5	586.6	100%

Sources: France Gouvernement (2021) and the data portal and own calculations. | Notes: The favourable expenditures include the "Recovery Plan" Mission (EUR 5.7bn). The sum of the parcels may not coincide with the total due to rounding effects

environment (74%), and 17% were still not yet tagged. Of the expenditures with an environmental impact (9% of the total), almost 3/4 were found favourable. The website informs that the largest budget appropriation with a favourable impact was the development of renewable energy, and the most relevant tax expenditure was the reduced VAT at 5.5% for the improvement of energy efficiency.

The 2022 Report envisages going further in the future in what regards the inclusion of a more specific estimate of the adequacy of public financing of the country's climate objectives and the adequacy of carbon pricing to achieve the climate objectives.

4 Portugal: Steps Taken and Lessons To Be Learned

4.1 What Has Been Done

Portugal has already taken some steps in relation to climate and environmental goals but still has a long way to go in terms of green budgeting. First of all, it is important to mention that Portugal has shown full commitment to climate and environment matters and was even one of the first countries to prepare a Roadmap for Carbon Neutrality by 2050.[53] Other national commitments are the National Energy and Climate Plan 2021–2030[54] (under which Portugal has committed to reach, by the year 2030, 47% of renewable sources in final energy consumption and to reduce primary energy consumption through energy efficiency gains of 35%), the National

[53] Approved by the Resolution of the Council of Ministers no. 107/2019.

[54] Approved by the Resolution of the Council of Ministers no. 53/2020.

Strategy for Adaptation to Climate Change,[55] and the Action Program for Adaptation to Climate Change (2019–2030).[56]

Recognizing the climate emergency and following the best practices (the United Kingdom being the pioneer with its Climate Change Act of 2008 that served as a model for other countries), Parliament approved the Portuguese Climate Law in the end of 2021 (Law No. 98/2021 of 31 December) which recognizes citizens' right to climate balance and commits to achieving climate neutrality by 2050. This law stipulates the creation of a Climate Action Council that will act as an independent advisory body with duties such as issuing opinions on the state budget and the state general account with regards to climate action; comment on scenarios for the decarbonization of the economy; presenting biennial recommendations on the development of energy and transport infrastructures and; if requested by the government and Parliament, comment about the elaboration, discussion, and approval of legislative acts, reports, and public policy instruments on climate action.

According to the Portuguese Climate Law, budgetary allocations for climate policy purposes should be consolidated into a specific account of the state budget, and climate scenarios should be integrated in the models underlying the macroeconomic scenarios that support the state budget. The law also determines that the government must create a "Climate Action Portal" (free and accessible on the internet, to allow citizens to participate in the path of climate action and to monitor all of the relevant information). Additionally, there must be a new category of tax deductions (Green Personal Income Tax) that benefits taxpayers that acquire, consume, or use environmentally sustainable goods and services and therefore adopt an individual behaviour that defends the environment and reduces the ecological footprint.

In the opinion of Mackaill-Hill & Mascolo,[57] the Portuguese Climate Law lacks ambition in some sections, such as the ban on the sale of combustion vehicles, lagging behind the EU's proposal in its Fit-for-55 package, or the end of subsidies for fossil fuels planned only for 2030. Not all Member States have adopted national climate laws yet, and not all climate laws are equally strong. This means the European Climate Law adopted in July of 2021 [Regulation (EU) 2021/1119] will be implemented against a background of highly inconsistent standards of national climate ambition and governance enabling conditions.[58]

Some other relevant decisions were taken previously by the Portuguese Government. In late 2014, a Green Taxation Reform[59] was introduced with the aim of simultaneously guaranteeing the balance of public accounts and sustainable growth. This reform revised and simplified taxation in the energy and transport, water, waste, urban planning and territorial planning, forests and biodiversity sectors, and

[55] Approved by the Resolution of the Council of Ministers no. 24/2020.

[56] Approved by the Resolution of the Council of Ministers no. 130/2019.

[57] Mackaill-Hill and Mascolo (2022).

[58] Mackaill-Hill and Mascolo (2022).

[59] Established by Law 82-D/2014, of 31 December.

introduced a tax regime for plastic bags and encouraged the scrapping of end-of-life vehicles. The Investment Tax Code[60] was also approved in 2014 aiming at the review of the investment and capitalization benefit regimes through the establishment of the Tax Incentive System in Business Research and Development which establishes that expenses related to R&D activities associated with ecological product design projects are considered at 110%.

In 2016, a carbon tax was introduced as a complement to the taxation on oil products which, in 2021, was extended[61] to the issuance of commercial passenger air transport tickets when departing from airports and aerodromes located in Portuguese territory as compensation for the polluting emissions from the sector and other negative environmental effects.

Additionally, in 2016, the Environmental Fund (*Fundo Ambiental*) was created[62] aiming at a more effective environment policy, concentrating the resources of existing funds (for this purpose, the Portuguese Carbon Fund, the Environmental Intervention Fund, the Water Resources Protection Fund, and the Fund for the Conservation of Nature and Biodiversity were extinguished). This fund's aim is to finance entities, activities, or projects that pursue sustainable development objectives, contributing to the fulfilment of national and international objectives and commitments, namely those relating to climate change, water resources, waste, and the conservation of nature and biodiversity.[63]

Although Portugal has not adopted the green tagging technique yet, in the letter with instructions for preparing the state budget issued by the Directorate-General for the Budget, public services are urged to use a specific measure to identify "Climate action initiatives" other than the ones included in the Recovery and Resilience Plan (Box 1).

Box 1 The Recovery and Resilience Plan in the context of climate objectives The Recovery and Resilience Mechanism (RRM) is the main instrument of the Next Generation-EU. In order to align the use of RRM financial resources (€750 billion, at 2018 prices) with European priorities, the RRM regulation[64] determined that its scope should be focused on six relevant pillars, the first of which corresponds to the green transition.

According to the article 18(e) of the RRM regulation, the recovery and resilience plan (RRP) of each member state must contain a qualitative explanation of how the measures contained therein are expected to contribute to the green transition, including biodiversity, or to addressing the challenges resulting therefrom, and whether these measures correspond to an amount representing at least 37% of the total RRP allocation.

---

[60] See Decree-Law No. 162/2014, 31 of October.

[61] See Ordinance No. 38/2021, 16 of February.

[62] Created by the Decree-Law 42-A/2016, of 12 August.

[63] The role of this Environmental Fund as an instrument for climate transition is detailed in (Marujo et al. 2022).

[64] https://eur-lex.europa.eu/legal-content/en/TXT/PDF/?uri=CELEX:32021R0241&from=en.

The RRP of Portugal[65] was approved by the European Council in July 2021 with a total allocation of €16.6 billion (of which around €14 billion in the form of grants), directed to three dimensions: Resilience (€11.1 billion); Climate Transition (€3.1 billion) and Digital Transition (€2.5 billion). Portugal's initial RRP contains measures to support climate objectives that account to €6.3 billion, which represents 37.9% of the plan's total allocation (Table 5, according to the EC's Analysis of the RRP of Portugal,[66] using the methodology for climate tracking set out in Annex VI of the RRM Regulation (Member States had to identify in advance whether the reforms and investments foreseen in their RRP contribute to supporting climate and environmental objectives in full [coefficient 100%], partial [40%] or if they have no impact on these goals [0%]).

The reforms and investments foreseen in Portugal's initial RRP are structured into 20 components, the majority (16) of which contribute to climate objectives. As would be expected, the structuring dimension related to the climate transition is the one with the highest percentage of investment allocation to climate requirements (95.2%), which will be channelled to each of its six components, with emphasis on investments aimed at promoting sustainable mobility (€967 million), the decarbonisation of industry (€715 million), the energy efficiency in buildings (€610 million). Within the scope of the structural dimension regarding resilience (with an allocation of 30.3% to those requirements), its nine components have a complementary relevance in terms of contribution to the green transition, with emphasis on housing (€1220 million) and forests (€615 million) (Fig. 2).

European Commission's first annual report on the implementation of the RRM states that the expenditure on climate in all the 22 RRP that have already been approved amounts to €177.4 billion. Those plans include €16.3 billion of additional environmental expenditure, taking the total amount of expenditure that is tagged as contributing to either climate or environmental objectives to €193.7 billion (equivalent to 43.5% of the total expenditure foreseen in the RRP of those 22 member states). About two-thirds of these countries' expenditure to support the green transition is focused in the areas of sustainable mobility and energy efficiency.

The RRP implementation process should ensure compliance with all applicable environmental standards, but also ensure that all measures included in the RRP respect the principle of the "do no significant harm"[67] to the following environmental objectives: (i) climate change mitigation; (ii) adaptation to climate change; (iii) sustainable use and protection of water and marine resources; (iv) circular economy; (v) pollution prevention and control; (vi) protection and restoration of biodiversity and ecosystems.

[65] https://recuperarportugal.gov.pt/wp-content/uploads/2021/10/PRR.pdf.

[66] https://commission.europa.eu/system/files/com_321_7_swd_en.pdf.

[67] https://eur-lex.europa.eu/legal-content/EN/TXT/PDF/?uri=CELEX:52021XC0218(01)&from=EN.

Component	Cost	Climate contribution	% allocation to climate requirement
CLIMATE TRANSITION	**3 059**	**2 911**	**95.2%**
Sustainable mobility	967	967	100.0%
Decarbonisation of industry	715	715	100.0%
Energy efficiency in buildings	610	610	100.0%
Hydrogen and renewables	370	370	100.0%
Sea	252	110	43.7%
Bioeconomy	145	139	95.9%
RESILIENCE	**11 125**	**3 372**	**30.3%**
Housing	2 733	1 220	44.6%
Forests	615	615	100.0%
Investment and innovation	2 914	521	17.9%
National Health Service	1 383	315	22.8%
Water management	390	157	40.3%
Social responses	833	211	25.3%
Qualifications and skills	1 324	182	13.7%
Infrastructures	690	91	13.2%
Culture	243	60	24.7%
DIGITAL TRANSITION	**2 460**	**9**	**0.4%**
Digital public administration	578	9	1.6%
Other components	1 882	0	0.0%
TOTAL	**16 644**	**6 291**	**37.9%**

Fig. 2 Portugal's initial RRP: Allocation to the climate requirement (EUR million). *Source*: European Commission (Analysis of Portugal's RRP, 16 June 2021 (https://eur-lex.europa.eu/legal-content/EN/TXT/PDF/?uri=CELEX:52021SC0146&from=EN)). CFP calculations. | Note: the amount of the total estimated costs of the initial RRP (16,644 M€) is higher than the global allocation of the plan (€16.606 million), which corresponds to the financial allocation after deducting the proportional part of Portugal's proportional share of expenses under the terms of article 6 (2) of Regulation (EU) 2021/241, plus support in the form of a loan requested by Portugal under the mechanism

Only a few member states have incorporated measures to support the implementation of green budgeting practices in their RRP.[68] Austria plans to create a structure in the Ministry of Finance that is responsible for implementing green budgeting standards in the budget process and conducting climate-related impact assessments. Spain plans to prepare a "green report" to accompany the annual budget, identifying "green" and "brown" expenditure items, and France intends to expand the spectrum of analysis to other expenditures. Italy plans to reclassify the state budget, with reference to environmental expenditures, in line with the sustainable development goals and 2030 agenda targets, and Slovenia plans to develop and implement a methodology to assess the impact of each budgetary appropriation on environmental objectives, in line with the EU taxonomy.

In its analysis of Portugal's RRP, published in June 2021, the European Commission underlines that Portugal does not use green budgeting practices, which could help fulfil national and international commitments on climate change and environmental protection.

[68] Battersby et al. (2021).

4.2 What Needs To Be Done: A Possible Roadmap

Portugal still misses the full implementation of a modern public financial management system based on the adoption of accrual accounting and performance budgeting.

The incomplete adoption of accrual accounting, namely the absence of a full financial balance sheet, makes the disclosure of the nonfinancial impacts of fiscal policy more difficult.[69] Despite the progress made in the adaptation of International Public Sector Accounting Standards (IPSAS) by the different public services, the full adoption of accrual accounting is quite delayed, particularly in what regards the consolidation of the accounts, the creation of the first State balance sheet, and its use in the budget itself which is still approved in cash accounting only.

Additionally, the practice of performance budgeting supports green budgeting as recognized by Battersby et al..[70] When the budget is organized around budgetary programmes, and particularly in a more advanced case of performance budgeting, it is easier to link inputs (public expenditure) with outcomes by means of performance indicators. In 2006, Portugal started to introduce programme budgeting seeking to achieve performance budgeting.[71] However, the practical progress on that front has been so limited that the 2015 Budgetary Framework Law still calls for the adoption of programme budgeting, and even that has not yet been implemented.[72]

The provisions of the Portuguese Climate Law should also be incorporated into the Budgetary Framework Law (BFL) in order to be applied to the budget process. As a matter of fact, Article 106 of the Constitution of the Portuguese Republic requires that "the Budget Law shall be annually drawn up, organised, put to the vote and implemented in accordance with the applicable framework law". As a result, for the dispositions of the climate law to have an impact on the budget process, they should necessarily be included in the BFL.

The accomplishment of all of these essential preconditions will lay the foundations for the implementation of green budgeting in Portugal but, even after that, a lot of work will have to be done. As suggested by Gonguet et al.,[73] the process for a successful adoption of a green budget requires the elaboration of an action plan that foresees the role to be played by each of the institutions involved, the agents responsible for coordinating this plan, and the deadlines to be met.

[69] Petrie (2021), p. 77.

[70] Battersby et al. (2021), p. 18.

[71] OECD (2009), pp. 160, 79. https://www.oecd.org/portugal/42007470.pdf.

[72] Formally, the Portuguese State Budget is organized as a programme budget but with just one programme per ministry (two for the Ministry of Finance) without any performance indicators associated which, in practice, is not different from the previous "organic classification of expenditure"

[73] Gonguet et al. (2021).

In view of the benchmark provided by the OECD,[74] the following procedures are still missing in Portugal: (i) Green tagging of budgetary items in order to identify the favourable, unfavourable, or neutral impact in climate and environmental terms; (ii) Environmental cost-benefit analysis of the fiscal policy measures to be implemented; (iii) Assessment of the state budget's environmental performance from the point of view of the proportion of environmental policy objectives contained therein; (iv) Auditing of the State Budget according to an environmental perspective by an independent entity such as the Court of Auditors or the Climate Action Council; (v) Regular reviews of tax expenditure and subsidies according to their impact on climate and environment; (vi) General government spending review from a green perspective in order to assess its contribution to the pursuit of defined environmental objectives; (vii) Quantification of greenhouse gases associated with the state budget and with each of the fiscal policy measures to be adopted; (viii) Inclusion of climate and environmental considerations in long-term fiscal sustainability analyses; and (ix) Adoption of a green balance sheet that includes assets and liabilities related to the country's natural resources.

In terms of the institutional framework on which the implementation of the green budgeting process in Portugal should be based, the following factors should be considered: (i) All of the procedural steps necessary for the preparation of a green budget (including green tagging of public expenditure and revenue) should be incorporated in the Budgetary Framework Law; (ii) A coordinating entity for the green budgeting process should be designated based on the knowledge and technical capacity to implement it. In Portugal, the most suitable institution to carry out this mission seems to be the Directorate-General for the Budget (DGO), notwithstanding it will need to work closely with the line ministries, particularly with the ministry of the environment; and (iii) Operationalization of the Climate Action Council (CAC), created by the recently approved Portuguese Climate Law. In the authors' opinion, as the Portuguese independent fiscal institution, the Public Finance Council (CFP) should be represented in the CAC given that the CFP is responsible for assessing compliance with the established budgetary rules and the sustainability of national public finances.

According to the best international practices, namely those of the most advanced countries in green budgeting (Italy and France), the reporting of green budget information should be based on the regular publication of the following documents: (i) An annex to the State Budget proposal including information about green tagging of the budgetary items by program and ministry, the ex-ante evaluation of the environmental performance of the budget regarding the pursuit of environmental objectives, the environmental cost-benefit analysis of the proposed policy measures, the forecast of tax expenditure according to its environmental impact, and the forecast of the impact of the State Budget proposal on the emission of greenhouse gases; (ii) An annual report about the execution of environmental expenditures and revenues in the previous year in order to provide an ex-post assessment; (iii) An

[74] OECD (2021c).

Annex to the Tax Expenditure Reports including the identification of tax expenditures and subsidies granted according to their favourable, unfavourable, or neutral impact on climate and the environment; and (iv) Publication of all relevant climate and environmental data in a public portal (as already envisaged in the Portuguese Climate Law).

5 Conclusions

Nowadays, it is rather consensual that the financial sustainability of public finances and environmental sustainability are intrinsically interconnected with each other. In fact, only sustainable public finances can provide the resources needed for counteracting the adverse effects of climate change, and only a sustainable environment can preserve the sustainability of public finances. Therefore, the traditional public debt sustainability analysis should be expanded to encompass the climate and environmental dimensions. In this context, greening national budgets is key for climate action and the green transition because budgets are one of the main expressions of how a government intends to implement its political ambition.

Green budgeting is a relatively new practice that is being adopted by a growing number of countries based on its potential to align fiscal policy objectives with climate and environmental goals. The green tagging technique allows the disclosure of the environmental and climate impacts (favourable, unfavourable, or neutral) of fiscal policy on both the revenue and spending sides of the State Budget. It makes clear the environmental costs and benefits underlying the economic policy measures and helps better identifying green financing needs. Therefore, one of the main advantages of green budgeting is to increase fiscal transparency, allowing policy makers to take more informed decisions and contributing to a more informed debate on sustainable growth.

The adoption of green budgeting might also pave the way to the issuance of green bonds to finance specific environmental and climate related projects. Such bonds might be a cost-effective way to finance the substantial green investment needs in a highly indebted country while contributing to the decrease of global risk.

In Europe, France and Italy stand out as the countries with the best green budgeting practices. A proper working fiscal framework including the adoption of accrual accounting and performance programme budgeting and the incorporation of climate and environmental risks into the fiscal risk statements seem to be instrumental in this domain. It is important that, in the near future, the coverage of green budgeting practices can be expanded to include subnational governments and other general government entities. Political commitment is also crucial for the implementation of green budgeting.

Portugal has already taken a few steps with the most recent being the approval of a climate law but still has a long way to go in terms of green budgeting. First of all, the reforms of its public accounting should be completed as well as the programme budgeting foreseen in the current Budgetary Framework Law reformed in 2015. The fulfilment of these preconditions will lay the foundations for the implementation of green budgeting in Portugal following the best international practices in terms of the procedures, the institutional framework, and the way of reporting green budget information.

Finally, it is important to stress that the real challenge is to make sure that green budgeting represents more than just a theoretical exercise and that concrete progress is made in taking the climate and environmental dimensions into the design of public policies that have their financial dimension in the elaboration and execution of the general government budget.

References

Bachelet MJ et al (2019) The green bonds premium puzzle: the role of issuer characteristics and third-party verification. Sustainability 11(4):1098. https://doi.org/10.3390/su11041098

Baker MP et al (2018) Financing the response to climate change: the pricing and ownership of U.S. green bonds. SSRN Electron J. https://doi.org/10.2139/ssrn.3275327

Balassone F, Franco D (2000) Assessing Fiscal Sustainability: a review of methods with a view to EMU.,Banca D'Italia, 21–60. https://www.bancaditalia.it/pubblicazioni/altri-atti-convegni/2000-fiscal-sustainability/021-060_balassone_and_franco.pdf?language_id=1

Battersby B et al (2021) Green budgeting: towards common principles. https://doi.org/10.2765/51675

Bova E (2021) Green budgeting practices in the EU: a first review, European Economy - Discussion Paper No. 140. https://doi.org/10.2765/94030

D'Incau F et al (2022) Identifying the 'greenium': How UNDP is contributing to a more efficient cost of capital for developing countries. https://www.undp.org/blog/identifying-'greenium'

Domínguez-Jiménez M, Lehmann A (2021) Accounting for climate policies in Europe's sovereign debt market, Policy Contribution No. 10/2021. https://www.bruegel.org/2021/05/accounting-for-climate-policies-in-europes-sovereign-debt-market/

Dorfleitner G et al (2022) The pricing of green bonds: external reviews and the shades of green. Rev Manag Sci 16(3):797–834. https://doi.org/10.1007/s11846-021-00458-9

European Commission (2021) Analysis of the recovery and resilience plan of Portugal, Commission Staff Working Paper SWD(2021) 146 final, June, https://eur-lex.europa.eu/legalcontent/EN/TXT/PDF/?uri=CELEX:52021SC0146&from=EN

Gonguet F et al (2021) Climate-sensitive management of public finances - "Green PFM, MF Staff Climate Note No. 2021/002. https://www.imf.org/en/Publications/staff-climate-notes/Issues/2021/08/10/Climate-Sensitive-Management-of-Public-Finances-Green-PFM-460635

Gutsche G, Zwergel B (2020) Investment barriers and Labeling schemes for socially responsible investments. Schmalenbach Bus Rev 72(2):111–157. https://doi.org/10.1007/s41464-020-00085-z

Hamilton JD, Flavin MA (1986) On the limitations of government borrowing : a framework for empirical testing. Am Econ Rev 76(4):808–819. https://doi.org/10.3386/w1632

Harrison C (2022) Green bond pricing in the primary market H2 2021. Climate Bonds Initiative, March, https://www.climatebonds.net/resources/reports/green-bond-pricing-primary-market-h2-2021

Harrison C, Filkova M (2019) Green bond pricing in the primary market July–December 2018. https://www.climatebonds.net/files/reports/cbi_gb_pricing_2h2018_08052019.pdf

Harrison C, Muething L (2021) Sovereign green, social, and sustainability bond survey. https://www.climatebonds.net/files/reports/cbi-sovereign-green-social-sustainability-bond-survey-jan2021.pdf

Lehmann A (2021) The EU green bond standard: sensible implementation could define a new asset class, Bruegel Blog, 12 July. https://www.bruegel.org/2021/07/the-eu-green-bond-standard-sensible-implementation-could-define-a-new-asset-class/

Mackaill-Hill H, Mascolo F (2022) Climate laws in Europe. Essential for achieving climate neutrality. https://caneurope.org/content/uploads/2022/05/2022_04_Climate-laws-briefing-ENG.pdf
Marinheiro CF (2006) The sustainability of Portuguese fiscal policy from a historical perspective. Empirica 33(2–3):155–179. https://doi.org/10.1007/s10663-006-9013-0
Marujo E, Gonçalves N Dias R (2022) Alterações climáticas: riscos e desafios macro-orçamentais, Occasional Publication of Conselho das Finanças Públicas no. 03/2022, May, https://www.cfp.pt/pt/publicacoes/outras-publicacoes/alteracoes-climaticas-riscos-e-desafios-macro-orcamentais
Petrie M (2021) The evolution of green budgeting. In: Petrie M (ed) Environmental governance and greening fiscal policy: government accountability for environmental stewardship. Springer International Publishing, pp 61–108. https://doi.org/10.1007/978-3-030-83796-9_4
Pizarro R et al (2021) Climate change public budget tagging: connections across financial and environmental classification systems. https://doi.org/10.18235/0003021
Radu D (2021) Disaster risk financing: main concepts and evidence from EU member states, European Economu - Discussion Paper No. 150. https://doi.org/10.2765/504147
Reichelt H, Keenan C (2017) The green bond market: 10 years later and looking ahead. https://thedocs.worldbank.org/en/doc/554231525378003380-0340022018/original/publicationpensionfundservicegreenbonds201712.pdf

Institutional References

Conselho das Finanças Públicas (2021) Riscos Orçamentais e Sustentabilidade das Finanças Públicas 2021. https://www.cfp.pt/pt/publicacoes/riscos-e-sustentabilidade/riscos-orcamentais-e-sustentabilidade-das-financas-publicas-2021
European Commission (2019) The European green deal, Communication from the Commission COM/2019/640 final. https://eurlex.europa.eu/legal-content/EN/TXT/?qid=1576150542719&uri=COM%3A2019%3A640%3AFIN
European Parliament (2019) Climate and environmental emergency. European Parliament resolution of 28 November 2019 on the climate and environment emergency (2019/2930(RSP). https://www.europarl.europa.eu/doceo/document/TA-9-2019-0078_EN.pdf
France Gouvernement (2021) Report on the environmental impact of the central government budget #PLF2022 September. https://www.budget.gouv.fr/documentation/file-download/15202
ICMA (2018) Green bond principles: voluntary process guidelines for issuing green bonds. https://www.icmagroup.org/assets/documents/Sustainable-finance/2021-updates/Green-Bond-Principles-June-2021-140621.pdf
OECD (2009) OECD review of budgeting in Portugal, OECD Journal on Budgeting, 2009, Supplement 1, 160. https://www.oecd.org/portugal/42007470.pdf
OECD (2017) OECD budget transparency toolkit. OECD Publishing, Paris. https://doi.org/10.1787/9789264282070-en
OECD (2021a) Green budget tagging: introductory guidance & principles
OECD (2021b) OECD sovereign borrowing outlook 2021. OECD, Paris. https://doi.org/10.1787/48828791-en
OECD (2021c) Green budgeting in OECD countries. OECD Publishing, Paris. https://doi.org/10.1787/acf5d047-en
Office for Budget Responsibility (2021) Fiscal risks report – July 2021. https://obr.uk/frs/fiscal-risks-report-july-2021/
United Nations General Assembly - UN (1987) Report of the World Commission on environment and development: our common future. https://doi.org/10.1080/07488008808408783
World Bank (2020) Climate change budget tagging: a review of international experience. World Bank, Washington, D.C. https://openknowledge.worldbank.org/handle/10986/35174

Government Procurement and Sustainable Development in the WTO

Pedro Infante Mota

Abstract If government authorities are committed to a more sustainable economy, a redirection of their public procurement can help to create the critical mass necessary for the existence and viability of important markets for the production of technologies, services and products with a reduced environmental impact (clean energy, electrical cars, smart buildings, etc.) and make an important contribution to the achievement of the goals established in relation to the fight against the main environmental and other problems at the local, national and international level. Although the preamble to the Government Procurement Agreement of 2012 does not mention the objective of sustainable development (contrary to the preamble to the Agreement establishing the World Trade Organization), it is very relevant that trade is mentioned nine times in the current Sustainable Development Goals, that national governments have formally recognized the role of public procurement in supporting sustainability (Goal 12.7) and that the WTO Government Procurement Agreement, far from being an obstacle for its Parties to use public procurement to pursue the objective of sustainable development, is increasingly a central force in public procurement worldwide.

1 Introduction

Although the public procurement dimension has always been wrapped in some mystery,[1] it is estimated that it represents between 25 and 30% of GDP in developing countries[2] and that expenditure by member countries of the Organization for

[1] Yang (2012), p. 373.

[2] United Nations Conference on Trade and Development, Competition policy and public procurement (TD/B/C.I/CLP/14), 24.4.2012, 3.

P. I. Mota (✉)
CIDEEFF, University of Lisbon, School of Law, Lisbon, Portugal
e-mail: pedroinfante@fd.ulisboa.pt

R. Saraiva, P. A. Pardal (eds.), *Sustainable Finances and the Law*, Economic Analysis of Law in European Legal Scholarship 16,
https://doi.org/10.1007/978-3-031-49460-4_10

Economic Co-operation and Development (OECD) on public procurement as a percentage of the GDP reached 12.6% in 2019 against 11.8% of the GDP in 2008.[3] This value can still increase between 2 and 12 percentage points of the GDP if the public contracts of companies owned by the state that provide public services are taken into account.[4]

Naturally, being considered as the largest business sector in the world,[5] the economic importance of public procurement[6] implies that policies adopted by government bodies as consumers can work "as a market trigger"[7] influencing trends in terms of investment, production, and consumption. It also creates important incentives for companies to invest in research and development of environmentally friendly goods and services and to play a strategic role in achieving the objective of sustainable development. If government authorities are committed to a more sustainable economy, a redirection of their public procurement can help to create the critical mass necessary for the existence and viability of important markets for the production of technologies, services, and products with a reduced environmental impact (clean energy, electrical cars, smart buildings, etc.), They can also make an important contribution to the achievement of the goals established in relation to the fight against the main environmental and other problems at local, national, and

---

[3] The size of general government procurement spending is estimated using data from the OECD National Accounts Statistics (database) based on the System of National Accounts (SNA). General government procurement is defined as the sum of intermediate consumption (goods and services purchased by governments for their own use such as accounting or information technology services), gross fixed capital formation (acquisition of capital excluding sales of fixed assets, such as building new roads), and social transfers in kind via market producers (purchases by general government of goods and services produced by market producers and supplied to households). Public corporations were excluded in the estimation of procurement spending. The distribution between central and sub-national governments' overall public procurement spending remains broadly unchanged with 64% of OECD-European Union countries' procurement spending taking place at the sub-national level. Health expenditures represented the largest share of public procurement spending, averaging 29.3% across OECD countries in 2019. In Italy, Japan, and the Slovak Republic, almost 45% of public expenditure for procurement was in the health sector. Notable exceptions to this include Lithuania and the United States where economic affairs represented the largest share of government spending and Switzerland where general public services, and social protection formed the largest share. The next largest areas of public procurement spending across OECD countries were economic affairs (16.7%), education (11.6%), defence (10.5%), and social protection (10%) with relatively little variability among countries. OECD (2021), p. 162.

[4] Woolcock and Grier (2015), p. 298.

[5] Grandia (2016), pp. 124, 183.

[6] According to recent estimates, the world's annual public procurement spending in 2018 was about USD 13 trillion, equivalent to one-sixth of the global GDP (Uehara, Thiago. 2020. Public procurement for sustainable development: A framework for the public sector, Royal Institute of International Affairs, London, November 4) and over USD 10 trillion (77% of the total) is spent by 16 countries. China is, by far, the largest procurer at USD 4.2 trillion, and the United States spends USD 1.8 trillion. *Id.* 2.

[7] Cheng et al. (2018), p. 771.

international levels.[8] For example, the city of Vienna saved over 15,000 ton of carbon dioxide a year through its "EcoBuy" initiative "mainly through saving electricity, emission limits for office materials, preferring ecologically sound construction or efficient lightning".[9] Further estimates suggest that if "all public authorities in the European Union switched to green electricity, they would save more than 60 billion tonnes of carbon dioxide, and another 830,000 tonnes of carbon dioxide if they used energy-efficient desktop computers".[10]

In the case of innovation, it is known, for example, that United States public authorities have long used public procurement to strategically promote it. A study published a few years ago concludes that "military and defense-related research and development and procurement" played an important role in the development of certain technologies in the United States during the twentieth century.[11] In each of the cases analysed (e.g., the Internet, the global positioning system, the space industries), commercial development would have been substantially retarded without the encouragement of military procurement.[12]

Agenda 21, an action program based on a 40-chapter document, which constitutes the most comprehensive attempt ever made to promote a new pattern of sustainable development on a planetary scale,[13] similarly states that:

> Governments themselves also play a role in consumption, particularly in countries where the public sector plays a large role in the economy and can have a considerable influence on both corporate decisions and public perceptions. They should therefore review the purchasing policies of their agencies and departments so that they may improve, where possible, the environmental content of government procurement policies, without prejudice to international trade principles. (4.23)

Additionally, Chapter III of the Implementation Plan of the World Summit on Sustainable Development adopted in Johannesburg in September 2002 reiterates the need for public procurement to take into account the objective of sustainable development and emphasizes its importance for the development and diffusion of goods and environmentally friendly services (No. 19).[14]

---

[8] At the same time, there is a risk that, if the price difference between environmentally friendly and conventional products increases, private consumers who previously purchased green products will begin to purchase other types of products. A sectoral legislation that establishes a higher environmental standard for all suppliers and not just for the public sector would leave no room for the so-called demand substitution. On the other hand, substitution risks depend on the share of private consumption in the relevant market. Halonen (2021), pp. 549–550.

[9] Koch (2020), p. 24.

[10] Witjes and Lozano (2016), pp. 112, 39.

[11] Ruttan (2006), p. 176.

[12] *Id.*, 177. See also Brenton et al. (2011).

[13] The Rio 92 summit and Agenda 21 were the first international policy documents of high profile to include a direct reference to the role and impact that public procurement could have on the environment. Correia et al. (2013), p. 59.

[14] http://www.un.org/esa/sustdev/documents/WSSD_POI_PD/English/WSSD_PlanImpl.pdf.

Reading the World Trade Organization Government Procurement Agreement (hereinafter GPA 2012 or simply GPA),[15] it was quickly concluded that some of its provisions clearly allow the objective of sustainable development to be pursued through various means or to be taken into account when interpreting its articles and annexes.[16]

2 Preamble to the Agreement Creating the WTO

The preamble to the GPA 2012 does not mention the objective of sustainable development (contrary to the preamble to the agreement establishing the World Trade Organization (WTO) and a preamble "did not by itself constitute a legal obligation of Parties to the Agreement."[17] But it should be borne in mind, given the importance recognized by the Appellate Body of the general rule of interpretation of the Vienna Convention on the Law of Treaties, that the context also includes the preamble for the purposes of interpreting a treaty (Article 31:2 of the Vienna Convention) and that the Appellate Body argued, shortly after the WTO took office, that:

> This language [in preamble of the Agreement establishing the WTO] demonstrates a recognition by WTO negotiators that optimal use of the world's resources should be made in accordance with the objective of sustainable development. As this preambular language reflects the intentions of negotiators of the WTO Agreement, we believe it must add colour, texture and shading to our interpretation of the agreements annexed to the WTO Agreement.[18]

Therefore, as the GPA 2012 is an agreement annexed to the agreement creating the WTO (Annex 4), the objective of sustainable development must clarify, organize, and qualify the interpretation of its provisions.

The *Shrimp/Turtles* case is, so far, the best example of the importance attached by the Appellate Body to the objective of sustainable development contained in the preamble to the Agreement Establishing the WTO:

---

[15] Since the new GPA was officially adopted at a meeting of the Government Procurement Committee held on 30 March 2012, it should be known as the GPA 2012 and not the GPA 2014 (the agreement entered into force on 6 April 2014). It is generally accepted that the relevant date for the purposes of Art. 30 of the Vienna Convention on the Law of Treaties of 23 May 1969 is the date of conclusion or adoption of a treaty regardless of whether the treaty may have been ratified or entered into force at different times. Pauwelyn (2002), pp. 40–41.

[16] The text of the GPA 2012 can be found in the Official Journal of the European Union L 68, 7.3.2014, 1–24.

[17] WTO Panel Report, *United States – Imposition of Anti-Dumping Duties on Imports of Fresh and Chilled Atlantic Salmon from Norway* (ADP/87), 27.4.1994, para. 369.

[18] WTO Appellate Body Report, *United States – Import Prohibition of certain Shrimp and Shrimp Products* (WT/DS58/AB/R), 12.10.1998, para. 153.

129. The words of Article XX(g), 'exhaustible natural resources', were actually crafted more than 50 years ago. They must be read by a treaty interpreter in the light of contemporary concerns of the community of nations about the protection and conservation of the environment. While Article XX was not modified in the Uruguay Round, the preamble attached to the WTO Agreement shows that the signatories to that Agreement were, in 1994, fully aware of the importance and legitimacy of environmental protection as a goal of national and international policy. The preamble of the WTO Agreement - which informs not only the GATT 1994, but also the other covered agreements - explicitly acknowledges 'the objective of *sustainable development*' (. . .).

130. From the perspective embodied in the preamble of the WTO Agreement, we note that the generic term 'natural resources' in Article XX(g) is not 'static' in its content or reference but is rather 'by definition, evolutionary'. It is, therefore, pertinent to note that modern international conventions and declarations make frequent references to natural resources as embracing both living and non-living resources (. . .).

131. (. . .) Moreover, two adopted GATT 1947 panel reports previously found fish to be an 'exhaustible natural resource' within the meaning of Article XX(g). We hold that, in line with the principle of effectiveness in treaty interpretation, measures to conserve exhaustible natural resources, whether *living* or *non-living*, may fall within Article XX(g).[19]

The Appellate Body's interpretation clearly departs from the literal meaning of the term "exhaustible natural resources" and constitutes a clear case of judicial activism *pur sang*.[20] When GATT Article XX(g) was drafted, the term "natural resource" was interpreted as targeting "minerals" or "raw materials" and the term "exhaustible natural resources" as including metals which is in contrast to renewables that would include animals, plants, and water (these would fall within the scope of GATT Article XX(b).[21] The history of the negotiations also supports the view that the GATT drafters had in mind goods such as oil and not animals.[22]

The Appellate Body's evolutionary interpretation was also heavily criticized by developing countries,[23] and it is all the more surprising when it is known that the WTO court was known to often adhere to a highly textual interpretation of the agreements[24] and calls into question the principle of useful effect as a fundamental principle in the interpretation of treaties. Since the exhaustion of renewable resources is possible, the inclusion of these in the category of "exhaustible" implies that this term ceases to have any meaning, and the term "exhaustible" now includes both types of resources, i.e. renewable and non-renewable.[25]

---

[19] WTO Appellate Body Report, *United States – Import Prohibition of Certain Shrimp and Shrimp Products* (WT/DS58/AB/R), 12.10.1998, paras. 129–131.

[20] In the *Shrimp/Turtles* case, the Appellate Body ignored "the State Consent aspects" of the WTO agreements and assumed "the legislative role of the Ministerial Council under the guise of interpretation." Kelly (2005), p. 476.

[21] Imperiale (2001), p. 242.

[22] Mavroidis (2008a), p. 354.

[23] Lida (2004), p. 219.

[24] The Appellate Body's decision in this case "was nothing short of shocking." Chaudhary (2005), p. 181.

[25] The application of the principle of evolutionary interpretation can also give rise to problems of conciliation with the principle of legal certainty as it results from the *Pacta sunt servanda* principle

At the same time, Professor John Jackson considered the Appellate Body report in the *Shrimp-Turtles* case to be the most important in WTO jurisprudence[26] and other authors argue that:

> By holding that the terms of the Article XX(g) exception can evolve with the views of the international community, the Appellate Body demonstrated a willingness to exercise significant interpretative discretion. In this case, that discretion was applied in a way that improved the ability of panels and the Appellate Body to apply WTO rules in ways that reflect changing notions in the international community regarding the appropriate balance between policing national regulatory measures that may improperly restrict trade and deferring to measures that legitimately promote non-commercial values.[27]

This is also the authors' understanding mainly because the Appellate Body's interpretation allows expanding the scope of the exception in GATT Article XX(g) to the conservation of practically any natural resource[28] "connects trade rules to the vast body of international environmental law (and the emerging field of 'international sustainable development law')",[29] This demonstrates that "the WTO is not just about trade and money".[30]

Although Petros Mavroidis understands that it is not possible to find space in the Vienna Convention on the Rights of Treaties for evolutionary interpretation,[31] the preference for a dynamic interpretation is reflected in the very structure of that convention. In accordance with the respective Article 31, the subsequent agreements and understandings between the parties as well as all relevant rules of international law (which obviously includes customs, which is necessarily evolutionary) are mandatory sources of treaty interpretation. Moreover, the preparatory work, acccording to Article 32 of the convention, are optional sources that may be used "when the interpretation obtained under article 31 leaves the meaning ambiguous or obscure or leads to a result that is manifestly absurd or unreasonable" or to "confirm the meaning resulting from the application of article 31."[32]

---

and from Art. 3:2 of the Memorandum of Understanding on the Resolution of Disputes. Canal-Forgues (2008), p. 122.

[26] Jackson (2008), p. 450.

[27] Reif and Eckert (2004), p. 686.

[28] The International Law Commission also applauded the evolutionary interpretation adopted by the Appellate Body. International Law Commission, 58th Session, *Fragmentation of International Law: Difficulties arising from the Diversification and Expansion of International Law*, Report of the Study Group of the International Law Commission - Finalised by Martti Koskenniemi (A/CN.4/L.682), 13.4.2006, para. 478.

[29] Reimers (2021), p. 222.

[30] Zarbiyev (2012), p. 276.

[31] Mavroidis (2008b), p. 445

[32] Howse (2001), p. 56.

3 Technical Specifications

It is now widely understood that the technical specifications and standards defined by public authorities must allow the opening of public contracts not only to competition but also to the pursuit of the objective of sustainable development. It is perfectly legitimate that they can be defined on the basis of performance criteria linked to the life cycle and sustainability of the production process of works, goods, and services.[33] Examples include requiring the use of a biodegradable materials or maximum emission threshold values for transport vehicles.

In the specific case of the GPA, Article I(u) proceeds with the following definition of technical specification:

> **Technical specification** means a tendering requirement that: lays down the characteristics of goods or services to be procured, including quality, performance, safety and dimensions, or the processes and methods for their production or provision; or addresses terminology, symbols, packaging, marking or labelling requirements, as they apply to a good or service.

Then, GPA contains some limitations that need to be considered when a party sets technical specifications:

1. Technical specifications shall not amount to "unnecessary obstacles to international trade" (GPA Article X:1).
2. Technical specifications shall be based on performance and functional requirements as well as on international standards (GPA Articles X:2 and X:4).
3. Contracting authorities need to consider equivalent offers when setting technical specifications in a restrictive way (GPA Articles X:3 and X:4).
4. Technical specifications cannot be defined in cooperation with persons with commercial interests in a manner that would be bad for competition (GPA Article X:5).
5. Technical specifications are subject to various publications and information obligations (GPA Articles X:7 and X:10).

It is important to note that GPA Article X:1 does not only refer to technical specifications; also "conformity assessment procedures" may not amount to unnecessary barriers to trade. These are defined in Annex 1.3 of the Technical Barriers to Trade Agreement as "any procedure used, directly or indirectly, to determine that relevant requirements in technical regulations or standards are fulfilled (...)". In other words, conformity assessment procedures are regulated procedures used to verify that the pertinent technical regulation (or technical specification in the case of public procurement) is fulfilled by the producer or supplier.

---

[33] The use of life-cycle costing or life-cycle cost (LCC) assessment in public procurement is not a recent idea:

> Already in the 1960s the Department of Defence of the United States Government applied LCC in the procurement of military equipment as they found that acquisition costs only accounted for a small part of the total costs of weapon systems, while operation and support costs represented up to two-thirds of overall costs. Querol et al. (2021), p. 50.

The obligation that the technical specifications prescribed by the contracting authorities be based, whenever possible, on international standards when they exist, avoids the uncertainty for a part of the GPA as to whether such specifications are legitimate.[34] In essence, the GPA recognizes that a contracting authority of a party that adopts a technical specification in compliance with the relevant international standards will be relatively immune to an attack by another party that sees it as an illegitimate protectionist measure; as a technical specification adapted to the capabilities of certain local suppliers; or established, adopted, or applied with the aim of creating unnecessary obstacles to international trade.

Additionally, while the GPA does not advance any definition of the condition of not "creating unnecessary obstacles to international trade", it is evident that it does not prohibit technical specifications that constitute a barrier to trade but only those that are "unnecessary". The absence of any jurisprudence on the concept of technical specifications within the scope of the GPA implies that we take into account the existing jurisprudence on conditions similar to those referred to in Article X. See, for example, Article 2:2 of the WTO Agreement on Technical Barriers to Trade:

> Members shall ensure that technical regulations are not prepared, adopted or applied with a view to or with the effect of creating unnecessary obstacles to international trade. For this purpose, technical regulations shall not be more trade-restrictive than necessary to fulfil a legitimate objective, taking account of the risks non-fulfilment would create. Such legitimate objectives are, inter alia: national security requirements; the prevention of deceptive practices; protection of human health or safety, animal or plant life or health, or the environment. In assessing such risks, relevant elements of consideration are, inter alia: available scientific and technical information, related processing technology or intended end-uses of products.

In the *United States - Measures Concerning the Importation, Marketing and Sale of Tuna and Tuna Products (Mexico)* case, the Appellate Body summarized the steps needed to determine whether a technical regulation is "more trade-restrictive than necessary":

> In sum, we consider that an assessment of whether a technical regulation is 'more trade-restrictive than necessary' within the meaning of Article 2.2 of the Technical Barriers to Trade Agreement involves an evaluation of a number of factors. A panel should begin by considering factors that include: (i) the degree of contribution made by the measure to the legitimate objective at issue; (ii) the trade-restrictiveness of the measure; and (iii) the nature of the risks at issue and the gravity of consequences that would arise from non-fulfilment of the objective(s) pursued by the Member through the measure. In most cases, a comparison of the challenged measure and possible alternative measures should be undertaken. In particular, it may be relevant for the purpose of this comparison to consider whether the proposed alternative is less trade restrictive, whether it would make an equivalent contribution to the

[34] At the same time, the Agreement on Technical Barriers to Trade specifically adds, with respect to the adherence to existing international standards, that these need not be followed when they would be "ineffective or inappropriate, for instance, because of an insufficient level of protection or fundamental climatic or geographical factors or fundamental technological problems" (Code of Good Practice for the Preparation, Adoption and Application of Standards, point F). This arguably amounts to a clear opportunity for states to determine their own level of desired protection and, even though scientific evidence may facilitate proof that no unnecessary obstacle to trade has been put in place, such proof is arguably not dependent upon the production of scientific evidence.

> relevant legitimate objective, taking account of the risks non-fulfilment would create, and whether it is reasonably available.[35]

Additionally, the more that the common interest or the common values pursued are vital or important, the easier it will be to admit the need for the measures in question to achieve those objectives. If the value pursued is both vital and important to the highest degree (for example, the protection of people's life and health through the ban on the use of asbestos in any construction service to be contracted), it remains to be seen whether there is an alternative measure that achieves the same objective and is less trade-restrictive than a ban.[36]

As the definitions of technical specifications and standards advanced by the GPA speak of labeling or symbols, contracting authorities may also require a specific label to certify that the characteristics (visible and invisible) of the works, goods, or services correspond to their requirements. However, about the use of labels, for example, on the energy efficiency of goods or services, such as the famous *Energy Star,*[37] it only will not pose any problem if certain requirements are met.[38] Labels must be appropriate to define the characteristics of the works, goods, or services to which the contract refers and be based on objective and non-discriminatory criteria. They must be established by a third party over which the economic operator applying for the label cannot exercise decisive influence; and contracting authorities that require a particular label must accept all labels that confirm that works, goods, or services comply with equivalent labeling requirements. At the same time, despite the fact that the last-mentioned requirement assumes great relevance in the context of the GPA, it should be borne in mind that:

> Worldwide, according to Ecolabel Index, there are 463 environmental labels in 199 countries and 25 industry sectors (Ecolabel Index, not dated). The increasing number of labels is a challenge for consumers as they are faced with a variety of logos, with different levels of reliability and Independence.[39]

Of course, the existence of hundreds of labeling schemes makes monitoring by public authorities extremely difficult and necessarily generates great confusion between consumers and producers who are often unable to even identify or differentiate products based on the information provided. In order for labels relating to "non-incorporated production processes and methods" to effectively constitute a

[35] WTO Appellate Body Report, *United States - Measures Concerning the Importation, Marketing and Sale of Tuna and Tuna Products* (WT/DS381/AB/R), 16.5.2012, para. 322.

[36] WTO Appellate Body Report, *European Communities – Measures Affecting Asbestos and Asbestos Containing Products* (WT/DS135/AB/R), 12.3.2001, para. 172.

[37] The Energy Star is the most widespread standard to estimate energy consumption (in kWh/year), which can easily be transformed into costs with the energy price of the contracting authority. Querol et al. (2021), p. 60.

[38] It is estimated that compliance with the Energy Star label by the United States Federal Administration resulted in a reduction in greenhouse gas emissions equivalent to 22 million tons of carbon dioxide. van Asselt et al. (2006), p. 220.

[39] Dragos and Neamtu (2021), p. 26.

commercial reality, it would be most useful for all interested WTO members to negotiate together with other relevant institutions (e.g., the International Tropical Timber Organization on the protection of tropical forests) for an international legal framework. It would unify criteria and put an end to much of the confusion prevailing in terms of labeling and reward companies for their efforts that really respect the objectives generally associated with sustainable development.

Furthermore, when defining "norm" in Article I(s) as "*a document approved by a recognized body*, which provides, for current or repeated use, rules, guidelines or characteristics of goods or services, or related processes and production methods, with which compliance is not mandatory" (italics added), the GPA seems to exclude that only standards emanating from international bodies (such as the International Organization for Standardization) or national standards organizations are relevant.[40] Therefore, there can be no exclusion *a priori* of the standardization efforts carried out by private organizations such as, for example, the Forest Stewardship Council (better known by its acronym FSC),[41] a non-governmental accreditation and certification organization based in Bonn, Germany. Its official mission is to promote environmentally sound, socially beneficial, and economically viable management of the world's forests.[42]

Finally, as there is no case law or decision of a WTO body on technical specifications in the context of the GPA, it is not known, for example, whether the principle of non-discrimination provided in the GPA accepts the distinction between incorporated and non-incorporated production processes or methods that has assumed so much importance in the context of the GATT 1947/1994.[43] Is it permissible to take into account not only the characteristics evident in the final product (e.g., that the materials used are recyclable) but also the supplier's production methods (e.g., emission levels of atmospheric pollutants)?

Briefly, the two GATT panels that settled the *United States Restrictions on Imports of Tuna* cases (1991 and 1994) concluded that product distinctions based on the characteristics of the production process or the producer that are not detectable in the final product are simply seen *a priori* as illegitimate. For example, the ban on the use of a trawl in fishing has no effect on fish as such or on its nutritional or taste value for the consumer, although such a measure can help to protect the environment. It is impossible to determine simply by looking at a table whether wood from sustainably managed forests was used in its manufacture or whether illegally harvested wood is involved. In contrast, livestock raised on growth hormones implies that hormone residues can be found in the meat, and exposure of tuna

[40] Van Calster (2009), p. 366.

[41] Van Calster (2002), p. 302.

[42] The *Forest Stewardship Council* has members of very diverse natures including environmental and social non-governmental organizations, private companies, academic institutions, religious organizations, and individuals from over 60 countries. Röben (2010), para. 10.

[43] On the distinction between product/process or production method, see, for example, Silva et al. (2015), pp. 97–132.

to chemicals in the water affects tuna as a product. In determining the similarity of two products, the national and the imported, a fundamental distinction is thus present. On the one hand, we have the so-called "incorporated processes and production methods" that give rise to an evident, detectable change in the final product; on the other hand are "non-incorporated production processes and methods" that do not cause any perceptible transformation in the final product.

In legal terms, the main consequence of the distinction mentioned previously is the fact that the very important national treatment clause enshrined in GATT Article III:1 does not allow two products to be treated differently on the basis of their "non-incorporated production processes and methods". For the purposes of the GATT national treatment clause, wood used in a construction work originating from sustainably managed national forests is similar to wood imported from illegally felled trees and, therefore, the latter must not receive less favourable treatment compared to the treatment granted to the first.[44]

Very few authors comment on the distinction in question in the context of the WTO agreements on public procurement. Christopher McCrudden, for example, argues that the GPA does not appear to support the distinction between embedded and non-embedded production processes or methods. This is because it refers to the "technical specifications laying down the characteristics of the products or services to be procured (...) or the processes and methods for their production".[45] Peter Kunzlik emphasizes that the use of the disjunctive "or" indicates that it is intended to cover "requirements that are different from those encompassed by the earlier reference to product characteristics".[46] Colleen Hanley also states that:

> It is submitted that unlike the present accepted interpretation of GATT, the provisions of the Government Procurement Agreement on technical specifications would clearly appear to assume that *both* product-related requirements and process production methods may in principle be included in the technical specifications of a contract. (...) It seems from the above text that under the Government Procurement Agreement technical specifications may in principle deal with Process Production Methods and may also require the use of symbols, labelling and marking which might for example include eco-labelling. To this extent it appears to depart significantly from the general approach of GATT taken in the *Tuna/Dolphin* cases.[47]

Therefore, the GPA does not prevent a contracting entity from establishing a technical specification for a good or service subject to a particular tender based on

[44]The subsequent *Shrimp-Turtles* case (1998) does not call into question the earlier GATT 1947 case law concerning the scope of application of Art. III, since the trade measures in question applied by the United States were analysed by the Appellate Body in the context of the general exceptions of Art. XX, with all of the resulting consequences in terms of the burden of proof. At the same time, the fact that the Appellate Body carefully reviewed the United States measure and specifically criticized the way in which the United States was implementing it clearly demonstrates that unincorporated production processes and methods can be justified under GATT Art. XX.

[45]McCrudden (1999), p. 36.

[46]Kunzlik (2003), p. 110.

[47]Hanley (2002), p. 722.

the energy efficiency of the respective production processes. The possibility that the technical specifications can be based on a "non-incorporated production process and method" certainly makes it easier to pursue the objective of sustainable development in terms of public procurement. In most cases, it is not possible to discern in the final product (or service) the amount of energy used in its production nor to physically distinguish between final products produced from renewable energy sources (green electricity) and those produced from non-renewable energy sources (fossil energy).[48]

The authors' understanding is also supported by two provisions of the GPA 2012, both of which did not exist in the previous GPA 1994.[49] The first establishes that: "For greater certainty, a Party, including its procuring entities, may, in accordance with this Article, prepare, adopt or apply technical specifications to promote the conservation of natural resources or protect the environment" (Article X:6). The second determines that: "The evaluation criteria set out in the notice of intended procurement or tender documentation may include, among others, price and other cost factors, quality, technical merit, environmental characteristics and terms of delivery" (Article X: 9).

Notwithstanding, Sue Arrowsmith defends that GPA Articles X:6 and 9 reflect the importance of environmental issues and emphasize the possibility for a party to incorporate environmental considerations into public procurement. However, the provisions in question do not resolve the issue of definitively knowing what types of environmental measures can be included as conditions or evaluation criteria and, in particular, whether production processes can be included.[50] Nevertheless, if that was the case, the useful effect of GPA Articles I(u) and X would certainly be reduced if production methods could not be taken into account[51] because the environmental characteristics referred to in GPA Article X:9 are not always reflected in the final product. The European Union, for example, understands that the environmental profile or the environmental attributes that a certain product can incorporate, even if they do not materialize in any particular physical characteristic, can legitimately form part of the specifications of the purchased product that are closely related to the object of the contract.[52]

It would also be difficult for many national governments to guarantee the fulfillment of internationally agreed targets regarding the reduction of carbon emissions if it was not possible to take into account the environmental impact of the life cycle of a product. In addition, many GPA countries and territories already include green criteria in their public procurement in order to reduce the environmental

---

[48] van Asselt et al. (2006), p. 223.

[49] The text of the GPA 1994 can be found in the Official Journal of the European Union C 256, 3.9.1996, 1–18.

[50] Arrowsmith (2011), p. 323.

[51] Davies (2009), p. 295.

[52] WTO Appellate Body Report, *Canada – Certain Measures Affecting the Renewable Energy Generation Sector/Measures Relating to the Feed-In Tariff Program* (WT/DS412/AB/R, WT/DS426/AB/R), 6.5.2013, footnote 499.

impact of government spending,[53] and the vast majority of labelling schemes are based on the product's life cycle, taking into account the energy performance of the products, the materials contained in the products, the production, return and recycling processes, etc. This is the case, for example, of ISO 14001 which is frequently required by public sector contracting authorities.[54]

Finally, the permeability of WTO agreements to values other than the liberalization of trade at the international level can help to remove some concerns about their legitimacy. As highlighted by Daniel Tarullo, "the World Trade Organization risks its own legitimacy further each time it appears to elevate trade over non-trade values".[55] Interestingly, or perhaps not, there is no reference in GPA Article X to other horizontal policies such as the promotion of human rights or minimum workers' rights.[56] However, the term "among others" contained in GPA Article X:9 may provide some coverage for the pursuit of such policies as well as the general exception provided in GPA Article III:2(a) (this provision concerns the protection of public morals, order, or security).

Moreover, one of the deepest preferential trade agreements completed in recent times, the Comprehensive and Progressive Agreement for Trans-Pacific Partnership (CPTPP), while replicating the GPA disciplines, clarifies that procurement can be designed to promote compliance with international labour rights:

> For greater certainty, this Article is not intended to preclude a procuring entity from promoting compliance with laws in the territory in which the good is produced or the service is performed relating to labour rights as recognised by the Parties and set forth in Article 19.3 (Labour Rights), provided that such measures are applied in a manner consistent with Chap. 26 (Transparency and Anti-Corruption), and are not applied in a manner that constitutes a means of arbitrary or unjustifiable discrimination between the Parties or a disguised restriction on trade between the Parties. (Article 15.8:5)

Some even defend that the GPA offers an opportunity to promote international human rights "by excluding corporations involved in violations of those rights from the WTO procurement market" because of its unique relationship connecting governments to private corporations.[57] In that sense, the Policy on Ethical Procurement of Apparel of Canada "requires suppliers of apparel to the government to certify that they and their first-tier subcontractors comply with local laws and international standards on labour and human rights".[58]

---

[53]Baron (2014), p. 25; Hollander and Marx (2014), p. 5.

[54]Rainville (2017), p. 1034. "Our analysis, based on ISO-14001 adoption levels in 147 countries over the 1999-2014 period, shows that a greater uptake of the ISO-14001 standard is associated with lower levels of emissions of greenhouse gases (GHGs), namely carbon dioxide (CO_2) and methane (CH_4)." Ubaldo et al. (2022), p. 2.

[55]Tarullo (2000), p. 173.

[56]Reich (2009), p. 1012.

[57]Giles (2018), pp. 407–408. See also Uysal (2021), p. 53: "Considering the role of the state in protection of human rights, it is only natural to expect the government to have business relations with the enterprises that are considerate of human rights effects of their conduct."

[58]OECD (2021), p. 164.

Finally, taking into account the exclusion criteria addressed in GPA Article VIII ("Conditions of Participation"), it is possible to defend that the:

> Failure to adhere to environmentally safe performance would readily qualify as 'significant or persistent deficiencies in performance of any substantive requirement (. . .)' under Article VIII.4.c GPA or as 'professional misconduct' under Article VIII.4.e GPA. Although, in general, the scope of including green exclusion criteria seems rather limited, it has to be borne in mind that the list in Article VIII.4 GPA is not exhaustive. It is, for example, entirely conceivable that the national procurement laws of GPA Parties would provide for the exclusion of suppliers that fail to meet environmental laws. How restrictive such an exclusion criterion is depends on the form and substance of the respective law.[59]

In short, although human rights or the so-called fundamental labour rights are not explicitly mentioned, nothing seems to prevent the parties to the GPA from imposing their observance provided that this condition of participation respects the fundamental principles of non-discrimination, transparency, and procedural fairness.

4 General Exceptions

Despite the advantages generally associated with the liberalization of trade, it is normal for treaties that promote it to provide for exceptions or limitations to its pursuit. The GPA is no exception and the recognition of the existence of certain values for which protection should not obey purely commercial considerations leads it to establish in its Article III:2 that:

> Subject to the requirement that such measures are not applied in a manner that would constitute a means of arbitrary or unjustifiable discrimination between Parties where the same conditions prevail or a disguised restriction on international trade, nothing in this Agreement shall be construed to prevent any Party from imposing or enforcing measures: b) necessary to protect human, animal or plant life or health.

Thus, even in cases when another provision of the GPA (for example, the one relating to technical specifications) is violated, a contracting entity of a party may justify such a violation by fulfilling the conditions imposed by the general exception provided in GPA Article III:2.

For reasons unknown to the authors, the GPA article referring to general exceptions does not contain a provision similar to that of GATT Article XX(g) which allows WTO members to adopt trade-restrictive measures with the aim of conserving "exhaustible natural resources". This absence has now lost relevance with Article X:6 of the GPA 2012 (*supra*), and it is still significant that the term "exhaustible" present in the text of the GATT is absent from the text of the GPA and that the protection of the environment is provided in GPA Articles III: 2(b), X:6, and 9, a situation that could cause some problems in terms of the burden of proof. Since established jurisprudence is that the party invoking an exception has the

[59] Koch (2020), p. 98.

burden of proving it, on whom should the burden of proof fall if a party maintains an environmental protection measure under GPA Article X? As there is no question of invoking one of the exceptions provided in GPA Article III, the Roman law maxim *quicunque exceptio invocat ejudem probate debet* does not seem to be applicable. Therefore, the burden of proof should fall on the party of the GPA that presents a complaint on the grounds that another party has not observed the conditions imposed by GPA Article X.[60]

Since the GPA provision on general exceptions has never been the subject of any analysis by either a panel or by the Appellate Body, there is no case law to clarify, for example, what is to be understood by the term "necessary" referred to in GPA Article III:2(b). However, given the case law relating to general exceptions in other WTO agreements (e.g., GATT Article XX and the General Agreement on Trade in Services Article XIV), it is important to note that, contrary to the established case law of the Court of Justice of the European Union, the WTO Appellate Body rejects the practice that exceptions should be interpreted restrictively.[61] Notwithstanding that Peter Van Den Bossche points out that it constitutes "an accepted principle of interpretation that exceptions are to be constructed narrowly (*singularia non sunt extendenda*)",[62] the authors believe that the Appellate Body's view finds support in Articles 31 and 32 of the 1969 Vienna Convention on the Law of Treaties. It does not follow from these two provisions that preference should be given to one part of the text over another, interpreting the first of a broadly and the second narrowly,[63] and there is no principle in international law that requires a different interpretation of rules and exceptions.[64] The International Court of Justice itself defends in the case *Dispute Regarding Navigational and Related Rights (Costa Rica v. Nicaragua)* that: "A treaty provision which has the purpose of limiting the sovereignty powers of a State must be interpreted like any other provision of a treaty, i.e., in accordance with the intentions of its authors as reflected by the text of the treaty and the other relevant factors in terms of interpretation."[65]

Moreover, the Appellate Body argues that an import ban or any other measure having restrictive effects on trade of which the contribution is not immediately perceptible may be justified by virtue of GATT Article XX(b), the GATT provision equivalent to GPA III:2(b):

---

[60] WTO Appellate Body Report, *United States – Tax Treatment for "Foreign Sales Corporations", Recourse to Article 21.5 of the DSU by the European Communities* (WT/DS108/AB/RW), 14.1.2002, paras. 132-133.

[61] WTO Appellate Body Report, *European Communities - Measures Concerning Meat and Meat Products (Hormones)* (WT/DS26/AB/R, WT/DS48/AB/R), 16.1.1998, para. 104.

[62] Van den Bossche (2006), 320.

[63] Orakhelashvili (2007), p. 166.

[64] Cottier and Delimatsis (2008), p. 337.

[65] International Courte of Justice, *Dispute Regarding Navigational and Related Rights (Costa Rica v. Nicaragua)*, Judgment of 13.7.2009, para. 48.

> We recognize that certain complex public health or environmental problems may be tackled only with a comprehensive policy comprising a multiplicity of interacting measures. In the short-term, it may prove difficult to isolate the contribution to public health or environmental objectives of one specific measure from those attributable to the other measures that are part of the same comprehensive policy. Moreover, the results obtained from certain actions—for instance, measures adopted in order to attenuate global warming and climate change, or certain preventive actions to reduce the incidence of diseases that may manifest themselves only after a certain period of time—can only be evaluated with the benefit of time. In order to justify an import ban under Article XX(b), a panel must be satisfied that it brings about a material contribution to the achievement of its objective. Such a demonstration can of course be made by resorting to evidence or data, pertaining to the past or the present, that establish that the import ban at issue makes a material contribution to the protection of public health or environmental objectives pursued.[66]

Finally, it is important to mention two aspects that are considered important. On the one hand, some authors point out that the general principle of non-discrimination and the prohibition contained in GPA Article IV:6 ("with respect to the contracts covered, the Parties, including their contracting entities, shall not seek to obtain, take into account, impose or apply any compensation") prevent that, outside of the exceptional cases expressly provided in the GPA (e.g. Articles V and III:1 referring to developing and least developed countries and the security exception, respectively), a GPA party uses its public procurement to support domestic industries that are developing, for example, environmentally friendly innovations. For the purposes of the GPA 2012, offsets, also known as counterparts, mean "any condition or undertaking that encourages local development or improves a Party's balance-of-payments accounts, such as the use of domestic content, the licensing of technology, investment, counter-trade and similar action or requirement" (Article I(l). Therefore, any public contract subject to the discipline of the GPA must observe the general principle of non-discrimination (GPA Article IV:1) and not impose, for example, any incorporation of national content as a condition or commitment to its execution.[67]

On the other hand, the GPA does not prevent its parties from ensuring the pursuit of certain horizontal policies through notes introduced in the respective annexes. For example, the United States has established in its Annex 2 that "nothing in this Annex may prevent any State entity included in this Annex from applying restrictions designed to promote the general quality of the environment in the State concerned, provided that such restrictions do not constitute hidden barriers to international trade" (Note 3). When talking about the general quality of the environment, the note in question seems to have a wider scope of application than that allowed by GPA 2012 Article III:2, excludes the applicability of some of the conditions imposed by this provision, and welcomes the so-called "California effect". This California effect concerns the influential role of powerful, wealthy, and environmentally friendly political jurisdictions in promoting race to the top regulation among their

---

[66] WTO Appellate Body Report, *Brazil – Measures Affecting Imports of Retreaded Tyres* (WT/DS332/AB/R), 3.12.2007, para. 151.

[67] Brenton et al. (2011), p. 22.

trading partners[68] and can be illustrated with the history of the emission levels of North American automobiles. In 1970, the so-called Clean Air Act Amendments specifically allowed California to adopt more stringent emission levels than other US states which led, for example, to the European Community (under pressure from Germany due to the importance of California markets for its automotive industry) to adopt the same level of emissions as California.[69] Developing countries themselves adopt stricter levels in terms of emissions from automobiles when the markets to which they export more automobiles and related parts adopt demanding emission levels.[70]

5 Awarding of Contracts

Pursuant to GPA Article XV:5:

> Unless a procuring entity determines that it is not in the public interest to award a contract, the entity shall award the contract to the supplier that the entity has determined to be capable of fulfilling the terms of the contract and that, based solely on the evaluation criteria specified in the notices and tender documentation, has submitted: a. the most advantageous tender; or b. where price is the sole criterion, the lowest price.

For many products and works, the environmental and health costs incurred during their use and disposal (e.g., of hazardous materials) at the end of their life can be very significant. Therefore, some authors argue that it makes perfect sense that the criterion of the lowest price can be considered from two perspectives, i.e., that of the lowest initial price and that of the lowest price during the product's life cycle.[71] The first perspective makes sense especially in the case of highly standardized products,[72] and the second makes it possible to reconcile the efficiency of public expenditure with, for example, environmental protection. Think, for example, of purchasing efficient LED lamps that are more expensive initially or electric cars that generally provide better results in terms of consumption, green energy, or repair frequency even though their initial purchase price is higher than that of traditional cars.[73]

Similarly, the European Commission argues that another complementary objective is to enable contracting authorities to make better use of public contracts to support common social objectives including environmental protection, greater resource and energy efficiency and the fight against climate change, the promotion

[68] Vogel (1995), p. 6.

[69] Vogel (2000), pp. 269–270.

[70] Perkins and Neumayer (2012), p. 232.

[71] Kullmann (2018), p. 122; Marty (2014), p. 7.

[72] Wiesbrock (2013), p. 121.

[73] European Commission, *Guidance on Innovation Procurement* (2021/C 267/01), Official Journal of the European Union C 267, 6.7.2021, 41.

of innovation and social integration, and the guarantee of the best possible conditions for the provision of high-quality public services. This objective can also contribute to achieving the first goal of greater efficiency of public expenditure in the long term, for example, by replacing the criterion of the lowest initial price with the criterion of the lowest life-cycle cost.[74]

Moreover, the GPA 2012 does not define the term "most advantageous" nor does it appear to limit the criteria that can be used to identify the most advantageous proposal.[75] As illustrated above, the new enumeration in GPA Article X:9 provides some guidance on how the most-advantageous tender could be identified ("price and other cost factors, quality, technical merit, environmental characteristics and terms of delivery"). It is even possible to argue that the latitude of the parties is greater in the case of the GPA since, unlike the Community directives, the WTO agreement speaks of "the most advantageous offer" and not "the most economically advantageous offer".

Contracting authorities must only ensure that the principles of non-discrimination and transparency are respected, the award criteria must be objective, and suppliers must have access to the tender documents and all of the information necessary for them to prepare and submit valid tenders.[76] In particular, contracting authorities must limit any conditions for participating in a tender to the essential conditions to ensure that a supplier has the legal and financial capabilities and the commercial and technical skills necessary to carry out the award of the relevant contract (GPA Article VIII:1). Fundamentally, contracting authorities should not be able to require tenderers to comply with certain requirements when these cannot be considered characteristic factors of the specific process of production or supply of the works, products, or services purchased. Some even argue that the "Life cycle of a good can only work with costs that have a clear monetary value. This removes the pressure from governments to engage with complicated pricing schemes for externalities that are difficult to monetize."[77]

So, there is nothing to prevent a contracting authority wishing to purchase buses from taking into account the carbon dioxide emissions or the noise level of the vehicles offered by the various competing companies. However, will it be possible (under normal circumstances) for that same entity to impose that they can only tender for the supply of the buses in question to suppliers of GPA parties who, for example, do not maintain diplomatic relations with Myanmar?[78]

[74]European Commission, *Green Paper on the modernisation of EU public procurement policy: Towards a more efficient European Procurement Market* COM (2011) 15 final, Brussels, 27.1.2011, 5.

[75]Tosoni (2013), p. 46.

[76]Kunzlik (2003), p. 115.

[77]Dragos and Neamtu (2021), p. 25.

[78]For example, because of Burma's (nowadays Myanmar) registration on the protection of human rights, Massachusetts adopted, on 25 June 1996, the so-called Act Regulating State Contracts with Companies doing Business with or in Burma, passing to apply an automatic 10% markup to the prices quoted by companies determined to do business with Burma. The increase applied to both US

If what is valued cannot be monetized (for example, respect for human rights), the criteria of price or the most advantageous proposal are metrics that raise enormous or unsurpassable difficulties in their use.[79] Therefore, issues such as respect for human rights can hardly be addressed at the award stage. As noted before, they may be taken into account only in connection with the conditions of participation in the contracting procedure (GPA Article VIII:4) or in the general exceptions provided in GPA Article III.

On the other hand, nothing prevents the two award criteria from being combined. For example, in 2010, the Norwegian Ministry of Transport launched a tender for the supply of a car transport ferry to connect two locations in Sognefjord. The so-called *Norwegian Public Roads Administration*, responsible for the tender, demanded as a minimum requirement an improvement of between 15 and 20% in energy efficiency compared to the diesel-powered ferry used until then. Offers were evaluated based on the following criteria and weights:

- Price (60%).
- Quality (40%) resulting from the sum of energy used per kilometer in the transport of passenger cars (energy use per passenger car-km) (18%); total energy

---

and foreign companies carrying out commercial transactions with Burma. One year after the adoption of the Burma Act by Massachusetts, the European Communities requested the United States to carry out consultations under Art. 4 of the WTO Dispute Settlement System, alleging that Massachusetts law violated, for example, the following provisions of the GPA 1994:

i) Art. VIII(b), as it imposed conditions on the bidding company that were not essential to ensure its ability to fulfill the contract;
ii) Art. X, since it applied qualification criteria based on political and non-economic considerations; and
iii) Art. XIII, as it allowed the award of contracts to be based on political rather than economic considerations (WTO, *United States – Measures Affecting Government Procurement, Request for Consultations by the European Communities* (GPA/D2/1, WT/DS88/1), 26.6.1997).

As the consultations did not put an end to the dispute, the European Communities requested, on 8 September 1998, the creation of a panel that was created at the meeting of the Dispute Settlement Body held on 21 October 1998. However, the Federal District Court of Massachusetts having declared the law of the state of Massachusetts unconstitutional on 4 November 1998, the European Communities applied to the WTO on 10 February 1999 for the suspension of the dispute settlement procedures because they understood that the Burma Law had become obsolete in practice. It should also be noted that some indicate that the security exception provided in the GPA 1994 was invoked by the United States in order to defend the so-called *Act Regulating State Contracts with Companies doing Business with or in Burma* adopted by Massachusetts on 25 June 1996 (Goodman 2001, pp. 101–102). Moreover, the security exception seems to be moving towards a greater scope in terms of its scope of application. For example, Annex 8-E to Art. 28.6 of the Comprehensive Economic and Trade Agreement (National Security) between Canada and the European Union states that "measures related to the maintenance of international peace and security" include the protection of human rights.

[79]Hamilton (2022), p. 24.

used annually (6%); tons of carbon dioxide emitted annually (6%); kilograms of nitrogen oxides emitted annually (4%); and innovation (6%).[80]

The ferry tender does not mention any technology in particular, merely setting a goal of greater energy efficiency and the associated weighting coefficients. The new ferry started operating in 2015, and known data reveals that its use has resulted in a 70% reduction in fuel costs and an 89% reduction in annual carbon dioxide emissions.[81]

Finally, when a contracting authority receives a tender at an abnormally lower price than the prices of the other tenders submitted, it can check with the supplier whether the supplier satisfies the conditions for participation and is in a position to fulfill the conditions of the contract (GPA Article XV:6). The inquiry may make it clear to the contracting authority that the abnormally lower price results, for example, from the fact that the tenderer concerned does not respect the relevant environmental legislation (for example, a construction work using wood originating from felled and smuggled trees illegally). However, unlike the relevant community directives on public procurement,[82] the GPA does not expressly impose its rejection, nor does it provide any examples that allow it to be rejected.[83]

6 Fight Against Corruption

According to the Implementation Plan adopted in 2002 at the World Summit on Sustainable Development held in Johannesburg:

---

[80] Baron (2014), p. 16.

[81] European Commission (2016), p. 22.

[82] Art. 69:3 of the current Public Procurement Directive provides that, if the reason why the tender is abnormally low is due to the fact that the obligations under Art. 18:2 are not complied with, the tender shall be rejected. It results from Art. 18:2 that "Member States shall take appropriate measures to ensure that in the performance of public contracts economic operators comply with applicable obligations in the fields of environmental, social and labour law established by Union law, national law, collective agreements or by the international environmental, social and labour law provisions listed in Annex X", ie: International Labour Organization (ILO) Convention 87 on Freedom of Association and the Protection of the Right to Organise; ILO Convention 98 on the Right to Organise and Collective Bargaining; ILO Convention 29 on Forced Labour; ILO Convention 105 on the Abolition of Forced Labour; ILO Convention 138 on Minimum Age; ILO Convention 111 on Discrimination (Employment and Occupation); ILO Convention 100 on Equal Remuneration; ILO Convention 182 on Worst Forms of Child Labour; Vienna Convention for the protection of the Ozone Layer and its Montreal Protocol on substances that deplete the Ozone Layer; Basel Convention on the Control of Transboundary Movements of Hazardous Wastes and their Disposal (Basel Convention); Stockholm Convention on Persistent Organic Pollutants (Stockholm POPs Convention); Convention on the Prior Informed Consent Procedure for Certain Hazardous Chemicals and Pesticides in International Trade (UNEP/FAO) (PIC Convention) and its 3 regional Protocols

[83] Semple (2017), p. 303.

> **4.** Good governance within each country and at the international level is essential for sustainable development. At the domestic level, sound environmental, social and economic policies, democratic institutions responsive to the needs of the people, the rule of law, anti-corruption measures, gender equality and an enabling environment for investment are the basis for sustainable development (. . .).
>
> **19.** Encourage relevant authorities at all levels to take sustainable development considerations into account in decision-making, including on national and local development planning, investment in infrastructure, business development and public procurement (. . .).[84]

More recently, the Sustainable Development Goals adopted in 2015 set as goal 16 to "promote peaceful and inclusive societies for sustainable development, provide access to justice for all and build effective, accountable and inclusive institutions at all levels" and as a target to "substantially reduce corruption and bribery in all their forms." (16.5).

In other words, achieving the objective of sustainable development is not limited to the environmental aspect[85] and as highlighted by some authors:

> Economically, corruption drains public funds: taxpayers pay an estimated 25% in additional costs for government due to bribery, kickbacks, theft, and other behaviours classified as corruption. The final quality of procured goods and services are also lower due to corruption – poorly engineered public works and incompetent service delivery stem from granting contracts to favoured suppliers rather than to the most qualified, defective infrastructure results from fraudulent substitution of low-cost materials and shortages of supplies due to their 'disappearance' en route are just two often-cited complaints about public purchases that are directly related to corruption. The costs of unnecessary contracts – projects planned and implemented in order to provide a source of corruption payments – are difficult to estimate but, are no less worrisome for that.[86]

Globally, corruption is estimated to cost about USD 1.5 to USD 2 trillion per year, roughly representing 2% of the global GDP, and 57% of known cases of corruption are related to public procurement.[87] As public procurement "represents between 15 and 25 per cent of GDP in OECD countries, the stakes in fighting corruption are high".[88]

Corruption in public procurement works as a barrier to trade (requires the foreign supplier to pay extra) by blocking competition and distorting the allocation of resources, it reduces economic growth and incentives for innovation; discourages

---

[84] Nações Unidas, *World Summit on Sustainable Development - Plan of Implementation of the World Summit on Sustainable Development* (A/CONF.199/20), 4.9.2002, paras. 4 and 19.

[85] Green Public Procurement (GPP) refers to the inclusion of environmental criteria in the public procurement process. Thereby, the term is narrower than the more frequently used term "sustainable public procurement" since the latter encompasses not only environmental but also social and economic aspects. The European Commission defines the GPP as a process whereby public authorities seek to procure goods, services and works with a reduced environmental impact throughout their life-cycle when compared to goods, services and works with the same primary function that would otherwise be procured. Koch (2020), p. 21.

[86] Schefer and Woldesenbet (2018), p. 1131.

[87] Chabrost (2021), p. 129.

[88] Chabrost (2021), p. 129.

foreign investment; weakens the legitimacy of governments; wastes resources that the government might otherwise invest productively in public goods, infrastructure, and social services (especially education and health); etc.

Bribery and corruption became an international issue in the mid-1970s as a result of several scandals involving payments to foreign government officials by Lockheed and other United States companies. In response to such scandals, the United States Congress passed the so-called Foreign Corrupt Practices Act in 1977 making it a crime to bribe foreign government officials in order to obtain business.[89] More recently, the corruption of Darleen Druyun, former assistant secretary general for United States air force procurement,[90] captured the attention of American society and occupies an important place "in the Pantheon of procurement horror stories".[91] Basically, Darleen Druyun negotiated (in 2003) a job with the Boeing company for herself, her daughter, and her son-in-law[92] at the same time that it was negotiating with that company for the contracting of a set of goods by the North American Air Force. Darleen Druyun acknowledged that she had agreed, on behalf of the Air Force, to pay a price higher than the real value for the goods in question and explicitly admitted that the inflated prices were intended to ingratiate himself with his future employer and function as a parting gift.[93] She also provided Boeing with information on the price submitted by a competing European bidder for the same procurement procedure. In the end: "She pleaded guilty and served nine months in federal prison [in 2005]. Boeing ultimately paid a record fine of $615 million to resolve various allegations stemming from procurement improprieties, including its dealings with Ms. Druyun."[94]

Unlike the GPA 1994, the new GPA mentions the word "corruption" (it is the first WTO agreement to do so),[95] the objective of combating corrupt practices, and the

[89] Abbott (2001), p. 275.

[90] Darleen Druyun "was the senior career civilian procurement official-second only to the political appointees that cycle through the Assistant Secretary of the Air Force for Acquisition position. In other words, she was the highest-ranking long-term procurement official providing continuity to the Air Force acquisition community throughout changes in administrations." Branstetter (2005), p. 444.

[91] *Ibid.*

[92] Dietrich (2005), p. 522.

[93] Branstetter (2005), p. 446.

[94] Yukins and Schooner (2007), pp. 548-549. Darleen Druyun was convicted in 2004.

[95] Pauwelyn (2013), p. 248. The GPA 1994 does not contain any special rules against or explicitly mention corruption in public procurement. However, indirectly, it is evident that the agreement contributed to fighting corruption through the principles of non-discrimination and transparency. On the other hand, there are other commercial instruments that have helped to strengthen the relationship between trade and the fight against corruption. For example, the European Union's system of generalized preferences has offered additional trade preferences to developing countries that ratify and implement certain conventions on principles of governance, including the United Nations Convention against Corruption.

United Nations Convention against Corruption[96] even if it does not advance any definition of corrupt practices.[97]

The GPA 2012 mentions the objective of fighting corruption twice. It is mentioned in the sixth recital of the preamble to the GPA 2012:

> *Recognizing* the importance of transparent measures regarding government procurement, of carrying out procurements in a transparent and impartial manner and of avoiding conflicts of interest and corrupt practices, in accordance with applicable international instruments, such as the United Nations Convention Against Corruption.

Although the preamble only mentions the United Nations Convention against Corruption, other international anti-corruption instruments should also be taken into account such as the OECD Convention against Corruption of Foreign Public Officials in International Business Transactions[98] and the Inter-American Convention Against Corruption.[99]

The other reference is found in GPA 2012 Article IV:4(c) which requires contracting entities to conduct the award of the covered contracts in a transparent and impartial manner, avoiding corrupt practices. If a party violates GPA Article IV:4 by not respecting, for example, the United Nations Convention against Corruption, the aggrieved supplier may resort to the internal appeal procedures provided in GPA Article XVIII.[100]

---

[96]The text of the United Nations Convention against Corruption, signed in 2003 and in force since 14 December 2005, can be found in Diário da República, I Série, No. 183, 21.9.2007, 6718-6738. It is interesting to note that many of the current parts of the GPA are not parties to the United Nations Convention and that this convention specifically contains an article for public procurement, Art. 9, entitled "Public Procurement and Management of Public Finances". It calls for transparency ex ante in the sense that clear criteria regarding the upcoming procurement should be established as well as ex post by stressing the need for accountability of the procuring entities.

[97]Despite the absence of a clear definition of corruption, this "can be defined as the abuse of entrusted power for individual or collective, direct or indirect personal gain, and whereas acts of corruption include the crimes of bribery, embezzlement, trading in influence, abuse of functions and illicit enrichment, as defined by the United Nations Convention against Corruption; whereas fraud, extortion, blackmail, abuse of discretionary powers, favouritism, nepotism, clientelism and illegal political contributions are closely linked to corruption." European Parliament, *Corruption in the public and private sectors: the impact on human rights in third countries European Parliament resolution of 8 October 2013 on corruption in the public and private sectors: the impact on human rights in third countries (2013/2074(INI))*, Official Journal of the European Union C/181, 19.5.2016, 4.

[98]The text of the OECD Convention on Combating Bribery of Foreign Public Officials in International Business Transactions (signed on 17 December 1997 and in force since 15 February 1999) can be found in Diário da República, I Série A, No. 77, 31.3.2000, 1408-1411.

[99]The text of the Inter-American Convention against Corruption adopted in Caracas on March 29, 1996 and in force since March 6, 1997 can be found in OAS :: SLA :: Department of International Law (DIL) :: Inter-American Treaties.

[100]Lo (2015), p. 39; Pauwelyn (2013), p. 256.

By comparison, even though the United Nations Convention against Corruption is the most important international effort to fight corruption[101] and its Article 66:2 stipulates that:

> Any dispute between two or more States Parties concerning the interpretation or application of this Convention that cannot be settled through negotiation within a reasonable time shall, at the request of one of those States Parties, be submitted to arbitration. If, six months after the date of the request for arbitration, those States Parties are unable to agree on the organization of the arbitration, any one of those States Parties may refer the dispute to the International Court of Justice by request in accordance with the Statute of the Court,

several parties have advanced a reservation on this provision (e.g., China, Colombia, India, Israel, South Africa, and the United States).[102]

In contrast, the GPA expressly determines that "no Party may enter a reservation in respect of any provision of this Agreement" (Article XXII:3), and it is significant that Ukraine (party to the GPA 2012 since 18 May 2016) and Moldova (became a party to the GPA 2012 on 14 July 2016) have expressly expressed their intention to use their accession to the WTO Agreement on Government Procurement as part of their anti-corruption strategy.[103] Similarly, a key motive for China to ask for accession (China tabled its first offer on 28 December 2007) was that it considered the GPA "a useful force for pushing domestic political anti-corruption efforts",[104] and the Brazilian Minister of Economy announced on 21 January 2020 that his country "will request to join the GPA to sending a powerful message that it is determined to grapple with corruption and collusion which has plagued its public procurement system in the past".[105]

Relevantly, the GPA provides measures aimed at increasing transparency of public procurement systems (sunlight is the best of disinfectants[106]), and better managed procurement can lead to significant savings in public budgets and to more investments. For example:

> An efficiency gain of 10% could yield significant savings of EUR 200 billion per year, without cutting the level of service offered to Europeans. Procurement has also a major impact on the European Union structural and investment funds, where almost half of these funds are spent via public contracts. Good contracting helps to get the best value for money from these European Union funds.[107]

On the other hand, some examples suggest that sustainable public procurement can be considerably more expensive than the conventional alternative. For instance,

---

[101] Lo (2015), p. 28.

[102] https://treaties.un.org/Pages/ViewDetails.aspx?src=IND&mtdsg_no=XVIII-14&chapter=18&lang=en (page visited on 9.6.2022).

[103] Anderson et al. (2017), p. 95.

[104] Harpaz and Peled (2020), p. 225.

[105] Anderson et al. (2019), p. 1293.

[106] Anderson, et al. (2019), p. 1236.

[107] European Commission, *Making Public Procurement work in and for Europe*, COM (2017) 572 final, Strasbourg, 3.10.2017, 2.

Swedish data revealed that an organic food basket was 65.6% more expensive and a carbon neutral pre-school building cost 5–7 times more than a conventional one.[108] So, it is absolutely vital to open up international public procurement markets and allowing new economic operators to enter procurement processes, especially in countries with smaller procurement markets and in sectors where supply is limited.

It is known that collusion has long been identified and treated as an important risk factor for efficient public procurement.[109] It is estimated to increase the costs that public authorities pay by up to 60% compared to what they would pay under normal market conditions. Even a single case of collusion in a multi-million-euro award procedure will cost the European taxpayer millions of euros of excess payments to the detriment of efficient and accountable public spending,[110] and the smaller the number of economic operators active in a public procurement market, the easier it is to engage in collusion.

GPA participation strengthens competition in at least three measurable ways: "(1) it increases the number and diversity of firms bidding for particular procurements, including by allowing foreign firms to bid; (2) it decreases the number of contracts with single bidders; and (3) it decreases the total number of contracts awarded to individual firms."[111]

Furthermore, exclusively using price as an award criterion facilitates collusive agreements as the outcome of the evaluation becomes more predictable and can be manipulated easier. Assessing tenders on the basis of quality criteria makes it more difficult for colluders to manipulate their offers as they would not be able to easily prejudge how the evaluation committee would evaluate them.[112]

Recently, a paper uses a unique data set provided by the European Union covering more than three million tenders conducted in the European Economic Area, Macedonia, and Switzerland between 2006 and 2016 and comes to the following main conclusions. First, the WTO GPA reduces barriers for foreign firms. Second, the WTO GPA promotes a competitive environment by increasing the number of offers, and foreign firms are more likely to win government procurement contracts when the contract is covered by the WTO GPA. Third, corruption risks, measured in two different ways, are lower in WTO GPA auctions. The first measure is the probability of a single-bid auction, and the second is the number of recurrent wins by a single firm. Finally, the WTO GPA improves procurement

---

[108] Halonen (2021), p. 546.

[109] In fact, collusion is a recurrent feature in some public procurement markets, and up to 20% can be added to the price otherwise paid in competitive markets. European Commission, *Making Public Procurement work in and for Europe*, COM(2017) 572 final, Strasbourg, 3.10.2017, 13.

[110] European Commission, *Notice on tools to fight collusion in public procurement and on guidance on how to apply the related exclusion ground* (2021/C 91/01), Official Journal of the European Union C 91, 18.3.2021, 3.

[111] Anderson, et al. (2019), p. 1294.

[112] European Commission, *Notice on tools to fight collusion in public procurement and on guidance on how to apply the related exclusion ground* (2021/C 91/01), Official Journal of the European Union C 91, 18.3.2021, 24.

cost-effectiveness by lowering the probability of the procurement price being larger than the estimated cost.[113]

7 Final Considerations

A specific goal of the Sustainable Development Goals[114] is to promote a universal, rules-based, open, non-discriminatory, and equitable multilateral trading system within the WTO (Goal 17.10). It is very relevant that trade is mentioned only once in the previous Millennium Development Goals but nine times in the current Sustainable Development Goals. It is also pertinent that national governments have formally recognized the role of public procurement in supporting sustainability: "Promote public procurement practices that are sustainable, in accordance with national policies and priorities" (Goal 12.7).

Currently, the GPA has the following 48 parties: Armenia, Australia, Canada, Chinese Taipei, the European Union and the 27 Member States, Hong Kong, Iceland, Israel, Japan, Liechtenstein, Moldova, Montenegro, the Netherlands regarding Aruba, Norway, New Zealand, the United Kingdom, Singapore, South Korea, Switzerland, Ukraine, and the United States.[115] Being a plurilateral trade agreement, the GPA only creates rights and obligations for WTO members who have accepted it (Article II:3 of the agreement creating the WTO), but it is important to note that the plurilateral nature of the GPA does not prevent its impact and influence from extending to countries and territories that are not formally part of it.[116] Many of the chapters of the preferential trade agreements relating to public procurement are based substantially or entirely on the text of the WTO Agreement on Public Procurement (in the 1994 text or in the revised version[117]), "a form of de facto

---

[113] Dawar et al. (2019), pp. 614, 621, 628 and 633.

[114] In September 2015, world leaders adopted the 2030 Agenda for Sustainable Development, a global effort under the auspices of the United Nations (UN) to tackle poverty, climate change, and violence while promoting more equal, inclusive, and prosperous societies. They agreed on 17 Sustainable Development Goals (SDGs) and 169 ambitious SDG targets covering all areas of human development and the environment to guide development efforts through the 2030 time horizon. Some of the SDGs explicitly call for the active use of trade measures, in particular Goal 2 (Zero Hunger) includes a call to correct and prevent trade restrictions and distortions in world agricultural markets, Goal 14 (Life Below Water) points to the need to reduce fishery subsidies to avoid overcapacity and overfishing, and trade benefits for poorer states are also explicitly raised in Goal 17 (Partnership for the Goals). From a broader economic perspective, general economic growth remains the most important channel through which trade can support the SDGs. The agenda itself affirms that "international trade is an engine for inclusive economic growth and poverty reduction, and contributes to the promotion of sustainable development" (United Nations 2015, para. 68).

[115] As of October 2022, the WTO had 164 members.

[116] Anderson. et al. (2011), p. 561.

[117] Anderson et al. (2015), p. 20.

multilateralization of the GPA".[118] On 21 July 2015, the World Bank's board of directors adopted a new policy with regard to public procurement for projects financed by it.[119] It recognizes that a GPA party may use its own public procurement system as an alternative procurement arrangement in the case of a project financed by the World Bank instead of the bank's regulations and procedures. Additionally, the Model Law of the United Nations Commission on International Trade Law (UNCITRAL) is largely harmonized with the GPA and, therefore, it can perfectly serve as a model for countries and territories that need to modernize their legislation in this area of public procurement and bring it into line with the GPA.[120]

In short, the GPA is far from being an obstacle for its parties when using public procurement to pursue the objective of sustainable development[121] and is increasingly "a central force" in public procurement worldwide.[122] The new GPA is estimated to apply annually to markets valued at USD 1.7 trillion while the value of public contracts reported by the parties to the GATT agreement on public procurement in 1992 amounted to only USD 62 billion.[123]

References

Abbott K (2001) Rule-making in the WTO: lessons from the case of bribery and corruption. J Int Econ Law 4:275

Anderson RD et al (2011) Government procurement provisions in regional trade agreements: a stepping stone to GPA accession? In: Arrowsmith S, Anderson RD (eds) *The WTO Regime on Government Procurement: Challenge and Reform*. Cambridge University Press, Cambridge, p 561

Anderson R et al (2015) Regional trade agreements & procurement rules: facilitators or hindrances?, European University Institute - Robert Schuman Centre for Advanced Studies - Global Governance Programme, EUI Working Paper RSCAS 2015/81, 20

Anderson R et al (2017) Promoting competition and deterring corruption in public procurement markets: synergies with trade liberalisation. Public Procurement Law Rev

[118] Gourdon and Messent (2019), p. 700. Countries are increasingly including disciplines on government procurement in their bilateral and preferential trade agreements. In 1990, only seven international trade agreements included provisions regarding government procurement; by 2010, this number had grown to at least 70, and these numbers have risen further since then. *Id.*, 682.

[119] World Bank, News Press Release, *New World Bank Procurement Framework Approved*, 21.7.2015.

[120] Yukins and Schnitzer (2015), p. 118.

[121] It is important to note that the European Union legislative public procurement framework and Member States' (all parts of the GPA) implementation laws have to meet the requirements of the GPA. See, for example, Article 25 of *Directive 2014/24/EU of the European Parliament ando f the Council of 26 February 2014 on public procurement and repealing Directive 2004/18/EC*, Official Journal of the European Union L 94, 28.3.2014, 65-242.

[122] Yukins and Schnitzer (2015), p. 91.

[123] Hoekman (2015), p. 4.

Anderson R et al (2019) Preventing corruption, supplier collusion, and the corrosion of civic trust: a procompetitive program to improve the effectiveness and legitimacy of public procurement. George Mason Law Rev 26(4):1233

Arrowsmith S (2011) The revised agreement on government procurement: changes to the procedural rules and other transparency provisions. In: Arrowsmith S, Anderson RD (eds) The WTO regime on government procurement: challenge and reform. Cambridge University Press, Cambridge

Baron R (2014) The role of public procurement in low-carbon innovation, background paper for the 33rd round table on sustainable development 12–13 April 2016. OECD Headquarters, Paris

Branstetter J (2005) Darleen Druyun: an evolving case study in corruption, power, and procurement. Public Contract Law J 34(3):443–468

Brenton J et al (2011) Issues and tensions in public procurement of 'green innovation': A cross-country study, The Graduate Institute/Genebra, The Centre for Trade and Economic Integration, Working Paper 2011–09

Canal-Forgues E (2008) Le règlement des différends à l'OMC. Bruylant, Brussels

Chabrost M (2021) Challenges in public procurement corruption and probity in public procurement. In: Castelli A et al (eds) The challenges of public procurement reforms. Routledge, Milton Park

Chaudhary O (2005) The Propriety of Preferences: An Evaluation of EC and U.S. GSP Schemes in the Wake of EC –Preferences, Asper Review

Cheng W et al (2018) Green Public Procurement, missing concepts and future trends - A critical review. J Cleaner Production

Correia F et al (2013) Low carbon procurement: An emerging agenda, Journal of Purchasing & Supply Management

Cottier T, Delimatsis P (2008) Article XIVbis GATS security exceptions. In: Wolfrum R et al (eds) WTO – trade in services, max Planck Institute for Comparative Public law and International law. Martinus Nijhoff Publishers, Leiden-Boston

Davies A (2009) Government procurement. In: Lester S, Mercurio B (eds) Bilateral and regional trade agreements: commentary and analysis. Cambridge University Press, Cambridge

Dawar K et al (2019) Does the WTO government procurement agreement deliver what it promises? World Trade Rev 18(4):609–634

Di Ubaldo M et al (2022) Voluntary programs and emissions revisited: what is the effect of EU trade agreements with environmental provisions?, working paper RSC 2022/05. Robert Schuman Centre for Advanced Studies

Dietrich E (2005) The potential for criminal liability in government contracting: a closer look at the procurement integrity act. Public Contract Law J 34:521–538

Dragos DC, Neamtu B (2021) Life-cycle thinking in EU public procurement moving beyond a simple 'buzz word'. In: Castelli A et al (eds) The challenges of public procurement reforms. Routledge, Milton Park

European Commission (2016) Buying green! A handbook on green public procurement, 3rd edn. Publications Office of the European Union, Luxemburg, p 22

Giles N (2018) The World Trade Organization's missed opportunity: how the agreement on government procurement can be transformed from a vehicle of trade to one of human rights. Public Contract Law J 47(3)

Goodman R (2001) Norms and National Security: the WTO as a catalyst for inquiry. Chic J Int Law 2:7

Gourdon J, Messent J (2019) How government procurement measures can affect trade. J World Trade 53

Grandia J (2016) Finding the missing link: examining the mediating role of sustainable public procurement behaviour. J Clean Prod

Halonen K-M (2021) Is public procurement fit for reaching sustainability goals? A law and economics approach to green public procurement. Maa J Eur Comp Law 28(4)

Hamilton S (2022) Public procurement – price-taker or market-shaper? Crit Perspect Int Bus ahead-of-print
Hanley C (2002) Avoiding the issue: the commission and human rights conditionality in public procurement. Eur Law Rev
Harpaz MD, Peled H (2020) The stalemate in China's GPA accession negotiations – is there a way out? Asian J Int Law 15(1):209–258
Hoekman B (2015) International Cooperation on Public Procurement Regulation, European University Institute - Robert Schuman Centre for Advanced Studies - Global Governance Programme, EUI Working Paper RSCAS 2015/88
Hollander D, Marx A (2014) Strengthening private certification systems through public regulation: the case of sustainable public procurement. Sustain Account Manag Policy J 5(1)
Howse R (2001) Adjudicative legitimacy and treaty interpretation in international trade law: the early years of WTO jurisprudence. In: Weiler J (ed) The EU, the WTO, and the NAFTA: towards a common law of international trade? Oxford University Press, Oxford
Imperiale V (2001) Characterizing air as an exhaustible natural resource. In: Jackson J, Weiss EB (eds) Reconciling environment and trade. Transnational Publishers, Ardsley-New York
Jackson J (2008) The case of the World Trade Organization. Int Aff 84:437–454
Kelly JP (2005) The seduction of the appellate body: shrimp/sea turtle I and II and the proper role of states in WTO governance. Cornell Int Law J 38:34
Koch R (2020) Green public procurement under WTO law: experience of the EU and prospects for Switzerland. In: European yearbook of international economic law monographs - studies in European and international economic law, vol 9. Springer, Cham
Kullmann M (2018) Promoting social and environmental sustainability: what role for public procurement. Comp Labor Law Policy J 40(1):109–129
Kunzlik P (2003) International procurement regimes and the scope for the inclusion of environmental factors in public procurement. OECD J Budg 3(4):155–191
Lida K (2004) Is WTO dispute settlement effective?, Global Governance
Lo C-F (2015) Making the anti-corruption provisions in the new government procurement agreement under the WTO operable. Trade, Law Dev VII(1):21–41
Marty F (2014) Les clauses environnementales dans les marchés publics: perspectives économiques, Working Paper No. 2012–01. Group de Recherche en Droit, Économie, Gestion, Paris, Revisée Mars
Mavroidis P (2008a) Legal eagles? The WTO appellate Body's first ten years. In: Janow M et al (eds) The WTO: governance, dispute settlement, and developing countries. Juris Publishing, New York
Mavroidis P (2008b) No outsourcing of law? WTO law as practiced by WTO courts. Am J Int Law 102
McCrudden C (1999) International economic law and the pursuit of human rights: a framework for discussion of the legality of 'selective purchasing' Laws under the WTO government procurement agreement. J Int Econ Law
OECD (2021) Government at a Glance. OECD Publishing, Paris, p 162
Orakhelashvili A (2007) Interpretation of jurisdictional instruments in international dispute settlement. In: Law and practice of international courts and tribunals. Brill, Leiden
Pauwelyn J (2002) The Nature of WTO Obligations, Jean Monnet Working Paper 1/02 – New York University School of Law
Pauwelyn J (2013) Different means, same end: the contribution of trade and investment treaties to anti-corruption policy. In: Rose-Ackerman S, Carrington P (eds) Anti-corruption policy can international actors play a constructive role? Carolina Academic Press, Durham-North Carolina
Perkins R, Neumayer E (2012) Does the 'California effect' operate across borders? Trading- and investing-up in automobile emission standards. J Eur Publ Policy 19:217–237
Querol ÁA et al (2021) LCC and GPP: competing or complementary approaches? In: Castelli A et al (eds) The challenges of public procurement reforms. Routledge, Milton Park

Rainville A (2017) Standards in green public procurement - a framework to enhance innovation. J Clean Prod
Reich A (2009) The new text of the agreement on government procurement: an analysis and assessment. J Int Econ Law
Reif T, Eckert J (2004) Courage you Can't understand: how to achieve the right balance between shaping and policing commerce in disputes before the World Trade Organization. Columbia J Transnational Law
Reimers LL (2021) International trade law legal: entanglement on the WTO's own terms. In: Krisch N (ed) Entangled legalities beyond the state. Cambridge University Press, Cambridge
Röben V (2010) Eco-labelling, max Planck Encyclopedia of public international law, Oxford University Press, Oxford
Ruttan V (2006) Is war necessary for economic growth? Military procurement and technology development. Oxford University Press, Oxford
Schefer K, Woldesenbet M (2018) The revised agreement on government procurement and corruption. J World Trade
Semple A (2017) Socially Responsible Public Procurement (SRPP) under EU Law and International Agreements: The GPA, CETA and the EU-Ukraine Deep and Comprehensive Free Trade Area, European Procurement and Public Private Partnership Law Review 2017/3
Silva MP et al (eds) (2015) A Organização Mundial do Comércio e a Proteção do Ambiente: A Distinção Produto/Processo de Produção, Anais do II Congresso Luso-Brasileiro do Núcleo de Estudos Luso-Brasileiro. Editora Vestnik, Brasília
Tarullo D (2000) The relationship of WTO obligations to other international arrangements. In: Bronckers M, Quick R (eds) New directions in international economic law: essays in honour of John Jackson. Kluwer Law International, Hague
Tosoni L (2013) The impact of the revised WTO government procurement agreement on the EU procurement rules from a sustainability perspective. European Procurement & Public Private Partnership Law Review
Uysal E (2021) Business and human rights: the state as a buyer. European Procurement & Public Private Partnership Law Review 16(1)
van Asselt H et al (2006) Greener public purchasing: opportunities for climate-friendly government procurement under WTO and EU rules. Clim Pol 6:217–229
Van Calster G (2002) Green procurement and the WTO – shades of Grey. Rev Eur Comp Int Environ Law 11:298–305
Van Calster G (2009) Procurement and the World Trade Organization: purchase power or pester power? In: Cottier T et al (eds) International trade regulation and the mitigation of climate change, world trade forum. Cambridge University Press, Cambridge
Van den Bossche P (2006) From afterthought to centerpiece: the WTO appellate body and its rise to prominence in the world trading system. In: Sacerdoti G et al (eds) The WTO at ten: the contribution of the dispute settlement system. Cambridge University Press, Cambridge
Vogel D (1995) Trading up: consumer and environmental regulation in a global economy. Harvard University Press, Cambridge
Vogel D (2000) Environmental regulation and economic integration. J Int Econ Law
Wiesbrock A (2013) An obligation for sustainable procurement? Gauging the potential impact of article 11 TFEU on public contracting in the EU. Legal Issues Econ Integr
Witjes S, Lozano R (2016) Towards a more Circular Economy: Proposing a framework linking sustainable public procurement and sustainable business models, Resources, Conservation and Recycling 112
Woolcock S, Grier JH (2015) TTIP and public procurement. In: Hamilton DS, Pelkmans J (eds) Rule-makers or rule-takers? Exploring the transatlantic trade and investment partnership, Center for Transatlantic Relations. Johns Hopkins University/Centre for European Policy Studies, Rowman & Littlefield International, Ltd, London
Yang J (2012) Expansion of the government procurement agreement: time to concentrate on depth as well as width. J East Asian Economic Integr 16(1):263–304

Yukins C, Schnitzer J (2015) GPA Accession: Lessons Learned on the Strengths and Weaknesses of the WTO Government Procurement Agreement. Trade, Law and Development VII(1):91
Yukins C, Schooner S (2007) Incrementalism: eroding the impediments to a global public procurement market. Georgetown J Int Law 38:529–576
Zarbiyev F (2012) Judicial activism in international law - a conceptual framework for analysis. J Int Dispute Settlement 3(2)

Part IV
Green Taxes

Environmental Taxation and ESG: Silent Partners

Janet E. Milne

Abstract Environmental, social and governance (ESG) perspectives have rapidly gathered speed and global reach over the past several years. Although often motivated by the desire to improve investor decision-making, ESG perspectives can also represent a broader ethic and understanding of the need for societal changes. This chapter focuses on the "E," or environmental, pillar of ESG. It explores the relationship between environmental taxation and the ESG environmental pillar. In working toward environmental protection, both share common characteristics. As environmental protection policies, they operate alongside but outside of traditional, environmental command-and-control regulations. They both send a strong educational signal that can influence behaviour in environmentally positive ways. At the same time, they play very different but symbiotic roles. For example, environmental taxation instruments that effectively change behaviour allow the private sector to show more positive results when they disclose ESG data on a voluntary or compulsory basis. Conversely, ESG programs may help policymakers develop stronger environmental taxation policies and build support for market-based environmental protection instruments. Drawing on selected current ESG developments in the United States and European Union, the chapter presents the relationship between environmental taxation and ESG as a silent partnership. The public ESG spotlight often places disclosures centre front, but the more nuanced relationship between environmental taxation and ESG principles works quietly in the background. The chapter considers how this potential relationship—the silent partnership—may have the capacity to improve environmental protection.

The author thanks Vanessa Fetter for her research, Patrick Parenteau for his review of a preliminary draft, and André Alfar for conforming footnotes to the book's style all errors and omissions remain at the author's door.

J. E. Milne (✉)
Environmental Tax Policy Institute, Vermont Law School, South Royalton, VT, USA
e-mail: jmilne@vermontlaw.edu

R. Saraiva, P. A. Pardal (eds.), *Sustainable Finances and the Law*, Economic Analysis of Law in European Legal Scholarship 16,
https://doi.org/10.1007/978-3-031-49460-4_11

1 Introduction

Environmental taxation is a longstanding concept. The recent environmental, social, and governance (ESG) perspectives have rapidly gathered speed and global reach over the past few years, motivated in large part by the desire to better inform investors' decision-making. The time seems right to think about the potential synergies between environmental taxation concepts and ESG concepts.

Environmental taxation and the "E" (environmental) pillar in the ESG concept bring both similar and different attributes to the environmental protection table. They share a common goal. They each seek to advance society's environmental sustainability by influencing private-sector behaviour. However, they each approach that goal from a different angle. Environmental taxation directly sends environmental *price signals* into the private-sector marketplace. By creating environmental taxation instruments, government directly influences the economics of private-sector decision-making. The ESG concept operates more indirectly, and its initiatives seek to enhance the *flow of information* to influence private-sector decision-making. This informational transparency in turn may affect the marketplace. Environmental taxation and the ESG concept also focus on different players in the private sector. Environmental taxation targets business enterprises and consumers while ESG policies seek to influence the investors, reaching explicitly up to the investor level in a way that environmental taxation generally does not. Investor decisions can then influence business entities' decisions. Environmental taxation requires governmental intervention to create the taxation instruments. ESG policies discussed in this chapter require government mandates, although ESG initiatives can also be voluntary. This chapter explores the relationship between environmental taxation and ESG environmental considerations. It posits that environmental taxation and the ESG concept may potentially have a low key, nuanced relationship that can work quietly in the background—a silent partnership. To provide a concrete context, the chapter looks through the lens of taxation and ESG policies that address climate change. It uses ESG policies that the United States (US) Federal Government and the European Union (EU) have put forward as examples to explore potential interactions between environmental taxation and ESG. The need to consider climate change policies, individually and in combination, is critical at this point in time. The United Nations Environment Programme in November 2022 issued "a call for the rapid transformation of societies" in light of inadequate action to address the climate crisis.[1] It identified tax policies and investor behaviour as two important areas for action.[2] According to its analysis, policies currently in place would lead to a 2.8 °C increase in global temperature over the century if additional measures are not put into effect; and to meet the Paris Agreement's goal of limiting global temperature rise to 1.5 °C,

[1]United Nations Environment Programme, Emissions Gap Report 2022: The Closing Window – Climate crisis calls for rapid transformation of societies (Nairobi 2022), XVI, https://www.unep.og/emissions-gap-report-2022

[2]Id. at XXIV, Table ES.3.

greenhouse gas emissions must fall 45 percent by 2030 relative to emissions levels projected under current policies.[3] In a parallel report, the environment programme also painted a daunting picture of the risks of climate change.[4] Even under low-emissions assumptions, the world faces severe climate risks before the 22nd century.[5] As explored below, environmental taxation and environmentally oriented ESG policies can work to shape private-sector behaviour in ways that can reduce greenhouse gas emissions and the risks that come with climate change. The chapter starts with a general description of environmental taxation and the ESG environmental pillar in order to introduce readers to these two approaches to addressing climate change (Sect. 2). It then describes ESG measures and proposals in the United States and the European Union (EU) (Sects. 3 and 4) and the important role of greenhouse gas emissions in climate-related environmental taxation and the ESG environmental pillar (Sect. 5). Building on that foundation, the chapter explores how, in the abstract, environmental taxation can help advance ESG goals (Sect. 6) and how ESG policies can help environmental taxation (Sect. 7), creating the potential for a mutually supportive, silent partnership. Drawing on the ESG case studies in the United States and the EU as illustrations, Sects. 6 and 7 consider potential interactions between the concepts of environmental taxation and ESG in the abstract. The chapter seeks to inspire thought about these interactions in general terms, not to critique any specific countries' policies.

2 Introducing the Partners

2.1 Environmental Taxation

Environmental taxation is an economic instrument for environmental protection.[6] It harnesses tax systems for environmental protection in three different ways of which all are relevant to the ESG environmental pillar as explored below—environmental taxes, green tax expenditures, and environmental fiscal reform more broadly. Governments can use taxes to increase the cost of environmentally damaging activities to correct for the market's failure to put a price on that damage, to influence behaviour, and possibly fund environmental remediation.[7] In the climate change context that dominates this chapter, the most significant form of environmental tax is a carbon

[3] Id. at XVI.

[4] See generally United Nations Environment Programme, Adaptation Gap Report 2022: Too Little, Too Slow—Climate adaptation failure puts world at risk (Nairobi 2022), https://www.unep.org/adaptation-gap-report-2022.

[5] Id. at IV.

[6] See, e.g., OECD (1989).

[7] See generally Milne and Andersen (2012), pp. 15–29.

tax.[8] Carbon taxes place a tax cost on carbon dioxide emissions and possibly other greenhouse gas emissions that are usually expressed in terms of the tax per tonne of emissions measured in carbon-dioxide equivalents (CO_2-e). CO_2-e converts the global warming potential of each greenhouse gas into a common metric based on the global warming potential of carbon dioxide. Carbon taxes that include greenhouse gases beyond carbon dioxide are sometimes still called carbon taxes. Carbon taxes often apply to fossil fuels based on the emissions that will occur upon combustion, but they can apply directly to the emissions.[9] Carbon pricing may also take non-tax forms, particularly through emissions trading systems such as those operating in the EU (the EU Emissions Trading Scheme), two regions in the United States, and elsewhere.[10] Emissions trading systems place a price on greenhouse gas emissions by requiring polluters to acquire emissions allowances that may be purchased at auction from the government (or allocated for free) or purchased in the marketplace. If a country or region uses carbon pricing in the form of a carbon tax or trading system, it sends a price signal into the marketplace to correct for market failures and reduce the level of greenhouse gas emissions.

According to a World Bank report, as of April 2022, 68 carbon pricing instruments were in operation around the world, including 37 carbon taxes and 34 emissions trading systems, attaching a price to 23% of global greenhouse gas emissions.[11] Carbon tax rates varied significantly by country. For example, the Swiss carbon tax rate in 2022 was USD 130 per tonne of CO_2; Canada's minimum carbon price was scheduled to increase to USD 136 per tonne of CO_2-e by 2030; and South Africa's carbon tax rate of USD 10 per tonne of CO2-e may increase over time under the government's proposal.[12] As these figures illustrate, carbon taxes and carbon pricing more broadly are real but have yet untapped global potential.

Conversely, governments can deliver tax benefits to encourage activities that are environmentally positive. Through tax expenditures, governments can directly reward certain kinds of activities that increase the level of participation in climate-friendly endeavours, making them more financially attractive. The term "tax expenditures" is often used to describe these incentives because government, in effect, is making an expenditure, albeit indirectly by foregoing tax revenue otherwise due.[13] Tax expenditures can take a variety of forms such as tax credits that reduce the amount of tax otherwise owed, tax deductions that reduce the amount subject to tax, tax exemptions for specific activities, or reduced tax rates. In the climate context,

---

[8] See, e.g., Krupnik and Parry (2012), pp. 1–21. Other taxes on fossil fuels, such as taxes on gasoline, can operate as implicit carbon taxes. The tax rate is not explicitly calibrated to the greenhouse gas emissions, but fuel taxes increase the cost of fossil fuels, and their tax rate can be translated into the cost per tonne of CO2-e emissions. See generally OECD (2021a).

[9] See United Nations (2021), pp. 79–99.

[10] See generally the World Bank (2022).

[11] World Bank (2022), p. 15.

[12] World Bank (2022), p. 22.

[13] See generally Surrey (1973), pp. 6–7, 126–154.

these tax expenditures might target, for example, investments in energy conservation, low-carbon technologies, and renewable energy. As just one example, in August 2022, US Congress passed legislation that included an array of climate-related tax expenditures for companies and individuals that is estimated to provide USD 270 billion in tax benefits over the next ten years.[14]

A government can also engage in environmental fiscal reform.[15] It can examine its fiscal system to determine whether it should shift its tax structure more toward environmental taxes, provide more fiscal incentives for green activities, and repeal fiscal subsidies (tax or otherwise) that finance environmentally harmful results. Environmental fiscal reform aligns relatively well with climate-oriented tax policies. Carbon taxes that apply substantial tax rates will generate significant revenue if a country relies heavily on fossil fuels. For example, if the United States adopted a carbon tax at the modest rate of USD 25 per tonne of carbon dioxide, the tax would generate an estimated one trillion dollars over a ten-year period from 2021 to 2030.[16] A significant new source of revenue could create an opportunity to reduce other tax burdens. In 2008, the Canadian province of British Columbia used the revenue from its new carbon tax to reduce other taxes on business and lower-income individuals, yielding a tax shift that was revenue neutral.[17] A report by the European Environment Agency suggests that the concept of environmental fiscal reform, which traditionally looked to tax shifting, might be reframed as sustainable tax reform to look more broadly at the present and future environmental, social, and fiscal challenges.[18]

Climate-related environmental fiscal reform also involves the repeal of tax and other subsidies that encourage the production of fossil fuels. The OECD and International Energy Agency estimated that support for fossil fuel through tax and other measures totaled USD 147 billion in 2020 for G20 countries and USD 362 billion for 51 countries that account for 85% of global energy supply—numbers that rose to USD 190 billion and USD 697 billion, respectively, in 2021 as the economy recovered.[19] International institutions and international negotiations

[14]US Department of the Treasury, Fact Sheet: Treasury, IRS Open Public Comment on Implementing the Inflation Reduction Act's Clean Energy Tax Incentives, Oct. 5, 2022, 1, https://home.treasury.gov/system/files/136/FactSheet-Implementing-IRA-Climate-CleanEnergy-TaxIncentives.pdf.

[15]See generally European Environment Agency (2022); European Court of Auditors (2022).

[16]Congressional Budget Office (2020), p. 85.

[17]Duff (2008).

[18]European Environment Agency (2022).

[19]OECD and IEA Support for fossil fuels almost doubled in 2021, slowing progress toward international climate change, according to new analysis from OECD and IEA, www.oecd.org/newsroom/support-for-fossil-fuels-almost-doubled-in-2021-slowing-progress-toward-international-climate-goals-according-to-new-analysis-from-oecd-and-iea.htm, visited Sept. 2, 2022.

pursuant to the Paris Agreement on climate change call for phasing out inefficient fossil fuel subsidies.[20] Doing so would advance environmental fiscal reform.

2.2 ESG

The ESG concept is still evolving in terms of its meaning, its boundaries, and its implementation and can be voluntary or governmentally mandated.[21] The "E" pillar in the ESG concept seeks to infuse sustainability considerations into investors' decisions about where to place their money.[22] It does so primarily through public disclosures by business entities and investment funds that enhance transparency. Its theory is that disclosures can allow investors who are concerned about climate risks and sustainability to make decisions that are more informed. Depending on the particular disclosure regime, disclosures may bring to light the extent to which investments are vulnerable to climate-related risks, the extent to which they contribute to climate change, thereby increasing risks, and whether they could benefit from climate-related business opportunities. ESG regimes may also set standards for defining sustainable business activities and the extent to which investment funds' corporate holdings meet sustainability standards, and they may target specific environmental issues, such as nature-related risks and opportunities.[23] Within this broad palette, this chapter focuses on regulatory ESG mechanisms that have strong climate components.

Sections 6 and 7 will explore how environmental taxation and the ESG "E" pillar might silently work in a partnership but, first, Sects. 3 and 4 describe environmentally oriented ESG initiatives in the EU and the United States in order to provide concrete contexts for considering that partnership. The descriptions of these two case studies cannot capture all the details of these intricate disclosure regimes. They instead highlight their substantive scope in broad terms—the types of information that must be disclosed and the extent to which climate-related disclosure applies at

[20] See, e.g. Sharm el-Sheikh Implementation Plan, Decision -/CP.27, paragraph 13, Advanced Unedited Version; G20 Bali Leaders' Declaration, Bali, Indonesia, Nov. 15–16, 2022, https://www.whitehouse.gov/briefing-room/statements-releases/2022/11/16/g20-bali-leaders-declaration/, visited Nov. 17, 2022; Report of the Conference of the Parties serving as the Meeting of the Parties to the Paris Agreement on the third session, held in Glasgow from 31 October to 13 November 2021, Decision I/CMA.3, Glasgow Climate Pact, paragraph 36 (March 8, 2022). The first major statement occurred at the 2009 meeting of the G20. G20 Leaders' Statement, The Pittsburgh Summit, Sept. 24–25, 2009, paragraphs 24, 29, 30.

[21] See, e.g., G20, G20 Sustainable Finance Roadmap (G20 Italia 2021, Oct. 7, 2021); Boffo and Patalano (2020).

[22] See generally Boffo and Patalano (2020); OECD (2021b, 2022).

[23] See Taskforce on Nature-related Financial Disclosures, The TNDF Nature-related Risk and Opportunity Management and Disclosure Framework Summary (Framework forthcoming September 2023).

the corporate and investment-fund level.[24] The case studies serve as illustrations of how ESG policies may operate when translating the general concepts above into specific regimes. Readers who are familiar with climate-related ESG might choose to proceed directly to Sects. 5, 6, and 7 which bring environmental taxation and potential interactions with ESG back into the picture. The author asks for other readers' indulgence along Sect. 3 and 4's journey through ESG measures. The highlighted aspects may sometimes seem a bit dry, but they offer signposts toward potential interactions between environmental taxation and the ESG environmental pillar. Please note that, as of fall 2022 when this chapter was written, the US provisions had been proposed but not yet adopted. The more expansive EU measures are a mix of provisions that have been adopted and those still under development. Thus, the descriptions below should be considered as conceptual illustrations of ESG approaches.

3 Climate-Related "E" Disclosure Proposals in the United States

In 2022, the US Securities and Exchange Commission (SEC) proposed two rules that directly address disclosures relevant to ESG policy and climate change. One is directed at disclosures by corporations, referred to here as the Company Rule. The second focuses on disclosures by managers of investment funds that invest in a portfolio of corporate holdings (and by other financial advisors, not discussed here), referred to here as the Investment Fund Rule. Thus, the first would provide information for people investing directly in the underlying companies while the second would provide information for people who are choosing among funds with multiple holdings. Each is described in turn below. The SEC is taking the proposals through the administrative rulemaking process based on its view that it has the legal authority to pursue the proposals under existing law.[25]

[24]The description does not delve into precisely which entities are subject to the disclosure requirements and which are exempted, but the US and EU measures have a broad reach into the corporate world and investment funds.

[25]At the closing of the comment period, over 10,000 comments had been filed in response to the notice of proposed rulemaking for the Company Climate Disclosure Rule. US Securities and Exchange Commission, Comments for Enhancement and Standardization of Climate-Related Disclosures for Investors, https://www.sec.gov/comments/s7-10-22/s71022.htm (visited Sept. 6, 2022).

3.1 Company Disclosure

The proposed Company Rule focuses entirely on climate-related disclosures. It concentrates primarily on disclosing risks. Although not framed in ESG terms, it is consistent with general ESG notions advocating environmental disclosures.

The Company Rule is designed to more effectively inform investors and the capital market about the impact of material climate-related risks on companies' finances so that investors will be in a better position to make investment decisions and to exercise their voting rights as shareholders. It would require publicly traded companies to disclose information about "climate-related risks that are reasonably likely to have a material impact on [the company's] business or consolidated financial statements."[26] Financial, climate-related risks to companies and their upstream and downstream value chain can be physical risks (acute or chronic) or transition risks that come with climate change mitigation and adaptation over the short, medium, and long term. Transition risks include government policies that can negatively affect companies' financial positions.[27] After identifying material risks, companies would then describe material financial impacts along the full value chain and how they are integrating climate risks and their management into their strategies.[28] Companies that have transition plans to address risks would describe the plans for mitigating or adapting to physical and transition risks.[29] Companies would also provide financial metrics of the impact of risks.[30] Disclosing financially beneficial opportunities is allowed but not mandated.

3.2 Investment Fund Disclosure

The proposed Investment Fund Rule[31] is framed explicitly in ESG terms and is not limited to climate change. The rule addresses the need for investors to have consistent, comparable information on ESG factors when choosing investment funds and the need to avoid greenwashing.[32] It applies to funds where one or more ESG factors

[26] Securities and Exchange Commission, The Enhancement and Standardization of Climate-Related Disclosures for Investors, 87 Federal Register 21334 (April 11, 2022), 21349.

[27] Securities and Exchange Commission, The Enhancement and Standardization of Climate-Related Disclosures for Investors, 87 Federal Register 21334 (April 11, 2022), 21349–51.

[28] Id. at 21354–56.

[29] Id. at 21362 (including imposition of a carbon tax).

[30] Id. at 21365–68 (including changes in revenue or costs as a result of "emissions pricing").

[31] Securities and Exchange Commission, Enhanced Disclosure by Certain Investment Advisors and Investment Companies About Environmental, Social, and Governance Investment Practices, 87 Federal Register 36654 (June 17, 2022).

[32] Securities and Exchange Commission, Enhanced Disclosure by Certain Investment Advisors and Investment Companies About Environmental, Social, and Governance Investment Practices, 87 Federal Register 36654, 36655 (June 17, 2022).

play a role in investment strategies.[33] It categories these funds into three types: (1) Integration funds in which one or more ESG factors are relevant but not dispositive to the funds' investment strategies; (2) ESG-focused funds in which one or more ESG factors, such as carbon emissions, are significant to investment strategies and engagement with the companies in their portfolio or when the name of the fund or marketing indicates that ESG is a significant factor; and (3) impact funds that seek to achieve specific ESG impacts,[34] such as goals for reducing greenhouse gas emissions. Each type has different disclosure requirements for greenhouse gas emissions (see Sect. 5 below).

From a climate change perspective, these two rules complement each other. Company disclosures can help potential investors and shareholders determine the degree of financial risk from climate change. Investment funds' disclosures then provide transparency about how companies in their portfolios are performing, allowing investors to consider environmental factors when they select investment funds. The company disclosures can help provide data to inform the investment funds' disclosures.

4 Climate-Related "E" Disclosure in the European Union

The EU has been a leader in translating general ESG concepts into specific principles and regulations. Its approach to climate change is broader than the US proposals described above. The European Commission's 2018 Action Plan: Financing Sustainable Growth[35] laid a foundation for significant ESG regulations directed at climate change issues. To work toward achieving the Paris Agreement's climate goals and the United Nation's Sustainable Development Goals, the plan called for sustainable finance and integrating ESG considerations into investment decision-making.[36] It defined sustainable finance as:

> the process of taking due account of environmental and social considerations in investment decision-making, leading to increased investments in longer-term and sustainable activities. More specifically, environmental considerations refer to climate change mitigation and adaptation, as well as the environment more broadly and related risks (e.g. natural disasters).[37]

---

[33] Id. at 36657.

[34] Id. at 36657.

[35] European Commission, Communication from the Commission to the European Parliament, the European Council, the Council, the European Central Bank, the European Economic and Social Committee and the Committee of the Regions, Action Plan: Financing Sustainable Growth, COM (2018) 97 final, March 8, 2018.

[36] Id. at 1.

[37] Id. at 2 (internal footnotes omitted). The "environment more broadly" is defined as "air and water pollution, resource depletion, and biodiversity loss". Id. at 2 n. 7.

Among its calls for specific actions were the issuance of corporate disclosure guidelines for ESG factors,[38] increased transparency for investors in funds,[39] the creation of ESG benchmarks that can measure the sustainability of investment funds,[40] and the development of a taxonomy that would identify "sustainable economic activities".[41] The EU has diligently pursued these sustainable finance goals. The following is a brief sketch of major, interlocking ESG regulations and proposals relevant to climate change.

4.1 Company Disclosure

The EU has been developing a system of environmental disclosures that applies to companies. A 2014 directive, the Nonfinancial Reporting Directive (NFRD), established the general principle that companies should disclose "non-financial" environmental information according to nonbinding guidelines that the European Commission would prepare.[42] Pursuant to its authority, the European Commission in 2019 issued nonbinding guidelines on reporting climate change information in line with the 2018 Action Plan.[43] In 2021, the European Commission proposed disclosure regulations for large companies and all listed companies—the Corporate Sustainability Reporting Directive (CSRD).[44] The CSRD responded to the need to mandate ESG disclosures and to do so on a broad, uniform basis for environmental, social, and human rights, and governance perspectives to better inform investors, actors in civil society, policymakers, and the companies themselves.[45] The CSRD substituted the term "sustainability information" for the NFRD's "non-financial information" in order to avoid the implication that sustainability information is not

[38] Id. at 9–10 ("Action 9").

[39] Id. at 8–9 ("Action 7").

[40] Id. at 7 ("Action 5").

[41] Id. at 4 ("Action 1").

[42] Directive 2014/95/EU of the European Parliament and the Council of 22 October 2014 amending Directive 2013/34/EU as regards disclosure of non-financial and diversity information by certain large undertakings and groups, Official Journal L 330/1, Nov. 15, 2014.

[43] European Commission, Communication from the Commission, Guidelines on non-financial reporting: Supplement on reporting climate-related information, C(2019) 4490 final, 17 June 2019.

[44] European Commission, Proposal for a Directive of the European Parliament and of the Council amending Directive 2013/34/EU, Directive 2004/109/EC, Directive 2006/43/EC and Regulation (EU) No. 537/2014, as regards corporate sustainability reporting, COM(2021) 189 final, 2021/0104 (COD), April 21, 2021. See generally European Commission, Communication from the Commission to the European Parliament, the Council, The European Economic and Social Committee and the Committee of the Regions, EU Taxonomy, Corporate Sustainability Reporting, Sustainability Preferences and Fiduciary Duties: Directing finance towards the European Green Deal, COM(2021) 188 final (April 21, 2021)

[45] Id. paragraphs 8–14, 23–25.

financially relevant.[46] In June 2022, the Council of the EU and the European Parliament reached a political provisional agreement on the CSRD subject to final approval that had not yet occurred as of fall 2022 when this chapter was written.[47]

The European Commission's nonbinding climate guidelines illustrate the types of disclosures relevant to climate change (referred to here as the European Commission Climate Guidelines). The guidelines apply a "double materiality" perspective that looks both inward and outward. Climate-related information may be *financially material* if it is necessary for understanding the company's development, performance, and position (looking inward).[48] Information is *environmentally material* if it is necessary for understanding the company's environmental impacts on the external world (looking outward). The guidelines consider both risks and opportunities. Risks of negative impacts can occur either in the internal perspective (risks to the company) or external perspective (risks that the company imposes on the climate). Climate risks to the company can include policy risks and physical risks from severe or chronic climate events.[49] Conversely, climate change may provide business opportunities that have an internal impact or provide opportunities to contribute to mitigation or adaptation and therefore reduce the external impact. In addition, the guidelines recommend determining materiality in light of the company's entire value chain both upstream and downstream.[50] The European Commission's approach is much broader than the US SEC's proposed Company Disclosure Rule that looks only at internal financial risks.

The CSRD bears similarities to the European Commission Climate Guidelines. It applies the dual materiality approach. It requires assessment of sustainability risks and opportunities for both the undertaking and the environment,[51] including adverse impacts connected with the value chain.[52] If the directive becomes law, the

[46] Id. paragraph 7, 23.

[47] Proposal for a Directive of the European Parliament and of the Council amending Directive 2013/34/EU, Directive 2004/109/EC, Directive 2006/43/EC and Regulation (EU) 537/2014, as regards corporate sustainability reporting, 10835/22 (30 June 2022); Council of the EU, Press Release, New rules on corporate sustainability reporting: Provisional political agreement between the Council and the European Parliament, updated June 30, 2022, https://www.consilium.europa.eu/en/press/press-releases/2022/06/21/new-rules-on-sustainability-disclosure-provisional-agreement-between-council-and-european-parliament/ (last visited 16 December 2022).

[48] European Commission, Communication from the Commission, Guidelines on non-financial reporting: Supplement on reporting climate-related information, Official Journal C209/1, June 20, 2019, Section 2.2, 209/4.

[49] Id. Section 2.3, C209/6.

[50] Id. Section 2.2, 8, Section 2.2, 209/5.

[51] Proposal for a Directive of the European Parliament and of the Council amending Directive 2013/34/EU, Directive 2004/109/EC, Directive 2006/43/EC and Regulation (EU) No 537/2014, as regards corporate sustainability reporting, 10835/22 (30 June 2022), paragraphs 25–27, 20–22, Art. 1(3).1-2, 58–60.

[52] Id., Art. 1(3).2(e), 60.

commission will be responsible for developing sustainability reporting requirements through delegated acts, including standards relating to climate change.[53]

4.2 *Investment Fund Disclosure*

The European Commission has actively advanced disclosure requirements for the financial services sector, including financial products such as investment funds, through its Sustainable Finance Disclosure Regulation (SFDR).[54] In brief summary, the regulation seeks to help inform investors about sustainability risks that can have a material negative impact on investments' value and principal adverse impacts of investment decisions on sustainability factors, including the environment. It also addresses greenwashing by increasing the transparency of products that are promoted as having environmentally positive characteristics or for which sustainability is a primary objective.[55]

The SFDR recognizes the ability to use reference benchmarks for financial products that promote environmental characteristics.[56] A regulation adopted the same day as the SFDR established a process for setting climate-related benchmarks to measure and compare the performance of financial products.[57] It creates two types of benchmarks: EU Climate Transition Benchmarks for portfolios that are on a decarbonization trajectory and EU Paris-aligned Benchmarks consistent with meeting the Paris Agreement's objectives.[58] Subsequent delegated regulations elaborate on the benchmark methodology and disclosure requirements for ESG factors and climate factors in particular.[59] The delegated regulation for EU Climate Transition

[53] Id., Art. 1(7b).1, 77–82). Recognizing the value of natural capital accounting methods, the CSRD interestingly recommends that sustainability reporting standards should include, when necessary, monetized values of companies' impacts on the environment. Id. paragraph 38, 31. This recommendation implicitly endorses concepts such as the social cost of carbon.

[54] Regulation (EU) 2019/2088 of the European Parliament and of the Council of 27 November 2019 on sustainability-related disclosures in the financial services sector, Official Journal L 317/1.

[55] Id., Arts. 2–9, 317/7-317/12.

[56] Id., Arts. 8, 9, 11, 317/11-317/14.

[57] Regulation (EU) 2019/2089 of the European Parliament and of the Council of 27 November 2019 amending Regulation (EU) 2016/1011 as regards EU Climate Transition Benchmarks, EU Paris-aligned Benchmarks and sustainability-related disclosures for benchmarks, Official Journal L317/17, Art. 1, 317/20-317/22.

[58] Id., Art. 1, 317/20-22.

[59] Commission Delegated Regulation (EU) 2020/1816 of 17 July 2020 supplementing Regulation (EU) 2016/2011 of the European Parliament and of the Council as regards the explanation in the benchmark statement of how environmental, social and governance factors are reflected in each benchmark provided and published, Official Journal L 406/1, December 3, 2020; Commission Delegated Regulation (EU) 2020/1817 of 17 July 2020 supplementing Regulation (EU) 2016/1011 of the European Parliament and of the Council as regards the minimum content of the explanation on how environmental, social and governance factors are reflected in the benchmark methodology,

Benchmarks and EU Paris-aligned Benchmarks sets specific minimum standards for the benchmarks.[60]

4.3 The Taxonomy

The EU has also created a taxonomy system to identify business activities that address climate change in positive ways. The Taxonomy Regulation establishes criteria for determining "environmentally sustainable economic activities" for investment purposes.[61] The criteria require that the activity must "contribute substantially" to one of six environmental objectives while also not significantly harming any of those objectives.[62] Two of the objectives are climate change mitigation and climate change adaptation. The criteria detail what constitutes a substantial contribution to climate change mitigation and adaptation.[63] Using its delegated authority, the European Commission has adopted meticulous, technical screening criteria for economic activities that qualify under this climate change standard.[64] Thus, the taxonomy creates consistent definitions of sustainability that apply across the EU.

The taxonomy directly contributes to disclosures. Under the European Commission Climate Guidelines, the taxonomy can help companies identify opportunities.[65] In a subsequent regulation, the European Commission also requires business

---

Official Journal, Vol. 63 L 406/12, 3 December 2020; Commission Delegated Regulation (EU) 2020/1818 of 17 July 2020 supplementing Regulation (EU) 2016/1011 of the European Parliament and of the Council as regards minimum standards for EU Climate Transition Benchmarks and EU Paris-aligned Benchmarks, Official Journal, Vol. 63 L 406/17, 3 December 2020.

[60] Commission Delegated Regulation (EU) 2020/1818 of 17 July 2020 supplementing Regulation (EU) 2016/1011 of the European Parliament and of the Council as regards minimum standards for EU Climate Transition Benchmarks and EU Paris-aligned Benchmarks, Official Journal, Vol. 63 L 406/17, 3 December 2020.

[61] Regulation (EU) 2020/852 of the European Parliament and of the Council of 18 June 2020 on the establishment of a framework to facilitate sustainable investment, and amending Regulation (EU) 2019/2088, Official Journal Vol. 63, L198/13, Vol. 63, June 22, 2020 (the "Taxonomy Regulation").

[62] Id. at Chapter II, Art. 3, Art. 9 (pages L 198/27, 198/29).

[63] Id. at Chapter II, Art. 10, Art. 11 (pages L 198/29–31). Regulations relating to the other environmental objectives will be forthcoming.

[64] Commission Delegated Regulation (EU) 2021/2139 of 4 June 2021 supplementing Regulation (EU) 2020/852 of the European Parliament and of the Council by establishing the technical screening criteria for determining the conditions under which an economic activity qualifies as contributing substantially to climate change mitigation or climate change adaptation and for determining whether that activity causes no substantial harm to any of the other environmental objectives, Official Journal Vol. 64, L 442, December 9, 2021.

[65] European Commission, Communication from the Commission, Guidelines on non-financial reporting: Supplement on reporting climate-related information, C(2019) 4490 final, 17 June 2019, Section 2.3, Table 2, 10.

enterprises and financial market participants to disclose the extent of their environmentally sustainable economic activities.[66] In ways appropriate for each type of reporting entity, the disclosure metrics quantify, in financial terms, the proportion of the undertakings' or financial products' investment in taxonomy-aligned activities.

Stepping back to consider the big picture and how these pieces fit together, the proposed CSRD for corporate reporting looks at sustainability risks and opportunities for business enterprises and the enterprises' risks and opportunities for the environment. The taxonomy can help identify environmentally positive activities within an enterprise. The company-level disclosures under the CSRD can potentially then inform investment fund managers' assessment of their funds' impacts, risks, and opportunities under the SFDR. The benchmarks define standards for identifying ESG-oriented investment funds. The pieces work together toward transparency, but their substantive scope and standards vary in light of different types of disclosures. When the European Commission exercises its delegated power under the proposed CSRD, it must consider disclosure obligations under the SRFD, the Benchmark Regulation, and the criteria under the taxonomy regulation to the extent possible[67] which is an instruction that should help integrate the various sets of requirements.

4.4 *Comparison of the US and EU Approaches*

Comparing the US and EU approaches in a broad brush, several features emerge. They each seek to increase transparency. The US SEC approaches this task from the traditional, financial perspective of wanting to ensure that investors and shareholders benefit from knowledge about material financial risks. The EU addresses climate disclosures as part of its affirmative plan to achieve a transition to a low-carbon, sustainable future. It has a substantive policy goal and uses disclosures as one tool. Consistent with this difference, the proposed US rules focus on climate-related risks to publicly traded companies and protect against funds' greenwashing. The EU's assembly of requirements looks at climate-based risks to companies and funds, but it considers risks and opportunities looking both inward and outward. It also identifies specific standards for climate-positive activities through the activity-specific taxonomy and through the benchmarks for investment funds.

---

[66] Commission Delegated Regulation (EU) 2021/2178 of 6 July 2021 supplementing Regulation (EU) 2020/852 of the European Parliament and of the Council by specifying content and presentation of information to be disclosed by undertakings subject to Articles 19a or 29b of Directive 2013/34/EU concerning environmentally sustainable activities, and specifying the methodology to comply with that disclosure, Official Journal, Vol. 64 L 443/9, Dec. 10, 2021.

[67] Proposal for a Directive of the European Parliament and of the Council amending Directive 2013/34/EU, Directive 2004/109/EC, Directive 2006/43/EC and Regulation (EU) No 537/2014, as regards corporate sustainability reporting, 10835/22 (30 June 2022), Art. 1(7b)(1), 78, Art. 1(7)(b)(3), 83–84.

5 The Central Role of Greenhouse Gas Emissions

Greenhouse gas emissions, of course, play a central role in the climate change plot: Greenhouse gas emissions contribute to climate change, and their reduction is essential for addressing climate change. It follows naturally that they also play a central role in the climate-oriented policy relationship between environmental taxation and the ESG "E" pillar. On the environmental taxation side, carbon taxes target greenhouse gas emissions (or their proxies), and green tax expenditures can focus on activities that reduce greenhouse gas emissions. On the ESG side, the level of greenhouse emissions serves as a proxy for measuring the degree of risk.[68] High emissions levels reflect heavy reliance on fossil fuels and therefore greater financial risk during the transition to a low-emissions world as well as continuing contributions to climate risks. This section briefly summarizes the US and EU ESG disclosure requirements for greenhouse gas emissions before moving on to explore interactions between environmental taxation and ESG policies and the role of greenhouse gas emissions in those interactions (Sects. 6 and 7). The focus in this chapter on greenhouse gas emissions as the common element does not preclude the possibility of other synergies between environmental taxation and environmentally oriented ESG policies.

The US SEC's proposed Company Rule would require disclosure of greenhouse gas emissions.[69] Companies subject to the disclosure requirements would annually disclose Scope 1 greenhouse emissions (direct emissions from companies' operations) and Scope 2 emissions (indirect emissions, such as emissions associated with electricity used by companies) measured by CO_2-e. Disclosure of Scope 3 emissions (emissions from upstream and downstream activities that are part of the companies' value chain from start to finish) depends on circumstances. Companies would disclose Scope 3 emissions if the emissions are material or if companies have set targets for reducing greenhouse gas emissions.[70] Companies would also disclose greenhouse gas intensity calculated by the tonnes of Scope 1 and Scope 2 greenhouse gas emissions per unit of total revenue and separately for Scope 3 emissions.[71]

Reporting requirements for greenhouse gas emissions under the US SEC's proposed Investment Fund Rule vary depending on the type of fund. If integrated funds' managers consider greenhouse gas emissions relevant in making investment decisions, they would disclose how they consider them and their methodology in

[68] Voluntary disclosures and ratings may put less emphasis on greenhouse gas emissions. See OECD (2022), pp. 13, 33.

[69] Securities and Exchange Commission, The Enhancement and Standardization of Climate-Related Disclosures for Investors, 87 Federal Register 21334 (April 11, 2022).

[70] Securities and Exchange Commission, The Enhancement and Standardization of Climate-Related Disclosures for Investors, 87 Federal Register 21334, 21373-81 (April 11, 2022). The proposed rule exempts small companies. Id. at 21390.

[71] Id. at 21382–21383.

doing so.[72] The notice of proposed rulemaking requests comments on whether to require quantitative information about emissions and possible metrics.[73] If the managers of ESG-focused funds or impact funds consider environmental factors, they would disclose the tonnes of CO_2-e emissions per million dollars invested in the funds, which will allow investors to track funds' contributions to emissions. They would also provide the weighted average carbon intensity measured in tonnes of CO_2-e per million dollars of revenue which allows investors to focus more on levels of risks during the transition to a lower-carbon economy.[74] The proposed rule requires funds to collect information about Scope 1 and Scope 2 emissions of companies in their investment portfolios.[75] It sets up a hierarchy of sources that looks first to the companies' emissions reported in regulatory filings, then to other sources the companies have made publicly available, and finally to the funds' good faith estimates.[76] The proposed rule requires disclosure of Scope 3 emissions only to the extent that companies in the portfolios have reported emissions; Scope 3 emissions would be disclosed separately from the Scope 1 and 2 emissions and according to the industry sector.[77] Impact funds must also specify their target impacts, indicate how they will measure progress and over what timeframe, and the relationship between impacts and financial returns.[78]

The EU also calls for disclosure of greenhouse gas emissions. The European Commission Climate Guidelines, which consider financial and environmental materiality, recommends determining materiality in light of the company's entire value chain both upstream and downstream.[79] Their suggested disclosure metrics include Scope 1, Scope 2, and Scope 3 greenhouse gas emissions.[80] If the CSRD becomes law, delegated regulations will provide more disclosure details.

---

[72] Securities and Exchange Commission, Enhanced Disclosure by Certain Investment Advisors and Investment Companies About Environmental, Social, and Governance Investment Practices, 87 Federal Register 36654, 36661 (June 17, 2022). The notice of the proposed rule requests comment on whether to require quantitative information about emissions and possible emissions metrics. Note that the proposed rule also details where and when the disclosures are made within the array of SEC filings, which is a topic that is not discussed in this chapter, information about emissions, and possible emissions metrics. The proposed rule also details where and when the disclosures are made within the array of SEC filings which is also a topic that is not discussed in this chapter. Id.

[73] Id.

[74] Id. at 36676–36679. The proposal treats Impact Funds as a subset of ESG-Focused Funds. Id. at 36662.

[75] Id. at 36667 & No. 155.

[76] Id. at 36681.

[77] Id. at 36682.

[78] Id. at 36662, 36668.

[79] European Commission, Communication from the Commission, Guidelines on non-financial reporting: Supplement on reporting climate-related information, (2019C), Official Journal June 20, 2019, C209/1, Section 2.2 and Section 2.3, C 209/4-209/7.

[80] Id., Section 3.5, C 209/12-209/14.

The EU Climate Transition Benchmarks and EU Paris-aligned Benchmarks for investment funds rely heavily on greenhouse gas intensity measurements that indicate greenhouse gas emissions in proportion to enterprise value or absolute emissions in the case of debt securities. The level of emission intensity can serve as an indicator of the extent to which investments face carbon risks and present opportunities.[81] The EU Climate Transition Benchmark requires that greenhouse gas intensity must be at least 30% lower than the intensity of the "investible universe" of all investible instruments in a given asset class. The EU Paris-aligned Benchmarks requires that emissions intensity must be 50% lower than the investible universe.[82] Greenhouse gas intensity and absolute emissions are calculated based on Scope 1 and Scope 2 emissions and, on a phased-in basis, Scope 3 emissions.[83]

In sum, ESG disclosure requirements potentially should yield a wealth of information about greenhouse emissions, where they occur along the full value chain (especially if Scope 3 reporting is required), and the allocation of greenhouse gas emissions to companies and investment funds. It is important to note, however, that the science and art of calculating greenhouse gas emissions along the full value chain is still developing. Hence, the role of greenhouse gas emissions in a partnership between environmental taxation and ESG disclosure is likely to be forward-looking as procedures and requirements develop. From an ESG perspective, it is also important to remember that greenhouse gas emissions are just one element in the calculation of ESG profiles. Emissions levels and emissions intensity are important measures of company and fund risks and opportunities but, as a recent OECD report found, other factors may plan significant roles in ESG profiles. As a result, levels of emissions may not always align with the ESG profiles.[84] Again, the methodology for determining ESG profiles is a work in progress. Thank you for bearing with this journey through the regulatory landscape.

With this background in mind, what is the potential relationship between environmental taxation and ESG disclosures in the climate change context based on these examples? The working relationship between environmental taxation and ESG policies is more implicit than explicit and hence the silent quality of the partnership. Having described the partners above, this chapter will now probe the character of that relationship, looking first at how environmental taxation can enhance ESG goals (Sect. 6) and then at how ESG processes can enhance environmental taxation (Sect.

---

[81] EU Technical Expert Group on Sustainable Finance, Report on Benchmarks (September 2019), 8–10, 38–39.

[82] Commission Delegated Regulation (EU) 2020/1818 of 17 July 2020 supplementing Regulation (EU) 2016/1011 of the European Parliament and of the Council as regards minimum standards for EU Climate Transition Benchmarks and EU Paris-aligned Benchmarks, Official Journal, Vol. 63 L 406/17, 3 December 2020, Article 9, Article 11, L 406/22–23.

[83] Commission Delegated Regulation (EU) 2020/1818 of 17 July 2020 supplementing Regulation (EU) 2016/1011 of the European Parliament and of the Council as regards minimum standards for EU Climate Transition Benchmarks and EU Paris-aligned Benchmarks, Official Journal, Vol. 63 L 406/17, 3 December 2020.

[84] OECD (2022), pp. 13, 33.

7). The points below are presented as arguably plausible speculation. There is not yet enough experience with the interaction between environmental taxation policies and ESG to prove relationships, nor does this author have the skills to statistically assess their interaction. The following discussion therefore attempts to think in the abstract about how the two might work constructively together in the climate change context as taxation and ESG policies evolve. It does not draw on specific tax policies now in effect but rather looks more generally at potential relationships.

6 Environmental Taxation's Contributions to ESG

As indicated in Sect. 2, environmental taxation has three conceptual branches—taxes (carbon taxes in the climate context), tax expenditures (measures aimed at reducing greenhouse gas emissions in the climate context), and the broader notion of environmental fiscal reform (which can involve carbon taxes, the repeal of fossil fuel subsidies, and the provision of climate-friendly tax expenditures). All three can potentially encourage stronger "E" profiles for ESG disclosure purposes. They are instruments that can help deliver on the ESG potential to shift investment towards sustainability. They are potential enablers.

6.1 Supportive Carbon Tax Signals

By placing a price on greenhouse gas emissions, carbon taxes can cause changes in behaviour that enhance ESG profiles at the level of the individual companies that are then reflected in disclosures by investment funds holding stakes in those companies. Whether executed through a carbon tax or an emissions trading system, a strong carbon price should steer companies toward reducing emissions to avoid paying that price. Companies can reduce their use of fossil fuels, increase reliance on renewable energy, and/or shift to less carbon-intensive activities. Companies, and funds holding investments in these companies, will then report lower greenhouse gas emissions and greenhouse gas intensity in mandated (or voluntary) disclosures and, therefore, stronger "E" profiles for ESG purposes. Under ESG theory, those disclosures should inform investors' decisions about where to place their money. Under the US SEC's proposals, the disclosures can allow investors to avoid material financial risks. Under the broader EU ESG regime, they also should encourage investors to pursue investments that will advance sustainability and the transition to net-zero carbon emissions.

Note that carbon taxes can constitute a downside risk for companies. For example, the US proposed Company Rule and European Commission Climate Guidelines recognize that carbon pricing may create a policy risk for companies: If the carbon price increases the companies' costs, it can pose an internal financial risk subject to disclosure.[85] By the same token, disclosure could send the message intended by the carbon price and the ESG concept: Companies and investors that change behaviour can reduce or avoid this risk.[86]

6.2 *Supportive Green Tax Expenditure Signals*

Climate-friendly tax expenditures that explicitly encourage climate-friendly activities such as investments in energy conservation, low-carbon technologies, and renewable energy can also advance ESG goals but in a very different way. Through tax expenditures, governments can directly reward selected activities that reduce companies' greenhouse gas emissions and increase the level of participation in climate-friendly entrepreneurial endeavours, making those activities more financially attractive. By offering tax expenditures, a government and its taxpayers underwrite part of the cost of these shifts in behaviour. In the EU, state aid rules govern when the provision of tax expenditures is appropriate[87] which is a constraint that does not exist in the United States.

In ESG terms, these tax-encouraged shifts in behaviour can enhance companies' and investment funds' ESG profiles. If tax expenditures encourage companies to reduce their greenhouse gas emissions, disclosures under the US and EU regimes would reflect those reductions over time. They can indicate reductions in material financial risks under the US SEC's proposed Company Rule and changes in risks and opportunities under the EU regime. Companies' performance would then flow into investment funds' disclosures.

If tax expenditures were to reward activities recognized by the taxonomy as substantially contributing to climate change adaptation or mitigation, they should increase the likelihood that companies will pursue those activities. The identification of business activities that qualify as environmentally sustainable economic activities under the taxonomy allows undertakings to report their qualification through disclosure requirements.[88] Qualification also contributes to results disclosed under the

[85] Securities and Exchange Commission, The Enhancement and Standardization of Climate-Related Disclosures for Investors, 87 Federal Register 21334, 21379 (April 11, 2022); European Commission, Communication from the Commission, Guidelines on non-financial reporting: Supplement on reporting climate-related information, C(2019) Official Journal, June 20, 2019, Section 3.2, C 209/6.

[86] An unanticipated, abrupt change in carbon pricing could significantly affect the financial markets' carbon-intensive industries that might be left with stranded assets in the transition to a low-carbon economy, but the transition to greener technologies can also generate "creative disruption". OECD (2020), pp. 46–47.

[87] European Commission, Guidelines on State aid for climate, environmental protection and energy 2022 (2022/C 80/01) Official Journal February 18, 2022 C 80/1.

[88] Commission Delegated Regulation (EU) 2021/2178 of 6 July 2021 supplementing Regulation (EU) 2020/852 of the European Parliament and of the Council by specifying content and presentation of information to be disclosed by undertakings subject to Articles 19a or 29b of Directive

CSRD, SFRD, and benchmark standards. Thus, tax expenditures help encourage positive ESG performance and investor response.

6.3 *Supportive Environmental Fiscal Reform*

Finally, environmental fiscal reform can reenforce ESG performance. For example, if a country imposes a carbon tax and uses the revenue to reduce other tax burdens, it is engaging in environmental fiscal reform. At the same time, the carbon tax should encourage stronger ESG profiles for the reasons stated above. Repealing fossil fuel subsidies can also steer companies and investors away from investments in fossil fuels in line with ESG objectives.

Environmental fiscal reform places the focus on government fiscal policies and not private-sector disclosure requirements, but the two can operate side-by-side under a broad view of sustainable finance. A 2021 report by the European Court of Auditors provides a useful illustration.[89] When it examined the extent to which the European Commission's 2018 Action Plan and implementing measures advanced sustainable finance, it considered transparency and disclosure measures that apply to the private sector but also the need for governments to examine fiscal policies. It found that the 2018 Action Plan did not acknowledge the market's failure to adequately reflect the cost of unsustainable activities' negative environmental externalities and did not propose remedial actions.[90] Hence, it recommended that the European Commission identify measures that would place a price on greenhouse gas emissions that would better reflect their negative externalities.[91] It also considered the role of government subsidies, finding that some Member States subsidize carbon-intensive products[92] and that sustainability criteria did not fully infiltrate EU spending programs.[93] The European Court of Auditors' report underscores the fact that fiscal policies, when viewed broadly, should play a role in achieving sustainable finance goals. Stated in partnership terms, environmental taxation and fiscal policies could play an even larger role alongside ESG policies in the broader partnership working toward sustainable finance.

2013/34/EU concerning environmentally sustainable activities, and specifying the methodology to comply with that disclosure, Official Journal, Vol. 64 L 443/9, Dec. 10, 2021.

[89] European Court of Auditors (2021).

[90] European Court of Auditors (2021), pp. 13, 15, 16.

[91] European Court of Auditors (2021), pp. 5, 48.

[92] European Court of Auditors (2021), p. 18.

[93] European Court of Auditors (2021), p. 50.

7 ESG's Contributions to Environmental Taxation

ESG transparency regimes offer the potential to increase the effectiveness of tax signals, inform the design of environmental tax policies, and improve the politics surrounding environmental taxation.

7.1 Enhanced Responsiveness to Tax Signals

The ESG "E" pillar holds the potential to help environmental taxation policies operate more effectively at the internal company level. First, disclosures' raw data about levels of greenhouse gas emissions and greenhouse gas intensity along Scopes 1, 2, and 3 should sensitize companies to their carbon footprint[94] (Here, "carbon" is used as a shorthand for greenhouse gases.) If carbon taxes apply to those emissions, companies will pay the tax cost directly (if they are the taxpayers) or indirectly (if upstream companies pay the tax and pass it down to the companies). Either way, carbon footprint disclosures may help focus corporate managers' attention on how to reduce the carbon tax burden that comes with that footprint. Corporate decisionmakers will more readily have the information available that they need to assess choices. Ongoing ESG disclosures may also provide additional motivation to reduce their emissions and therefore their tax cost, assuming that the market rewards positive ESG profiles. Thus, managers may respond to a carbon price more astutely and more robustly. Disclosures may, in effect, amplify the tax message. Similarly, if tax expenditures are available, the greenhouse gas emissions disclosures can draw heightened attention to opportunities to take advantage of tax benefits in order to reduce the carbon footprint.

Second, ESG disclosure requirements can potentially build tax policies into the internal corporate planning process. For example, the US SEC's proposed Company Rule requires companies to disclose how they identify and propose to manage material climate-related risks as well as whether the risks are integrated into the companies' overall risk-management strategies.[95] The European Commission Climate Guidelines recommend that companies disclose how risks and opportunities affect business strategies and financial planning.[96] This analytical process should

[94] The European Commission's proposed CSRD includes the premise that disclosures can raise companies' awareness of risks and opportunities. European Commission, Proposal for a Directive of the European Parliament and of the Council amending Directive 2013/34/EU, Directive 2004/109/EC, Directive 2006/43/EC and Regulation (EU) 537/2014, as regards corporate sustainability reporting, COM(2021) 189 final, 2021/0104(COD), April 21, 2021, paragraph 10, 24.

[95] Securities and Exchange Commission, The Enhancement and Standardization of Climate-Related Disclosures for Investors, 87 Federal Register 21334, 21361 (April 11, 2022).

[96] European Commission, Communication from the Commission, Guidelines on non-financial reporting: Supplement on reporting climate-related information, Official Journal C209/1, June 20, 2019, Section 3.1, 209/9.

logically encourage interest in available tax policies that might help address risks. The US SEC's rule also focuses attention on carbon pricing. Companies that have transition plans to reduce climate-related risks would disclose their plans, including how they would deal with factors such as the imposition of carbon pricing.[97] Generally applicable financial metrics of the impact of risks include changes in costs as a result of carbon pricing.[98] These requirements may heighten internal sensitivity to the role of carbon taxes and companies' responses. In addition, transition plans may—but are not required to—identify climate-related opportunities[99] in which tax expenditures might play a part.

Finally, and relatedly, disclosure requirements may raise the visibility of climate-related tax policies to the highest levels within companies. The US SEC's proposed Company Rule would require companies to disclose the degree and type of oversight for climate-related risks, strategies, and oversight at the board level and the management level.[100] The European Commission Climate Guidelines also recommend disclosure of information about board and management involvement in climate-related matters.[101] These transparency requirements do not demand a substantive result. However, they implicitly encourage companies that want to achieve strong ESG profiles to integrate climate issues, including climate-related taxation policies, into their agendas corporate-wide and up to the highest levels. As a result of disclosure policies, taxation policies have the opportunity to gain strategic attention that can sharpen managerial minds and responses. Taxation may move out of the corners of accounting departments into decision-making companywide. Broadened awareness can add weight and heft to the tax signals.

The potential dynamics contemplated above focus on the company level but not the investment fund level because companies will decide how to respond to environmental taxation's signals. They are the frontline taxpayers. Nonetheless, investment funds can benefit vicariously from enhanced sensitivity at the company level.

7.2 *Informing Environmental Taxation Design*

ESG transparency also holds the potential to enhance understanding that can contribute to tax policy design. The following discussion notes several possibilities.

---

[97] Securities and Exchange Commission, The Enhancement and Standardization of Climate-Related Disclosures for Investors, 87 Federal Register 21334, 21362 (April 11, 2022).

[98] Id. at 21367.

[99] Id. at 21362.

[100] Id. at 21359–21360.

[101] European Commission, Communication from the Commission, Guidelines on non-financial reporting: Supplement on reporting climate-related information, Official Journal C209/1, June 20, 2019, Section 3.2, 209/9-209/10.

Greenhouse gas emissions reporting over time could allow policymakers to revisit carbon tax design assumptions. The US and EU regimes apply to the disclosure of greenhouse gas emissions along the full value chain—Scope 1, Scope 2, and Scope 3 emissions. As reporting methodologies improve and address thorny issues, such as the double-counting of Scope 3 emissions by companies along the value chain, companies will be able to more accurately pinpoint the sources of emissions and their responsibility for contributions to emissions. As a result of disclosures, policymakers will also better understand the relative contribution of emissions along the value chain.[102]

This improved understanding may allow policymakers to reconsider carbon tax design. For example, carbon taxes on fossil fuels often operate at the "upstream" level when fossil fuels enter a country's economy or when they are purchased for industrial use or the generation of electricity. An upstream tax is generally regarded as administratively feasible because fewer taxpayers are involved than when a tax is imposed closer to consumers. The assumption is that upstream taxpayers will pass the tax down through the price system until at least some of the tax cost falls on the ultimate consumer of electricity or products. Query whether a robust understanding of Scope 1, 2, and 3 emissions might allow policymakers to consider whether a carbon tax could be imposed at some downstream points closer to the consumer, more fully capturing emissions along the value chain. Issues of administrative feasibility, of course, would be highly relevant, as would sufficient accuracy of allocations of the carbon emissions to downstream activities or consumer products.

Robust data about upstream emissions within Scopes 2 and 3 might also facilitate the implementation of border carbon adjustments within carbon taxes, also known as border tax adjustments. A country that applies a carbon tax (or carbon price) to activities within its borders may choose to adopt a carbon border adjustment. The border adjustment would apply a carbon tax cost to designated imports comparable to the cost born by products produced within the country. Without a border adjustment, companies might relocate activities to countries that do not apply a similar carbon tax, causing greenhouse gas emissions and economic activity to move from one country to another (what is commonly known as carbon leakage).[103] The EU has opted to use a "carbon border adjustment mechanism" to place a carbon price on certain imported products comparable to the EU Emission Trading System's (ETS) carbon price on domestic products.[104]

One of the challenges of implementing a border carbon adjustment is determining the upstream greenhouse gas emissions attributable to imported products. As ESG

[102] The CSRD recognizes, in general terms, that ESG disclosures can inform policymakers and public policy. Proposal for a Directive of the European Parliament and of the Council amending Directive 2013/34/EU, Directive 2004/109/EC, Directive 2006/43/EC and Regulation (EU) 537/2014, as regards corporate sustainability reporting, 10835/22 (30 June 2022), paragraph 8, 8.

[103] See generally Keen et al. (2021).

[104] European Commission, A proposal for a Regulation of the European Parliament and of the Council establishing a carbon border adjustment mechanism, COM (2021) 564 final, 2021/0214 (COD), 14 July 2021.

disclosure of greenhouse gas emissions matures, it might again be wondered whether its methodologies and data might help policymakers design and implement border carbon adjustments. ESG reporting of greenhouse gas emissions reflects company-wide data whereas border tax adjustments and emissions calculations operate at the level of individual products. Nonetheless, companies gathering ESG information about Scope 2 and Scope 3 emissions associated with materials they use from the upstream value chain may yield data or methodologies relevant to policymakers' decisions about whether and how to use border tax adjustments. The question is posed here and left for readers to ponder.[105] Carbon tax design questions such as these may warrant investigation in the future—as well as the political question of whether using disclosure information to inform tax policy design could dampen the ESG movement.

Even if enhanced understanding of emissions along the value chain does not open the door to new carbon tax designs, it would at least provide policymakers with more knowledge about how carbon pricing flows through the value chain to end users, such as which products are likely to have a larger carbon footprint and therefore any carbon tax burden. Policymakers and others could use this information to accentuate public awareness of the tax cost and therefore enhance the behavioural effectiveness of the tax. A better understanding of the emissions along the full life cycle could also refine the ability to design equity measures in order to avoid a carbon tax's unwanted hardships for vulnerable populations.

ESG policies can also inform tax policy by systematically creating standards for significant environmental improvement, such as the EU's Taxonomy criteria. If a government decides to award tax expenditures to encourage green activities, it might consider whether to define eligibility according to selected business activities identified in the taxonomy. A taxonomy-style classification system could help provide a rational basis for choosing which activities the government should subsidize through the tax system (or otherwise). For example, the European Commission has indicated that the taxonomy can assist with the assessments of measures that qualify for state aid.[106]

In short, the new knowledge flowing out of ESG disclosures may allow policymakers and other stakeholders to consider whether new understandings open new possibilities for tax policy design.

[105] A full analysis would also inquire into the compatibility with World Trade Organization rules.

[106] See, e.g., European Commission, Questions and Answers, Guidelines on State Aid for Climate, Environmental Protection and Energy 2022, January 27, 2022 (discussing the link between the State Aid Guidelines and the Taxonomy).

7.3 Politics

Finally, if ESG disclosures raise awareness of environmental footprints and if they put an investor premium on shrinking them, it might wonder whether ESG policies at least theoretically might smooth the political resistance to carbon pricing or other environmental taxes. If companies and investment funds have carbon footprints that they want to reduce in order to improve their ESG profiles, might they be more willing to accept carbon taxes as a vehicle to help achieve that improvement? Companies presumably would prefer approaches such as internal carbon pricing that leaves the "tax" revenue within companies.[107] However, carbon taxes on less carbon-efficient competitors could create a competitive advantage in both image and the bottom line. In addition, financial market participants that tout ESG values could find it politically contradictory to oppose carbon pricing. Governments, of course, would still need to address potential regressivity, competitiveness, and carbon leakage questions, but ESG disclosures might subtly shift the political dynamics around carbon pricing.

In the broader context of environmental fiscal reform, if a government construes the ESG concept broadly to include an examination of government's spending policies, ESG proponents should support the idea of repealing subsidies (tax or otherwise) for fossil fuels and carbon-intensive undertakings. Beneficiaries of subsidies are likely to resist but, again, perhaps the balance of power might shift. A commitment to ESG principles might also create more support for targeted green tax expenditures that can hasten the sustainability transition.

It is difficult to predict politics either in general or even in any specific country. Only time will tell, but political economists may want to consider and investigate the political ramifications of this silent partnership.

8 Conclusion

Using climate change policies as a testing ground, this chapter has pursued the thesis that environmental taxation and ESG policies can work quietly together. It cannot provide proof, but the author hopes that it has at least presented the potential for plausible interactions that are mutually supportive. In the abstract, climate-related environmental taxation can improve ESG profiles which is important if the market in fact rewards companies and investment funds by sending them capital. That capital

[107] The proposed US Company Rule and the European Commission both identify internal carbon pricing as an emissions-reduction strategy that should be disclosed. Securities and Exchange Commission, The Enhancement and Standardization of Climate-Related Disclosures for Investors, 87 Federal Register 21334, 21355–21356 (April 11, 2022); European Commission, Communication from the Commission, Guidelines on non-financial reporting: Supplement on reporting climate-related information, Official Journal C209/1, June 20, 2019, Section 3.4, 209/12.

will help fuel progress toward climate change goals in the transition to a low- or no-carbon world. ESG policies can help climate-oriented environmental taxation by heightening sensitivities to price signals, providing data that can inform design, and possibly improving the political context for taxation instruments.

The ability of the partnership to significantly contribute to climate change goals will depend on specific policies in any given country. The EU's broad approach to the ESG concept that takes into account risks and opportunities to companies and to the environment creates more potential for interaction than the US's narrower ESG proposals that focus only on financial risks. On the tax side, a country that does not use significant carbon pricing or draw on green tax expenditures leaves the prospect of a partnership with the ESG concept weak until that the country chooses to harness tax policy to achieve climate goals. Country-specific analyses could investigate the actual or potential strength of the partnership given specific tax and ESG policies. Future analysis could also consider the role of voluntary ESG regimes.

For the moment, this chapter closes with the suggestion that this silent partnership has the potential in the future to address climate change and possibly other environmental challenges. Stakeholders and policymakers who work in each of these fields might think about relations that could grow between environmental taxation and ESG policy and how each can contribute to the other's potential. The walls of all silos need to break down if we are to meet the daunting promise of a net-zero world in 2050.

References

Boffo R, Patalano R (2020) ESG investing: practices, progress and challenges. OECD, Paris

Congressional Budget Office (2020) Options for reducing the deficit: 2021 to 2030

Duff D (2008) Carbon taxation in British Columbia. Vermont J Environ Law 10(87)

European Court of Auditors (2021) Sustainable finance: more consistent EU action needed to redirect finance towards sustainable investment

European Court of Auditors (2022) Energy taxation, carbon pricing and energy subsidies

European Environment Agency (2022) The role of (environmental) taxation in supporting sustainability transitions

Keen M et al (2021) Border carbon adjustments: rationale, design and impact. IMF Working Paper WP/21/239

Krupnik A, Parry I (2012) In: Parry IWH et al (eds) What is the best policy instrument for reducing CO_2 emissions in fiscal policy to mitigate climate change: a guide for policymakers. International Monetary Fund

Milne JE, Andersen MS (2012) Introduction to environmental taxation concepts and research. In: Milne JE, Andersen MS (eds) Handbook of research on environmental taxation. Edward Elgar

OECD (1989) Economic instruments for environmental protection

OECD (2020) Sustainable and resilient finance: OECD business and finance outlook 2020

OECD (2021a) Effective carbon rates 2021

OECD (2021b) ESG investing and climate transition: market practices, issues and policy considerations

OECD (2022) ESG ratings and climate transition: an assessment of the alignment of E pillar scores and metrics
Surrey SS (1973) Pathways to tax reform: the concept of tax expenditures. Harvard University Press
United Nations (2021) United Nations handbook on carbon taxation for developing countries
World Bank (2022) State and trends of carbon pricing 2022

International Fiscal Cooperation to Better Integrate Public and Private Efforts on Sustainability: The Case of Carbon Offset Credits

María Amparo Grau Ruiz

Abstract Currently, carbon offset credits are gaining momentum in the voluntary and compliance markets. Many investors, private companies, or public entities look at them as a way to implement or supplement their decarbonization strategies. These tools are easily available to utilize for meeting the declared sustainability goals by compensating carbon emissions that are impossible or just hard to mitigate. At the same time, they can serve to comply with the regime of nationally determined contributions according to the Paris Agreement. However, they often pose challenges from a public and private perspective, both in a domestic or multinational scenario. There is a blatant lack of legal certainty concerning their treatment for tax purposes. This affects the agents involved in the different processes of the carbon offset credits' lifecycle (their generation, trade, and use). The growing nature of this problematic situation simultaneously derives from qualitative and quantitative factors. A greater dose of international cooperation among the stakeholders is needed to provide balanced solutions between public and private interests. Special attention should be paid to the developing and developed countries' positions. The following pages describe the state of the art and explain what the main concerns are with regard to the application of these credits in the framework of the existing tax systems. In many cases, carbon taxes are not mature enough, or their interaction with other economic instruments is not well defined. The innovative work of the United Nations Subcommittee on Environmental Taxation in this regard is reviewed. In an attempt to sort out the observed obstacles due to the configuration and features of the schemes up to date, some alternative proposals are mentioned. Final remarks stress that future regulations should not only facilitate but ensure a global positive environmental impact on society in line with the UN 2030 Agenda. Public finances,

Principal Investigator of AudIT-S project (PID2019-105959RB-I00) https://www.ucm.es/proyecto-audit-s/.

M. A. Grau Ruiz (✉)
Financial and Tax Law, Universidad Complutense de Madrid, Madrid, Spain

Transnational Taxation, Northwestern University, School of Law, Chicago, IL, USA
e-mail: grauruiz@ucm.es

R. Saraiva, P. A. Pardal (eds.), *Sustainable Finances and the Law*, Economic Analysis of Law in European Legal Scholarship 16,
https://doi.org/10.1007/978-3-031-49460-4_12

particularly, tax legislators and authorities have a decisive role to play in this uncharted area.

1 Introduction

Nowadays, public and private efforts to deliver more sustainable outputs checking diverse environmental footprints are frequently increasing around us in view of the climate emergency that human beings face on Earth. However, in this phenomenon, there is a manifest handicap as the lack of real integration among the multiple actions taken by different actors still locks their full potential resulting in unsought gaps and overlaps. This problem is often happening at a domestic level and can also be observed globally although it is exacerbated because of geographical dispersion. Therefore, to try to solve it, there is an urgent need to further develop the scope of international fiscal cooperation to better support progress towards the Sustainable Development Goals. The United Nations architecture for cooperation in tax matters is currently struggling to keep pace with the recently enhanced cooperation in environmental matters. The following pages aim to explain how the implementation of this tactic would have meaningful impact on the case of carbon offset credits. A carbon offset credit is a transferable instrument certified by governments or independent certification bodies that represents an emission reduction or removal of one metric tonne of CO_2 or an equivalent amount of other GHGs that are measured against a counterfactual baseline. How it is treated for tax purposes in the countries to which it is connected can make a difference in stakeholder attitude towards more efficient credit use for a healthier atmosphere apart from the effects on the revenue that is collected.

For administrations to efficiently cooperate, a minimum prior legislative coordination is inevitably decisive in both the environmental and tax areas. In principle, this approach requires considering several connections in parallel circuits, exceeding the traditional public-private perspective that is domestically limited in most cases. In fact, in the international framework, movements of various natures are being simultaneously orchestrated beyond borders often between public-public, private-private and, finally, some public-private agents. Properly aligning the national tax systems to promote all sorts of the longtime desired pro-sustainability activities from all of these agents becomes a challenge for academic researchers in theory and policymakers in practice. It entails assuming, as a starting point, the necessity to allow an adequate flow of resources (both financial and sustainable) to be used where they can produce the maximum benefits to society. Obviously, the systems soon to be devised will have to exploit, in a reasonable manner, other ones previously available and hopefully count on a certain degree of effective supervision.

2 A Look at the Companies' Side in the Midst of a Changing Environment

Carbon offset credits are becoming more important universally as more and more companies assess and report their environmental, social, and governance (ESG) goals and activities.[1] Many companies are not able to fully eliminate their carbon footprint because certain emission sources are inevitably involved in some businesses' processes or inputs until green research, development, and innovation (R&D +i) deliver an alternative solution. Others cannot do it speedily because current technologies may be too expensive and, consequently, unaffordable for them. They may then decide to buy carbon credits to offset their emissions under those or similar circumstances.

Ideally, companies should disclose their GHG emissions from operations and plans to eliminate them or purchase and retire carbon credits in the event of residual emissions that they will not be able to eliminate. Carbon offset credits could cover any remaining GHG emissions from sources that the organization owns or controls and, if possible, from its supply chain and product use. This may evidently have an eventual impact on the process of counting emissions reduction.[2]

From a company's perspective, carbon offsets can be part of a comprehensive strategy for corporate social responsibility, combining efforts to address climate change with contributions to other public goods. The number of companies with net zero pledges is continuously growing and many often show commitments to reduce GHG emissions or make up-front agreements with project developers. There is currently a compliance market on top of a voluntary market with both going forward. There are a lot of new standards and new areas coming up under the voluntary market. Many companies are interested in it due to the onerous nature of the compliance market (that, in turn, ensures higher quality credits). Anyhow, all offset claims should be only defensible under a set of rigorous conditions. The offsetting should be legitimate and should not disincentivize these companies' own mitigation efforts.

Whether an entity decides to acquire carbon credits may depend in part on the legal certainty that the entity can obtain with respect to the nature of the instrument that a carbon credit represents. For example, whether the relevant authority considers and treats a carbon credit as a commodity, financial instrument, or tangible or intangible assets or simply as a set of contractual rights to benefit from the verification process performed by the project developer.[3]

---

[1] Also named "voluntary carbon offsets (VCOs)" that allow a business to create a net reduction in GHG emissions by funding atmospheric carbon reduction actions of another party. White (2022).

[2] There are different types of double counting, i.e., for credit, finance, and reporting. Authorization by a government should not be required unless the credit was to be counted towards Nationally Determined Contributions (NDCs).

[3] Colombia considers carbon credits as intangible property under a form of a right to offset or reduce the purchaser's carbon footprint for exchange of a price (Estatuto Tributario Nacional, Article 420)

It is important to note that the socially expected entrepreneurial behaviours in environmental matters can be voluntary or mandatory depending on the legal framework in which the companies conduct their businesses. The current landscape is quickly evolving in this regard in numerous countries. It is key to clarify whether the voluntary market is used or not for accounting towards the Nationally Determined Contribution (NDC) that would lead to corresponding adjustments and the bureaucracy attached to Article 6 of the Paris Agreement in the compliance market.[4] In the future, the voluntary market will probably stay because not every project is related to NDCs, and there may be companies that need credits to offset their self-imposed targets for reputational and SDGs' reasons.[5]

The complexity of the situation grows when assessed with a dynamic perspective: What is voluntary at a moment in a certain place can change and become mandatory later after considering some specific events (energy transition, for example). Countries normally take their country target and devolve it to companies. When the targets on companies are derived from compulsory or mandatory regulation, ascertaining whether an action is under the umbrella of voluntary market or Article 6 (except for contractual agreements) can become a gray area. This explains "the difficulty in developing the rule book" in Article 6. In addition, the classification of a carbon credit for legal purposes may be vital for project developers and buyers of carbon credits as it impacts the financial model of the carbon reduction project. It may also ultimately affect its tax treatment at both a domestic level and under double taxation conventions or the way that it is recognized in financial reporting.

---

and therefore regards them as a supply of services. Through tax ruling 13505 from 2017, these intangible assets represent a right for one tonne of CO_2 removal or reduction which is transferable for exchange of a price. Australia defines carbon credits as financial instruments in the Corporations Act 2001. The potential categorization of a carbon credit as a set of contractual rights to benefit from the verification process is considered and suggested by the ISDA in its paper on the legal implications of voluntary carbon credits (https://www.isda.org/a/38ngE/Legal-Implications-of-Voluntary-Carbon-Credits.pdf). Salway et al. (2022).

[4] Companies would have to get authorization by the government to sell or trade those credits because it has a direct impact on the NDC. Article 6.2 on bilateral actions contains guidelines covering internationally transferred mitigation outcomes that must be reported and recorded in registries. Article 6.4 establishes a multilateral mechanism with a supervisory board to approve projects adjusted to the circumstances. Article 6.8 addresses non-market international cooperation among governments.

[5] "Companies that have announced climate targets (for instance: becoming 'net zero' by 2050) represent a market capitalization of over $20 trillion. Almost all of them will rely on carbon offsets purchased on the voluntary carbon market (VCM) to reach their target." Battocletti et al. (2023).

3 The Complex Situation of the States' Public Policies at a Glance

Decarbonization is no longer an exclusive matter of corporate social responsibility in the private sector. Even states themselves are also bound by their own pledges in this field. Thus, there is tension between private and public agents interacting in related markets. A question immediately arises: Could one carbon offset credit be computed for a country's NDC and also for private purposes? This demand has recently caused a relatively rapid evolution of the compliance and the voluntary markets[6] which shows the importance of clarifying the interactions between the carbon offset market and taxation as soon as possible. The market has grown tenfold in the last year, and it is necessary to start reconciling the transactions in the voluntary field with what can be utilized for compliance purposes. Uncertainty and changing rules may create some expectations that may not be achieved in the future. Tax authorities, just as investors in carbon credits, require legal certainty to grant and control any possible environmental tax benefit and avoid unnecessary revenue losses when the climate purpose is not met.

Currently, there is no settled law in many countries about how (environmental) tax rules should apply to carbon offset credits. Many governments and stakeholders still need to figure out the general tax treatment of carbon. This is particularly relevant in the context of a carbon tax, i.e., if and when carbon offset credits may be used to reduce liability in full or in part. The characterization for tax purposes (dependent or not of the character of the asset or activity from which the carbon credit is created) and the overall tax treatment (e.g., like expenses or intangible assets[7]) are being strongly debated. This emerging-asset class is still relatively new, not well-defined, and often varies based on the taxpayer's facts and circumstances.

It is important to highlight that this lack of legal certainty and the different characterization at a domestic level might have negative consequences for facilitating further international cooperation in tax matters at a later stage. This may lead to double taxation for companies, limiting consensus on the application of the Model Conventions on Double Taxation and restricting the effectiveness of the transfer pricing expected guidance.[8]

---

[6]Michaelowa et al. (2019).

[7]In the United States, the cost of carbon credits may be currently deductible under Section 162 of the Internal Revenue Code if it can be shown that the cost of voluntary carbon offsets is a taxpayer's current ordinary and necessary expense. However, if they provide a long-term benefit, under Section 263 of the Internal Revenue Code and the regulations, the cost may be capitalizable. Some companies obtain them by funding projects undertaken by a not-for-profit entity. Payments made to entities related to such projects can generally be treated as a charitable contribution to not-for-profit organizations.

[8]The best solution for carbon offsets must still be sought irrespective of whether they are linked to an immovable or a movable project or intangibles. A thorough discussion on the qualification of the income is crucial. Coverage might be provided by Articles 7 and 9 of the model treaties although, for the kind of credits linked to change of land use or nature-based solutions, this qualification may not be evident. Setting a different system may entail a risk of lowering investments in that country.

Two basic worries can be observed in the current debate among tax experts about this topic, mainly from temporal and territorial perspectives. First, there cannot be evergreen credits; they must have a sunset period. Second, why would a country allow a company to buy carbon offsets (potentially in another jurisdiction) instead of paying a carbon tax in its territory? This would reduce its own revenue.

These concerns explain why several governments have decided to initially limit the use of carbon offset credits and allow only a partial "offset"[9] of carbon tax liability through credits obtained from a domestic market. Their intention is usually to keep the revenue and the benefits within their own country. For instance, South Africa has only allowed carbon offset credits for certain sectors excluded from its tax net (in order to avoid double reduction of the tax burden). This behaviour is reasonable in the context of a relatively new carbon tax. It is prudent to maintain an uncomplicated offset market as a starting point and later adopt transitional measures (contingent on revenue and benefit flow) to expand it to the international market.

A better understanding of how the carbon offset credit system works and its economic and health impacts on a jurisdiction could help to sort out confusion. However, a small preliminary question regarding the misleading terminology must be addressed. Some states have already explicitly mentioned some internationally well recognized tools (like the Clean Development Mechanisms (CDMs)) in their carbon tax legislation. This does not really mean that the projects taken into consideration may happen abroad as they may be restricted to those developed in their territory. Policymakers should distinguish between the two meanings associated with the word "international" as either a tool covered by an international agreement used with a domestic focus or a reduction of emissions that effectively happens elsewhere resulting from a project carried out outside territorial borders.

Accepting international credits in the framework of a domestic carbon tax is frequently seen as a risk among tax officials, especially when their nature is not clear enough. Breaking the barrier of territoriality entails a policy choice to recognize them without being completely sure if they will be part of Article 6. Beyond the sacrifice of country revenues, the "official" public recognition for having provided the associated environmental benefit is uncertain. However, this line of thinking is deeply rooted in a narrow view of state sovereignty. Setting aside national achievements, that decision would be positive on a global scale. Choosing global advancement leads to environmental benefits that reach the state's own citizens and extend to those in foreign countries.

Bearing in mind a time-line perspective, a deadline should be imposed to avoid the repeated consideration of "evergreen credits" for tax purposes or the creation of bubbles by storing them in only a few hands.

[9]Sometimes the word "offset" is understood as what is obtained when employing a carbon credit towards reducing its overall carbon price (by offsetting its carbon footprint or by offsetting the carbon tax liability).

4 Multilayered Control: Roles of Carbon Offset Programs and Tax Authorities

The nature of carbon credits is heterogeneous, and there is a lot of inconsistency among these credits. Carbon offset programs are already amending quantification methodologies and reconsidering the eligibility of certain project types in order to prevent over-estimation of GHG reductions and ensure the quality of carbon offset credits.

A monitoring, reporting, and verification system for reductions as well as a reliable intermediary to record and verify them are needed for a carbon market to exist. These tasks have basically been performed by carbon offset programs. They range from international or governmental regulatory bodies to independent non-governmental organizations (NGOs). Historically, governmental bodies certified offset credits for regulatory purposes (compliance programs) while NGOs primarily served voluntary buyers (voluntary programs). More recently, both types of programs have begun to serve both types of markets. Each carbon offset program issues its own labelled brand of credit.

Nowadays, however, there is room for some degree of manipulation of voluntary carbon markets. The prospect is that some rules for regulation of voluntary markets will be approved in 2030, so there is a risk because many of these credits could have their eligibility questioned over time and might eventually be disallowed. A consensus on the basic concepts (like additionality, double counting, etc.) was established after the Glasgow Pact, and work is now being carried out to discuss the details in several fora (although with the same voices habitually resonating in them). The matter of integrity has scaled the agenda and recent initiatives have been presented around the voluntary market to introduce more rigorous measures (like the principles developed by the Integrity Council for the Voluntary Carbon Market) and disclosures.[10]

The situation may be a bit confusing for newcomers as many self-regulated entities with (competing?) interests in the voluntary market act as certifying agencies in this environment. Criticisms spin around their role and the standards by which they operate. They may differ so much from each other, although there are some similar approaches as well. There is no actual regulatory body looking at their standards to identify which ones are best, and the proposed applicable principles are quite broad.

Therefore, when tax authorities are dealing with the introduction of carbon offset credits (already contemplated by policymakers in Chile, Colombia, Mexico,

[10]For the Voluntary Carbon Markets Integrity initiative, the Science Based Targets initiative and Climate Impact X. See respectively https://vcmintegrity.org https://sciencebasedtargets.org https://www.climateimpactx.com.

Singapore, and South Africa),[11,12] they must focus carefully on the conditions imposed on the available tools for verifying the quantity and quality of emission reductions and removals related to the credits that could be accepted in the tax system. In South Africa, companies can use carbon offsets to reduce their carbon tax liability by up to 5–10% of their actual emissions. Carbon offset projects must be developed in South Africa, and three standards are accepted (CDM, Verified Carbon Standards, and Gold Standards). In Mexico, 20% of the Special Tax Upon Services and Production can be paid through CDM offset credits if developed in Mexico and emitted after 2014, among other requirements. Colombia specifies that the GHG emission reductions valid for the purpose of the carbon neutrality non-charge application must come from mitigation initiatives implemented in the national territory using certification programs or certain carbon standards. Companies may use high quality international carbon credits to offset up to 5% of their taxable emissions from 2024 in Singapore. Additionally, all international carbon credits used under the carbon tax regime will need to adhere to a set of eligibility criteria to ensure that they are of high environmental integrity and compliant with Article 6 of the Paris Agreement. Policymakers can learn from these comparative examples about the tax treatment of the lifecycle of carbon offset credits thereby establishing new opportunities to strengthen international tax cooperation.[13]

The Chilean experience deserves attention as an example of a detailed consideration of tax matters. Some decisive elements in the design for policymakers are underlined in the following paragraphs:

> Article 3. Taxpayers subject to the tax may offset all or part of their taxable emissions by means of emission reduction certificates for the purpose of determining the amount of tax payable.
>
> Article 4. Emission reductions used to offset taxable emissions must be additional, measurable, verifiable and permanent.
>
> Article 5. The owners of those projects that correspond to the mitigation or integration components established in the Nationally Determined Contribution in force, when submitting applications for approval of emission reduction projects, shall declare this fact to the Ministry and describe how such projects or activities relate to the criteria or conditions that the Nationally Determined Contribution establishes for such projects.
>
> Article 6. Emissions of carbon dioxide (CO_2), particulate matter, nitrogen oxides and sulphur dioxide taxed under the Act may only be offset through the implementation of emission reduction projects carried out in the national territory.

---

[11] Pizarro (2021), p. 70.

[12] "Section 12K of the Income Tax Act is an incentive available for any person holding a CDM [Clean Development Mechanism] project registration while that person implements the project. Essentially, amounts received or accrued upon disposal of these CERs [Certified Emission Reductions] are exempt from normal tax and capital gains tax purposes". Steenkamp, L.A. 2017. To incentivise or penalise: an analysis of the proposed carbon tax in South Africa, in Weishaar et al. (2017), p. 51. "Under the carbon tax policy framework, firms will be able to reduce their carbon tax liability by using offset credits up to a maximum of 5 or 10 per cent of their GHG emissions, depending on the time of emissions". Machingambi (2017), p. 69.

[13] "[T]he Canadian federal carbon tax and its various provincial surrogates would do well to consider the benefits of the South African offset allowance". Gilder and Stiles (2019), pp. 270–279.

The taxed emissions may only be offset through the implementation of emission reduction projects for the same pollutant. For the purposes of CO_2, the emission reduction must correspond to CO_2 or CO_2 equivalent.

For emission offsets, there may not be a difference of more than three years between the year of emission reductions used for offsetting and the year in which the taxed emissions are generated.

Taxed emissions of particulate matter, nitrogen oxides and sulphur dioxide may only be offset through the implementation of emission reduction projects carried out in the same commune in which such emissions are generated or in the communes adjacent to it. For these purposes, adjacent shall be understood as those communes whose geographical boundaries are adjacent to the commune in which the emissions to be offset are generated.

Emissions of particulate matter, nitrogen oxides and sulphur dioxide taxed with the tax, generated in an area declared as saturated or latent, may only be offset through the implementation of emission reduction projects that are executed in the area declared as saturated or latent in which they are generated.

Only emission reductions corresponding to the mass fraction of particulate matter with an aerodynamic diameter less than or equal to 2.5 microns of this pollutant may be used to offset emissions of particulate matter.

Article 7. The following projects are inadmissible for the purpose of offsetting emissions:

(a) Consider reductions in emissions from activities or establishments that close or must close due to: the end of their useful life indicated in the permits or resolutions authorising their operation; due to an administrative sanction; due to a final or enforceable court ruling; or due to an act of authority imposing such a measure;
(b) Generate an increase in the emissions of any other pollutant subject to the tax, unless it is demonstrated that in order to minimise this impact, the best available technology has been used to control the emissions generated, as determined by the Ministry; or
(c) involve reductions in emissions from emission sources subject to the tax itself.[14]

5 Reflections About Recent Proposals, Agreements, and Other Pending Issues

Corporations purchasing carbon offsets certified by the leading standard setters can pay lower taxes in some countries, as explained in the previous section. Therefore, companies have "incentives to purchase as many offsets at as little cost as possible to cut their tax bill. Thus, offset buyers have no interest in punishing standard setters, VVBs [Verification and Validation bodies] and project developers to inflate offsets".[15] To address the problem of inflation, academic proposals have been made

[14]Unofficial translation. Agreement No.17/2022 for a Regulation of projects for the reduction of pollutant emissions to offset taxed emissions in accordance with the provisions of article 8 of Act 20,780.

[15]"If offset buyers were interested in purchasing only offsets that correspond to true reductions of CO2, then reputational sanctions might prevent market players from inflating offsets. But most of the demand of the VCM comes from corporations that have all the interest in purchasing cheap and inflated offsets. Cheap and inflated offsets allow corporations to reach their climate target at a lower cost. And, given that their end-consumers are unable to assess the quality of the offsets they purchase, the expected reputational sanctions that corporations face for relying on inflated offsets

arguing that policymakers should not implement ex-ante regulation or impose ex-post liability on standard setters and VVBs that inflate offsets. Implementing either of these solutions in an effective manner is difficult due to a lack of information. It has therefore been stressed that "policymakers should avoid that certifications from leading standard setters are associated with regulatory benefits, as this further displaces the reputational mechanisms that should limit rating inflation".[16] Apart from these reputational sanctions, administrative or criminal sanctions could be considered when tax legislation has been applied and benefits have been unduly enjoyed. Here, the reinforcement of quality with another extra layer of tax control could have some additional deterrent effect.

The advent of bilateral agreements for climate cooperation under the Paris Agreement is worth mentioning as a new phenomenon within the international arena. For instance, the Swedish Energy Agency has signed a Memoranda of Understanding—expressing a common interest to cooperate through Article 6—with the Dominican Republic, Ghana, and Nepal.[17] This again shows the importance of combining public and private initiatives in the international field involving developed and developing countries. All agents are facing this process of learning by doing, and pilot programs at an early stage may be a good solution.

At a certain point, all countries will need to decide under national law whether the value of the credits is deductible as a tax payment in the carbon tax. For that purpose, to some extent, they will need to consider how taxpayers are treating the original cost of the credits for tax purposes. For example, if polluters can deduct some or all of the offsets' purchase cost, should they also be able to deduct the value of the offset used as a carbon tax payment? These tax issues will affect the real cost of offsets for the polluters who are paying the carbon tax.

In addition, tax liability is usually paid with cash, and the only question is the tax treatment of that payment—whether taxes are deductible—which may vary

are extremely low. Further, carbon offsets certified by the leading standard setters increasingly provide regulatory benefits". Cf. Battocletti et al. (2023).

[16] "Instead, we argue that any attempt to improve the functioning of the VCM should simultaneously achieve three things: i) increase the transparency of the market, ii) provide agents that possess the relevant information with the necessary and sufficient incentives to identify low-quality offsets, and iii) strengthen reputational sanctions for inaccurate certifications". Cf. Battocletti et al. (2023).

[17] The framework bilateral agreement "establishes the conditions and rules for both the cooperation between the countries and the activities that will result in the transfer of mitigation outcomes, e.g., ITMOs (Internationally Transferred Mitigation Outcomes). Such an agreement thereby confirms the host country's willingness to make a so-called corresponding adjustment when the mitigation outcomes are transferred to Sweden." https://www.energimyndigheten.se/en/cooperation/swedens-program-for-international-climate-initiatives/paris-agreement/bilateral-climate-agreements/.

depending on the country. The situation is slightly different when it comes to the carbon tax because tax liability is paid with an asset.[18]

Certainly, carbon offset credits may also be relevant in the framework of the corporate income tax to the extent that they can lead to deductible expenses for a company that has bought them (i.e., as business costs in the context of sustainable management when making climate claims[19]) or to taxable profits in the case of a company that has sold them. Hence, considering the complex, often cross-border, lifecycle of carbon offset credits, it is important to clarify who taxes what and where.[20] The tax systems should embrace the happenings in markets under current development and pay attention to predictability around costs.

In addition, the potential tax aspects that restrict the creation of and effectiveness to trade could be taken into account. One concern is how prices are calculated in the tax field. Could partial (private/public) claims be made over the same carbon offset credit? The corresponding adjustments could impact companies that wish to source credits internationally,[21] thus, cooperation and/or competition between public and private agents may lead to problems. Governments should act while considering how private actors can deliver benefits to society. Governments can directly sell offsets for projects in their own territory or can tax them to increase their revenue. There are, however, several additional justifications for government action in the field of environmental tax apart from the revenue expectations that carbon credits represent.

Carbon offset credits could serve as a payment method or deduction against an environmental tax liability, providing the impulse needed to support environmental action. Doing so may lead to governments receiving less cash carbon tax revenues. Recognizing carbon offset credits formally as a mode of payment for carbon tax purposes could serve to transmit a signal to the market showing that the carbon credit

[18]For example, as stated in Chile: Article 2. e. "Offset of emissions: act by which emissions reductions that are included in an emissions reduction certificate issued by the Ministry of the Environment, in accordance with the respective regulation, are discounted from the emissions taxed with the tax established in Article 8 of the Law". The Ministry of the Environment Regulation establishes the obligations and procedures related to the identification of the taxpayers affected and that establishes the administrative procedures necessary for the application of the tax levied on emissions into the air of particulate matter, nitrogen oxides, sulfur dioxide, and carbon dioxide as provided in Article 8 of Law No. 20,780, as amended by Law No. 21,210. No. 63.- Santiago, November 2, 2022. Official Journal of the Republic of Chile, No. 43,465, January 31, 2023.

[19]White (2022), pp. 18–24.

[20]For an extended explanation in Spanish, Grau Ruiz (2022) https://revistatecnicatributaria.com/index.php/rtt/article/view/2308/4777.

[21]Porsborg-Smith et al. (2023). There is an ongoing debate on whether a double claim may be appropriate, however, i.e., once against a host country's Nationally Determined Contribution (NDC) and once by a company in the private sector using a voluntary credit to compensate their GHG emissions. If credits are to be used once, it should be used either by the private company to offset its emissions or by the host country as a tool to meet its NDCs. A counterargument to this is that forbidding host countries to use credits produced in their territory and used by private companies as offsets would slow down the deployment of carbon projects.

is considered legitimate. This recognition could support mobilizing capital through a large, transparent, verifiable, and environmentally robust market.[22]

Allowing for the application of carbon credits against an environmental tax liability could perhaps indirectly help avoid climate and financial fraud as it assumes proper verification of the carbon offset credits that are used to pay a carbon tax. The addition of an eventual second layer of tax control with respect to carbon offset credits (through tax risk assessments and audits) could reinforce any previous validation made by a carbon offset program. However, this would require integration at the tax authority level of some knowledge provided by environmental authorities. Bogus carbon credits could jeopardize a country's ability to meet its climate goal.[23] The current noticeable lack of price transparency can lead to undetected (eventually illicit?) financial flows. Carbon taxation may allow focusing on the commercial (market) price for carbon credits that may, in turn, help fight money laundering.

Carbon offset projects that promote co-benefits being treated more favourably by a carbon tax can serve as an incentive for taxpayers to engage in them. Some carbon offset projects could have additional benefits like innovation, improved energy access, biodiversity and habitat protection, job creation, and education or public-health improvement for community economic development. Some programs actively require that projects not only avoid harm but demonstrate social and environmental co-benefits as well as monitor and report on them. The main problem is the proper definition of the credit's co-benefits. The types of projects that make higher-quality carbon offsets tend to be those with fewest co-benefits—and vice versa.[24]

A project should demonstrate its compliance with all legal requirements in the jurisdiction where it is located. Depending on a project's type and the jurisdiction to which it belongs, additional reviews and safeguards may be necessary to guard against negative outcomes unrelated to GHG emissions. For example, this could be the case if workers involved in carbon projects, such as subsistence farmers, are paid below applicable (local) market rates while contributing to a carbon offset program.

[22] "Clearer demand signals would help give suppliers more confidence in their project plans and encourage investors and lenders to provide with financing" Blaufelder et al. (2021).

[23] A new analysis of large-scale forest protection schemes in the Colombian Amazon by Carbon Market Watch claims that they may be dramatically overstating their impact on preventing deforestation. The report warns that millions of carbon credits have likely been generated with no benefit to the climate. https://carbonmarketwatch.org/publications/two-shades-of-green-how-hot-air-forest-credits-are-being-used-to-avoid-carbon-taxes-in-colombia/.

[24] There are a number of "add-on" certification schemes focused on the social and environmental impacts of carbon offset projects. The certifiers can be organizations like the Climate, Community & Biodiversity Alliance (CCBA) and SOCIALCARBON, for example. Broekhoff et al. (2019). Available at: https://www.offsetguide.org/wp-content/uploads/2020/03/Carbon-Offset-Guide_3122020.pdf.

6 Final Remarks

The United Nations Tax Committee is, in its current mandate, analysing the main issues around the taxation of carbon offset credits in the Transfer Pricing Subcommittee and the Subcommittee on Environmental Taxation.[25] The expert team from the latter specific workstream has been working to offer an overview of what is happening in emerging markets regarding carbon offset credits—and how it justifies timely tax authority action. It has aimed to raise awareness of the framework provided by Article 6 of the Paris Agreement by capturing current problems and possible ways to further develop carbon taxation. The team has targeted core issues to address in order to ensure a coherent approach in qualification and valuation of those credits. Its purpose has been to have both policy considerations and implementation costs assessed, focusing on carbon taxation and leaving aside income taxation. The subcommittee has recognized that these commodities contribute to lowering the amount of carbon emissions, that they serve to meet the NDCs pledges under the Paris Agreement, and that there is an urgent need to assess their cross-border impacts. A document has been presented for the committee's consideration at the twenty-seventh session.[26]

Any future regulation, irrespective of the level of government adopting it, should not only facilitate but ensure a global positive environmental impact in line with the UN 2030 Agenda. The Addis Ababa Action Agenda already pointed out that private participation should be stimulated to reach the SDGs. Cooperation in tax matters is still relatively precarious, and a serious attempt should be made to facilitate the achievement of extra-fiscal objectives in a coordinated manner. This could be done by establishing the appropriate controls on tax incentives and monitoring their real impact through the use of available digital means.[27] The costs—economic but also environmental, social, and governance—arising from the lack of sufficient cooperation should no longer be ignored.

[25] Committee of Experts on International Cooperation in Tax Matters, Twenty-sixth session New York, 27–30 March 2023 E/C.18/2023/CRP15 - Co-Coordinators' report https://financing.desa.un.org/document/crp15-environmental-taxation-co-coordinators-report-0 E/C.18/2023/CRP7 - Co-Coordinator's Report, Annex C https://financing.desa.un.org/document/ec182023crp7 The Report of the 25th Session of the Committee of Experts on International Cooperation in Tax Matters (E/2023/45-E/C.18/2022/5) at para. 52. https://financing.desa.un.org/document/report-25th-session-committee-experts-international-cooperation-tax-matters.

[26] Committee of Experts on International Cooperation in Tax Matters, Twenty-sixth session, Geneva, 17–20 October 2023. E/C.18/2023/CRP35 - Co-Coordinators' report https://financing.desa.un.org/sites/default/files/2023-10/CRP.35%20Environmental%20Co-Coordinators%20Report_1.pdf and CRP.35 Annex D (Carbon Offsets) https://financing.desa.un.org/sites/default/files/2023-10/CRP.35%20Annex%20D%20%28Carbon%20Offsets%29_1.pdf.

[27] In preparing his report in response to General Assembly Resolution 77/244, the secretary-general invited written input from Member States and relevant stakeholders on the range of issues addressed in the resolution. Grau Ruiz (2023).

References

Battocletti V et al (2023) Can voluntary carbon markets be fixed? Oxford Business Law Blog, Posted 14 March. https://blogs.law.ox.ac.uk/oblb/blog-post/2023/03/can-voluntary-carbon-markets-be-fixed

Blaufelder C et al (2021) A blueprint for scaling voluntary carbon markets to meet the climate challenge, McKinsey Report 29 January. Available at: https://www.mckinsey.com/business-functions/sustainability/our-insights/a-blueprint-for-scaling-voluntary-carbon-markets-to-meet-the-climate-challenge

Broekhoff D et al (2019) Securing climate benefit: a guide to using carbon offsets. Stockholm Environment Institute & Greenhouse Gas Management Institute, 9

Gilder A, Stiles G (2019) Comparative approaches to carbon taxation in Canada and South Africa. Carbon Climate Law Rev 13(4)

Grau Ruiz MA (2022) Los créditos por compensaciones de emisiones de CO_2 a la hora de 'descarbonizarse': el complejo debate mundial sobre el régimen tributario aplicable a los *carbon offset credits*, Revista Técnica Tributaria, No. 138

Grau Ruiz MA (2023) Input for promotion of inclusive and effective tax cooperation at the United Nations, UN, NY. https://financing.desa.un.org/sites/default/files/2023-03/Grau%20Ruiz%2C%20Mar%C3%ADa%20Amparo_%20Input%20Tax%20Report%20combined.pdf

Machingambi M (2017) Is the use of carbon offsets in the South African carbon tax a smart mix? In: Weishaar S et al (eds) The green market transition: carbon taxes, energy subsidies and smart instrument mixes. Edward Elgar Publishing

Michaelowa A et al (2019) Evolution of international carbon markets: lessons for the Paris Agreement. Wiley Interdiscip Rev Clim Change 10(6). John Wiley & Sons, Inc. https://doi.org/10.1002/wcc.613

Pizarro R (2021) Sistemas de instrumentos de fijación de precios del carbono en América Latina y jurisdicciones de las Américas relevantes, Documentos de Proyectos (LC/TS.2021/41), Santiago, Comisión Económica para América Latina y el Caribe (CEPAL)

Porsborg-Smith A et al (2023) The voluntary carbon market is thriving, 19th January. https://www.bcg.com/publications/2023/why-the-voluntary-carbon-market-is-thriving

Salway H et al (2022) Carbon credit rights under the Paris Agreement. How Article 6 and the implementation of NDCS may shape government approaches to the carbon market, and what this mean for rights related to carbon credits, EY-Goldstandard, November

Weishaar S et al (eds) (2017) The green market transition: carbon taxes, energy subsidies and smart instrument mixes. Edward Elgar Publishing

White C (2022) Voluntary carbon offsets: the evolution of a business expense. Tax Adviser 53(1). American Institute of CPA's

The Use of Windfall Taxes on the Energy Sector to Support the Green Transition in the EU

Karolina Tetłak

Abstract On 6 October 2022, Council Regulation (EU)2022/1854 on an emergency intervention to address high energy prices was adopted. The regulation introduced two fiscal measures: A "temporary solidarity contribution" imposed on the oil, gas, coal, and refinery sector to recover surplus profits generated during the fossil fuel crisis and a "cap on market revenues" for electricity producers. The regulation also outlines the use of these revenues in the Member States of the European Union (EU). The objective of this chapter is to demonstrate that these EU policy measures serve as fiscal instruments for accelerating the green transition. By imposing tax measures on windfall profits resulting from the energy crisis and requiring the Member States to use the proceeds for the purposes listed in the regulation, the EU created a redistribution tool to support its transition to renewable resources. The chapter examines in detail whether the solidarity contribution and the cap on market revenues as defined in the regulation can effectively contribute to sustainable financing as part of the EU's energy and climate policy measures.

1 Introduction

On 6 October 2022, Council Regulation (EU)2022/1854 on an emergency intervention to address high energy prices was adopted.[1] The regulation includes measures to counter soaring electricity prices in Europe, including instruments referred to as a "temporary solidarity contribution" imposed on the oil, gas, coal, and refining sector and a "cap on market revenues" obtained by certain electricity producers. The

[1] Council Regulation (EU)2022/1854 on an emergency intervention to address high energy prices of 6 October 2022 (OJ L 261I, 7.10.2022, pp. 1–21; hereafter referred to as Regulation).

K. Tetłak (✉)
Faculty of Law and Administration, Warsaw University, Warsaw, Poland
e-mail: karolina.tetlak@wpia.uw.edu.pl

R. Saraiva, P. A. Pardal (eds.), *Sustainable Finances and the Law*, Economic Analysis of Law in European Legal Scholarship 16,
https://doi.org/10.1007/978-3-031-49460-4_13

regulation also sets rules for redistribution of the proceeds obtained in the Member States.

Explaining the background and objectives of the adopted measures, the European Commission indicated in the legislative proposal that the sharp increase in natural gas and hard coal prices after the Russian invasion of Ukraine in February 2022 and the resulting demand for alternative fuels led to an increase in electricity prices which causes hardship for households and businesses in the EU and fuel inflation while the necessary support measures increase public spending.[2] Very high energy prices generate excessive financial profits for electricity producers and for companies operating in the fossil fuel sector. These entities could not count on such profits in normal circumstances if unforeseeable events did not occur in the energy markets.[3] However, while rising prices of fossil resources translate into electricity generation costs for gas and coal-fired power plants, electricity prices have also increased for technologies with much lower marginal costs such as renewables, nuclear, and lignite (infra-marginal technologies). The resulting profits are primarily due to favourable external market factors caused by the Russian war and not due to additional efforts or investments by the companies themselves.[4]

As a result, the Commission proposed a package of urgent market interventions including two windfall profit taxes. Excess profits generated by EU companies and permanent establishments operating in the fossil fuel sector are subject to a mandatory temporary solidarity contribution unless Member States have introduced equivalent national measures. The Commission believes that the temporary solidarity levy on companies from oil, gas, coal and refining activities will allow to recover excess revenues generated by the crisis.[5]

The windfall revenues of electricity producers with lower marginal costs are temporarily targeted and reduced by setting a revenue cap of up to a maximum of EUR 180/MWh electricity generated. The Commission explained that, by reducing the revenues of electricity producers, the measure is designed to mimic the market outcome that producers could expect if global supply chains functioned normally without disruption to gas supplies and Russia's use of energy as an economic weapon. Importantly, the budget revenues from these taxes on excess profits are to be used in accordance with EU guidelines, as part of the implementation of the energy and climate policy.

---

[2]Commission proposal of 14 September 2022 for a Council Regulation on emergency intervention to address high energy prices (COM(2022)473).

[3]Recital (14) of the Preamble of the Regulation.

[4]Recital (50) of the Regulation states: "Without substantially changing their cost structure and increasing their investments, Union companies and permanent establishments generating at least 75% of turnover with activities in the crude petroleum, natural gas, coal and refinery sectors, have seen their profits spike due to the sudden and unpredictable circumstances of Russia's war of aggression against Ukraine, reduced supply of energy and increasing demand due to record high temperatures".

[5]See also Erdős and Czoboly (2023), pp. 36–41.

2 Windfall Taxes

In general, windfall taxes are levied on unexpected or excessive profits earned by individuals, businesses, or industries due to factors beyond their control such as natural resource discoveries, sudden price increases, or regulatory changes.[6] By targeting windfall profits, governments can ensure that those who have benefited disproportionately from unforeseen circumstances contribute a larger share of their gains back to the community.[7] This helps to reduce income disparities and create a more level playing field for all members of society.

Windfall taxes can be applied in various sectors, including oil and gas, mining, real estate, financial services, and technology. For example, in the oil and gas industry, windfall taxes may be imposed when oil prices rise significantly above a certain threshold.[8] This allows governments to capture a portion of the additional profits generated by companies operating in this sector and allocate them towards addressing social and economic inequalities.[9]

The revenue generated from windfall taxes can be used for various redistributive purposes. One common approach is to allocate these funds towards social welfare programs aimed at supporting vulnerable populations such as low-income families, the elderly, or individuals with disabilities. This can include initiatives like healthcare subsidies, education grants, affordable housing projects, or unemployment benefits.[10]

Another way windfall tax revenue can be redistributed is through investments in infrastructure development. By allocating funds towards building or improving public infrastructure such as roads, bridges, schools, hospitals, and public transportation systems, governments can enhance overall societal well-being and stimulate economic growth. These investments not only create job opportunities but also improve access to essential services for all citizens.[11]

It is important to note that the implementation of windfall taxes should be carefully designed to avoid unintended negative consequences.[12] Excessive taxation can discourage investment, innovation, and economic growth. Therefore, it is crucial for governments to strike a balance between capturing windfall gains and maintaining a favourable business environment.[13]

---

[6] Zodrow (1988), pp. 387–424. https://doi.org/10.1177/109114218801600401. Access: 17 August 2023.

[7] Chennels (1997), pp. 279–291.

[8] Drapkin and Verleger (1981), p. 631; Matikonis (2022), pp. 330–340.

[9] McIntyre (1981), p. 705; Feldstein (1976a), pp. 123–130.

[10] Tickell (1998), pp. 83–90. http://www.jstor.org/stable/20003853. Access: 17 August 2023.

[11] See Matikonis (2023), pp. 8–19.

[12] Gamponia and Mendelsohn (1985), pp. 165–181, https://doi.org/10.2307/1885740, access: 17 August 2023.

[13] Van der Ploeg and Venables (2011), p. 1, https://doi.org/10.1111/j.1468-0297.2010.02411.x, access: 17 August 2023; Goode (1987), pp. 159–169.

In summary, the redistributive function of windfall taxes lies in their ability to capture unexpected or excessive profits and allocate them towards addressing social and economic inequalities. By targeting windfall gains, governments can promote fairness and equity within society, reduce income disparities, support vulnerable populations, invest in infrastructure development, and finance progressive taxation systems. The redistributive function of windfall taxes refers to the role these taxes play in redistributing wealth or income within a society.

Traditionally, the following roles of taxes are distinguished: Fiscal (revenue-raising), allocative, redistributive, and stimulating (interventionist). The fiscal function is primarily related to the collection of budgetary funds. The revenue collected from taxation is then used to finance the implementation of public tasks which corresponds to the allocative function of taxes. The redistributive function of taxes consists of the fact that taxes are used as instruments to regulate the distribution of income and wealth among different groups of taxpayers and the state (budget) and local government. The funds collected from taxation are subsequently used to finance the implementation of various public tasks. The order of implementing these tasks is determined by the economic and social programs of the state and its authorities and is supported by the political parties currently forming the government and holding the majority in parliament. The redistributive function is therefore strongly determined by political and social factors.

The stimulative function pertains to the government's intervention in taxpayers' activities by stimulating desirable behaviours and eliminating (preventing) or reducing undesirable behaviours through appropriate tax incentives or oppressive taxation.[14] The implementation of the functions of taxes (such as the distribution of resources among different social groups, elimination of undesirable behaviours) is achieved through the appropriate design of tax structure (subjective and objective scope of taxation, differentiated tax rates). However, combining repressive goals with fiscal goals should not take on a confiscatory and discriminatory character.

3 Cap on Market Revenues

A mandatory cap on market revenues was introduced by Article 6 of Regulation (EU) 2022/1854 that, in section 1, provides: Market revenues of producers obtained from the generation of electricity from the sources referred to in Article 7(1) shall be capped to a maximum of 180 EUR per MWh of electricity produced.

According to the definition in Article 2.38 of Directive (EU) 2019/944,[15] "producer" means a natural or legal person who produces electricity. Other entities operating in the energy sector including producers of heat and other types of energy,

[14] Feldstein (1976b).

[15] Based on Article 2, for the purposes of this regulation, the definitions in Article 2 of Directive (EU) 2019/944 and in Article 2 of Regulation (EU) 2019/943 apply.

producers of RES technologies, and energy sales intermediaries (energy trading brokers) will remain outside the scope of the discussed regulations.

Article 7(1) of the regulation specifies that the "revenue cap" shall apply to the market revenues obtained from the sale of electricity produced from the following sources:

(a) wind energy;
(b) solar energy (solar thermal and solar photovoltaic);
(c) geothermal energy;
(d) hydropower without reservoir;
(e) biomass fuel (solid or gaseous biomass fuels), excluding biomethane;
(f) waste (whereby "waste"—pursuant to Article 2.9—means any substance or object which the holder discards or intends or is required to discard as defined in Article 3(1) of Directive 2008/98/EC);
(g) nuclear energy;
(h) lignite;
(i) crude petroleum products; and
(j) peat.

The above provision contains a closed catalog of energy sources to which the revenue cap is applicable. It should be emphasized that, in the enumerative catalog, natural gas and hard coal are missing.[16] Natural gas, in accordance with the justification to the draft regulation, was considered a raw material setting the limit price. Recital (33) of the regulation states:

> The cap on market revenues should not apply to technologies with high marginal costs relating to the price of the input fuel necessary to produce electricity, such as gas and hard coal-fired power plants, as their operating costs would be significantly above the level of the cap on market revenues and its application would jeopardise their economic viability.[17]

It is worth noting that, since the revenue cap should not apply to technologies with high marginal costs, the inclusion of biomass, crude oil, and lignite in this measure should be critically assessed as technologies with high variable costs and, as a result, total costs often significantly higher than EUR 180/MWh.[18] There is no provision in the regulation that would exclude the application of the cap when the related production costs are above the threshold. In such a case, power plants would have negative margins which could discourage them from operating, result in a decrease in production and, as a result, threaten the security of supply (especially in a tight

[16] In the original version of the draft, the catalog did not include petroleum products, but crude shale oil was included in the list.

[17] The explanatory memorandum to the proposal for a regulation further notes that: "If gas and coal-fired power plants were subject to an income ceiling, they would not be able to cover their operating costs and would be forced out of the market."

[18] Position paper on draft Council Regulation proposing a price cap on electricity producers' market revenues COM(2022)473, 25.9.2022, https://www.eurelectric.org/publications/position-paper-on-draft-council-regulation-proposing-a-price-cap-on-electricity-producers-market-revenues-com-2022-473/ [access: 6.02.2023].

balance of supply and demand). Such a risk applies to biomass which should not be treated on an equal footing with other renewable energy technologies such as wind, photovoltaics, and water. Biomass plants are affected by soaring fuel costs and much higher maintenance costs. As a result, the marginal costs of the technology exceed the proposed revenue threshold of EUR 180/MWh. Therefore, biomass installations as well as biogas plants should be exempt from the revenue limit.[19] The same applies to lignite for which the proposed fixed cap of EUR 180/MWh is not enough to cover variable costs. The situation may even worsen given the possible increase in the price of CO2 emissions. Member States should be able to exempt from the application of the cap technologies or producers generating energy from the sources listed in Article 7, section 1 who demonstrate to the regulatory authority that their current leveled costs of generated energy exceed the maximum specified in Article 6(1) of the regulation. Regarding Article 7(1)(e) of the regulation, which excludes biomethane from the scope of the measure, recital (34) explains:

> The cap on market revenues should not apply to technologies using as input fuels that are substitutes for natural gas, such as biomethane, so as not to jeopardise the conversion of existing gas-fired power plants in line with the REPowerEU objectives set in particular in the Commission Communication of 18 May 2022 on a REPowerEU Plan.

The provision of Article 6 of the regulation defining the scope of the measure in question should be interpreted in conjunction with the legal definition of the term "market revenue" contained in Article 2.5. According to this definition, "market revenue" means realized income that a producer receives in exchange for the sale and delivery of electricity in the Union regardless of the contractual form in which such exchange takes place including power purchase agreements and other hedging operations against fluctuations in the wholesale electricity market and excluding any support granted by Member States. The latter reservation means that the scope of taxation does not include any subsidies or other forms of co-financing received from the state. The scale of such subsidies is significant in the case of renewable energy sources, e.g., in Germany.[20]

It is worth noting that the concept of "market revenue" caused some definitional difficulties for the Commission. The EU legislature did not expressly decide that

---

[19] *Ibidem.*

[20] The report commissioned by the European Commission shows the value of subsidies that the EU-28 countries allocated in 2012 to support individual energy sectors. The largest support was received by solar energy (EUR 14.7 billion), onshore wind energy (EUR 10.1 billion), biomass power plants (EUR 8.3 billion), hydropower (EUR 5.2 billion), and subsidies for offshore wind energy amounted to EUR 1.3 billion. On the other hand, among the sectors of conventional energy in the EU, in 2012, the biggest support was given to coal energy (EUR 10.1 billion), nuclear energy received EUR 7 billion, and gas energy—EUR 5.2 billion. The value of energy subsidies granted by the Polish Government in 2012 amounted to EUR 970 million. The Germans paid more—EUR 25 billion, the British—EUR 13 billion, the Spaniards—EUR 10.4 billion, and the Italians—EUR 10.3 billion (*Ile kosztuje produkcja energii z węgla, gazu, atomu, wiatru i słońca?*, Gramwzielone.pl, 14.10.2014, https://www.gramwzielone.pl/trendy/13075/ile-kosztuje-produkcja-energii-z-wegla-gazu-atomu-wiatru-i-slonca [access: 6.02.2023].

taxes and fees should be excluded from the concept of income, but the solidarity contribution proposed later was clearly regulated in this respect. Therefore, it is not known, for example, whether the amount of VAT should be excluded from the amount of revenue and whether the new tax will be deductible for income tax purposes, whether it will be levied on the amount constituting revenue (price) or on the amount of income after deduction of costs. It seems that the wording suggests the income nature of the tax based on the selling price and not on income less tax-deductible costs.[21] This is suggested both by the provisions of the regulation and the legislative proposal as well as by different terms (profits, taxable income) used in the case of the solidarity contribution imposed by the regulation on fossil fuel companies.[22]

The tax base for the "cap on market revenue" is measured in EUR per MWh (megawatt-hour[23]) of electricity, indicating the taxable amount in a value-quantity manner. This format expresses the tax base as a monetary ratio per unit of measurement, highlighting the quantitative relationship between currency (EUR) and the specific measurement (MWh) used by gas and electricity suppliers to gauge energy consumption. By adopting this value-quantity approach, the tax assessment encompasses both the financial aspect and the measured quantity of the taxable item.

The regulation establishes that the revenue of electricity producers "shall be capped to a maximum of EUR 180 per MWh of electricity generated". Any revenue above this limit is subject to confiscation as the tax rate is set at 100% above the limit. Essentially, a tax-free allowance applies up to this threshold beyond which the confiscation tax rate is applied.

Confiscation rates are typically implemented to seize assets or income and discourage certain behaviours. In this case, the tax serves as a means to discourage producers from setting prices higher than EUR 180 per MWh of electricity and earning revenues exceeding this limit.

The nature of this windfall tax rate is expropriatory as it involves the state taking over all revenues beyond the specified limit. The "cap" effectively entails mandatory forfeiture of any income exceeding EUR 180 per MWh of electricity generated as indicated by the regulation. However, when determining the tax rate, no mechanism was established to individualize the burden in a way that ensures the taxpayer retains sufficient amounts to cover their costs. The regulation allows for the application of the revenue ceiling irrespective of the level of energy production costs. Consequently, power plants with high costs and negative margins may face the risk of

---

[21] A similar tax introduced in the United States in 1980 was considered an excise tax and not a profit tax (see Lazzari 2006, p. 28, https://liheapch.acf.hhs.gov/pubs/oilwindfall.pdf, access: 17 August 2023).

[22] See broadly: Tetłak (2022), pp. 188–201.

[23] 1 megawatt hour (MWh) equals 1000 kWh of energy. In turn, 1 kilowatt-hour (kWh) is a unit of work, energy, and heat that corresponds to the amount of energy consumed by a device with a power of 1000 watts, i.e. one kilowatt, for an hour. The megawatt hour (MWh) is used as a unit of measurement in industry, for example, to indicate the amount of energy produced annually by power plants.

the tax having a confiscatory impact and potentially discouraging their operations. This risk is particularly relevant for biomass and lignite plants for which the proposed fixed limit of EUR 180 per MWh may not adequately cover their variable costs. Despite the unstable economic situation and rising prices, the EU legislature omitted the impact of inflation on the depreciation of this rate. The regulation does not specify the possibility of its valorization, and no mechanism for changing the rate based on the increase in inflation has been introduced.[24] It is possible that this was not done due to the envisaged temporary nature of the revenue cap.

Although the regulation does not preclude the application of the revenue cap beyond a certain level of energy production costs, the EU legislature undoubtedly took into account the issue of taxpayers' ability to pay as recital (27) of the regulation emphasizes:

> The level at which the cap on market revenues is set should not jeopardise the ability of the producers to which it is applied, including renewable energy producers, to recover their investment and operating costs and should preserve and incentivise future investments in the capacity needed for a decarbonised and reliable electricity system. The cap on market revenues, being a uniform cap across the Union, is best suited to preserve the functioning of the internal electricity market, as it maintains price-based competition between electricity producers based on different technologies, in particular for renewables.

Nevertheless, the legislative procedure consisting in indicating the amount of the mandatory income ceiling from the normative point of view does not contain mechanisms to protect the taxpayer's ability to pay in changing economic conditions. The adopted amount of EUR 180 is more or less arbitrary and vulnerable to inflation. This increases the confiscation potential of this rate and makes it difficult to assess, a priori, the maximum effective tax rate (the relation of the tax on a specific amount of the tax base to that amount) and the amount of taxation in global terms.

In the case of the revenue cap, the effective tax rate depends on the amount of revenue actually obtained from the sale of electricity by its producers. For example, if it is EUR 360/MWh, the effective tax rate is 50%. However, this does not take into account the costs of energy production that will determine the actual burden of taxation. If the amount of revenues is lower but costs are higher, the effective tax rate will increase. The income tax should also be taken into account as the revenue cap constitutes a system of two-stage taxation of producers of energy from specific sources. Taking the gross production (turnover) value as the tax base entails the accumulation of tax, i.e., the obligation to pay tax on tax.

Some flexibility is allowed under Article 7(5) of the regulation pursuant to which Member States may decide that the cap on market revenues only applies to 90% of the market revenues exceeding the cap on market revenues provided for in Article 6(1). By adjusting the tax base, the Member States may effectively reduce the applicable tax rate.

A mechanism that ensures that the taxpayers retain the amounts necessary to cover their costs is included in Article 8(1)(a) applicable to national crisis measures.

[24] See Thuronyi (2000), p. 434.

Under this provision, Member States may set a higher cap on market revenues for producers generating electricity from the sources listed in Article 7(1) provided that their investments and operating costs exceed the maximum set in Article 6(1) of the regulation.

Regarding the moment when the tax obligation arises, Article 6(4) of the regulation states that Member States shall decide whether to apply the cap on market revenues at the settlement of the exchange of energy or thereafter. According to the glossary contained in Article 2(6) of the regulation, "settlement" means a payment that is made and received between counterparties against delivery and receipt of electricity where applicable in fulfillment of the counterparties' respective obligations pursuant to one or more clearing transactions.

The provisions in question also introduce tax exemptions. According to Article 7(2) of the regulation, the cap on market revenues provided in Article 6(1) shall not apply to demonstration projects, i.e., projects demonstrating a certain type of technology for the first time in the Union and constituting a significant innovation that significantly departs from the state of the art.[25]

Pursuant to Article 7(2) of the regulation, the cap on market revenues provided in Article 6(1) shall not apply to producers whose revenues per MWh of electricity produced are already capped as a result of state or public measures not adopted under Article 8.

Article 7(3) of the regulation gives Member States the competence to introduce another exemption particularly in cases when the application of the cap on market revenues provided in Article 6(1) leads to a significant administrative burden to the smallest producers. Member States may decide that the cap on market revenues does not apply to producers generating electricity with power-generating facilities with an installed capacity of up to 1 MW. Considering the average power of the installations, in practice, it would mainly concern photovoltaic and wind installations, including small and micro-installations.

According to Article 8(1) applicable to national crisis measures, Member States may:

- maintain or introduce measures that further limit the market revenues of producers generating electricity from the sources listed in Article 7(1), including the possibility to differentiate between technologies, as well as the market revenues of other market participants, including those active in electricity trading;
- set a higher cap on market revenues for producers generating electricity from the sources listed in Article 7(1) provided that their investments and operating costs exceed the maximum set in Article 6(1);
- maintain or introduce national measures to limit the market revenues of producers generating electricity from sources not referred to in Article 7(1);

[25] Article 2 point 24 of Regulation (EU) 943/2019. Interestingly, "project which demonstrates a technology as a first of its kind" is ambiguous, and it is not clear whether the project is to be the first project of this type or the technology being demonstrated.

- set a specific cap on the market revenues obtained from the sale of electricity produced from hard coal; and
- subject the hydropower units not referred to in Article 7(1)(d) to a cap on market revenues or maintain or introduce such measures that further limit their market revenues, including the possibility to differentiate between technologies.

Pursuant to Article 8(2) of the regulation, the measures referred to in paragraph 1 shall, in line with this regulation:

- be proportionate and non-discriminatory;
- not jeopardize investment signals;
- ensure that the investments and operating costs are covered;
- not distort the functioning of electricity wholesale markets, and particularly not affect the merit order and the price formation on the wholesale market;
- and be compatible with Union law.

Article 7(3) of the regulation specifies that Member States may, in particular in cases when the application of the cap on market revenues provided in Article 6(1) leads to a risk of increasing CO2 emissions and decreasing renewable energy generation, decide that the cap on market revenues does not apply to electricity produced in hybrid plants that also use conventional energy sources. In accordance with Article 7(4), Member States may decide that the cap on market revenues does not apply to the revenues obtained from the sale of electricity in the balancing energy market and from compensation for redispatching and countertrading.

4 Temporary Solidarity Contribution

Profit surpluses generated by EU companies and permanent establishments from oil, gas, coal, and refining activities are subject to a mandatory temporary solidarity levy unless Member States have introduced equivalent national measures. The legal definition of the term was formulated in the glossary in Article 2.19 of the regulation according to which "solidarity contribution" means a temporary measure intended to address surplus profits of Union companies and permanent establishments with activities in the crude petroleum, natural gas, coal, and refinery sectors to mitigate exceptional price developments in the energy markets for Member States, consumers, and companies.

The legislative measure in question was named in the regulation as a "contribution", however, the mere fact that the EU legislature used such a term does not mean that the measure in question is not of a tax nature. Giving a specific public levy a different name does not automatically mean that it will cease to be a tax. The nature of a measure is determined by its character and not its name.

According to the literal meaning, a "contribution" is "a collection of money for some purpose" or "a sum of money paid regularly and obligatorily by one person to a common fund for some common purpose". The legal nature of the "solidarity contribution" in question may not be clear considering only its name. Therefore, it becomes necessary to study the material features of this measure and to search for the goal that the legislature followed in connection with its introduction. The regulation directly uses terms referring to the tax character of this measure such as the basis for calculation or the rate and also regulates other elements of the solidarity contribution structure such as the subject and object.

In the light of Articles 14–15 of the regulation, the subjects of taxation with the solidarity contribution are EU enterprises and permanent establishments operating in the oil, natural gas, coal, and refining sectors, including those that are part of a consolidated group merely for tax purposes. According to the glossary contained in Article 2.15 of the regulation, "Union company" means a company established in a Member State which, according to the tax laws of that Member State, is considered to be resident in that Member State for tax purposes and, under the terms of a double taxation agreement concluded with a third state, is not considered to be resident for tax purposes outside the Union.

Under Article 2.16, "permanent establishment" means a fixed place of business located in a Member State through which the business of a company established in another state is wholly or partly carried on insofar as the profits of that place of business are subject to tax in the Member State in which it is located.

Under Article 2.17, "Union companies and permanent establishments with activities in the crude petroleum, natural gas, coal and refinery sectors" means Union companies or permanent establishments generating at least 75% of their turnover from economic activities in the field of the extraction, mining, refining petroleum, or manufacturing coke oven products as referred to in Regulation (EC) 1893/2006 of the European Parliament and of the council.

It should be noted that the solidarity contribution does not apply to electricity producers but only to entities that acquire and process energy resources. Exceeding 75% of the turnover for the indicated activity results in covering all income of such entities with an additional tax. In practice, this may result in the division of energy companies and the separation of activities that do not generate burdened income into separate companies. It is also worth noting that the oil sector will be subject to two new taxes—the solidarity contribution will apply to entities extracting oil and refineries, and producers of electricity from crude oil and other petroleum products will be covered by the revenue cap.

The solidarity contribution applies to surplus profit from activities in the oil, natural gas, coal, and refining sectors. According to Article 2.18 of the regulation, "surplus profits" means taxable profits as determined under national tax rules in the fiscal year 2022 and/or the fiscal year 2023[26] and for their full duration accrued from activities carried out at the level of Union companies and permanent establishments with activities in the crude petroleum, natural gas, coal, and refinery sectors that are above a 20% increase of the average of the taxable profits in the four fiscal years starting on or after 1 January 2018. Article 15 of the regulation further specifies that,

[26]The fiscal year is determined by reference to the rules in place under Member States' national law.

if the average of the taxable profits in those four fiscal years is negative, the average taxable profits shall be zero for the purpose of calculating the temporary solidarity contribution. Member States that tax only distributed corporate profits should apply the temporary solidarity contribution to the calculated profits irrespective of their distribution (recital (52) of the regulation).

It is worth noting that this tax is based on actual windfall profits (i.e., profits above the historical average). Recitals (53)-(54) of the regulation clarify:

> Only profits made in 2022 and/or 2023 above a 20% increase of the average taxable profits generated in the four fiscal years starting on or after 1 January 2018 should be subject to the solidarity contribution. [. . .] This approach would ensure that part of the profit margin, which is not due to the unpredictable developments in the energy markets following Russia's war of aggression against Ukraine could be used by Union companies and permanent establishments concerned for future investment or for ensuring their financial stability during the ongoing energy crisis including for the energy intense industry. This approach to determining the calculation base would ensure that the solidarity contribution in different Member States is proportionate.

In the case of this levy, there is no doubt that the intention of the EU legislature was to tax profits generally understood as gross income less the costs of obtaining it (net income). However, the exact rules regarding the tax base will differ depending on the domestic law of the Member States. The reference to the rules of taxation with the national tax means that, despite the seemingly uniform tax base resulting from the regulation, the tax base for this tax, i.e., one of the key elements of its structure, will vary from country to country.

The solidarity contribution has a cascading nature, i.e., it is levied on taxable income. The assumption of double taxation also follows directly from Article 16(2) of the regulation pursuant to which the temporary solidarity contribution shall apply in addition to the regular taxes and levies applicable according to the national law of a Member State. This intention is also expressed in recital (14) of the regulation which states that this measure should be applied in parallel to the normal corporate taxes levied by each Member State on the companies concerned.

Pursuant to Article 16(1) of the regulation, the rate applicable for calculating the temporary solidarity contribution shall be at least 33% of the base referred to in Article 15. According to the Commission, the proposed rate guarantees

> covering part of the profit with this contribution, without making it unnecessarily difficult for energy companies operating in the oil, gas, coal and refinery sectors to use this profit for future investments or to ensure their profitability. Therefore, the rate proposed in the Regulation is limited to one-third of the excess taxable profit after applying the buffer to the tax base. However, in order to ensure that the specific circumstances of Member States are taken into account, the proposed rate is a minimum rate and Member States may apply a higher rate if deemed necessary (page 21 of the proposal for the regulation).

In the Commission's view, this minimum rate approach ensures that the solidarity contribution is fair and proportionate. "Member States should remain free to apply a rate higher than 33% for their solidarity contribution. This should enable those

Member States to set a preferred rate which they consider acceptable and appropriate under their national legal systems."[27]

Profit surpluses generated by EU companies and permanent establishments from oil, gas, coal, and refining activities are subject to the mandatory solidarity levy unless Member States have introduced equivalent national measures. According to Article 2.21 "enacted equivalent national measure" means a legislative, regulatory, or administrative measure adopted and published by a Member State by 31 December 2022 that contributes to the affordability of energy. Pursuant to Article 14(2), Member States shall ensure that enacted equivalent national measures share similar objectives and are subject to similar rules as the temporary solidarity contribution and generate comparable or higher proceeds to the estimated proceeds from the solidarity contribution. This provision requires EU Member States to coordinate their internal policy instruments with the new EU tax. Member States that already have a national tax in place at a rate above the proposed solidarity contribution rate may continue to apply the existing higher rate to take account of the national specificities that led to the adoption of that rate.

5 Distribution of Windfall Profits

According to Article 17(1) of the regulation, Member States shall use the proceeds from the temporary solidarity contribution with *sufficiently timely impact* for any of the following purposes:

(a) financial support measures for final energy customers and in particular vulnerable households to mitigate the effects of high energy prices in a targeted manner;
(b) financial support measures to help reduce the energy consumption such as through demand reduction auctions or tender schemes, lowering the energy purchase costs of final energy customers for certain volumes of consumption, *promoting investments by final energy customers into renewables, structural energy efficiency investments, or other decarbonization technologies*;
(c) financial support measures to support companies in energy intensive industries *provided that they are made conditional upon investments into renewable energies, energy efficiency, or other decarbonization technologies;*
(d) financial support measures to develop the energy autonomy, in particular investments in line with the REPowerEU objectives set in the REPowerEU Plan and in the REPowerEU Joint European Action such as projects with a cross-border dimension; and
(e) in a spirit of solidarity between Member States, Member States may assign a share of the proceeds of the temporary solidarity contribution to the common

[27] Recital (63) of the regulation.

financing of measures to reduce the harmful effects of the energy crisis including support for protecting employment and reskilling and upskilling the workforce or to promote investments in energy efficiency and renewable energy including in cross-border projects and, in the Union, a renewable energy financing mechanism provided for in Article 33 of Regulation (EU) 2018/1999 of the European Parliament and of the Council.[28]

The uniform obligation to pass on excess income to final recipients established by the regulation will ensure that all Member States allocate these additional resources for the same purpose. In recitals (57–58) of the regulation, the Commission underlines:

> The use of the proceeds for those purposes reflects the solidarity contribution's exceptional and temporary nature as a measure that intends to reduce and mitigate the harmful effects of the energy crisis for households and companies across the Union with the objective of protecting the internal market and preventing the risk of further fragmentation. [...] In particular, Member States should target financial support measures to the most vulnerable households and companies, which are most affected from the soaring energy prices. [...] Moreover, the proceeds of the solidarity contribution should be used for fostering the reduction of energy consumption. In this respect, such proceeds should be used, for instance, for the purpose of demand reduction auctions or tender schemes, lowering the energy purchase costs of final energy customers for certain volumes of energy consumption, or promoting investments by final energy customers, both vulnerable households and companies, into renewables, energy efficiency investments or other decarbonisation technologies. The proceeds from the solidarity contribution should also be used for financially supporting companies in energy intensive industries, and in regions relying on those industries. [...] Financial support measures are to be made conditional upon investments into renewable energies, energy efficiency, or other decarbonisation technologies. Furthermore, measures which help making the Union more autonomous in the energy field should be supported with investments in accordance with the objectives set in the [...] REPowerEU Plan.

Similarly, under the provision of Article 10 of the regulation entitled "Distribution of the surplus revenues", Member States shall ensure that all surplus revenues resulting from the application of the cap on market revenues are used to finance measures in support of final electricity customers that mitigate the impact of high electricity prices on those customers in a targeted manner. According to the definition in Article 2.9, "surplus revenues" means a positive difference between the market revenues of producers per MWh of electricity and the cap on market revenues of 180 EUR per MWh of electricity provided in Article 6(1).

According to Article 10(4) of the regulation, these support measures may include, for example:

> granting financial compensation to final electricity customers for reducing their electricity consumption, including through demand reduction auctions or tender schemes;
>
> direct transfers to final electricity customers, including through proportional reductions in the network tariffs;

[28] The common financing aspect covers both project-based cost-sharing between Member States and channeling through a Union instrument on the basis of Member States voluntarily assigning revenues to the Union budget in a spirit of solidarity.

> compensation to suppliers who have to deliver electricity to customers below costs following a state or public intervention in price setting pursuant to Article 13;
> lowering the electricity purchase costs of final electricity customers, including for a limited volume of the electricity consumed; and
> promoting investments by final electricity customers into decarbonization technologies, renewables, and energy efficiency investments.

Recital (47) of the regulation explains:

> The revenues from the cap should help Member States finance measures such as income transfers, rebates on bills, compensating suppliers for supplying below cost, as well investments that would lead to a structural reduction of consumption, in particular from electricity produced from fossil fuel sources. When support is granted to non-household customers, those should work towards undertaking investments in decarbonisation technologies, including renewable energies, for example through power purchasing agreements or direct investments in renewables generation, or towards undertaking investments in energy efficiency.

Articles 10(4) and 17(1) of the regulation list several examples of support measures for end recipients. These provisions together constitute a redistribution clause requiring Member States to use the budget revenues obtained from the measures for specific purposes. They contain positive indications, i.e., prescriptive guidelines, regarding the use of revenue. As compared to the original version of the proposal for the regulation, negative indications have been removed from the catalog, i.e., prohibition guidelines, excluding the allocation of funds for direct support to consumers other than households (e.g., schools, hospitals, public universities, offices). Under the current wording of the regulation, the proceeds must be used to finance measures to support end-users of energy (customers who purchase energy for their own use), in particular those final customers, both private and commercial, who are most vulnerable to high electricity prices. It is worth noting that the catalog of exemplary support measures financed from the revenue obtained from the solidarity contribution contained in Article 17(1) of the regulation is closed which means that Member States are free to use the proceeds from the contribution only within the framework of the objectives set out in the regulation. This limits the powers of Member States to decide on the allocation of their budgetary resources. The catalog of measures to be financed from the revenue cap listed in Article 10(4) is open and exemplary which means that Member States are free to allocate tax revenues also to other forms of support of a similar nature. Nevertheless, both provisions in question limit the powers of the Member States to decide on the allocation of their budgetary resources.

What is more, pursuant to Articles 10(2) and 17(2), support measures should be clearly defined, transparent, proportionate, non-discriminatory, and verifiable. The expressions contained in this provision are of a general and vague nature which gives the Commission the right to arbitrarily assess the use of the proceeds from windfall taxes by the Member States.

The provision of Article 10(3) provides that, when revenues obtained directly from the implementation of the cap on market revenues in their territory and revenues obtained indirectly from cross-border agreements are insufficient to adequately support final electricity customers, Member States shall be allowed to use other appropriate means such as budgetary resources for the same purpose and under the same conditions.

According to Article 11 of the regulation entitled "Agreements between Member States", in situations when a Member State's net import dependence is equal or higher than 100%, an agreement to share the surplus revenues adequately shall be concluded by 1 December 2022 between the importing Member State and the main exporting Member State. All Member States may, in a spirit of solidarity, conclude such agreements which may also cover revenues coming from national crisis measures under Article 8, including electricity trading activities.

The provision in question introduces obligatory and optional agreements on the transfer of budget revenues from the new tax to electricity importing countries from electricity exporting countries. Recital (38) explains:

> Given that by application of the cap on market revenues, not all Member States can support their final customers to the same extent due to circumstances relating to their dependence on imports of electricity from other countries, it is necessary for Member States with net imports of electricity equal or higher than 100% to have access to agreements to share the surplus revenues with the main exporting Member State in a spirit of solidarity. Such solidarity agreements are also encouraged, in particular, to reflect unbalanced trading relationships.

6 Temporary Character of the Windfall Taxes, Monitoring the Implementation of the Measures, and Reporting Obligations of the Member States

The regulation repeatedly emphasizes the temporary character and limited time span of the solidarity contribution and revenue cap. The windfall taxes on the EU energy industry were introduced for the 2022–2023 winter season. The regulation entered into force on the day following that of its publication in the Official Journal of the European Union, i.e., on 7 October 2022 and applies, as a rule, until 31 December 2023. The measures are therefore immediately applicable from 8 October 2022. Member States are required under Article 14 sec. 3 of the regulation to adopt and publish measures implementing the mandatory temporary solidarity contribution by 31 December 2022. Since it applies to surplus profits earned in the tax years of 2022 and 2023, in practice, it basically means that it applies retroactively for the entire year of 2022 for those entities whose tax year coincides with the calendar year. The revenue cap on the surplus income of energy producers from renewable sources was introduced for seven months in the period from 1 December 2022 to 30 June 2023 with the possibility of extension based on the Commission's proposal.

Prolonged application of the regulation regards distribution of surplus income and certain reporting obligations imposed on Member States. While the windfall taxes were introduced for a limited period of time, the redistribution of proceeds obtained therefrom is not limited and may exceed the timeframe of the taxes.

The provision of Article 19 of the regulation requires the relevant state authorities to monitor the implementation of the measures, including reporting obligations on the collection of revenue as well as the use of these funds. By 31 January 2023 and again by 30 April 2023, Member States shall report to the Commission on, *inter alia*, the surplus revenues generated pursuant to Article 6 and the measures concerning the distribution of the surplus revenues applied to mitigate the impact of high electricity prices on final electricity customers pursuant to Article 10.

Moreover, pursuant to Article 19(4), Member States shall report to the Commission on:

(a) the introduction of the temporary solidarity contribution pursuant to Article 14, including in which fiscal year(s) they will apply it, by 31 December 2022;
(b) any subsequent amendments to the national legal framework within one month of the date of publication in their respective national official journals;
(c) the use of the proceeds pursuant to Article 17 within one month of the date on which the proceeds have been collected by them in accordance with national law; and
(d) the enacted equivalent national measures referred to in Article 14 by 31 December 2022; Member States shall also provide an assessment of the amount of proceeds generated by those enacted equivalent national measures and on the use of those proceeds within one month of the date on which the proceeds have been collected by them in accordance with national law.

The proceeds from the solidarity contribution should be distributed starting 1 December 2022. The regulations mentioned above require Member States to report on the collection of income from the solidarity contribution as well as the use of this income and on any changes they introduce in relation to this contribution. As follows from the provisions on the reporting deadline, Member States should distribute the proceeds from the temporary solidarity contribution and equivalent national measures within one month from collection. This sets a very short deadline for disbursement of the sums collected and runs the risk of doing so in haste.

It should be emphasized that the imposition of reporting obligations on Member States also means that the Commission has been given the power to monitor the application of the measures set out in the regulation. Recital (60) of the preamble to the regulation states that: "Regular and effective monitoring and reporting to the Commission is essential to assess the progress made by Member States in meeting the demand reduction targets, the implementation of the market yield cap, the use of surplus revenue and the use of regulated prices."

7 Conclusions

A windfall tax is a special tax levied on unexpected and unusually high profits earned by companies or individuals due to specific economic conditions, natural resource discoveries, or other unforeseen events. The purpose of such a tax is to capture windfall gains that would not have been generated under normal circumstances and redirect them towards public financing needs. Windfall taxes on energy refer to tax schemes that are imposed on energy companies when they realize unexpected or excessive profits due to price increases or other factors. Windfall taxes can help to reduce income inequality by ensuring that those who have benefited the most from windfall gains contribute a larger proportion of their income towards public goods and services.[29]

Windfall taxes on energy in the European Union have been proposed as a means to address both high energy prices and environmental concerns. Council Regulation (EU) 2022/1854 introduced two windfall taxes: the market revenue cap on electricity producers and the solidarity contribution from the fossil fuel industry. Both are aimed at imposing additional charges on energy companies that benefit from unexpected or excessive profits due to changing market conditions. It also strictly regulated the use of proceeds from windfall profit taxes, strengthening the role of these EU policy measures in transitioning to a green economy.

The rationale behind windfall taxes on energy is to ensure a fair distribution of wealth and mitigate the negative impacts of high energy prices on consumers, particularly those with limited financial means such as low-income households. By taxing excessive profit margins, the EU hopes to generate revenue that can be used for various purposes in alignment with the EU environmental and energy policy such as funding renewable energy projects, subsidizing energy costs for vulnerable populations, or investing in energy efficiency initiatives. These taxes may also serve as a way to incentivize energy companies to invest in renewable energy sources and reduce their reliance on fossil fuels. By imposing higher taxes on profits generated from non-renewable sources, companies may be encouraged to shift their focus towards more sustainable energy sources. Hence, these windfall taxes are viewed as a means of redistributing wealth from energy companies to encourage a shift towards renewable energy sources and support the green transition envisaged by the EU.

It is important to note that the implementation of windfall taxes on energy is subject to political debates and considerations within each EU Member State. Each country has its own energy resources, infrastructure, and socio-economic conditions as well as policy priorities that influence the viability and effectiveness of such tax measures. Therefore, the approach to windfall taxes on energy may vary across EU countries[30] just like the redistribution effects of energy taxation and the timing of a complete transition to green energy. The transition involves various policy measures beyond just energy taxes. It requires a comprehensive approach that includes renewable energy incentives, research and development funding, investment in infrastructure, and regulatory frameworks that support clean energy adoption. Energy taxes can be part of this broader strategy by providing economic signals that encourage the deployment of renewable energy sources while driving innovation and market competition.

Ultimately, the objective of windfall taxes on energy in the EU should be to strike a balance between promoting sustainable and affordable energy while addressing income disparities. The design and impact of these taxes require careful

[29] Baunsgaard and Vernon (2022), p. 2.

[30] See e.g., Veress (2023), pp. 264–268.

consideration, taking into account the broader socio-economic context and long-term sustainability goals.

The windfall taxes on energy companies in the European Union have been designed to play a redistributive role by promoting sustainable sources of energy while mitigating the impact on vulnerable groups and low-income households. Governments can allocate the revenue generated from these taxes to help those who may be disproportionately affected by higher energy costs. This can include measures to alleviate energy poverty, improve energy efficiency in low-income housing, or provide financial support for renewable energy projects. Furthermore, energy taxes attempt to incentivize the transition to green energy by making traditional fossil fuel-based energy sources less economically attractive. By imposing higher taxes on carbon-intensive energy sources, governments may try to encourage businesses and individuals to adopt cleaner alternatives to reduce greenhouse gas emissions and promote the development and investment in renewable energy technologies.

Overall, energy taxes in the EU can contribute to both a more equitable distribution of wealth and the transition to green energy by providing economic incentives, generating revenue for social programs, and supporting the development of renewable energy technologies.

It should also be noted that the discussed windfall taxes constitute part of the EU tax policy. Despite labelling them as a "contribution" and "cap", the measures adopted by the Commission are of a fiscal nature not only because of the way they are collected but also because of their purpose. The regulation explicitly uses terms referring to the tax structure of these measures such as the basis for calculation or the rate. It also regulates their distributive role in detail.

Recital (45) of the preamble to the regulation explicitly states that:

> "The temporary solidarity levy should be a redistributive measure to ensure that the companies concerned, which have realized excess profits as a result of unexpected circumstances, contribute proportionately to the recovery of the internal market affected by the energy crisis." The explanatory memorandum to the draft regulation also emphasized that: "The solidarity contribution introduced by this regulation will increase state budget revenues and will allow Member States to finance measures from them to reduce the burden of high energy costs on consumers, in particular people and companies in difficulty."

The use of taxes to achieve various non-fiscal goals is conditioned by the involvement of the state and its organizational structures in economic and social processes. By introducing the windfall taxes—an unusual fiscal solution of a strongly interventionist nature as a tool of financial redistribution—the European Union strengthens the links between the financial system and the political and economic tasks typical of a socialist state. The tax, serving specific intervention purposes, also becomes a regulator of the amount of disposable profit of enterprises. The Commission decided not to introduce the tax at the EU level probably due to possible controversy and opposition of Member States resisting the imposition of taxes by the EU. While the regulation does not impose a tax directly on the Member States and requires it to be implemented by Member States, it secured very strong competences for the European Commission both in regard to its design as well as supervising spending by requiring the proceeds of the windfall taxes to be used in a specific way. This is undoubtedly another step in the EU's fiscal and climate policy.

Regarding the way windfall taxes can potentially contribute to sustainable public finance, it should be noted that windfall taxes can be applied to industries that heavily rely on natural resources such as oil, gas, or minerals. When these industries experience a sudden surge in profits due to factors like rising commodity prices, a windfall tax can ensure that a fair share of those profits is directed to the government. This revenue can then be invested in sustainable development projects, renewable energy initiatives, or other environmentally friendly programs. In the case of the discussed taxes, they have also been imposed on unexpected profits from certain renewable resources excessively concentrated in the hands of certain energy producers. By implementing a windfall tax, the government can redistribute some of these gains to support more sustainable and long-term business practices instead of focusing solely on short-term gains. This can align business interests with broader societal and environmental objectives.

However, there are also potential drawbacks and challenges associated with windfall taxes. Excessive taxation on windfall profits may discourage investment and innovation in certain industries. If companies feel that they are penalized for their success, they may be less inclined to take risks or invest in projects with uncertain outcomes. If not implemented carefully by striking a balance between capturing windfall gains and ensuring a favourable business environment, windfall taxes could lead to unintended negative consequences on economic growth, job creation, and competitiveness. To ensure that windfall taxes contribute to sustainable public finance, policymakers need to carefully design and implement them, taking into account the specific context of their economy, the industry in question, and the potential long-term impacts. Properly managed windfall taxes can help finance sustainable initiatives, reduce inequality, and promote responsible business practices while considering potential economic implications. Evaluated from this perspective, the windfall taxes on energy have not proven successful.

On 5 June 2023, the European Commission submitted its report on the review of emergency interventions to address high energy prices in accordance with Council Regulation (EU) 2022/1854.[31] The report concludes that the measures have overall contributed to a stabilization of the energy markets and finds a prolongation of the emergency measures not necessary. Concerning the inframarginal revenue cap, the report concludes that all Member States have not implemented the set level of the revenue cap as well as the temporal scope of the measures. Considering that the revenues generated were below what was expected and since the differences in implementation among Member States have created regulatory uncertainty—which may have affected existing power purchase agreements and discouraged the conclusion of new ones—the Commission reckons that a prolongation is not desirable.

[31] Report from the Commission to the European Parliament and the Council on the review of emergency interventions to address high energy prices in accordance with Council Regulation (EU) 2022/1854, June 5, 2023.

Moreover, it has been argued that the role that Member States have played in driving up energy prices by filling their natural gas storages much more than the EU's filling trajectory prescribes raises questions as to whether the EU Solidarity Contribution could be in conflict with the proportionality principle.[32]

It should also be mentioned that the discussed taxes raise significant doubts of a constitutional nature not only due to its legal basis and imposition by an EU regulation under Article 122(1) of the Treaty on the Functioning of the European Union but also due to reservations regarding the principles of decent legislation resulting from the principle of the rule of law expressed in Article 2 of the EU Treaty. Under this rule, in general, taxes should not be introduced retroactively. The relevant *vacatio legis* was not taken into account since the provisions entered into force immediately. While the application of these taxes will not be prolonged, the European Commission will have to face charges regarding unlawful adoption of these taxes since a claim against it has been brought to the Court of Justice of the European Union by fossil fuel companies.

References

Baunsgaard T, Vernon N (2022) Taxing windfall profits in the energy sector, IMF Notes 2022/002. International Monetary Fund

Chennels L (1997) The windfall tax, fiscal studies. J Appl Public Econ 18(3)

Drapkin DB, Verleger PK Jr (1981) The windfall profit tax: origins, development, implications. Boston Coll Law Rev 22(4)

Erdős G, Czoboly G (2023) New legislative tool for introducing EU-wide windfall taxes. Eur Tax 63(1):36–41

Feldstein M (1976a) Compensation in tax reform. Natl Tax J 29:2

Feldstein M (1976b) On the theory of tax reform. J Public Econ 6(1–2)

Gamponia V, Mendelsohn R (1985) The taxation of exhaustible resources. Q J Econ 100(1)

Goode R (1987) Disappointed expectations and tax reform. Natl Tax J 40(2)

Lammers JM, Kuźniacki B (2023) The EU solidarity contribution and a more proportional alternative: a study under EU and international investment law. Intertax 51(6/7)

Lazzari S (2006) The crude oil windfall profit tax of the 1980s: implications for current energy policy, CRS Report for Congress, Congressional Research Service, The Library of Congress

Matikonis K (2022) Shortcomings of the energy (oil and gas) profits levy. Br Tax Rev 4

Matikonis M (2023) Implications of expanded levies on energy producers. Br Tax Rev 1

McIntyre RS (1981) Lessons for tax reformers from the history of the energy tax incentives in the Windfall Profit Tax Act of 1980. Boston Coll Law Rev 22(4)

Tetłak K (2022) Składka solidarnościowa od nadwyżek zysku z działalności w sektorze paliw kopalnych, Kwartalnik Prawa Międzynarodowego, No. 3 (III)

Thuronyi V (2000) Adjusting taxes for inflation. In: Thuronyi V (ed) Tax law design and drafting. The Hague

Tickell A (1998) A tax on success? Privatization, employment and the 'windfall tax'. Area 30(1)

[32] Lammers and Kuźniacki (2023), pp. 451–471.

Van der Ploeg F, Venables AJ (2011) Harnessing windfall revenues: optimal policies for resource-rich developing economies. Econ J 121(551)
Veress J (2023) Changes to Hungarian windfall taxes and transfer pricing rules for 2022 and 2023. Eur Tax 63(6)
Zodrow GR (1988) The windfall recapture tax: issues of theory and design. Public Finance Q 16(4)

The European "*Fit for 55*" Package and the Portuguese Tax Benefits System: Prospective Analysis and Reform Proposals

Filipe de Vasconcelos Fernandes

Abstract The purpose of this brief chapter is to offer a broad-spectrum analysis of the connection between environmental sustainability—under the European "*fit for 55*" package—and tax policy options in Portugal, particularly at the level of the existing tax benefits system.

Based on the main environmental sustainability standards and principles on a European and global scale, a constructive rationale will be followed in order to analyse the tax benefit options adopted in the Portuguese tax system and possible needs for reform. The purpose is to make it more rational and efficient in a context of energy transition and the pursuit of demanding environmental goals as they ultimately derive from the Paris Agreement.

The reform proposals presented will focus mainly on tax benefits applicable on personal income tax, corporate income tax, excise taxes, and property taxes.

1 Preliminary Framework

Sustainability is one of the most relevant and discussed topics, and its growing importance in tax law is no exception—not in the least because, ultimately, tax instruments have been of enormous importance in the pursuit of sustainability goals with emphasis on the environmental dimension.[1]

This text seeks to replicate, without major changes and with an open and tax policy perspective, the intervention at the Conference "*Sustainable Finance: Between the Public and the Private*", on 4th July 2022, promoted by the Centre for Research in European, Economic, Financial and Tax Law (CIDEEFF) – University of Lisbon School of Law.

[1] For an introduction to the subject with no claim to completeness, see Amatucci (1975), p. 351 ss.; Hertzog (1984); Arndt (1995), pp. 11–24; Molina (1996), pp. 108–127; Marchetti (1999), pp. 115–148; Alfano (2012). Additionally, in the Portuguese tax literature, see Lobo (1994),

F. de Vasconcelos Fernandes (✉)
CIDEEFF, University of Lisbon, School of Law, Lisbon, Portugal
e-mail: filipefernandes@fd.ulisboa.pt

R. Saraiva, P. A. Pardal (eds.), *Sustainable Finances and the Law*, Economic Analysis of Law in European Legal Scholarship 16,
https://doi.org/10.1007/978-3-031-49460-4_14

Already in 1987, the well-known United Nations Brundtland Commission mentioned, particularly impressively, that

> [h]umanity has the ability to make development sustainable – to ensure that it meets the needs of the present without compromising the ability of future generations to meet their own needs. The concept of sustainable development does imply limits – not absolute limits but limitations imposed by the present state of technology and social organization on environmental resources and by the ability of the biosphere to absorb the effects of human activities.[2]

More recently, the topic of sustainability has proliferated through various strongholds with proximity to tax law with also a growing influence at the tax policy level[3] with a rapid expansion of environmental taxes, exemptions, or other tax benefits for new energy transition realities (such as renewable gases). In the meantime, the tax burden on directly or indirectly more polluting (or not so environmentally friendly) activities progressively increases.

While sustainability has seen very different manifestations on an international scale, at the European level, the European Commission is undertaking a range of actions to support the move to a more circular economy—these cover the cycle from production and consumption to waste management and the market for secondary raw materials.

In this context, and although sustainability is not limited to the environmental field, the authors will focus mainly on the relationship between environmental sustainability and tax policy options with emphasis on tax benefits. The key concept of "*tax benefit*" will be followed as defined in Article 2 (2) of the Portuguese Statute of Tax Benefits (EBF) and which includes therein *exemptions*; *tax rate reductions; deductions from the tax base* and *(deductions) from taxable income*; *accelerated depreciation and amortizations;* and *other tax measures that are exceptional in nature and are instituted to protect relevant extra–tax public interests that are over and above the taxation they prevent.*

As there is no Europe-wide definition of what should be understood as a tax benefit—while having to respect the general principles of European law, including non-discrimination—the authors will continue to adhere to this definition of the Portuguese tax law.

---

pp. 11–49; Ferreira (2001), pp. 9–32; Soares (2001); Soares (2003), pp. 23–48; Soares (2014), pp. 59–82; Nabais (2003), pp. 23–42 and, more recently, Nabais (2008), pp. 107–144.

[2] World Commission on Environment and Development, Report of the World Commission on Environment and Development (1987), p. 24. The Sustainable Development Goals form the framework for improving the lives of populations around the world and mitigating the hazardous man-made effects of climate change. SDG 13: Climate Action peremptorily requests integrating measures to prevent climate change within development frameworks. SDG 14: Life Below Water, and SDG 15: Life on Land, also call for more sustainable practices in using the earth's natural resources.

[3] See, at this level, Schratzenstaller (2015), pp. 57–77.

2 The Connection Between Tax Benefits and Sustainability in Modern Tax Policy

Whenever talking about tax benefits, values, or interests other than the collection of revenue by the states are always at stake, including environmental sustainability targets.

With reference to the original definition of a tax expenditure—as originally formulated by Surrey[4]—the justification for supporting a certain level of one will be, in a cost-benefit analysis, the importance given to certain values or interests, including environmental ones, compared to the costs associated with the tax expenditure they represent for taxpayers (since they will have to pay for them now or in the future, in the latter case, covering also the tax burden of next generations[5]).

In the specific case of tax expenditure associated with environmental sustainability measures—pursued wholly or partially through tax solutions—its legitimacy seems easily perceptible since the pursuit and achievement of environmental sustainability goals have, as their ultimate beneficiaries, the citizens and society in general. Therefore, although tax benefits around environmental sustainability necessarily generate a tax expenditure, there is a large consensus on the superiority of the resulting interests or advantages, both for the states and for society in general.[6]

This approach will be of great importance for understanding the evolution that the "*fit for 55*" package implies at the level of existing tax benefits regimes in Member States like Portugal, especially considering the needs for reform or amendments resulting therefrom.

3 The Current Role of Sustainability for Tax Policy Options

Nowadays, any tax policy option ends up having a connection with sustainability goals: if considering personal income taxation, certain behaviours can be induced or prevented as well as at the level of special consumption taxation. Similarly, by encouraging or discouraging certain business options of performances through tax benefits or additional tax burden (whether by increasing the effective rate, reducing deductible expenses, or introducing specific forms of taxation on expenses, such as autonomous taxation existing in the Portuguese corporate income tax, for example), effects will be felt in the factor and product markets exactly where the paradigm shift towards a circular economy model is intended.

---

[4] See, in this respect, Surrey (1973).

[5] See Musgrave and Musgrave (1989), p. 552.

[6] See, at this level, Chapman (2019), pp. 1–42.

In this sense, the authors not only consider the so-called "*Green Tax Reforms*"[7] but, in broader terms, any and all legislative changes in tax matters that are guided by sustainability goals—which focus mainly on taxes on the purchase or use of motor vehicles and fuels, including taxes on petrol and diesel.[8]

Considering that taxes, subsidies, and other economic instruments provide important market signals that can influence (or even induce) the behaviour of producers and consumers,[9] the authors will analyse the effect that environmental sustainability goals may have on the design of existing tax benefits in the Portuguese tax system.

3.1 The Role of "Standards" *and the Limits of Self-Regulation in Sustainability Area: Brief Background on* ESG *Frameworks*

As is readily apparent at the present time, sustainability has received more and more attention and its environmental, social, and governance (*ESG*) factors even more so.[10] Although this article is not specifically about the *ESG*, some brief background on their scope is important, not in the least because this nomenclature will underpin the main developments around the sustainability in the coming decades—including in the tax field.

In general terms, an ESG *framework* is a systematic approach for identifying, assessing, and integrating the economic, environmental, and social impacts of a business on society as well as the environment. Within each *framework*, *standards* (even with a *soft-law* dimension) occupy a very significant role, especially considering that its application is always the consequence of a certain context or paradigm motivated by the movements of the main influencing groups or agents—from politics, academia, industry, and media, among others.

In a first general definition, *standards* are a repeatable, harmonized, agreed, and documented way to achieve a certain goal not necessarily of an environmental nature—once again, within the conceptual architecture provided by each framework. Therefore, resulting from collective work by experts in a specific field and providing

---

[7]Over the last decade, economic instruments have been playing a growing role in environmental policies of OECD countries. As has been highlighted by the OECD, a distinctive feature of tax reforms in recent years is the increasing role of environmentally related taxes defined as "as any compulsory, unrequited payment to government levied on tax bases deemed to be of environmental relevance, i.e., taxes that have a tax base with a proven, specific negative impact on the environment". See OECD. 2020. Policy Instruments for the Environment (PINE) Database, available at: https://pinedatabase.oecd.org/.

[8]See OECD. 2017. Policy Instruments for the Environment – Database 2017.

[9]This is even relevant for statistical purposes—as is the case of Policy Instruments for the Environment (PINE) Database containing key quantitative and qualitative information on six types of policy instruments in 80 countries—OECD members and many others.

[10]More recently, with great interest, see Câmara and Morais (2022).

a consensus at the time they are developed, *standards* contain technical specifications or other criteria designed to be used consistently as a *rule*, *guideline*, or *definition*.

Additionally, in the field of sustainability—including, but not exclusively, environmental sustainability—there are several *ESG frameworks* with tax relevance on a global scale such as:

(i) The Principles of Responsible Investment (PRI) developed by an international group of institutional investors reflecting the increasing relevance of environmental, social, and corporate governance issues to investment practices and convened by the United Nations Secretary-General;
(ii) The Global Reporting Initiative (GRI) standards which enable any organization—large or small, private, or public—to understand and report on their impacts on the economy, environment, and people in a comparable and credible way. This thereby increases transparency on their contribution to sustainable development—more recently, (partially) absorbed by the Corporate Sustainability Reporting Directive (CSRD[11]);
(iii) The World Economic Forum's International Business Council (IBC) metrics;[12] and
(iv) The principles of the Task Force for Climate-related Financial Disclosures (TCFD[13]).

Each one of these frameworks, with different degrees of bindingness (because some are already law and others are not), is part of the wider movement to which the "*fit for 55*" package seeks to respond. This is based on a new paradigm of sustainability (not only environmental) towards energy transition and carbon neutrality, again with the target of 2050.

Making the connection with the next points of analysis, it is already clear that the "*fit for 55*" package is mainly designed for the "*E*" component of the *ESG*. It seeks side by side with legislative changes in each sector to introduce a new paradigm of environmental sustainability characterized by several specified quantitative goals and measures to decarbonize the economy and promote greener energy.

[11] Directive (EU) 2022/2464 of the European Parliament and of the Council of 14 December 2022 amending Regulation (EU) 537/2014, Directive 2004/109/EC, Directive 2006/43/EC and Directive 2013/34/EU, as regards corporate sustainability reporting.

[12] This set of 21 core and 34 expanded metrics and disclosures were published in September 2020 in the World Economic Forum Report "*Measuring Stakeholder Capitalism: Towards Common Metrics and Consistent Reporting of Sustainable Value Creation*". Focused on four themes, People, Planet, Prosperity and Principles of Governance, these metrics and disclosures reflect a six-month consultation process with more than 200 companies, investors, and other interested parties.

[13] The Task Force consists of 31 members from across the G20 representing both preparers and users of financial disclosures.

3.2 *The Role of* **Rules and Principles***: In Particular, the* **"Fit for 55"** *European Package and Its Foreseeable Tax Impacts*

Alongside the relevance occupied by *frameworks* and *standards*—now the topic of (environmental) sustainability in the ESG context—is also subject to formal regulation at the legal level.

On 14 July 2021, the European Commission adopted a package of the legislative proposals "*fit for 55*" as part of the European Green Deal, a set of policy initiatives by the European Commission with the overarching aim of making the EU climate neutral by 2050.

The "*fit for 55*" package aims to modernize existing legislation in line with the EU's 2030 climate target and introduce new policy measures to help bring about the transformative changes needed in the economy, society, and industry to achieve climate neutrality by 2050 and to support it and reduce net emissions by at least 55% (compared to 1990) by 2030.

Energy taxation can help the EU achieve its climate and environment objectives by encouraging a transition to cleaner energy and greener industry.

Therefore—and just as an example—within the framework of the "*fit for 55*" package, the Energy Taxation Directive[14] will be revised to align the taxation of energy products with the EU's current energy and climate policies with the necessary consequences for the tax legislation of the Member States implementing the directive (in Portugal, for the so-called Tax on Oil and Energy Products (ISP), the Excise Duty Code[15]).

As a true legislative package, "*fit for 55*" will have different impacts on each of the sectoral legislations that will be amended, and the impact of these changes should be analysed on a *case-by-case basis*.

4 Review of Legislation Included in "*Fit for 55*" and *Case-by-Case* Assessment of Its Tax Impact

As mentioned above, the "*fit for 55*" package is a set of proposals to revise and update EU legislation and to put in place new initiatives with the aim of ensuring that EU policies are in line with the climate goals agreed by the Council and the European Parliament. In quantitative terms, the "*fit for 55*" refers to the EU's target

[14] Council Directive 2003/96/EC of 27 October 2003 restructuring the Community framework for the taxation of energy products and electricity.

[15] Approved by Decree-Law No. 73/2010, of 21 June. Obviously, since we are dealing with Excise Duties, this decree-law serves mainly to transpose Council Directive (EU) 2020/262 of 19 December 2019 laying down the general arrangements for excise duty (which repealed the previous Council Directive 2008/118/EC).

of reducing net greenhouse gas emissions by at least 55% by 2030—and thus bring EU legislation in line with the 2030 goal.

In this context, the "*fit for 55*" package includes proposed legislation on the following areas:

(i) EU Emissions Trading System;
(ii) Efforts Sharing Regulation;
(iii) Land Use and Forestry (LULUCF);
(iv) Alternative Fuels Infrastructure;
(v) Carbon Border Adjustment Mechanism (CBAM);
(vi) Social Climate Fund;
(vii) RefuelEU aviation and FuelEU maritime;
(viii) CO_2 emission standards for cars and vans;
(ix) Energy Taxation;
(x) Renewable energy;
(xi) Energy Efficiency; and
(xii) Energy performance of buildings

Considering the potential tax dimension of each of these elements included within the "*fit for 55*" package, the authors will briefly describe those that may have some tax importance and impact for changes to the Portuguese tax system with special emphasis on the level of tax benefits.

4.1 Changes in EU Emissions Trading System (EU ETS)

The EU's Emissions Trading System (ETS) is the world's first international emissions trading scheme and the EU's flagship policy to combat climate change.

The EU ETS was launched in 2005 and covers about 45% of EU greenhouse gas emissions. The latest revision of Directive 2003/87/EC of the European Parliament and of the Council of 13 October 2003 establishing a scheme for greenhouse gas emission allowance trading within the Community and amending Council Directive 96/61/EC—EU ETS Directive—sets the total quantity of emission allowances for phase 4 (2021–2030). This is in line with the previous EU emission reduction target (40% reduction below 1990 levels by 2030).

On July 14, 2021, as part of the "*Fit for 55*", the European Commission adopted a legislative proposal for a revision of the EU ETS in order to align it with the target of a 55% reduction of EU GHG emissions by 2030 compared to 1990 levels.[16]

The Commission proposal to amend EU ETS Directive concerns the ongoing phase 4 of the ETS (2021–2030). It consists of five main elements:[17]

[16] See https://www.consilium.europa.eu/pt/infographics/fit-for-55-eu-emissions-trading-system/.

[17] See https://www.consilium.europa.eu/en/policies/green-deal/fit-for-55-the-eu-plan-for-a-green-transition/#package.

(i) Include emissions from maritime transport in the EU ETS;
(ii) Phase out free allocation of emission allowances to aviation and to the sectors that are to be covered by the carbon border adjustment mechanism (CBAM);
(iii) Implement the global carbon offsetting and reduction scheme for international aviation (CORSIA) through the EU ETS;
(iv) Increase funding available from the modernization fund and the innovation fund; and
(v) Revise the market stability reserve in order to continue ensuring a stable and well-functioning EU ETS.

A separate self-standing emissions trading system for fuel distribution for road transport and buildings would be established starting from 2025.

The regulated activity will be "release for consumption" because the GHGs are emitted by small entities like households and car drivers. The regulated entities will be fuel distributors for which a monitoring and reporting system already exists under the excise duty system of the Council Directive (EU) 2020/262 of 19 December 2019 mentioned previously.

In December 2021, the Commission presented a legislative proposal for a Council Decision amending the system of own resources of the European Union by adding new sources of revenue, including the EU ETS and the CBAM, complemented in March 2022 by a proposal for a council regulation on the methods and procedure for making available own resources based on the ETS and CBAM.[18]

4.2 *Amendment to the Renewable Energy Directive (RED II) to Implement the Ambition of the New 2030 Climate Target*

The EU Renewable Energy Directive (RED[19]) was originally adopted in 2009 to deliver the EU goal of a minimum 20% share of renewable energy sources (RES) in final energy consumption by 2020—and was revised in 2018 to deliver the EU objective of a minimum 32% share of RES in final energy consumption by 2030.

At this level, a key element in the "*fit for 55*" package is the revision of the Renewable Energy Directive (RED II) currently in force—Directive (EU) 2018/2001 of the European Parliament and of the Council of 11 December 2018 on the

[18] See Proposal for a Council Regulation on the methods and procedure for making available own resources based on the Emissions Trading System, the Carbon Border Adjustment Mechanism and reallocated profits and on the measures to meet cash requirements (available at: https://eur-lex.europa.eu/legal-content/EN/TXT/?uri=celex%3A52022PC0101).

[19] Directive 2009/28/EC of the European Parliament and of the Council of 23 April 2009 on the promotion of the use of energy from renewable sources and amending and subsequently repealing Directives 2001/77/EC and 2003/30/EC.

promotion of the use of energy from renewable sources—to help the EU deliver the new 55% GHG target.

The revised RED II sets a new EU target of a minimum 40% share of the RES in final energy consumption by 2030 accompanied by new sectoral targets.[20] As part of the REPowerEU plan, the European Commission proposes to further raise this RES target to a 45% share by 2030.

4.3 Revision of the Energy Efficiency Directive (EED)

This Energy Efficiency Directive (EED)—Directive (EU) 2018/2002 of the European Parliament and of the Council of 11 December 2018 amending Directive 2012/27/EU on energy efficiency—is currently designed to meet the existing goal of 32.5% energy efficiency improvements by 2030.

The recast EED would require Member States to almost double their annual energy savings obligations, make exemplary efforts in the public sector, address energy poverty, and take other measures to deliver 9% more energy savings than foreseen under existing EU legislation.[21]

As part of the REPowerEU plan to address the ongoing energy crisis, the Commission proposed a targeted EED amendment requiring 13% more energy savings by 2030.[22]

4.4 Revision of the Energy Taxation Directive (ETD)

In line with the strong link between environmental sustainability and taxation, a revision of the Energy Tax Directive (ETD) (Council Directive 2003/96/EC of 27 October 2003 restructuring the Community framework for the taxation of energy products and electricity) is also foreseen in the context of "*fit for 55*".

The topics of energy taxation requiring the most urgent revision are the level and structure of minimum rates, replacement of the volume-based approach to energy taxation with one based on energy content and environmental performance, and the introduction of an indexation mechanism.[23]

---

[20] See https://www.europarl.europa.eu/thinktank/en/document/EPRS_BRI(2021)698781.

[21] See https://www.europarl.europa.eu/thinktank/en/document/EPRS_BRI(2021)698045.

[22] See Proposal for a Directive of the European Parliament and of the Council amending Directive (EU) 2018/2001 on the promotion of the use of energy from renewable sources, Directive 2010/31/EU on the energy performance of buildings and Directive 2012/27/EU on energy efficiency.

[23] See https://www.europarl.europa.eu/thinktank/en/document/EPRS_BRI(2022)698883.

Therefore, the revision of the Energy Tax Directive proposed aligning the taxation of energy products with EU energy and climate policies at the following levels:[24]

(i) Promoting clean technologies;
(ii) Removing the outdated exemptions and reduced rates that now encourage the use of fossil fuels;
(iii) Fuels will start being taxed according to their energy content and environmental performance rather than their volume, helping businesses and consumers alike to make cleaner, more climate-friendly choices;
(iv) Exemptions for certain products and home heating will be phased out. Thus, fossil fuels can no longer be taxed below minimum rates;
(v) Fossil fuels used as fuel for intra-EU air transport, maritime transport, and fishing should no longer be fully exempt from energy taxation in the EU.

4.5 Carbon Border Adjustment Mechanism (CBAM)

The key measures envisaged in this context also include the proposal for a CBAM for selected sectors with the aim to ensure that the EU's climate objectives are not undermined by a relocation of carbon-intensive productions outside the EU.[25,26]

Designed in compliance with the World Trade Organization (WTO) rules and other international obligations of the EU, the CBAM system will work as follows: EU importers will buy carbon certificates corresponding to the carbon price that would have been paid had the goods been produced under the EU's carbon pricing rules.

Conversely, once a non-EU producer can show that they have already paid a price for the carbon used in the production of the imported goods in a third country, the corresponding cost can be fully deducted for the EU importer. This reduces the risk of carbon leakage by encouraging producers in non-EU countries to green their production processes.

Therefore, under the CBAM, EU importers would buy carbon certificates corresponding to the carbon price that would have been paid had the production taken place in the EU. When a non-EU producer has already paid a price for the carbon used in the production in a third country, the EU importer can fully deduct the corresponding cost.

---

[24] See https://www.europarl.europa.eu/RegData/etudes/BRIE/2022/698883/EPRS_BRI(2022)698883_EN.pdf.

[25] See https://www.consilium.europa.eu/pt/infographics/fit-for-55-cbam-carbon-border-adjustment-mechanism/.

[26] Not disregarding the importance that carbon taxation has been object of by the United Nations - even so, outside the scope of "*fit-for-55*". On this aspect, see Falcão (2021), pp. 897–914; Grau Ruiz (2022), pp. 247–256.

The CBAM would be phased in gradually and would initially apply only to a selected number of goods at high risk of carbon leakage: iron and steel, cement, fertilizer, aluminum, and electricity generation.

As from 2026, EU importers would start paying a financial adjustment by surrendering the amount of CBAM certificates that correspond to the emissions embedded in their imports. Correspondingly, under the proposal for the revision of the EU ETS, the free allowances under the ETS would gradually be phased out for the CBAM sectors as from 2026.

To complement the ETS, the CBAM will be based on a system of certificates to cover the embedded emissions in products being subsequently imported into the EU.

5 Analysis of the Portuguese Tax Benefits System and Proposals for Reform

After delimiting the assumptions, it is now time to move on to the analysis of the existing tax benefits system in Portugal in order to identify the main inconsistencies and, above all, the reform needs arising from the "*fit for 55*" legislative package. This is in accordance with the proposals to amend European legislation already known and without prejudice to changes in policy choices that may occur in the meantime.

Disregarding some residual legislation, the core of the tax benefits existing in the Portuguese tax system is condensed as follows:

(i) On the one hand, the excise duty code, the investment tax code, the corporate income tax code, and the personal income tax code; and
(ii) On the other hand, the tax benefits code.[27]

5.1 *Excise Duty Code*

In this context, considering the scope of the excise duty code mentioned previously, the special tax on petroleum and energy products (ISP) is relevant. In particular, considering the projected revision of the ETD, it is expected that some structural changes in the ISP may be introduced, namely, a structural worsening of the tax burden applicable (in particular, nominal tax rates provided for in Article 92 of the code) to petroleum products as well as a very significant change in exemptions structure (Article 89 of the code).

Of particular note will be the review of the exemptions for the aviation and shipping sectors as provided for in Article 89 (1)(b) and (c) as well as the impacts of

[27] We will not include any specific aspect linked to VAT, because (at least directly) it does not result in any aspect specifically linked to the "*fit-for-55*" package. Even so, more recently, on the environmental dimension of VAT, see Traversa and Timmermans (2021), pp. 871–884.

the changes to the EU ETS for the purposes of the exemption provided for in Article 89 (1)(f), all of the excise duty code.

In the opposite direction, it is expected that the exemption enshrined in Article 90 (for biofuels and gases of renewable origin) will be somewhat extended.

5.2 *Investment Tax Code*

The investment tax code was approved by Decree-Law No. 162/2014 of 31 December, and includes:

(i) The contractual tax benefit regime for productive investment;
(ii) The investment support tax regime (RFAI);
(iii) The system of tax incentives in research and business development II (SIFIDE II); and
(iv) The deduction for retained and reinvested profits regime (DLRR).

None of these tax regimes are specifically linked to environmental sustainability, although tax benefits linked to environmental sustainability already exist.[28] As an example, at the level of the objective conditions for access to contractual tax benefits to productive investment projects, the investment projects must, among others, contribute to the improvement of the environment (Article 4, No. 1, c) of the investment tax code).

In any case and since the contractual tax benefits regime for productive investment and the RFAI are included in the national map of state aid with regional purposes for the period from 1 January 2022 to 31 December 2027 approved by the European Commission on 8 February 2022, the authors are of the opinion that very significant short and medium-term changes should not be expected due to the "*fit for 55*" package.

5.3 *Corporate Income Tax Code*

The corporate income tax[29] does not have many tax benefits within its own structure, even less connoted with environmental sustainability—not in the least because, focusing on profit (in the case of companies), the corporate income tax has a tendency towards competitive neutrality in relation to the impact of tax benefits.

The only properly environmental tax benefit regime—given that it materializes in a deduction—is that of provisions with charges for repairing damage of an

[28] More recently, in a comparative perspective, on the role of incentives, see Kymenvaara (2020), pp. 58–69; Lind (2021), pp. 885–896.

[29] Approved by Decree-Law No. 442-B/88, of November 30.

environmental nature to the sites affected by the exploitation (Article 40 of the corporate income tax code), thus assuming the existence of an extractive activity.

Even so, particularly in line with the changes projected for the RED II, the authors are of the opinion that this special regime could have some kind of expansion in order to cover any and all types of charges associated with renewable explorations, including those relating to matters such as noise or the landscape.

At the same time, based on the fact that the autonomous taxation regime (established in Article 88 of the code that implements a special form of taxation of certain expenditure acts within the corporate income tax code) does not subject the acquisition of purely electric cars, the authors understand that this must necessarily happen with vehicles powered by Hydrogen.

5.4 *Personal Income Tax Code*

As with corporate income tax, it is difficult to establish a direct relationship between personal income taxation and tax benefits that are totally or partially contrary to standards, rules, or principles relevant for environmental sustainability.

However, in line with "*fit for 55*" priorities, the authors have identified one measure that could be reintroduced in the personal income tax code,[30] especially in line with the EED revision (although not in a direct way as an obligation included in its transposition). This is the establishment (in terms more or less similar to the regime repealed in the meantime—as provided for in former section 85-A of the personal income tax code) of environmental deductions namely related to the replacement of inefficient windows with windows of class 'A+'; the application of thermal insulation to roofs, walls, or floors; ambient and/or water heating and/or cooling systems using class 'A+' renewable energy; or the installation of photovoltaic panels or other renewable energy equipment.

5.5 *Tax Benefits Code (in Particular, Property Tax)*

The tax benefits code[31] addresses the topic of environmental sustainability essentially at three different levels:

(i) First, in terms of tax benefits applicable to an entities' regime applicable to entities licensed in the Madeira Free Zone, a special deduction may be applied (to the collection) if they contribute to the improvement of environmental conditions (Article 36-A, paragraph 6, d)) which is a matter that, due to its

[30] Approved by Decree-Law No. 442-A/88, of November 30.

[31] Approved by Decree-Law No. 251/89, of July 1.

special framework (currently authorized until 31 December 2023), does not seem to change as a result of the "*fit for 55*" package.

(ii) Second, the patronage tax regime (Articles 61 to 66) that can be applied to donations granted to entities that pursue environmental purposes, such as Environmental Non-Governmental Organizations (ENGOs). Although the authors do not expect the "*fit for 55*" package to change the basic structure of the patronage tax regime, the recent news that indicates that the Portuguese Government is going to create specific legislation for voluntary carbon markets allows anticipating the emergence of bonds/carbon certificates for which the subscription may, in some way, have a framework similar to that of the patronage tax regime (deduction and eventual increase to taxable income of the corresponding expenses or losses).

(iii) Third, tax benefits will be applicable to properties that, under the terms of Article 44-B, may be related to energy efficiency. Therefore, it is not excluded that, in line with the EED review, the applicable benefits, especially at the level of a municipal property tax, may be expanded (decrease in the nominal tax rate).

Additionally, the authors have many doubts that the legislative context raised by the "*fit for 55*" package is compatible with the taxation of wind turbines (or even dams) at the municipal property tax level. This is especially valid when these assets are exclusively allocated to the production of electricity—so it seems to be an aspect that, sooner or later, will also have to be reconsidered.

6 Conclusions and Reform Proposals

The above analysis allows concluding that there is significant room for improvement and reform in the Portuguese tax system, having the main *standards* and principles of environmental sustainability as references (i.e., above all the "*E*" of *ESG*), especially those arising from "*fit for 55*" package and the legislative changes that will follow from it, both at European and national levels.

The main and most relevant changes, in a short and medium-term perspective, can be expected for excise duties, particularly in terms of the applicable exemptions (ceasing to apply, in particular, to aviation and maritime sectors) and nominal tax rates (general increase for petroleum products according to energy content and environmental performance).

Additionally, other changes can be envisaged in terms of income and property taxation with special emphasis on the energy efficiency component (revision of the EED) and the continuous promotion of renewable energies (revision of the RED II).

References

Alfano R (2012) Tributi ambientali. Profili interni ed europei. Giappichelli, Torino

Amatucci A (1975) Qualità della vita, interessi diffusi e capacità contributiva, RDFSF

Arndt H-W (1995) Die Lenkungsfunktion des Umweltrechts. In: Eichhorn P (Hrsg) Ökosoziale Marktwirtschaft, Ziele und Wege. Springer Fachmedien Wiesbaden, pp 11–24

Câmara P, Morais F (eds) (2022) The Palgrave handbook of ESG and corporate governance. Palgrave Macmillan

Chapman R (2019) Managing the transition to a climate neutral economy in cities and regions. Background Paper for an OECD/EC Workshop on 17 May 2019. OECD, Paris

Falcão T (2021) Policy note: highlights of the United Nations handbook on carbon taxation. Intertax 49(11)

Ferreira EP (2001) "Fiscalidade Ecológica: Uma ideia em busca de afirmação", RDAOT, Ns. 6/7

Grau Ruiz MA (2022) Policy note: smooth implementation of carbon taxation: an overview of the main proposals in the UN handbook. Intertax 50(3)

Hertzog R (1984) La fiscalité de l'environnement: bilan critique du droit positif, Année de l'Environnement, Actes du Colloque Fiscalité-Environnement||, PUF

Kymenvaara S (2020) Towards low-emission transport: biofuels' tax incentives and state aid for climate change mitigation. Eur Energy Environ Law Rev 29(2)

Lind Y (2021) Attracting multinational tech-companies through environmental tax incentives. Intertax 49(11)

Lobo CB (1994) Imposto Ambiental. Análise Jurídico-financeira, RJUA, No. 2

Marchetti F (1999) I presupposti della tassazione ambientale, in Rassegna Tributaria, No. 1

Molina PH (1996) Desgravaciones tributarias y protección del medio ambiente. Análisis a la luz de los princípios constitucionales y del Derecho europeo, Impuestos, No. 15/16

Musgrave RA, Musgrave PB (1989) Public finance in theory and practice, 5th edn. McGraw-Hill, International Editions

Nabais JC (2003) Direito Fiscal e Tutela do Ambiente, RevCEDOUA, No. 2/6, 23–42

Nabais JC (2008) Tributos com fins ambientais, RFPDF, Ano 1, No. 4, Almedina

Schratzenstaller M (2015) Sustainable tax policy – concepts and indicators beyond the tax ratio. Revue de l'OFCE, No. 141

Soares CD (2001) O imposto ecológico: contributo para o estudo dos instrumentos económicos de defesa do ambiente, Stvdia Juridica 58, Coimbra Editora

Soares CD (2003) A inevitabilidade da tributação ambiental. In: de Melo Rocha M (Coord) Estudos de Direito do Ambiente. UCP, pp 23–48

Soares CD (2014) O enquadramento constitucional dos tributos ambientais: sua natureza e regime. RFPDF, A. 7, No. 1, Almedina

Surrey S (1973) Pathways to tax reform – the concept of tax expenditure. Harvard University Press

Traversa E, Timmermans B (2021) Value-Added Tax (VAT) and sustainability in the European Union: a radical proposal design issues, legal aspects, and policy alternatives. Intertax 49(11)

“*Fit for 55*”: The EU Plan for a Green Transition

André Alfar Rodrigues

Abstract This article focuses on the importance of the “*fit for 55*” legislative package, which has as its main objective the transformation of the economy, society, and industry towards climate neutrality. Fit for 55 aims to ensure that the European Union meets the target of a 55% reduction in net greenhouse gas emissions by 2030 compared to 1990. There are several legislative proposals with regulations for areas as diverse as climate, energy and fuels, transport, buildings, land use, forests, or taxation. The legislation is presented as a comprehensive package, but will this package remain intact? Obviously, there are major political and legal challenges ahead. These various measures are positioned as inter-related and inter-dependent. They reflect a chosen policy mix of legal instruments that in turn represents a careful balance between pricing, targets, standards, and support measures. In this paper a critical analysis will be made of some of the main legislative proposals that are included in the “*fit for 55*” package, namely: (i) Reform of the Emissions Trading System; (ii) Effort Sharing Regulation (ESR); (iii) Revision of the Regulation on the inclusion of greenhouse gas emissions and resulting from activities related to land use, land use change and forestry (LULUCF); (iv) Revision of the Directive on the implementation of alternative fuels infrastructure; (v) Revision of the Regulation setting CO_2 emission performance standards for new passenger cars and new light commercial vehicles.

A. A. Rodrigues (✉)
CIDEEFF, Lisboa, Portugal

R. Saraiva, P. A. Pardal (eds.), *Sustainable Finances and the Law*, Economic Analysis of Law in European Legal Scholarship 16,
https://doi.org/10.1007/978-3-031-49460-4_15

1 Introduction

On 14 July 2021, the European Commission adopted a package of legislative proposals called "*fit for 55*"[1] as part of the European Green Deal[2] that aims to strengthen the EU's position as a global leader on climate.[3] The objective of the package is to modernize existing legislation in line with the European Union's (EU) 2030 climate target and introduce new policy measures to help bring about the necessary transformational changes in the economy, society, and industry to achieve climate neutrality by 2050 and to support it by reducing net emissions by at least 55% (compared to 1990) by 2030.[4]

The proposed package actively contributes to raising the EU's level of ambition regarding climate change and related policies as it provides legislative instruments and actions for several critical sectors. With the objective of making the EU Green Deal work, the package aims at: (a) reviewing the (EU-ETS) emissions trading system[5] including maritime, aviation, and CORSIA[6] as well as a proposal for ETS as an own resource; (b) creating a border carbon adjustment mechanism (CBAM);[7] (c) an effort sharing regulation (ESR);[8] (d) reviewing the energy taxation directive;[9] (e) amendment of the Renewable Energy Directive to implement the ambitions of the new 2030 climate target (RED); (f) amendment of the Energy Efficiency Directive to implement the ambition of the new 2030 climate target;[10] (g) reduction of methane emissions in the energy sector; (h) reviewing the regulation on the inclusion of greenhouse gas emissions and resulting from activities related to land use, land use

[1] Elkerbout and Egenhofer (2021). https://www.mdpi.com/2071-1050/14/7/3947.

[2] Sabato and Frontedu (2020). https://papers.ssrn.com/sol3/papers.cfm?abstract_id=3699367.

[3] AA. VV. (2021).

[4] Business Europe position paper on the 'Fit for 55' Package - November 2021.

[5] Proposal for a Directive of the European Parliament and of the Council amending Directive 2003/87/EC establishing a scheme for greenhouse gas emission allowance trading within the Union, Decision (EU) 2015/1814 establishing and operating a market stabilization reserve for the Union greenhouse gas emission allowance trading scheme and Regulation (EU) 2015/757.

[6] Proposal for a Directive of the European Parliament and of the Council amending Directive 2003/87/EC as regards the contribution of aviation to the EU's economy-wide emissions reduction target and implementing an appropriate overall market mechanism - general approach.

[7] Cosbey et al. (2021). https://papers.ssrn.com/sol3/papers.cfm?abstract_id=3838167.

[8] Proposal for a Regulation of the European Parliament and of the Council amending Regulation (EU) 2018/842 on mandatory annual reductions of greenhouse gas emissions by Member States between 2021 and 2030 as a contribution to climate action to meet their commitments under the Paris Agreement.

[9] Proposal for a Council Directive restructuring the Union framework for the taxation of energy products and electricity (recast).

[10] Proposal for a Directive of the European Parliament and of the Council on energy efficiency (recast).

change, and forestry (LULUCF);[11] (i) reviewing the directive on the implementation of alternative fuels infrastructure;[12] (j) revision of the regulation setting CO_2 emission performance standards for new passenger cars and new light commercial vehicles;[13] (k) revision of the energy performance of the buildings directive (EPBD); and (l) revision of the third gas energy package (Directive 2009/73/EU and Regulation 715/2009/EU) to regulate competitive markets for decarbonized gas.[14]

In the present text, the author will focus on: (i) the reform of the Emissions Trading System (ETS); (ii) the Effort Sharing Regulation (ESR); the (iii) revision of the regulation on the inclusion of greenhouse gas emissions resulting from activities related to land use, land use change, and forestry (LULUCF); the (iv) revision of the directive on the deployment of alternative fuels infrastructure; and the (v) revision of the regulation setting CO_2 emission performance standards for new passenger cars and new light commercial vehicles.

2 Reform of the Emissions Trading System (ETS)[15]

The European Union Emissions Trading Scheme (EU ETS) is a mechanism for regulating greenhouse gas (GHG) emissions in activities such as mineral oil refining, ceramics, pulp and paper, chemicals, fuel combustion, and aviation that are responsible for about 45% of GHG emissions in the EU.

The EU ETS is one of the two main pillars of the EU's climate policy to reduce greenhouse gas emissions (the second is the Effort Sharing Decision and Regulation).[16] The ETS encompasses all EU Member States as well as Iceland, Liechtenstein, and Norway and generally covers heavy industries, electricity installations, and aviation.

---

[11] Proposal for a Regulation of the European Parliament and of the Council amending Regulation (EU) 2018/841 as regards the scope, the simplification of the rules on compliance, the setting of Member State targets for 2030 and the commitment to collectively achieve climate neutrality in the land use, forestry and agriculture sectors by 2035, and Regulation (EU) 2018/1999 as regards improved processes for monitoring, reporting, progress monitoring and review.

[12] Proposal for a Regulation of the European Parliament and of the Council on the deployment of alternative fuels infrastructure and repealing Directive 2014/94/EU of the European Parliament and of the Council.

[13] Proposal for a Regulation of the European Parliament and of the Council amending Regulation (EU) 2019/631 on enhanced CO_2 emission performance standards for new passenger cars and new light commercial vehicles in line with the Union's increased climate ambition.

[14] Berghmans (2021).

[15] Proposal for a Directive of the European Parliament and of the Council amending Directive 2003/87/EC establishing a scheme for greenhouse gas emission allowance trading within the Union, Decision (EU) 2015/1814 establishing and operating a market stabilization reserve for the Union greenhouse gas emission allowance trading scheme and Regulation (EU) 2015/757.

[16] Woerdman (2015). https://papers.ssrn.com/sol3/papers.cfm?abstract_id=2654641.

It is currently in its fourth phase (2021–2030) with the other three having taken place, respectively, between 2005 and 2007, 2008 and 2012, and 2013 and 2020.[17] Phase 4 was subdivided into two stages, i.e., 2021 to 2025 and 2026 to 2030.

The Commission proposal to amend Directive 2003/87/EC relates to the ongoing phase 4 of the ETS (2021–2030). It consists of five main elements: (i) a lower cap and a more ambitious linear reduction factor for GHG emissions; (ii) revised rules for the free allocation of allowances and the market stability reserve; (iii) extension to maritime transport; (iv) a new separate ETS for buildings and road transport; and (v) an increase in the Innovation and Modernization Funds and new rules on the use of the ETS.

To align the directive establishing the European Union Emissions Trading System (EU ETS) with the greenhouse gas emission reduction targets set out in the European Climate Act, the Commission proposes to reduce emissions from the EU ETS sectors by 61% by 2030 compared to 2005 levels. To reach this target, the proposal increases the linear emission reduction factor from 2.2% per year to 4.2% to be applied after the entry into force of the revised directive.

In addition, the cap on emission allowances would be adjusted downwards as if the linear reduction factor (LFR) had increased from 2021 (rebasing). The cap will be increased by allowances corresponding to shipping emissions to be included in the EU ETS derived from reporting under Regulation (EU) 2015/757 of 29 April 2015 (MRV Regulation).

The ETS provides for free allocation of a proportion of allowances in the rules in order to avoid "carbon leakage" which may involve shifting production to countries where emission restrictions are less stringent.[18]

The free allocation of emission allowances began by covering about 95% of the allowances in 2005. However, this has been reduced. Except for district heating, free allocation will no longer be possible by 2030. Emission allowances for electricity production and carbon dioxide capture, transport, and storage are excluded from free allocation from the third ETS period (2013–2020). Benchmarks for free allocation exist and are based on the results of the most efficient installations in the European Union for each sector.

In this way, the aim is to increase the use of more efficient technologies and increase investment in alternative production processes to reduce greenhouse gas emissions. As for determining the number of licenses to be allocated free of charge, they are based on the list of facilities covered by the ETS, also known as the NIMs List (National Implementation Measures). It includes the history of the facilities submitted by operators on production activity, heat and gas transfers, electricity production, and emissions at the sub-installation level. However, the number of free allowances will be gradually reduced with a decreasing emissions cap.

Entities covered by the Border Carbon Adjustment Mechanism (BCMF) receive 90% of the free allowances until 2026 and, after that date, they will receive around

[17] Alberola et al. (2008). https://papers.ssrn.com/sol3/papers.cfm?abstract_id=1117411
[18] Appun (2021).

10 percentage points less each year. Regarding the sectors covered by the MACF, the Council endorsed the proposal to phase out free emission allowances for the sectors covered by the MACF over a 10-year period from 2026 to 2035. The support to the decarbonization of these sectors will be possible through the Innovation Fund.

This mechanism will also introduce a price on greenhouse gas emissions for products imported into the EU. The aim is clear to ensure that the EU's climate objectives are not undermined by less ambitious climate policies in other countries.

To encourage the adoption of low-carbon technologies, the free allocation of allowances will be reduced by 25% for installations that fail to implement the recommendations of the energy audits required by the Energy Efficiency Directive or fail to take equivalent measures to reduce GHG emissions.

This means that, overall, emissions allowances will decrease at a faster rate. From 2021 onwards, they will decrease by 2.2% per year instead of 1.74%. To proceed with this reform, the Commission proposes: (a) a review of the system of free allocation of allowances that focuses on those sectors most at risk of relocating their production outside the EU (covering some 50 sectors); (b) setting aside a considerable number of free allowances for new and growing installations; (c) more flexible rules to better align the volume of free allowances with production figures; and (d) an update of all benchmarks used to measure emissions performance to reflect technological advances since 2008.

The European Commission estimates that around 6.3 billion allowances worth EUR160 billion will be allocated free of charge to businesses between 2021 and 2030 alone.

3 Effort Sharing Regulation (ESR)[19]

Regulation (EU) 2018/842 of 30 May sets out the Member States' obligations regarding their minimum contributions for the period from 2021 to 2030 to achieve the Union's target of a 30% reduction of its greenhouse gas emissions by 2030 compared to 2005 levels and contributes to achieving the objectives of the Paris Agreement.

This regulation lays down the rules for determining the annual emission allocations as well as the assessment of Member States' progress and compliance with the minimum contributions required. It concerns emissions not covered by the ETS/CETS directive with the latter accounting for 60% of total emissions relating to buildings, transport, agricultural activity, waste management operations, and

[19]Proposal for a Regulation of the European Parliament and of the Council amending Regulation (EU) 2018/842 on mandatory annual reductions of greenhouse gas emissions by Member States between 2021 and 2030 as a contribution to climate action to meet their commitments under the Paris Agreement.

small industry. This methodology is to be continued until 2030 with efforts being shared based on the relative gross domestic product (GDP) per capita.

Thus, all Member States have scaled targets ranging from 0% to 40% compared to 2005 data. National targets for the group of Member States with a GDP per capita above the Union average should be adjusted in relative terms to reflect cost-effectiveness in a fair and balanced manner.

Achieving these greenhouse gas emission reductions should enhance efficiency and innovation in the Union economy and should promote improvements in, inter alia, buildings, agriculture, waste management, and transport insofar as they are within the scope of this regulation. It should cover greenhouse gas emissions from the IPCC categories energy, industrial processes and product use, agriculture, and waste as determined in accordance with Regulation (EU) 525/2013 except for greenhouse gas emissions from activities listed in Annex I to Directive 2003/87/EC.[20]

In this way, more ambitious targets are set whereby Member States are challenged to seek to develop and implement additional measures regarding the sectors covered. The regulation empowers Member States to take measures to enable them to tackle emissions in the buildings, transport, agriculture, waste, and small industry sectors by stipulating strengthened emission reduction targets.

In the specific case of Portugal, it should reduce its emissions by 17% in 2030 and should achieve this goal.

To consider previous efforts undertaken since 2013 by Member States that had a GDP per capita below the Union average in that same year, it was considered appropriate to create a limited special buffer corresponding to a maximum of 105 million tonnes of CO_2 equivalent.

The emergency buffer should also benefit those Member States in which greenhouse gas emissions are below their annual emission allocations for the period from 2013 to 2020 and have difficulties in reaching their 2030 greenhouse gas emissions target despite making use of other flexibilities provided for in this regulation.

The emergency buffer should be available for those Member States in 2032 subject to certain conditions and provided that its use will not compromise the achievement of the Union's target of a 30% reduction of greenhouse gas emissions for 2030 in the sectors covered by this regulation.

[20] Labello et al. (2022). https://papers.ssrn.com/sol3/papers.cfm?abstract_id=4010386.

4 Revision of the Regulation on the Inclusion of Greenhouse Gas Emissions Resulting from Activities Related to Land Use, Land Use Change, and Forestry (LULUCF)[21]

Regulation (EU) 2018/841 sets out Member States' commitments for the land use, land use change and forestry (LULUCF) sectors that contribute to achieving the objectives of the Paris Agreement and meeting the Union's greenhouse gas emission reduction target for the period 2021 to 2030.

The LULUCF sector, including agricultural soils, has a direct and significant impact on biodiversity and ecosystem services. For this reason, any policy affecting these sectors should set one of its key objectives as ensuring coherence with those of the Union's biodiversity strategy.

This regulation seeks to establish the rules for the accounting of emissions and removals from the LULUCF sector and for the verification of Member States' compliance with these commitments.[22]

Considering this, EU Member States must ensure that the accounted greenhouse gas emissions from land use, land use change, or forestry are balanced by at least an equivalent removal of CO_2 from the atmosphere in the period 2021 to 2030.

To achieve the climate target set for 2030 and the goal of carbon neutrality by the year 2050,[23] more greenhouse gases need to be sequestered. To this end, the long-term stability and adaptability of carbon pools is essential for ensuring the effectiveness of measures aimed at increasing carbon sequestration. Furthermore, sustainable management practices can maintain the productivity, regeneration capacity, and vitality of the LULUCF sector and thus promote economic and social development while reducing the carbon and ecological footprint of that sector.[24]

---

[21] Proposal for a Regulation of the European Parliament and of the Council amending Regulation (EU) 2018/841 as regards the scope, the simplification of the rules on compliance, the setting of Member State targets for 2030 and the commitment to collectively achieve climate neutrality in the land use, forestry, and agriculture sectors by 2035, and Regulation (EU) 2018/1999 as regards improved processes for monitoring, reporting, tracking progress and review.

[22] In order to accurately account for emissions and removals in accordance with the 2006 Intergovernmental Panel on Climate Change (IPCC) guidelines (IPCC guidelines), the values reported annually under Regulation (EU) No 525/2013 of the European Parliament and of the Council for land use categories and conversion between land use categories should be used. This should thereby simplify the approaches used under the UNFCCC and the Kyoto Protocol. Land that is converted into another land use category should be considered to be in transition to that category for a period of 20 years, which is the default value defined in the IPCC guidelines. Member States will be able to derogate from this default value only when dealing with forested land and only in very limited circumstances that are justified by virtue of the IPCC guidelines. Amendments to the IPCC guidelines adopted by the Conference of the Parties to the UNFCCC or by the Conference of the Parties serving as the Meeting of the Parties to the Paris Agreement should be reflected, as appropriate, in the reporting requirements under this regulation.

[23] Valenduc (2022). https://papers.ssrn.com/sol3/papers.cfm?abstract_id=4013350.

[24] Leal-Arcas (2022), pp. 223–240. https://papers.ssrn.com/sol3/papers.cfm?abstract_id=3999019.

Forests, which are the largest carbon sink in the LULUCF sector, should be managed sustainably, thus contributing to climate change mitigation. In the reporting period 2000 to 2009, the reported average removal of sinks created by forest soils[25] was 372 million tonnes of CO_2 equivalent per year for the Union as a whole.

The regulation sets out the duty of Member States to ensure that sinks and reservoirs, including forests, are conserved or enhanced as appropriate to achieve the Paris Agreement objective and to meet the Union's ambitious greenhouse gas emission reduction targets by 2050.

A two-stage approach with rolling targets is proposed by the Commission for the periods between 2021 and 2025 and between 2026 and 2030. These are based on the average level of removals or emissions with a reference period between 2016 and 2018.

The goal is for the European Union to achieve climate neutrality in the land use, forestry, and agriculture sectors by 2035, also including non-CO_2 agricultural emissions such as from fertilizer use and livestock breeding, by balancing all greenhouse gas emissions from land use, forestry, and agriculture with removals from these three sectors at the EU level.

Member States should increase net carbon removal in the land use and forestry sector between the period 2026 to 2030 and to significantly simplify *compliance* rules.

Another important objective is to ensure that primary food production and biomass are climate neutral by 2035. The revision of the regulation also aims to seek improved monitoring, reporting, and verification of emissions and removals such as through increased use of geo-referenced data and remote sensing so that Member States' progress can be recorded with high accuracy. This is especially true for sensitive areas with high biodiversity or high carbon stocks.

The proposed rules also address, in a proportionate and adequate manner, the negative impacts of natural disturbances such as pests and forest fires on the achievement of Member States' targets. To implement the proposal, the incentive framework is improved for carbon storage in long-life and circular wood products.

The increased sustainable use of harvested wood products can substantially limit emissions by substitution and enhance removals of greenhouse gases from the atmosphere.

[25] Removals resulting from managed forest soils should be deducted from the projected forest reference level. Projected future removals by sinks should be based on an extrapolation of forest management practices and intensity from a reference period. A decrease of a sink relative to the reference level should be accounted for as emissions. The specificity of the national situation and practices such as, for example, lower than usual felling intensity or ageing of forests in the reference period, should be taken into account.

5 Review of the Directive on the Deployment of Alternative Fuels Infrastructure[26]

Directive 2014/94/EU of the European Parliament and of the Council of 22 October 2014 on the deployment of alternative fuels infrastructure sets out a common framework of measures for the deployment of an alternative fuels' infrastructure in the European Union to minimize dependence on oil and mitigate the environmental impact of transport. It sets out minimum requirements for the deployment of this infrastructure, including recharging points for electric vehicles and refueling points for natural gas and hydrogen.[27]

The proposed regulation that will replace Directive 2014/94/EU seeks to ensure the necessary deployment of an interoperable and user-friendly infrastructure for recharging and refueling of cleaner vehicles across the EU, including rural and remote areas.

It is also underlined in the proposed regulation that it seeks to provide alternative solutions to the use of on-board engines for docked vessels and stationary aircraft to ensure full interoperability in the EU and the ease of the infrastructure's use.

The general approach adopted by the Council maintains the key aspects of the Commission's proposal particularly in light of electric vehicle charging, heavy electric vehicle charging, hydrogen refueling, and electricity supply to vessels at berth in ports while improving and adapting them.

According to the proposed regulation, the electric vehicle fleet is expected to reach 30 million units by 2020. For each electric car, 1 KW of installed charging capacity should be provided. Setting mandatory targets for this type of infrastructure is considered essential to support the further penetration of cleaner fuels and the continued growth of a market that presents opportunities for the EU automotive industry.

This proposal will require Member States to extend the charging capacity in line with sales of zero-emission cars and to implement charging and refueling points at regular intervals on the main motorways (TEN-T core network: Trans-European Transport Network) every 60 kilometers for electric charging (300 kW of capacity provided by fast charging points by 2025 and 600 kW by 2030) and every 150 kilometers for hydrogen refueling.

The Commission's Sustainable and Smart Mobility Strategy auspiciously points to the production of more than 1 million recharging points by 2025 and approximately 3.5 million by 2030. For heavy electric vehicles, recharging points must be provided along the TEN-T core network every 60 km and at least 1400 kW of power will have to be provided by 2025 and 3500 kW by 2030. In the global TEM-T network, these targets will have to be met every 100 km by 2030 and 2035, respectively.

---

[26]Proposal for a Regulation of the European Parliament and of the Council on alternative fuels infrastructure and repealing Directive 2014/94/EU of the European Parliament and of the Council.

[27]Marcu et al. (2021).

These recharging points will have to be implemented in car parks suitable for this purpose and should exist in large cities and agglomerations of the TEN-T network (urban nodes) to allow the recharging of urban delivery trucks. Any existing gaps in the LNG refueling infrastructure for trucks should be filled by 2025.

6 Revision of the Regulation Setting CO_2 Emission Performance Standards for New Passenger Cars and New Light Commercial Vehicles[28]

The proposed "*fit for 55*" package strengthens CO_2 emission reduction targets for new passenger cars and commercial vehicles.[29]

The overall objectives of this proposal are to contribute to achieving climate neutrality by 2050 and, to this end and in line with the European Climate Act, to contribute to achieving at least a 55% reduction of net greenhouse gas emissions by 2030 compared to 1990 levels.

The proposal has three specific objectives. The first is to contribute to the climate objectives and targets set for 2030 and 2050 by reducing CO_2 emissions from passenger cars and light commercial vehicles.[30] The second specific objective is to provide consumers and citizens with the benefits of increased availability of zero-emission vehicles. The main expected benefits concern not only the improvement of air quality, in cities. The third objective is to promote innovation in zero-emission technologies thereby enhancing the technological leadership of the automotive value chain and boosting employment in the EU.

This proposal sets a CO_2 emission reduction target of 55% for new passenger cars and 50% for new commercial vehicles compared to 2021 levels to be achieved by the year 2030. An ambitious CO_2 emission reduction target of 100% for new passenger cars and commercial vehicles to be achieved by 2035 is also highlighted.

With the application of more stringent targets for the EU fleet from 2030 onwards, manufacturers will have to make significantly more zero-emission vehicles available on the Union market. In this context, the incentive mechanism for zero or low emission vehicles (ZLEV) would no longer meet its initial objective and would risk undermining the effectiveness of Regulation (EU) 2019/631.

---

[28] Proposal for a Regulation of the European Parliament and of the Council amending Regulation (EU) 2019/631 on enhanced CO_2 emission performance standards for new passenger cars and new light commercial vehicles in line with the Union's increased climate ambition.

[29] The CO_2 emission standards that promote the availability of new zero-emission vehicles on the market are also a complementary measure to Directive (EU) 2018/2001 on energy from renewable sources.

[30] Finally, while CO_2 emission standards guarantee the supply of zero-emission vehicles, Directive 2014/94/EU on the alternative fuels infrastructure that encourages the deployment of charging and refueling infrastructure is a necessary complementary instrument to remove the market barrier to the creation of such infrastructure.

The incentive mechanism for ZLEV should therefore be abolished from 2030. Before that date, i.e., during this decade, the incentive mechanism for ZLEV will continue to support the availability of vehicles with emissions between 0 g CO_2/km and 50 g CO_2/km, namely battery electric vehicles, hydrogen fuel cell vehicles, and efficient plug-in hybrid electric vehicles. After that date, plug-in hybrid electric vehicles will continue to be included in the fleet targets imposed on vehicle manufacturers.

Under this mechanism, if a manufacturer reaches certain benchmarks for sales of zero or low emission vehicles, it can be rewarded with less stringent CO_2 emission targets.[31] The co-legislators agreed to increase the benchmark to 25% for passenger cars and 17% for commercial vehicles by 2030.

Under the regulation, all manufacturers must ensure that the average CO_2 emissions of their newly registered fleet in a calendar year do not exceed their specific annual emissions target.[32] Such a proposal does not exclude cars with combustion engines, however, it is defined that, if manufacturers decide to place vehicles with such characteristics on the market and if they exceed their emission target each year, they will have to pay a charge of EUR 95 per gram of CO_2/km above the target for each registered vehicle.

Thus, thanks to the new agreed targets, zero-emission vehicles will eventually become cheaper than fossil fuel-powered vehicles.

The new EU rules will not affect older cars still on the road until 2035, but the aim is to ensure that all vehicles within the EU area are zero-emission by 2050 via fleet turnover.

References

AA. VV. (2021) Fit for 55?: A progressive business perspective on the EU's transformative climate package. University of Cambridge, Institute for Sustainability Leadership, Policy Briefing

Alberola E et al (2008) European carbon prices fundamentals in 2005-2007: the effects of energy markets, temperatures and sectoral production. EconomiX Working Paper No. 2007-33

Appun K (2021) Emission reduction panacea or recipe for trade war? The EU's carbon border tax debate. Clean Energy Wire

Belmans R et al (2021) Electrification and sustainable fuels: competing for wind and sun (Complement to the Policy Brief). Robert Schuman Centre for Advanced Studies Research Paper, No. RSC 2021/55

Berghmans N (July 2021) EU climate ambition: four challenges for the Fit-for-55 legislative package. Institut du Développement Durable et des Relations Internationales (IDDRI)

Cosbey A et al (5 May, 2021) CBAM for the EU: a policy proposal. SSRN Electron J

Daskalakis G et al (2009) Modeling CO_2 emission allowance prices and derivatives: evidence from the European Trading Scheme. J Bank Finance 33(7)

[31] Daskalakis et al. (2009), pp. 1230–1241. https://papers.ssrn.com/sol3/papers.cfm?abstract_id=912420.

[32] Belmans et al. (2021). https://papers.ssrn.com/sol3/papers.cfm?abstract_id=3858536.

Elkerbout M, Egenhofer C (12 July, 2021) Fit for 55 - is the European Green Deal really leaving no-one behind? Centre for European Policy Studies (CEPS)
Labello M et al (2022) Not Fit for 55: the Hdi spatial injustice of residential energy consumption in the European Union. SSRN Electron J
Leal-Arcas R (2022) A legal exploration of the European Union's carbon border adjustment mechanism. Eur Energy Environ Law Rev 31(4):223–240
Marcu A et al (2021) ERCST hydrogen paper: the Fit for 55 package and its implications for the EU hydrogen economy. European Roundtable on Climate Change and Sustainable Transition
Sabato S, Frontedu B (2020) A socially just transition through the European Green Deal? ETUI Research Paper - Working Paper 2020.08
Valenduc C (2022) The carbon pricing proposals of the 'Fit for 55' package: an efficient and fair route to carbon neutrality. ETUI Research Paper - Working Papers 2022.03
Woerdman E (2015) The EU greenhouse gas emissions trading scheme, essential EU climate law. Edward Elgar, Cheltenham (Forthcoming), University of Groningen Faculty of Law Research Paper No. 2015/34

Jurisdictional Assessment of Environmental Taxation

Solange Juvandes

Abstract This reflection on environmental tax jurisprudence deals with some of the relevant jurisdictional decisions in which the legality of taxes on grounds of environmental protection purposes was syndicated. Despite its extra-fiscal purpose, the environmental tax respects the constitutional configuration of a tax legal instrument subject to the principles of the Fiscal and Economic Constitution, which, when interpreted by the courts, must be subjected to the strict proportionality test in its adequacy standpoint.

1 Introduction

The present reflection on environmental tax jurisprudence addresses some of the relevant jurisdictional decisions in which the legality of taxes with ecological objectives has been syndicated. Emphasis is given to the relevance of the effects of jurisdictional judgments that go far beyond the concrete case.

Legislative practice has been moving towards an exponential increase of environmental taxation which has merited the attention of the doctrine and generated some perplexity in the scope of tax science concepts.

Disputes related to the formal and material legitimization of such taxes force the tax jurisdiction, particularly the Constitutional Court (TC), to constant ponderation.

The authors proceed to the analysis of the particular role of tax law in environmental law, of its vocation as a modelling or corrective instrument, and of its distinct nature from command-and-control instruments, such as impositions of a sanctionary nature.

As a science, taxation requires unity and order and cannot be characterized as a disorderly system of measures. If taxation is not subject to the general principles of law, it will be a social regression and a contribution to its discredit as a science.

S. Juvandes (✉)
Lisbon Tax Court, Lisbon, Portugal

R. Saraiva, P. A. Pardal (eds.), *Sustainable Finances and the Law*, Economic Analysis of Law in European Legal Scholarship 16,
https://doi.org/10.1007/978-3-031-49460-4_16

After the legislative intervention, it is up to the courts, when they are called upon to do so, to verify compliance with the fiscal, economic, and environmental constitutional principles that legitimize and materialize a tax based on ecological preservation objectives.

The authors analyse the case law produced so far in the area of environmental taxation, highlighting decisions that have changed the direction followed until then and seeking to demonstrate that the premises of necessity, adequacy, and effectiveness constitute the legitimacy of a tax created for environmental protection reasons.

The environmental principles such as the polluter pays, the rational management of resources or prevention are the only legally acceptable justifications for the existence of deviations from the principle of substantive tax legality.

In the ambit of environmental taxation, jurisprudential control should not only be negative.

This work ends with the necessary conclusions after the excursus made on the most relevant jurisprudence.

2 Environmental Protection Tax Law

The tax system is one of the instruments available to the state to pursue the purposes constitutionally assigned to it. This means that, even in the purest form of taxation erected solely to obtain revenue for the pursuit of the general objectives of the state, the economic and social repercussions exist, leading some authors to refer to undue extra taxation. The fact that some taxes have in their genesis extra-fiscal purposes serving economic, social, or environmental objectives, as is the case of ecological taxes, does not deprive them of their classification as taxes and, as such, as fiscal instruments.[1]

Environmental preservation as an asset of public and collective interest naturally constitutes an area of state intervention as a constitutionally consecrated task and incumbency. Furthermore, it is enshrined as a fundamental right that immediately prefigures citizens' access to the law and the courts to demand its pursuit.[2]

The Constitution of the Portuguese Republic (CRP) provides in its part I, relating to the fundamental rights and duties of citizens, in paragraph 1 of Article 66, the

[1] Ollero (1991), p. 457; Garcia (2020), p. 05.

[2] Regarding the actual judicial protection, the mechanisms of popular action constitutionally foreseen in Article 53(2)(a), as provided in Law No. 83/95 of 31 August that allows the universalization of the right of action at the end of Article 9 of the Code of Procedure in Administrative Courts (CPTA) stand out. Furthermore, the role of the public prosecutor's office as a defender of legality, public interest and, naturally, guardian of the environment by Article 219(1) of the CRP is translated into the public prosecutor's right of public action provided for in Articles 9 and 62 of the CPTA.

"right to a healthy and ecologically balanced human living environment" as a fundamental right autonomous from the others.[3,4]

In truth, more than a subjective fundamental right, Article 66, paragraph 1, 2nd part, consecrates a fundamental duty to protect the environment given the impossibility of appropriation of the collective good. This is a duty that is multiform because it includes duties of *non facere*, duties *of facere* that fall on citizens and the state to which are also associated duties of *dare* and provision of which the imposition of environmental taxes are an example.

Simultaneously, the constitutional text consecrates the objective protection of the environment as an objective and fundamental task of the state [see Articles 9(d) and (e), 66(2), 81(m) and 93(1)(d) and (2)], i.e., as a legal good that should condition the positions taken by the legislature and the enforcer of the law. It not only prohibits actions that may compromise its preservation but also requires favourable actions for the prosecution of efficient legal protection.

The use of tax planning in environmental protection is foreseen in Article 192(2)(a) of the Treaty on the Functioning of the European Union (TFEU) and in Article 66(2)(h) of the CRP.

In infra-constitutional legislation, the Environment Framework Law (LBA)[5] in paragraph e) of paragraph 2 of Article 17 establishes environmental taxation as one of the instruments at the service of environmental policy. The previous Law No. 11/87 of April 7 already provided for taxation as an instrument in its Articles 24(1)(c) and 27(1)(r).

As the legislature rightly states in the Environment Framework Law, taxation is one of the instruments at the service of environmental politics and not the main instrument.

Tax law emerges as an instrument for shaping behaviours through tax increases or decreases or through the creation of taxes that may be aimed at correcting externalities, ideally eliminating them. It may also be aimed exclusively at obtaining revenue

---

[3] About the environment as a fundamental right, see Canotilho (2004), pp. 177–189.

[4] Pereira da Silva argues that "The right to the environment, which stems from the third generation of human rights, simultaneously presents a negative aspect, which guarantees its holder defence against illegal aggression in a constitutionally guaranteed area, and a positive aspect, which requires public entities to act to make it effective. Thus - and answering the question formulated at the beginning - the legal regime of rights, freedoms, and guarantees, in the measure of its negative dimension, and the legal regime of economic, social, and cultural rights, in the measure of its positive dimension, must be applied to the right to the environment" in "Green is one of the colours of Constitutional Law."

"O direito ao ambiente, oriundo da terceira geração dos direitos humanos, apresenta em simultâneo uma vertente negativa, que garante ao seu titular a defesa contra agressões ilegais no domínio constitucionalmente garantido, e uma vertente positiva, que obriga à actuação das entidades públicas para a sua efectivação. Assim – e respondendo à questão formulada no início – ao direito ao ambiente é de aplicar o regime jurídico dos direitos, liberdades e garantias, na medida da sua dimensão negativa, e o regime jurídico dos direitos, económicos, sociais e culturais, na medida da sua dimensão positiva." *in* Pereira da Silva (2021).

[5] Law No. 11/87, of April 7, amended by Law No. 19/2014, of 14/4.

for ecological purposes for which effectiveness will most certainly depend not only on environmental ethics but, above all, on tax ethics and essentially on the interconnection of the fundamental principles of environmental law and tax law.

The design of an environmental tax instrument requires prior scientific work supported by economic, social, and behavioural science of which the conclusions allow affirming that the planned tax measure can produce the intended positive environmental effects.

In 1997, the OECD and Eurostat defined a "green tax" as one for which the tax base "consists of a physical unit that contains specific and clear evidence of negative impact on the environment". This definition is incomplete since all human activity tends to produce an environmentally negative impact which would justify the proliferation of taxes targeting all types of activities. However, not all taxes based on specific evidence of adverse effects are a tool that can generate ecological benefits.

Without forgetting the legislature's need for freedom of interpretation, the system of scientific tax values and parameters is essential to ensure fairness and balance in the design of taxes for extra-fiscal purposes.

The same requirement of prior scientific support to prove or at least sustainably presume that the tax measure can produce the environmental benefits for which it was created is also essential in the appraisal of its legality by the courts when challenged.[6,7]

3 The Fiscal Constitution and the Economic Perspective

The General Tax Law (LGT) in Article 1 defines its scope as the law that regulates tax relations. In paragraph 2, the legal-tax relations are defined as those established between the tax administration, acting as such, and natural and legal persons. Paragraph 3 defines, in general terms, the entities that comprise the tax administration considering "the other public entities legally in charge of the assessment and collection of taxes".

In Article 3 of the LGT, two types of taxes are enumerated, i.e., fiscal and parafiscal and, in No. 2, taxes, fees, and other financial contributions are included. In this sense, tax law also includes the legal tax relations resulting from unilateral, bilateral, fiscal, and parafiscal taxes.[8]

The environment is indeed a fundamental right, but so are the property right and the right to free economic initiative, requiring the promotion of a simultaneous policy of protection and integration that reconciles the various interests. It starts

---

[6]The expert evidence is provided in Articles 388 and 399 of the Civil Code.

[7]Judicial presumptions are admitted under the terms of Article 351 of the Civil Code based on the judge's conclusion based on judgments of experience, probability, logic, and intuition itself.

[8]In a different sense, Nabais (2003a), p. 24.

from rational premises in which the presumption of an abstract danger is based on the maxims of experience, on concrete judgments of logic, and probability.[9]

The economic perspective tempered by the tax law necessarily implies the consideration of parameters of social justice in the contribution to public charges and intergenerational solidarity, tax equality, and proportionality of burdens. These are essential for the efficient functioning of the market to ensure balanced competition between companies (see Article 81, f) of the CRP).[10]

Like Baptista Lobo points out, "When we talk about the necessary state intervention in regulating market failures and promoting equality in environmental, land use and urban planning matters, we can never forget the issue of administrative failures and government failures."[11]

Public intervention as a guarantee of market efficiency in correcting negative externalities with environmental repercussions is an essential but subsidiary element to private action insofar as, in cases when there are no market failures to be corrected, public intervention, besides being unnecessary, may contribute to imbalances that cause even more damage. It requires a balance between the benefits to be achieved and the underlying costs. This cost-benefit consideration is essential in tax intervention as it can otherwise strangle economic initiatives and distort economic competitiveness.

This economic principle of subsidiarity of public intervention in efficient market dynamics is close to another principle of fiscal science, i.e., the neutrality of the tax system. It is structural in international tax law and defends that the tax system should intervene as little as possible in the decisions of economic agents.[12]

The principle of tax neutrality as one of the priority tasks of the state is addressed constitutionally in part II of the CRP on economic organization, in Article 81, f) of the CRP in the 1st part "to ensure the efficient functioning of markets to ensure balanced competition between companies (. . .)".

Of course, environmental taxation will intrinsically aim to influence or change certain behaviours, benefiting or penalizing according to its inherent extra-fiscal objectives. However, the principles of subsidiarity and neutrality aim to ensure that this influence on the decisions of economic agents is limited to what is indispensable to achieve the objectives pursued and that, together with the environmental purpose

---

[9]On the perverse effects of a totalitarian environmental concern, see the position defended by Saraiva in her doctoral thesis. (2009), p. 224 e ss.

[10]Cf. Article 61(1) of the CRP.

[11]"Quando falamos da necessária intervenção do Estado na regulação das falhas de mercado e na promoção da igualdade nas matérias do ambiente, ordenamento do território e do urbanismo, não poderemos nunca esquecer a questão das falhas administrativas e das falhas de governo." Lobo (2019).

[12]The principles of international tax law are divided into two major groups, i.e., structural and operational. The former is the most important in the structuring of the legal and fiscal order. For the study of the principles of international tax law, see Pereira (2020).

or the excuse of the environmental purpose, no unnecessary market distortions are created.[13]

An environmental tax is not launched separately from other strategic measures to achieve the proposed ecological objective. It is a subsidiary promotion and incentive measure that should be part of a strategy to maximize environmental benefits and minimize economic costs.[14]

The legal classification given to the various taxes does not always correspond to their true legal nature. Thus, only the analysis of each specific tax in light of constitutional, tax, and legal principles clarifies its definition and classification.

As instruments of environmental policy, the characteristics of each tax will dictate their suitability for the intended ecological purpose.

The environmental tax, despite its essentially extra-fiscal purpose, respects the constitutional configuration of the duty to contribute, the principle of equality of contribution and its progressivity, mitigated by the principle of commutative justice (the principle of benefit) to the extent that it is subordinated to the principle of the polluter-payer (the polluter pays) limited by the principle of non-confiscation.

The principles of law are the pillars that support and allow a legal system to be coherent and fair,[15] they do not configure absolute rules of mathematical application,[16] or consent to unique readings. On the contrary, they are dependent on weighing judgments for their application to objective reality, and their interpretation must obey the principles of prohibition of abuse and practicability.[17]

The collision between different principles will lead to a preference for the acceptability of one without implying total disregard for the other with graduation to be performed only through the proportionality principle.[18]

---

[13] The legislative response always requires a careful analysis and in-depth study as, otherwise, the legislative response will become an inefficient and costly placebo with no corrective function, paraphrasing Saraiva: "Even with good intentions in the pursuit of the common good, it fails in certain and determined circumstances" Saraiva (2011a), pp. 1085–1118.

[14] As a good example, see the tax on low energy efficient light bulbs created by Decree-Law 108/2007 of 12 April, a tax measure that was accompanied by initiatives arising from synergies between private operators, the regulatory authority of the sector (ERSE) for promotion and information as well as labelling rules. On the misclassification of this tax, see Dias and da Costa (2010).

[15] As affirmed by José de Oliveira Ascensão the principles are "great orientations of the positive order, which pass through it and vivify it." The same author adds that the "legal order is not a casual accumulation of elements, but is illuminated by great coordinates that give it its basic outline.". - Os princípios são "grandes orientações da ordem positiva, que a percorrem e vivificam". Acrescenta o mesmo autor que "a ordem jurídica não é um amontoado casual de elementos, é iluminada por grandes coordenadas que lhe dão o travejamento básico" cf. de Oliveira Ascensão (2008), p. 419.

[16] Novais (2012), p. 114 e ss.

[17] Dourado (2020), p. 35.

[18] "The principle of relativity in Germanic Law (*verhältnismässig*) that determines the search for a "compromise solution" respecting more, in a particular situation, one of the principles in conflict and trying to disrespect the minimum to the other(s) without ever lacking the minimum respect, that is, hurting their "essential core"." Our translation of: "Princípio da relatividade no Direito Germânico (verhältnismässig), o qual determina a busca de uma" solução de compromisso",

Fairness is achieved to the extent that pollutant charges are not imposed on the whole community, preventing the subsidization by the community of environmentally harmful activities.

Considering the objectives of raising revenue to restore the environment in the case of *improper* environmental taxes, obtaining resources for carrying out the environmental functions should have this further destination.

The introduction of an environmental tax requires a specific objective, a concrete definition of the taxable event, and an appropriate tax base; the choice of the taxpayer is to be considered and justified for reasons of efficiency and fairness.

The pursuit of sustainable economic development (social and environmental) requires a strong technical and strategic dimension of the political decision and the legislature.

A tax that is not based on consideration of its effectiveness, efficiency, fairness, or proportionality and for which diffuse effects are not controlled and mitigated by other measures is reduced to a political price or a diversion of resources.

A tax measure with an environmental rationale but aimed at short-term revenue will only lead to economic and social distortions and divert resources from the environmental cause.

4 Case Law, Tax Instruments for the Environment

4.1 South Administrative Central Court Ruling of 6/6/2013[19]

The Water Resources Charge (TRH) was specifically regulated in Decree Law No. 97/2008 of June 11.[20]

The unconstitutionality of this fee was invoked on the grounds that it does not have the typical bilateral nature of fees since the component (U) refers to the environmental costs arising from the use of water applies to the use of private water. This claim was contradicted by the court which highlighted the fact that the subjection to a fee is not voluntary nor does the service at the origin of the fee have to be desired by the taxpayer. It is sufficient that there is an individually provided service for its payment to qualify as a fee.[21]

respeitando-se mais, em determinada situação, um dos princípios em conflito, e procurando desrespeitar o mínimo ao(s) outro(s), sem jamais lhe(s) faltar minimamente com o respeito, isto é, ferindo-lhes o "núcleo essencial" (...)" Guerra Filho and Cantarini (2017). https://enciclopediajuridica.pucsp.br/verbete/15/edicao-1/proporcionalidade.

[19] Case No. 08573/12, Relator, Judge Counselor Paulo Pereira Gouveia.

[20] Amended by Law No. 82-D/2014 of December 31.

[21] In the same sense, Ruling No. 357/99, handed down by the Constitutional Court on June 15, 1999, reported by Judge Counsellor Artur Maurício; Ruling No. 76/88, handed down on April 7, 1988, reported by Judge Counsellor Raul Mateus.

Despite ruling out the theory of exact economic equivalence between the fee and the service rendered, the court pointed out that the value of a fee is based on a relation of proportionality between the specific benefit provided by the service rendered or the cost supported by the community with the use of the public domain asset or the removal of the legal limit to the exercise of the activity of the private individual.[22]

The court concluded that this water resources fee created by a law of the regional government (Article 78 of Law No. 58/2005) is a fee and not a tax or contribution. This is because it constitutes a legal equivalent related to the negative impact of the authorized activity on water resources, the direct or indirect discharge of effluents, and the use of waters subject to public planning and management.[23]

Through Decree-Law No. 46/2017 of 3 May, the economic and financial regime of water resources was changed. In the calculation of the TRH, several components of objective incidence are used cumulatively having been added the component (S) which its purpose is to promote the sustainability of urban water systems. This revenue is consigned to the Environmental Fund under the terms of paragraph d) of n. 1 of Article 4 of Decree-Law No. 42-A/2016 of August 12 which, in turn, will transfer the necessary amounts to the beneficiary systems.[24]

The (S) component is intended to compensate for the high costs supported by municipal water systems located in low-density regions or with supply problems resulting from scarcity in a logic of sustainability and universality of the good.

The fact that one of the components of a fee has the solidarity between present and future generations as its express scope in the sense of allowing a sustained use of a given resource throughout the territory and over time covering technical, administrative, and monitoring costs does not remove its bilaterality or legal equivalence that characterizes it as a fee. This is because the alternative method to the definition of these costs in the different components of the fee can always be the monetization of the costs inflated by the rarity of the good of universal utility.[25]

In addition to the purpose of behavioural modelling, environmental taxes have the scope of redistributing the costs of financing environmental policy and preserving natural resources that are essential to human survival such as air quality, drinking water, energy, and soil.[26]

---

[22] Judgment No. 177/2010, rendered by the plenary on 5/5/2010, Case No. 742/09, Judge Counsellor Joaquim de Sousa Ribeiro.

[23] In the same sense, Judgment No. 0929/17, rendered by the Supreme Administrative Court on 12/12/2018, Case No. 0621/12.9BEALM, reported by Judge Counsellor Francisco Rothes.

[24] The preamble to Decree-Law No. 46/2017, of May 3.

[25] Article 3(1)(c), of Law 58/2005 of December 29, refers to the principles of water law, namely, "The principle of the economic value of water, which includes the recognition of the current or potential scarcity of this resource and the need to ensure its economically efficient use, with the recovery of the costs of water services, even in environmental and resource terms, and based on the principles of polluter pays and user pays."

[26] On the right to sustainable energy, see Saraiva (2011b).

As stated by Gomes Canotilho "The protection of the environment is a task of solidarity and not solitary and it is not compatible with the unilateral imposition of restrictive constraints on some in favour of others. This was, moreover, the fundamental dimension of the classic principle of equality before public costs."[27]

Justice in the distribution of public costs and solidarity are intrinsic values and concerns of both tax law and environmental law. The principle of solidarity has been part of tax law since the evolution from a liberal state to a social state and, in addition to making citizens self-responsible for increasing their sustenance and ensuring free economic availability, its function is to guarantee more individual freedom, mitigating inequalities of access to essential goods that allow the development of the personhood of the individual. This goal is expressed in tax law in the principle of contributive capacity, in the progressivity of the tax system, and in the qualitative discriminations of income and assets, constituting one of the fiscal objectives pursued by taxes.[28]

The subjective right to a healthy environment is, by itself, an expression of the principle of solidarity in the realization of intra- and intergenerational justice.

The fact that the component relating to the costs of universal access to scarce natural resources is expressed is a determinant for more transparent and participatory taxation that would no longer happen with the mere inflation of costs.

With regard to the internalisation of negative externalities and taking into account the polluter pays principle, bilateral taxes, such as fees, given their synallagmatic structure, seem to be the most appropriate and adequate instruments to directly impose the payment of environmental recovery on the agent causing measurable and quantifiable external environmental costs.

However, in the field of environmental damage, the fundamental characteristic of these externalities is precisely the frequent impossibility of divisibility and concrete attribution of responsibilities. This is because pollution naturally originates from diffuse sources and usually results from the interaction of a large number of causative agents.

The ecological charge may arise as compensation for environmental services or the use, occupation, or exploitation of ecological assets in the public domain when such use could be individualized. For this reason, except in the case of licensing fees[29] for polluting, dangerous, or high-risk environmental productive activities and the case, for example, of the treatment, removal, and disposal of industrial waste, the costs or negative externalities are more easily imputed in a group or sector manner, the quantification is presumed, and costs that intended to compensate have a diffuse character.

[27]"A defesa do ambiente é uma tarefa solidária e não solitária e não se compadece com a unilateral imposição de vínculos restritivos a uns a favor dos outros. Era esta, de resto, a dimensão fundamental do clássico princípio da igualdade perante os encargos públicos." Canotilho (1995).

[28]Nabais (2004), pp. 573–588.

[29]Ruling No. 581/2012, rendered by the Constitutional Court on 5/12/2012, Case No. 204/12, Judge Counsellor Pedro Machete.

The difficult measurement and quantification of the specific consideration required by the rate's synallagmatic nature and the need for proportionality of this type of fiscal measure mean that its application in environmental legal protection is not as ideal as it might first appear.

Dias Soares[30] understands that the need to comply with an objective bilaterality conditions the potential of the fee as an instrument to promote behavioural changes. Its utility is predominantly expressed at the level of financing specific public interventions to which can be added the licensing of activities of exploration or use of public or semi-public assets such as natural resources.

The absence of an infra-constitutional rule requiring a concrete financial and economic justification does not allow the courts to take a more specific and objective approach to the relationship between the benefit, utility, cost, or proportionality between the deviation from the equivalence principle and the intended additional fiscal objective, leaving the concept of equivalence devoid of objective substance.

In the case of environmental fees, the existence of a general regime that presupposes adequate rules of quantification and qualification is of great help in understanding the values involved that are not always monetizable.

In the constitutional revision of 1997, the legislature consecrated the reservation of law for this type of tribute to a general framework law or a general regime. However, constitutional jurisprudence does not judge the legislative omission of their existence as a condition of the legality creation of new fees and financial contributions.

The legislative omission[31] of the regulatory framework and the absence of prior economic and financial justification imply opacity and a consequent lack of understanding by taxpayers of the extra-fiscal objectives on which an environmental fee may be based.

The Constitutional Court has ruled that unconstitutionality by omission can only be verified when there is a specific concrete duty that the Constitution assigns to the legislative authorities and the latter refrain from fulfilling it.[32]

The creation of the general system of fees and other financial contributions as a relative competence of the Assembly of the Republic is contained in Chapter II, Title III, Part III of the Constitution entitled "Organization of Political Power" which makes it hard to understand the legal doctrine[33] when it intends to attribute a purely programmatic content to this legislative provision.

---

[30] Soares (2004), pp. 459–496.

[31] de Andrade (2001), p. 380, note 24.

[32] See, among others, Judgment No. 276/89 of 28/2/1989 and Judgment No. 359/91 of 9/7/1991, available at http://www.tribunalconstitucional.pt/tc/acordaos/.

[33] In the sense of the attribution of a programmatic character to the relative reserve of the parliament on the general regime of financial contributions, see de Vasconcelos Fernandes (2019b), p. 127.

Regarding the fees that existed prior to the constitutional revision of 1997, the Constitutional Court, on 10 July 2001, ruled about the justice fee in the terms contained in Ruling No. 333/01.[34]

In exercising its supervisory functions, the assembly of the republic is responsible for "overseeing compliance with the Constitution and the laws and reviewing the acts of the Government and the Administration" under the terms of Article 162(1)(a) of the Constitution. The president of the republic is also responsible for "requesting the Constitutional Court to prior review of the constitutionality of rules contained in laws, decree-laws, and international conventions". However, until now, this general regime only exists for local authorities, materialized in the General Regime of Local Authority Fees (RGTAL) approved by Law No. 53-E/2006, of 29/12.

In Article 4(1) and (2) of the RGTAL, the legislature provides for the attribution of an extra tax purpose to fees, such as environmental protection through conduct guidelines, so the principle of objective bilaterality will be less restrictive and be more related to the relationship of proportionality between the purpose and the sacrifice. This requirement allowed taxpayers to challenge municipal fees where there is no financial or economic justification for the amounts levied.[35]

The economic-financial justification of municipal fees required by the general regime allows taxpayers to verify the legitimization of the rate imposed and the courts to carry out a concrete assessment of the proportionality relationship between the cost and the benefit or utility which constitutes a normative instrument for measuring proportionality in terms of adequacy.

The absence of an infra-constitutional rule requiring a concrete financial and economic justification does not allow the courts to take a more specific and objective approach to the relationship of benefit, utility and cost, or proportionality between the deviation from the principle of equivalence and the intended additional tax objective, leaving the concept of equivalence devoid of objective content.

In the Judgement of the Supreme Administrative Court, delivered on 3 December 2014 in Case No. 01273/13, the court proceeded to assess the legality of a fee related to the existence of "towers with wind turbines and other radio communication infrastructures with their respective accessories" created by the Municipality of Lousã.[36] In reading this decision, the importance of the economic and financial statement of reasons is emphasised in order for the court to analyse the structure, purpose and legality of the charge whose existence is required by the RGTAL. After classifying the contested tax as a special contribution, it decided that its creation would be subject to a reservation of law, as required by Article 103 of the CRP.

---

[34] Case No. 233/2001, Relator Counsellor Messias Bento.

[35] Judicial appeals for lack of economic and financial justification have been occurring, as can be seen, for example, in the judgments of the Supreme Administrative Court of 27/9/2017, in Case No. 479/16 and of 6/11/2019 in Case No. 01014/08.

[36] Rapporteur: Counsellor Fonseca Carvalho.

Vasques[37] defends that both legal equivalence and economic equivalence must be present to the extent that "the contraposition between legal equivalence and economic equivalence serves to distinguish two levels of analysis of commutative fees, the first respecting the notion at the level of conceptual delimitation and the second at the level of material legitimation of these fees."

The material legitimization of a tribute is essential in a tax system that is intended to be transparent, coherent, and effective because it is closely linked to its social acceptance and understanding.

The Constitutional Court[38] has considered that the principle of equivalence of rates—as not only the basis of its incidence but also the justification for its amount—does not necessarily have to be the "cost coverage" of the service provided as its specific counterpart. It may also be the so-called principle of legal equivalence that rightly refers to the "value of the utility" earned with that service by the respective beneficiary.

The authors agree with this position of the Constitutional Court when it considers the legal equivalence and not the economic equivalence as an essential assumption of the fee. However, the operability of this perspective presupposes the existence of a general regime or a framework regime which has unfortunately also been abdicated.

In fees created for extra-fiscal purposes, the equivalence ratio is not strict but is subject to corrective, functional, and deviation objectives that require specific consideration of the cost/benefit ratio that could be expressed in the economic-financial report.

The creation of taxes and levies, hybrid taxes based on extra-fiscal reasons such as the environment, without precise control based on an economic and financial justification and a previously constructed typification of the tax base, can lead to a tax system that is materially illegitimate, incoherent, obscure and, above all, burdensome for individuals.

It is a drain on resources with little room for the extra-fiscal objectives that justified its creation and which, instead of providing solutions, creates new problems.

The absence of a general framework for fees also leads to the question as to what is the specific meaning of the principle of legality of fees in constitutional law. Has it been part of the difficult task of the constitutional legislature's ponderation, in the Herculean task of creating a fundamental diploma of legislation able to ensure the

---

[37]"The contrast between legal equivalence and economic equivalence serves to distinguish two levels of analysis of commutative taxes, respecting the first notion at the level of conceptual delimitation and the second at the level of material legitimization of these taxes". Our translation of: "A contraposição entre a equivalência jurídica e equivalência económica serve para distinguir dois planos de análise dos tributos comutativos, respeitando a primeira noção ao plano da delimitação conceitual e a segunda ao plano da legitimação material destes tributos." Vasques (2008), pp. 344–348.

[38]Among many others, Judgments No. 1140/96, 288/2010, Judge Counsellor Maria Fernanda Palma and Judge Counsellor Maria João Antunes, and Judgment No. 410/2000, Judge Counsellor Tavares da Costa.

Democratic state of law for as long as possible and to face the most varied vicissitudes to provide the political system with internal mechanisms of balance, weights, and counterweights?

The absence of a general regime for fees and other financial contributions implies ab initio that any review of the substantial legality of one of these tributes is only possible through the invocation of unconstitutionality.

Regarding financial contributions, since the constitutional revision of 1997, the Constitutional Court has considered that their creation was subject to parliamentary reservation. This position was followed by the Constitutional Court until 2014, of which an example, among others,[39] is the Judgement of the TC No. 152/2013, of 20/3/2013, Rapporteur: Councillor José da Cunha Barbosa in which the court proceeded to analyse the constitutionality of the settlement of fees for the use of the radioelectric spectrum and concluded:

> Therefore, the solution is to weigh the risk of paralysis of government activity, on the one hand, with the risk of proliferation, uncontrolled by Parliament, of hybrid taxes or imperfect *synallagmatic*, on the other. From this consideration it follows that the financial contributions must be created by Parliament law, requiring that at this level some of its essential elements are already sufficiently defined (. . .).[40]

However, this jurisprudential approach was abandoned in the TC Judgement No. 80/2014 of 21 January 2014[41] in which it was understood that the creation of financial contributions belongs to the concurrent competence of the parliament and the government. This understanding was later reaffirmed in Judgement No. 539/2015, regarding the "Food Safety Levy".

[39]The ruling of the Constitutional Court No. 365/2008, of 23/10/2007, in Case No. 22/2008, reported by Councillor João Cura Mariano, regarding the Regulation and Supervision Fee due to the Regulatory Authority for the Media (ERC).

[40]"Therefore, the solution involves balancing the risk of paralyzing Government activity, on the one hand, with the risk of proliferation, uncontrolled by Parliament, of hybrid taxes or imperfect synagmaticity, on the other. From this consideration it follows that financial contributions must be created by law of the Parliament, requiring that at this level some of their essential elements are already sufficiently addressed (. . .)." Our translation of: "Assim sendo, a solução passa por ponderar o risco de paralisação da atividade do Governo, por um lado, com o risco de proliferação, não controlada pelo Parlamento, de tributos híbridos ou de sinalagmaticidade imperfeita, por outro. Dessa ponderação deflui que as contribuições financeiras devem ser criadas por lei do Parlamento, exigindo-se que a este nível estejam já suficientemente recortados alguns dos seus elementos essenciais (. . .)."

[41]Case No. 911/12, Judge Councillor João Cura Mariano.

4.2 Constitutional Court Ruling No. 80/2014 Delivered on 22 January 2014

This judgment was proffered in the context of a compulsory appeal brought by the Public Prosecutor's Office on the grounds that Article 25(1) and (2) of Decree-Law No. 233/2004 of 14 December was organically unconstitutional, as it encroached on the legislative function of the Assembly of the Republic (Article 165 of the CRP).

At issue was the decision to annul the administrative decision of the Director General of the Portuguese Environment Agency, which imposed a penalty for the excess emission of 1778 tonnes of carbon dioxide in 2006, amounting to €71,120.00, under the provisions of Article 25(1) and (2) of Decree-Law No. 233/2004 of 14 December.

It should be noted that this legal regime was established in Decree-Law No. 233/2004 of 14 December.[42] It has since been repealed by Article 36 of Decree-Law No. 38/2013 of 15 March and resulted from the transposition of Directive No. 2003/87/EC of the European Parliament and of the Council of 13 October (as modified by Directive No. 2004/101/EC).

This directive aims at "implementing a European market for greenhouse gas emission allowances that is efficient and has the least possible impact on economic development and employment" (see recital 5 of the Directive thus implementing the European Union Emissions Trading Scheme-CELE). With the creation of the CELE, the intention was to pursue both an environmental objective expressed in the prior establishment of a maximum limit on pollution that may be emitted globally and another of an economic nature achieved through the free circulation of emission licenses.

Article 16 of the directive under the heading "Penalties" provides in paragraph 3 that the Member States must ensure that any operator who does not surrender sufficient allowances by 30 April of each year to cover its emissions during the preceding year must pay an excess emissions penalty. The excess emissions penalty shall be EUR 100 for each tonne of carbon dioxide equivalent emitted by that installation for which the operator has not surrendered allowances.

Payment of the excess emissions penalty does not release the operator from the obligation to surrender several allowances equal to the excess emissions when surrendering allowances for the following calendar year.

In the appealed judgment, it was understood that these "excess emissions penalties" were considered to constitute an environmental administrative infraction and, to that extent, it was decided to disapply the rule set out in Article 25 of Decree-Law No. 233/2004. This was based on its organic unconstitutionality resulting from the invasion of the Assembly of the Republic's reserve legislative function (Article 165 of the CRP).

[42] Modified by Decree-Laws No. 243-A/2004, of 31 December, 230/2005, of 29 December, 72/2006, of 24 March, 154/2009, of 6 July, 30/2010, of 8 April, 93/2010, of 27 July, and 252/2012, of 26 November.

The Constitutional Court, in the scope of the appeal of this decision, has considered that the fixing of the penalty for excess emission does not integrate the concept of environmental administrative offense.[43] For this purpose, the Constitutional Court concluded that, in substantial terms, the legal provision of the penalty does not follow a legal punishment framework between a minimum and a maximum, its concrete measure is not based on guilt, it is not applied based on intent or negligence, and the application procedure does not fit into the framework provided in the general regime regarding the application of sanctions.

It also pointed out that the destination of the revenue resulting from the penalties referred to is far away from the general regime (see Article 33 and following Decree-Law No. 433/82 of 27 October) and is not identified with the procedure established for environmental administrative offenses in Article 45 of Law No. 50/2006 of 29 August.

The Constitutional Court, contrary to what was decided by the appealed court, considered that the legal regime admitted excess emissions, the emission of gases exceeding the limit of allowances does not constitute an illicit behaviour, and the failure to present in the following year the number of licenses equivalent to the excess emissions does not constitute an illicit act. In other words, the legal configuration of the fixed overcharge does not have the purpose of punishment but only a dissuasive purpose, concluding that the rule in question does not provide for a contravention punishable by a fine. As such, it does not integrate the relative reserve of legislative competence of the Assembly of the Republic established in Article 165(1)(d) of the Constitution.

The Constitutional Court finally concluded that the payment of the excess emissions penalty was in the nature of a financial contribution.

Dourado[44] warns that the solution found by the Constitutional Court is not legally correct since the sanctioning idea derives from the directive itself and, moreover,

---

[43] Article 1, paragraph 2 of Law No. 50/2006, of 29 August which approves the framework law on environmental administrative offences, "all illicit and censurable facts that fulfil a legal type corresponding to the violation of legal and regulatory provisions on the environment that consecrate rights or impose duties, for which a fine is imposed, constitute an environmental administrative offence." Our translation of: "constitui contraordenação ambiental todo o facto ilícito e censurável que preencha um tipo legal correspondente à violação de disposições legais e regulamentares relativas ao ambiente que consagrem direitos ou imponham deveres, para o qual se comine uma coima".

[44] Dourado (1987). In this regard, the illustrious professor also refers to the inadmissibility in a state under the Rule of Law of the absence of a general regime of financial contributions and other extra fiscal contributions not requiring the reservation of law that applies to taxes "... given the similarity they have with taxes and the fact that the Constitutional Court does not establish material criteria for quantitative control to be charged: for example through the principle of equivalence if it is understood that there is a group signalman; but this is not the case in the excess emissions, even because art. 25, no. 4 of the Decree-Law does not establish that the Environment Institute must allocate the amounts collected to the compensation of carbon dioxide emissions." Our translation of: "... dada a similitude que têm com os impostos e o facto de o Tribunal Constitucional não estabelecer critérios materiais de controlo quantitativo a cobrar: por exemplo através do princípio da equivalência, se se entender que há um sinalagma de grupo; mas não é o caso nas

emphasizes: "While in the case of the atypical sanction, it would be advisable to approve a general regime of a law of the Parliament or an authorized Decree-Law, similarly to what happens regarding the general regime of administrative offenses, in the case of an extra fiscal tax, this general regime is required by law."[45]

The authors fully agree with this understanding. While it is acknowledged that sanctioning systems are characterized by a repressive component, the true dimension of any penalty is prevention and education which is revealed in the signalling of the error about the values that should be respected. The penalization of excess emissions aims to internalize the externality produced by the defaulter and simultaneously highlight the incorrectness of its conduct in environmental and competition terms by increasing the cost attributed to it in an attempt to discourage agents from its practice.

It should be noted that the generalized practice by agents of excessive emissions without the corresponding permits would void the CELE of its practical effect.

By deciding as it did, the court removed the penalizing nature of the legally established value and the negative qualification intended for the behaviour of greenhouse gas emissions beyond the limit of allowances. In agreement with the objectives underlying the creation of the CELE expressed in Directive No. 2004/101, the acceptance of this behaviour is not conditional on the payment of a contribution; on the contrary, it is erratic and sanctioned behaviour. The borderline between the nature of environmental administrative offenses and the environmental taxation regime has thus become unclear.

The TC also examined the claimed organic unconstitutionality of Article 25 of Decree-Law No. 233/2004, the domestic legal provision that establishes a penalty for excess carbon dioxide emissions, because it violates the Assembly of the Republic's reservation of legislative powers (Article 165 of the CRP). The court then concluded that this was a financial contribution falling within the category of financial contributions set out in Article 165(1)(i) because that it primarily pursues an extra-fiscal purpose of "guiding behaviour".[46]

In the lack of a general regime for financial contributions, the court pointed out that, in previous decisions, the court's jurisprudence already accepted legislative acts of the government creating those contributions provided that they are covered by parliamentary legislation that previously defined their essential elements.[47]

However, in this case, in the absence of any prior definition by the Assembly of the Republic, the court took into account the constitutional framework of

---

emissões excedentárias, até porque o art. 25.°, n.° 4 do Decreto-Lei não estabelece que o Instituto do Ambiente deva afetar os montantes cobrados à compensação das emissões de dióxido de carbono."

[45] Our translation of: "Enquanto no caso da sansão atípica seria recomendável a aprovação de um regime geral por meio de lei da A.R. ou de Decreto-Lei autorizado, à semelhança do que acontece quanto ao regime geral das contraordenações, no caso de um tributo extrafiscal, esse regime geral é exigido por lei."

[46] On the legal nature of this financial contribution, see Pina (2006), pp. 493–502.

[47] Judgments No. 365/2008, 613/08, concerning the regulation and supervision fee (TRS) due to the Regulatory Authority for the Media (ERC) and Judgment No. 152/2013, concerning the radio spectrum usage fee.

environmental protection as a fundamental task of the state and the fact that the basic law of the environment contemplates the instrumentalization of tax rules for the pursuit of environmental objectives.

The court considered that, in the absence of a general regime for financial contributions, the environmental guidelines set out in the Constitution and the Environmental Framework Law could be understood to enable the government's legislative intervention in the matter. This would allow the creation of specific contributions to be "applied to the use of natural resources and environmental components" without a prior definition of their essential elements by the Assembly of the Republic.

Finally, the Constitutional Court stated that Article 25 of Decree-Law No. 233/2004 resulted from the transposition of Directive No. 2003/87/EC which is binding under the terms of Article 288, paragraph 3 of the TFEU and has a very precise content. Under the terms of Article 8, paragraph 4 of the CRP, the norms of the directive would always prevail over any legal norms that were contrary to it so that the national legislature had no margin of conformation.

In the absence of a general regime for financial contributions, the court considered that, in this case, the intervention of the Assembly of the Republic in the definition of the essential elements of the new contribution was not required given the virtual absence of freedom of the national legislature in that matter.

It affirmed that the government had the power to provide for the existence of the taxation provided for in Article 25(1) and (2) of Decree-Law No. 233/2004 of 14 December in the absence of a general regime for financial contributions. Such a provision did not offend the requirement of a formal law reserve imposed by Article 165 (1)(i) of the Constitution given the provision for environmental taxation created by the LBA and the binding and precise nature of Directive No. 2003/87/EC.

Despite the already expressed disagreement with the typological characterization made by the Constitutional Court in this case as a "financial contribution," the authors also disagree with the position taken regarding the principle of legality.

The environmental guidelines contained in the CRP are part of the fundamental tasks and duties of the Portuguese state. However, this Constitutional provision does not imply that the constituent legislator has foreseen or admitted that, to pursue those priorities, it is necessary to change the competencies it has attributed to the sovereign powers. On the other hand, there is no doubt that European Union Law has contributed to the shaping of the Constitutional Law of all the Member States, and the inverse is also true since the relationship established between national constitutions and EU law is one of complementarity, interpenetration, and dialogue within a framework of multilevel and plural constitutionalism. It integrates the constitutional law of the Member States, EU law, and the law of the European Convention on Human Rights in the field of fundamental rights.[48]

In this relationship with domestic law, national rules will not be applied in the concrete case when they contradict Union law. However, this primacy of EU law

[48] Martins (2017), p. 37 ss.

enshrined in Article 8(4) of the CRP does not in itself justify the non-application of a constitutional rule of attribution of competencies to sovereign bodies just because its substantial content is in accordance with EU law. [49]

In the constitutional revision of 1992, some of the constitutional changes made were precisely towards the power of the Assembly of the Republic to monitor the participation of Portugal in the EU (Article 166(f), now Article 163(f) of the CRP) as well as the obligation of the Government to present, in due time, the necessary information (cf. Article 200(i), now Article 197(i) of the CRP).[50]

The transposition of EU Directives into national legislation must comply with the constitutional requirements of the reservation of the tax law as stated by the plenary of the Constitutional Court on 5 May 2010 in Ruling No. 176/2010.

The jurisprudential understanding that was subsequently followed in this ruling that the mandatory nature of directives and the precise content of the rules to be transposed to national law could affect the constitutional rules attributing competencies to sovereign bodies is not supported by the primacy of Union law enshrined in Article 8(4) of the CRP.

The rhetoric of imperative financial need, celerity, government expediency, and extraordinary circumstances do not constitute a justification or even reasonable grounds for the disregard of material constitutional principles such as the principle of legality and the separation of powers as foundations of the democratic rule of law.

Special political requirements depend on a rigorous legislative technical performance; complacency does not generate effectiveness.

The constitutionally defined that parliamentary reserve on taxes, financial contributions, and fees cannot be ignored by jurisprudence based on the particular mobility and mutability of economic activity. It is not up to jurisprudence to modify the competencies constitutionally enshrined to accompany the mobility of economic objectives or environmental urgency.

The competence to speed up legislative procedures and to comply with constitutionally enshrined legality falls to the respective political entities through strategic and institutional relationship measures. Any deviation from a constitutional rule or principle should be constitutionally justified. The creation of a fiscal duty with extra-fiscal objectives is not an economic competence of the executive power; it is a fiscal competence that is placed at the service of a certain economic or environmental purpose.

The constitutional rules concerning the competencies of the sovereign entities constitute a complex system with the objective of constantly rebalancing the political system. They were not created to respond to a certain time or conjuncture but to ensure the desired balance in any situation until a considered revision. The destructive movement of any complex system is easier and faster than the constructive movement which is, by nature, slow and requiring pondering and planning.

[49] The principle of separation and interdependence of powers (Article 2 and Article 111 of the CRP) is a fundamental principle of the democratic rule of law, in this sense, Miranda (2007), p. 50.

[50] Constitutional Law No. 1/92, of November 25th.

This position of the TC by admitting the creation of a financial contribution by the government without the respective legislative authorization brought significant consequences at the level of the principle of formal legality required to the contributions' regime. This can be seen in the analysis of the subsequent Ruling No. 539/2015 regarding the Food Safety Tax Plus in which it decided that no legislative authorization was necessary using the position of this ruling as grounds.

4.3 *Judgment No. 539/2015, Delivered on 20 October 2015*[51]

In this ruling concerning the "Food Safety Plus" fee, the scrutiny of the organic constitutionality of Article 9 of Decree-Law No. 119/2012 of 15 June was at stake as well as of the rules of Articles 3 and 4 of Ministerial Order No. 215/2012 of 17 July. The Constitutional Court classified it as a contribution to finance the activity of guaranteeing food safety and quality. It is not intended to finance public expenditure in general but rather an expenditure associated with certain public services. Being a contribution that cannot be subsumed under the concept of tax or fee, it reverts to a public entity and falls within the category of the financial contribution referred to in Article 165(1)(i) of the Constitution.

However, about the question of whether a financial contribution may be created by a government decree without legislative authorization, the Constitutional Court has taken a crucial position contrary to what has been decided in the jurisprudence produced to date in the cases that have been subject to its appreciation basing itself on Judgment No. 80/2014.

As the Constitutional Court had already admitted the approval of individualized rates by an unauthorized legislative act of the government, the court considered that there were no reasons to take a different position regarding the creation of financial contributions. Additionally, a different solution had to exist for them, making a distinction where the constitutional text does not distinguish.

Thus, the court concluded that the absence of approval of a general regime of financial contributions by the Assembly of the Republic cannot prevent the government from approving the creation of individualized financial contributions in the exercise of a concurrent competency without prejudice to the Assembly always being able to revoke, amend, or suspend the respective diploma in the exercise of its constitutional powers.

In the opposite direction, the dissenting vote of Counsellor Judge Carlos Fernandes Cadilha:

> The inclusion in the formal law reserve of the general regime of financial contributions seems to have been intended to ensure standardization of criteria about how the financial needs of public entities should be ensured and to preserve the coherence and fairness of the

[51] Case No. 27/15, Judge Councillor João Cura Mariano and Carlos Fernandes Cadilha with dissenting vote.

> tax system, also taking into account the principles of legal certainty and fair distribution of public expenses. It was not the purpose of the legislator to unconditionally allow the Government to create public financial contributions while a situation of legislative omission regarding the definition of the general regime continues. . .[52]

He also points out that, in the field of financial contributions, a new area based on a more complex framework of economic benefits and social relations is being dealt with for which there is no consistent legislative tradition in which the parliamentary definition of the structuring principles and essential elements of tax is essential.

Councillor Judge Joaquim de Sousa Ribeiro also voted in dissent. The authors highlight his considerations regarding the constitutionally conferred competencies and the alleged blocking effects of the governmental action that are much used as an argument for the deviation from the constitutional dictum of the creation of a general framework regime for fees and other financial contributions.

This cannot be so, because what is unitarily at stake, in both segments of the constitutional rule, is the enabling projection of prior parliamentary control over the concrete acts of taxation. What changes is only the form of implementation and intensity, not the tutelary objective.

Therefore, to claim that the persistence of the legislative omission in editing the general regime allows the free and unconditioned creation of financial contributions by means of a governmental diploma entirely subverts the guaranteeing reach that the reserve inescapably possesses.

> I am not unaware that attributing an inhibitory effect to the inertia of the legislative assembly in enacting the general regime for these taxes may, in certain regulatory areas, cause serious difficulties for a modern and effective administrative apparatus. But on the one hand, this should serve as an additional incentive to legislative action according to the legal reservation, and on the other hand, pragmatic reasons should not override clear constitutional determinations. . .[53]

---

[52]Our translation of: "A inclusão na reserva de lei formal do regime geral das contribuições financeiras parece ter tido em vista garantir uma uniformização de critérios relativamente ao modo como deverão ser asseguradas as necessidades financeiras das entidades públicas e preservar a coerência e justiça do sistema tributário, tendo também em linha de conta os princípios da segurança jurídica e da justa repartição dos encargos públicos. Não terá sido propósito do legislador constituinte facultar incondicionalmente ao Governo a criação de contribuições financeiras públicas enquanto se mantenha uma situação de omissão legislativa em matéria de definição do regime geral. . ."

[53]Our translation of: "Não pode ser assim, pois o que está unitariamente em causa, em ambos os segmentos da norma constitucional, é a projeção habilitante de um prévio controlo parlamentar sobre os atos concretos de tributação. O que muda é apenas a forma de realização e a intensidade, não o objetivo tutelador.

Deste modo, pretender que a persistência da omissão legislativa em editar o regime geral faculta a criação livre e incondicionada de contribuições financeiras, por meio de diploma governamental, subverte inteiramente o alcance garantístico que a reserva iniludivelmente possui.

Não ignoro que atribuir efeito inibitório à inércia da assembleia legislativa em promulgar o regime geral destes tributos pode, em certos domínios regulatórios, causar sérias dificuldades a um aparelho administrativo moderno e eficaz. Mas, por um lado, isso deve valer como um incentivo suplementar à atuação legislativa, em conformidade com a reserva, não podendo exclusivas razões pragmáticas sobrepor-se a claras determinações constitucionais."

From this ruling, for the constitutional jurisprudence, the creation of financial contributions has been inserted in the competitive competence of the government and the parliament without any increased requirement of predictability and legal reinforcing value of the act of its forecast.

It should be noted that this is a contribution for the purpose of protecting animal health and ensuring the safety of food products of animal and plant origin.[54] However, the tax base is based on the area of the establishment on an *ad valorem* basis that is not very adequate for achieving the objective of creating this contribution if it is considered that the annual quantity of supplies of products of vegetable and animal origin obtained by the commercial establishment is recorded in the accounts and is easily verifiable in the event of a tax inspection.

The greater or lesser effectiveness of the tax base calculated directly or indirectly for the pursuit of the purpose, expresses the work of the tax legislature and must be judicially syndicated to the extent that it diverges from the principle of legal equivalence, and it is possible to assess the existence of other equally effective but more equitable tax bases.[55]

The Court of Justice in its ruling *Commission v Belgium* of 20 March 1984, Case No. 314/82, on health inspection services, considered that such control services, rather than benefiting the importer/exporter, benefit the community in general.

However, in the *Bauhuis* judgment of 25 January 1977, Case No. 46/76, concerning sanitary inspection fees on poultry meat, confronted with inspection fees related to supervision imposed by the European Union itself, the Court of Justice finally admitted to their legality in light of Article 25 of the Community Treaty but with the condition that the taxes were limited to the actual cost of the services on which they were based.

In the *Ford España* judgment of 11 July 1989, Case No. 170/88, the court ruled out the possibility of using an *ad valorem* taxable amount based on the value of the goods.

In the *Bakker Hilligom* judgment of 2 May 1990, Case No. C-111/89, the court demanded that, in view of the alleged impracticability of establishing the real cost of the service, the cost must be calculated in advance and must correspond to an average cost of the service, for example, on the basis of an average hourly cost.

In its judgments, the Court of Justice has been particularly strict with regard to the principle of equivalence regarding the objective bilateral nature of financial contributions.

In the case law cited above, the Court of Justice entrusts the national courts with the task of verifying that there is an economic correspondence between the service and the tax, but the national absence of a general regime imposing an economic and financial justification for the contribution precludes such an objective verification. That task can be exercised by national courts only by means of a financial economic report that must be required by law.

[54] The preamble of Decree-Law No. 119/2012 of 15 June.

[55] Nabais (2004), p. 622.

Considering the importance of the information and justification of environmental measures, regard should be had to Article 2(c) to (e) of Directive No. 2003/4/EC of the European Parliament and of the Council of 28 January 2003. The path taken by national constitutional jurisprudence in these two rulings is not understandable in view of the constitutional law in force and constitutes a step backward from the principle of tax legality. The requirement of a general framework law or a Parliamentary legislative authorization for the creation of a rate becomes even more pressing in the establishment of financial contribution in view of the diffuse and presumptive nature of the respective bilateral relations that are the basis for them. They are taxes of a hybrid nature as they are based on complex and diffuse relations of a presumptive nature for which its imperfect reciprocal nature should be particularly justified and understood.

The risk of this jurisprudential sense by allowing the creation of financial contributions with no previous general legislative framework and without parliamentary reservation as to their essential elements increases exponentially if allied in the future to conceptual confusions between financial contributions and special contributions.

4.4 *Judgment No. 7/2019 Delivered on 8 January 2019*[56]

In this judgment, the TC was called to assess the constitutionality of the Extraordinary Contribution to the Energy Sector (CESE) instituted during the period of the financial rescue of the Portuguese State by Article 228 of Law No. 83-C/2013 of 31 December (State Budget Law for 2014).

This measure was justified as a corrective tax mechanism to reduce the tariff debt of the national electricity system (SEN) and as a mechanism to promote the systemic sustainability of this sector through the financing of social and environmental policies and the adoption of measures related to energy efficiency. Nevertheless, the extraordinary nature attributed to it by the legislature has been subject to annual extensions. Its prediction has remained in the state budgets up to the present.

The court began by stating that the classification of the contribution results from its specific legal regime that is legally defined, the *nomen juris* attributed by the legislature, or the express classification of the measure being irrelevant.[57]

Qualified it as a financial contribution proper to the economic model of a regulatory state aimed at financing energy sector policies of a social and environmental nature related to energy efficiency measures and the reduction of the tariff debt stock of the SEN.

---

[56] Case No. 141/16, Judge Councillor Catarina Sarmento e Castro.

[57] Affirmation already made before; see among many regarding the analysis of the constitutionality of the "Food Safety Fee" Judgement No. 539/2015 of 20/10, available for consultation at www.dgsi.pt.

It identified a quid pro quo presumably caused and exploited by taxpayers operating in the energy sector.

Regarding the issue of proportionality between the benefit and the consideration imposed by the CESE, the Constitutional Court has understood that the assets do not appear as a manifestation of the ability to pay. Instead, it is an indicator that allows presuming the potential utility of the public benefits that operators benefit from and the presumed costs that they cause "since the assets are essential elements to the development of the activity, being sufficiently adequate to differentiate that impact".

Finally, the Constitutional Court reaffirms the understanding explained in several previous judgments based on the premise that "in tax matters, it is not the Constitutional Court's role, in principle, to control the options of the legislator or the Administration in the choices they make to establish the *quantum* of taxes, whether they are taxes, fees or special contributions".[58]

The purpose of the CESE is, naturally, to create revenue and correct the economic effects resulting from the market failure caused by the liberalization of the energy sector and energy transition, namely due to the so-called inefficiencies and extra costs associated with the production and use of resources. The legislature's intention with the CESE was to tax behaviours and practices that it considered to be the source of very high economic costs for the SEN and the National Natural Gas System (SNGN).[59]

For compensating for the additional costs generated by the energy sector, the legislature intended to socialize the negative structural externalities generated by a state-regulated price policy.

It would be publicly instituted for reasons of economic competitiveness and social solidarity and contracted with those subjects to the CESE who, in their normal activity at market price, generated an increase in the tariff debt. Although not a true environmental tax measure, the grounds for its creation were essentially the negative

---

[58] Among others, see Judgment No. 640/1995 of 15/11/1995.

[59] In the recent Judgment No. 101/2023, of 16/3/2023, the Constitutional Court decided to declare unconstitutional, for violation of article 13 of the Constitution, article 2(d) of the EESC legal regime (approved by article 228 of Law No. 83-C/2013, of 31 December, whose validity was extended to 2018 by Law No. 114/2017, of 29 December), insofar as it determines that the tax is levied on the value of the asset elements referred to in paragraph 1 of article 3 of the same regime. Article 3(1) of the same regime, owned by legal persons that are part of the national energy sector, with tax domicile or with registered office, effective management or permanent establishment in Portuguese territory, which, on 1 January 2018, are concessionaires of the activities of transmission, distribution or underground storage of natural gas.

We held that, in its initial configuration, the EESC was intended not only to help solve the problem of the SEN tariff deficit, but mainly to finance energy sector policies of a social and environmental nature, regulatory actions and measures related to energy efficiency. However, from 2018 onwards, the largest share of the revenue was intended to reduce the tariff debt of the electricity sector, without it being clear why the legislator saw fit to require operators not integrated in this subsector to participate in the resulting charges, when they did not cause them, nor to extract a special benefit. It should be noted that the mere fact that all the operators are part of the 'energy sector' is clearly not sufficient to affirm that there is group liability of the natural gas subsector for the charges relating to a problem specific to the electricity subsector.

externalities inherent in the activity carried out in the National Energy System, the sustainability of the sector and the financing of environmental policies.

This tax measure has been contested by taxpayers and by the majority of tax doctrine[60] that criticizes the jurisprudence for ignoring the fact that this tax is not based on group equivalence. This is due to the lack of homogeneity in the group of taxpayers whose tax base is based on the ability to pay revealed in the value of the taxpayer's assets without any relationship with the benefits that the taxpayers presumably may receive or have received.

Much of the doctrine[61] qualifies the CESE as a real sectoral tax given the alleged lack of bilaterality due to its national subjective incidence being extended to all energy sub-sectors such as electricity, natural gas and oil as well as the respective intermediate activities such as transport, storage, and distribution.

The qualification as a tax is also defended, considering its objective incidence that falls on tangible fixed assets, intangible assets, except industrial property and financial assets allocated to concessions or licensed activities and that, in the case of the SNGN supplier, falls on the equivalent economic value of the take-or-pay contracts and additionally on the surplus calculated for the said economic equivalent value.

Considering the vocation of the CESE for the amortization of the SEN tariff debt, a negative externality that the legislature recognizes and intends to compensate with a ability to pay specially revealed by the sector operators, the qualification as a "special contribution" made by Vasconcelos Fernandes proves to be more appropriate than the qualification made by case law. This is because it corresponds to the internalization of an extra cost or damage in the sector considered by the legislature as being attributable to the taxpayers themselves.

This author classifies the CESE in the subspecies of special contributions, i.e., "contributions for increased expenditure", that he defines as "levies imposed to tax increases in revenue, maintenance or conservation in the value of property or assets of taxpayers that are, exclusively or predominantly, attributable to public intervention.".[62]

Thus, while financial contributions are justified by the existence of benefits presumably enjoyed or caused by certain groups of taxpayers, "special contributions" are based on a special ability to pay by certain groups of taxpayers resulting from a public activity or framework. To this extent, Casalta Nabais argues that these taxes are effectively special taxes because "they have the particularity of being based on manifestations of the ability to pay off certain groups of persons resulting from the exercise of a public administrative activity and not, or not exclusively, from the exercise of an activity of the respective taxpayer as happens in taxes".[63]

---

[60] In this regard, Lobo (2019), p. 421 ss; Dourado (2019).

[61] Lobo (2019), p. 421 ss; Dourado (2019).

[62] de Vasconcelos Fernandes (2019a).

[63] Nabais (2003b). Our translation of: "apresentam a particularidade de terem por base manifestações de capacidade contributiva de determinados grupos de pessoas resultantes do

In the case of special levies, which often pursue non-tax purposes, an objective economic justification identifying the investments made or to be made, in the case of improvement levies, and the expenditure incurred, in the case of levies that increase expenditure, should be required in order to fully justify the imposition of a special tax, in particular a selective one.

Regarding the principle of legality concerning "special contributions", it is important to have in mind Article 4, No. 3 of the LGT which equates its legal regime with that of taxes.

The legislator will have taken into account that the so-called improvement contributions, or higher expenditure contributions, are indicative of a certain "ability to pay" and have a diffuse and presumed bilateral nexus, which brings them substantially closer to selective taxes.

The absence of subjective bilaterality (group) and objective bilaterality (only presumed) brings its legal regime closer to the tax and subject to the reservation of the law in its formal aspect (Article 165(1)(i) of the CRP) and to the material reservation under the terms of Article 103(2) of the CRP.

However, it constitutes a fiscal figure that is close to but distinct from the tax since it is based on an individualized and presumed benefit reflexively resulting from the action of a public entity, or on the need to compensate the public entity for the abnormal use of public goods or services by certain taxpayers which, in some way, more seriously encumber state finances or deteriorate public assets.

> It is, therefore, a general, individualizable, and abnormal situation that justifies the imposition of tax liability. The individual situation is occasional and indirect - it is not intentional and directly connected with the purposes of the state activity which gives rise to it.[64]

In Ruling No. 277/86 pronounced on 8/11/1986 by the Constitutional Court, this definition was adopted about the parking deficiency compensation charge that the court qualified as a "special contribution" subject to the tax regime, determining that its creation is a legislative competence reserve of the parliament.[65] The typical examples of these special contributions are those levied on the increase in the value of the property as a result of major public works such as the two bridges over the Tejo, the CREL, the CRIL, the CREP, the CRIP, and EXPO/98.[66]

---

exercício de uma atividade administrativa pública e não, ou não exclusivamente, do exercício de uma atividade do respetivo contribuinte como acontece nos impostos".

[64]Our translation of: "É, pois, uma situação geral, individualizável e anormal, que justifica a imposição de uma prestação tributária. A situação individual é ocasional e diretamente – não é intendiretamenteectamente conexa com os fins da actividade estadual que lhe dá origem". Nabais (2003b), pp. 27–30.

[65]Case No. 9/84, Judge Councillor Nunes de Almeida.

[66]On the case law analysis of these improvement contributions, see, among others, Constitutional Court Decision 63/2006, of 24/1/2006, in Case No. 392/2005, Reporting Judge Counsellor Maria Helena Brito, defeated vote Counsellor Judge Carlos Pamplona de Oliveira.

For the distinction between special contributions and financial contributions, Vasconcelos Fernandes[67] highlights the fact that the latter are based on specific financial needs of certain public entities in the exercise of a certain framework of functions generating potential private benefits. Regulatory contributions are an example, considering them to be close to those designated by the German doctrine of "Sonderabgaben" characterized by being based on a certain group homogeneity with a common interest or an activity generating financial needs and by this fact being attributed the responsibility for financing.

In the "special contributions", whose parallelism with the "*Breitäge*" of the German system is raised by this author, differentiated assessments of the contributory capacity obtained by non-socialised or internalised benefits are evident.

These include betterment contributions, of which special contributions for public works and contributions for higher expenditure stand out, with the aim of compensating for economic losses or damage reflexively resulting from the actions of a group of taxpayers in society at large.

Vasques[68] equates the commutative basis of these special contributions to excise duties, referring to the recognition of the Portuguese legislature in the Excise Duty Code introduced by Decree-Law No. 566/99 of 22 December and amended by Decree-Law No. 73/2010 of 21 June. Its Article 2 states that "excise duties obey the principle of equivalence, seeking to burden taxpayers to the extent of the costs they cause in the areas of environment and public health, in the realization of a general rule of fiscal equality".

This author highlights the tax on petroleum and energy products and Directive No. 2003/96 in which European legislators extend this taxation to other products, linking energy taxation to climate change as well as Directive No. 2003/30 with a provision for tax incentives/benefits for biofuels.

> Current excise duties have commutative - strictly speaking, para-commutative - contours that increasingly attempt to establish an exchange between the State and certain groups of people who presumed to cause certain costs.[69,70]

[67] de Vasconcelos Fernandes (2020), pp. 74–77 e 92–93.

[68] Vasques (2018), p. 268.

[69] Although Article 104 of the Portuguese Constitution states that consumption taxation aims to assess a certain taxable income "luxury consumption", this will certainly not be the present and future objective of consumption taxation considering Article 113 of the TFEU of which Council Directive No. 2008/118/EC of 16/12/2008 is an expression.

[70] Despite the reference to extra-fiscal purposes, for Dourado (2020): "...excise duties are taxes in the strict sense, as they are allocated to the State budget and are not consigned to environmental or health purposes. In other words, there is always a tax purpose - that is the collection of revenue - even if such purpose is secondary and the predominating objectives are those of behavioral orientation (decrease in the consumption of such products, either because they are harmful to the environment or health)". Our translation.

> These excise duties are also sometimes classified as "relevant environmental taxes" since they do not have ecological protection as their principal objective, but whose tax base translates into a polluting reality.[71]

In the case of "special contributions", there is no subjective bilateralism, since they presuppose the existence of a consideration that translates into advantages that cannot be determined for each taxpayer (as in the case of taxes).

They are only determinable and objectively quantifiable from the perspective of a closed group of taxpayers who are presumed to benefit from the corresponding administrative activity or expense.

In reality, they are "special taxes" that follow the tax system as regards the application of the principle of fiscal legality. They are distinguished from other taxes by the fact that the relevant manifestation of the ability to pay is that of a specific group of persons to whom the public utility causes a positive manifestation of the ability to pay, in the case of improvement contributions. Alternatively, the public utility prevents the appearance of negative manifestations of that capacity, in the case of contributions to increase expenditure.

Tavares da Silva[72] identifies them as "special equal or fairness contributions" that, in his view, essentially aim to "rebalance the accounts between should and should have" between taxpayers and the state when they have benefited specially or abnormally from state interventions in the creation of infrastructures, services, planning, or protectionism.

As Vasques says,[73] the negative scope of the equivalence principle is to disallow the creation of contributions when no costs or benefits exist to be compensated.

4.5 The Constitutional Court Ruling No. 70/2004 of 28/1/2004 on the Fixation of the Rates of Tax on Oil Products (ISP)

The development of the legal framework of this tax has been subject to jurisprudence concerning compliance with the principle of legality regarding some of its provisions. The ruling of the Plenary of the Constitutional Court No. 70/2004 of 28/1/2004[74] for which a request for appraisal was raised by the Ombudsman using the powers conferred to him by Article 282(2) of the CRP stands out.

In this ruling, the Constitutional Court decided not to declare the unconstitutionality of the provisions of Nos. 1, 2, 3, and 4 of Article 32 of Law 32-B/2002 of 30 December (state budget for 2003) based on an alleged violation of the principle of legality enshrined in Article 103(2) and Article 165(1)(i) of the constitution.

---

[71] Vasques (2018).

[72] da Silva (2013), p. 86.

[73] Vasques (2008), p. 46.

[74] Case No. 57/03, Rapporteur, Councillor Judge Benjamim Rodrigues.

The alleged unconstitutionality lies in the violation of the principle of legality with regard to the referral to the ministers of finance and economy and to the regional governments, in the case of the autonomous regions of the Azores and Madeira, of the competence to set the unit rates of tax on petroleum products.

Within the ranges provided for in Article 32(2) and (3), the rate may vary from EUR 18.00 to EUR 149.64 or at least a zero rate, which may mean exemption from the tax by administrative means.

In practice, given the normal variations in the prices of petroleum products, such a broad scope of the remissive rule means that the Assembly of the Republic is relieved of the power to fix the rate of tax whereas it is for the legislature to determine the rate of tax as its essential component.

The Constitutional Court has decided that this compression of the principle of tax legality is justified by the need to adapt to the instability of economic life and to make the system more flexible. It has indicated that the parliamentary legislature, by defining the quantification of the tax translated into a rate only by indicating its minimum and maximum limits, does not fail to act in the exercise of taxing power in the political representation of the taxpaying citizens, expressing it in a tax consent that translates into the possibility of determining the rate between a minimum and a maximum level.

As mentioned by Judge Councillor Paulo Mota Pinto in his dissenting vote:[75]

> Such excessive amplitude of the range of the space for fixing the rate, left to free regulatory intervention - between margins that could easily reach 100% variation (...). On the other hand, it seems clear to me that in this matter, where a truly structural principle and rules of competence are at stake - and on an issue which, as we know, is in fact at the origin of "Parliament - there is no room to invoke, in support of the constitutional conformity of the setting of the tax rate by regulatory means, any "applicability of the general principles of necessity, appropriateness and proportionality" of laws restricting fundamental rights (...).

In the same vein of manifest unconstitutionality, the dissenting vote of Judge Mário José de Araújo Torres, who considered that the fact that the Constitutional Court had not recognised the unconstitutionality of this solution represented a manifestation of excessive complacency that completely distorts the meaning of the parliamentary reserve of law on the setting of tax rates, as an instrument for defining tax policy.

The argument that the legislative option is inevitable and feasible is distorted in view of the feasibility of the tax rate-setting system provided for in Decree-Law No. 261-A/91 of 25 July 1991, in which the formula for calculating the rate was directly determined by law, as well as comparative law with Spain, where the rate of

[75] Our translation of: "...Tal excessiva amplitude do intervalo do espaço de fixação da taxa, deixado à livre intervenção regulamentar – entre margens que poderão facilmente chegar a 100% de variação (...). Por outro lado, parece-me evidente que, nesta matéria, em que estão em causa um princípio e normas de competência verdadeiramente estruturantes – e num tema que, como se sabe, está, aliás, na origem do parlamentarismo –, não cabe de todo invocar, a favor da conformidade constitucional da fixação da taxa do imposto por regulamento, qualquer "aplicabilidade dos princípios gerais de necessidade, de adequação e de proporcionalidade" das leis restritivas dos direitos fundamentais. (...)"

the 'Impuesto sobre Hidrocarburos' provides for a fixed amount for each type of fuel concerned directly determined by law (Article 50 of Law No. 38/1992 of 28 December 1992).

In addition to the violation of the legal reserve in the setting of the tax rate, an essential element, the final price of the products to which the ISP applies, has a direct impact on domestic economic activity and affects taxpayers in general. Thus, both from the point of view of the formal and material reservation of law, the parliamentary waiver of responsibility for fixing the tax rate or its calculation formula is incompatible with the constitutional principle of tax legality.

With regard to the principle of typicality, relating to the subjective incidence of the tax, we highlight Judgement No. 176/2010,[76] delivered by the Plenary of the Constitutional Court on 5/5/2010.

This decision analysed the alleged unconstitutionality of Article 3(2)(e) of the Excise Duty Code and Article 7 of Ordinance No. 234/97 of 4 April, on the grounds of violation of Article 103(2) and Article 165(1)(i) CRP.

The court considered that the CIEC[77] approved by Decree-Law No. 566/99 was issued under the legislative authorization granted by Article 35 of Law No. 87-B/98 of 31 December. It only stated that the government was authorized to codify in a single act the excise duty regime on alcohol and alcoholic beverages, on petroleum products. and on manufactured tobacco.

This was then provided for in separate acts in order to harmonize the various regimes with each other with the general tax law and with European directives without altering the rules of assessment and the rates.

Until then, the subjective incidence of the ISP[78] was set out in Article 6 of Decree-Law No. 123/94 of 18/5 which established as taxable persons "the natural or legal persons in whose name the products ... are declared for release for consumption" and "in cases of detention or irregular release for consumption, (...) the natural or legal persons who hold, use or have benefited from the consumption of the products".

In Article 3(2)(e) of the CIEC, the government established as taxable persons of the IEC, among others, "natural or legal persons who, in an irregular situation, produce, hold, transport, release for consumption, sell or use products subject to excise duty".

The court concluded that the legislative authorization that the legislative assembly granted to the government did not contain any reference to the possibility of modifying and/or extending the range of taxable persons of the said special taxes and, specifically, the tax on petroleum products. As a consequence, it ruled that the rule in paragraph 7 of Ministerial Order No. 234/97 of 4 April and the rule in Article 3(2)(e) of the Excise Duty Code were organically unconstitutional for breach of Articles 103(2) and 165(1)(i) of the Constitution.

---

[76] Case No. 400/09, Reporting Judge Counsellor Joaquim de Sousa Ribeiro.

[77] Code of Excise Duties.

[78] Nabais (2019).

It should be noted that, in this ruling concerning the obligation to transpose EU Directives, the Constitutional Court stressed that, even if the rule of Article 3(2)(e) of the Income Tax Code resulted from the obligation to transpose EU Directives, such a transposition would have to comply with the constitutional requirements of tax law reservation. Subsequently, in the Constitutional Court ruling No. 80/2014 concerning the penalties for excess emissions, the court ruled in the opposite direction.

In Judgment No. 358/92 pronounced by the Constitutional Court on 11 November 1992,[79] the unconstitutionality decision was based on the understanding that the normative program of the mentioned rule of parliamentary was not sufficiently complete since it did not contain a guiding criterion for the use of delegated powers.

In the grounds of that judgment, the court recalled the parliament's historical role in the democratic rule of law, in particular its political function in the definition of taxes deriving from its representativeness which presupposes its legitimacy to set limits on the executive power in terms of sacrificing citizens' property.

The Court emphasised the seriousness of rendering Parliament's enabling function meaningless by allowing the existence of "blank authorisations".

About the fact that the norm under analysis is included in the state budget which could induce parliamentary legitimization given its systematic insertion in a diploma that was subject to parliamentary approval, the court was clear in stating that the alteration introduced by the constitutional legislature in the 1989 constitutional review in Article 168(5) of the Constitution:

> (...) legitimizes constitutionally, legislative authorizations on tax matters and even the 'extravagant authorizations' (on non-tax matters), in the case of authorizations on tax matters - (except only the regime on the caducity date) - authorizations that are part of the Budget Law are subject to the rules and limits of Article 168 of our Fundamental Law, and cannot, therefore, proceed today, a less rigorous and demanding view that would be based on the argument of systematic order of the insertion of such authorizations in the Budget Law itself.[80]

In these decisions, the application of the principle of legality in its formal and material aspects is at stake. Formal because the reservation of law was called into question by a vague legislative authorization, and material because of the infringement of the principle of typicality by the failure to define the essential elements of the tax.

The principle of legality requires that the prevision of taxable events be made in sufficient detail[81] so that taxpayers can have some certainty as to the extent of their wealth or income that will be affected by taxation or that the law "takes the discipline

---

[79] Case No. 120/92, of 11/11/1992, Reporting Judge Counsellor António Vitorino.

[80] In the same sense, the ruling of the Constitutional Court No. 606/95 of 8/11, in Case No. 258/94, Reporting Judge Counsellor Guilherme da Fonseca

[81] Cfr. Cardoso da Costa (1972), p. 309.

of those essential elements, that is, the essential discipline of each tax, as far as it is possible to go.[82]

Among the principles of the rule of law and the legal security inherent to it is the principle of typification and determinability according to which, when designing the type of tax, the legislature has to ensure the predictability of the legal effects of any act that amputates the wealth or income of taxpayers.

It should be noted that this principle of the reservation of substantive law does not exclude a margin of free appraisal in the application of the law. The use of indeterminate legal concepts is only unacceptable if it confers on the tax authorities an arbitrary power to define the essential elements of the tax.

There is a "margin of free typification"[83] resulting from the principle of practicability, efficiency, and fairness as it enables the monitoring of spatial, temporal changes of reality itself that is naturally endowed with unlimited creativity. However, it is only admitted when the essential elements of the tax are legally established, namely the objective and subjective incidence, the rate, the tax benefits, and the taxpayers' guarantees under Article 103(2) of the CRP.

The principle of substantive tax legality also does not allow the integration of gaps by analogy in tax incidence rules as provided by the legislature in Article 11(4) of the LGT.

As decided in the judgment rendered by the South Central Administrative Court on 26 January 2017,[84] the legality of including wind turbines as part of a wind farm in the concept of the edifice in Article 2 of the Municipal Property Tax Code (CIMI) in order to be taxed as an edifice was denied. This decision was subsequently confirmed in the judgment rendered by the Supreme Administrative Court on 15 March 2017[85] which considered the definition of the edifice in Article 2 of the CIMI to reaffirm the principle of material tax legality, namely with regard to the tax incidence element.[86]

As for the scope of taxes, the principle of ability to pay is taken from Articles 103 and 104 of the Constitution and Article 4(1) of the LGT. It is firmly established

[82]Nabais (2003b), p. 138.

[83]Dourado (2020), p. 158.

[84]In Case No. 516/15, Rapporteur: Judge Councillor Joaquim Condesso.

[85]Case No. 0140/15, Rapporteur: Judge Councillor Dulce Neto.

[86]Subsequently, in a path that dissented from the use of taxation as an environmental instrument, namely regarding the incentive to the production of renewable energy, Law No. 7-A/2016, of 30 March, introduced amendments to the CIMI, specifically in Article 38 in which the general rule for determining the taxable asset value of urban properties is established as "the additional land cost method" provided in Article 46(2) of the CIMI. Ministerial Order No. 11/2017, of 9 January, defined the typology of urban buildings to which the method provided in Article 46(2) of the CIMI would be applicable in which wind energy-producing centers and wind farms are included. This is a rare revenue tax measure that may lead to double taxation since there is already a municipal tax levied on income from the operation of wind farms that generates double, unequal, and disproportionate taxation in breach of the constitutional provisions contained in Articles 103(2) and 104(3) of the Portuguese Constitution.

in jurisprudence and doctrine[87] as a hallmark of fiscal justice and as a criterion that expresses and concretizes the principle of tax equality in its aspect of uniformity.

The tax aims to tax the economic capacity or ability to pay and is therefore based on ad valorem incidence criteria, namely on income, assets, or other manifestations of that ability to pay. This is not very appropriate for the underlying objectives of the eco-tax in which the obtaining of revenue tends to be combined with the modulating of ecological behaviours of individuals and groups, penalizing anti-environmental behaviour or favouring green behaviour.

The legislature takes into account environmental circumstances such as pollutant emissions, the discharge of effluents or the exploitation of natural resources, or the harmfulness of a product for the environment in the selection of the taxable event. It applies the polluter-pays principle as a criterion for justice in the distribution of the sacrifice and not the ability-to-pay principle which is the central criterion for equality in taxation.

The closer the link between the tax base and the taxpayer's participation in the event giving rise to pollution, the fairer and more effective the tax will be. It is the purpose for which the tax is created and not its chargeable event that allows it to be classified as environmental.[88] However, there is no unanimous definition of "environmental tax".

In environmental taxation, two types of environmental taxes are systematized, i.e., those that pursue an extra-fiscal purpose of encouraging behaviour (*reine Lenkungssteuern*) and those that have a revenue or redistributive purpose (*reine Umweltfinanzierungsabgaben*).

Classified among us by Dias Soares,[89] the first in environmental taxes in the proper sense, inserted in a line of prevention of environmental damage and the second in environmental taxes in the improper meaning, aimed at the recovery of (ecological balance).

Since if the main objective is to raise revenue, they will be as environmental as any other tax that allows collecting financial means allocated to the purpose in question.[90]

Both can allow the internalization of externalities and have an incentive or disincentive effect, although to a different degree, while collecting funds to be

---

[87] Constitutional Court Ruling No. 84/2003 of 12 February; Nabais (2004), p. 445 ss.

[88] Soares (2002).

[89] Soares (2002), p. 14; "Taxes with a general revenue-raising purpose, i.e., which are intended to raise revenue for the State to apply indiscriminately to the performance of any of its functions, even if they are levied on unsustainable goods or behaviour, cannot be called environmental. Their presentation as such can only be aimed at seeking political support for their collection by deceiving the citizen." Our translation of: "Impostos com um intuito recaudatório de âmbito geral, isto é que se destinam a obter receitas para o Estado aplicar, indiferenciadamente, na realização de qualquer uma das suas funções, ainda que incidam sobre bens ou comportamentos insustentáveis, não podem ser denominados de ambientais. A sua apresentação como tal só pode ter como objetivo a busca de um apoio político para a sua cobrança através do engano do cidadão."

[90] Azevedo (2010), pp. 85–128.

applied to public environmental expenditures or the redistribution of costs associated with the defense of ecological balance and sustainability.[91]

However, environmental taxes in the strict sense created with the purpose of modelling the behaviour of taxpayers will tend to be more effective when they produce lower revenue since the decrease in revenue indicates that their purpose is being fulfilled.[92]

The double dividend theory argues that the application of eco-taxes is not only fundamental to reveal and eliminate environmentally harmful behaviours. It can also help to remove the economic inefficiencies generated and finance research and development projects in the area of environmental protection or even help to reduce other classic taxes. However, an eco-efficient tax tends to reduce the revenue generated in the medium term.[93,94] It tends to be so because alternatives to polluting behaviours do not always exist or, when they do, they are sometimes limited or inflated, especially in investment costs. Any production or consumption activity has an inherent degree of environmental impact so the growing demand for environmental impact reduction and sustainability has led to a gradual growth of these revenue-generating taxes.[95]

The legitimacy of taxes with extra-fiscal purposes, namely improper environmental or relevant environmental taxes, resides precisely in the destination of their revenue for those same purposes.

The application of the polluter-pays principle is not sufficient even in commutative or para-commutative environmental taxes since, despite the payment of the tax, the environmental damage continues to exist. Therefore, the effective allocation of revenue to its correction and prevention is necessary.[96]

[91] Nabais (2004), pp. 266, 267.

[92] An example of a tax with this effect is found in Article 30 of Law No. 82-D/2014 of 31/12, the contribution on lightweight plastic bags by the definition of packaging in Directive No. 94/62/EC of the European Parliament and of the Council of 20 December.

[93] A good example of a tax that shapes behaviour and, at the same time, provides a source of revenue for environmental protection is the carbon tax that has been in place since 1992 in Denmark. It is levied indiscriminately on the state and on companies based on the amount of fuel and electricity consumed, and the tax revenue has been used to subsidize industries to adapt to green technologies and renewable energies; see Martinzes (2015).

[94] Without excluding the threat of regressivity given the fact that eco-taxes are predominantly indirect taxes.

[95] The transversal nature of law requires the application of methodologies outside law for its improvement, with economic-behavioural analysis being an added value in the behavioural reflexes of a certain normative for the design and implementation of policies. In this sense, Saraiva (2011a), pp. 105–118.

[96] About the functions attributed to municipal funds for environmental sustainability by the Basic Law of Territorial Land Policy and Urbanism (Law No. 31/2014, of 30 May - LBPSOTU) See Gomes et al. (2017), pp. 117–143.

Alongside the doctrine,[97] there are numerous examples of jurisprudence[98] that consider the revenue earmarking[99] factor essential for the qualification and assessment of the legality of taxes with extra-fiscal motives.

Many environmental funds have been created benefiting from numerous and diverse tax incomes that are legally directed to areas of ecological relevance such as water, carbon, forests, and biodiversity. However, the activities carried out by these environmental funds are unknown, their work is not known, and the evidence of their positive work is not demonstrated.

An example of the possible passivity and/or opacity of the environmental funds to which most of the taxes instituted with environmental justifications are consigned is demonstrated in Report No. 3/17 - 2nd section, Audit Process No. 26/2015 - AUDIT, prepared by the Court of Auditors on 26/1/2017. The objective was to analyse the activity carried out by the Permanent Forest Fund, the Conservation and Biodiversity Fund, and the Baixo Sabor Hydroelectric Exploitation Fund.[100]

Dourado,[101] in systematizing the contributions with pure extra-fiscal purposes, which are of particular interest because they include the contributions aimed at environmental protection and qualification, states that regarding this category in systematizing the contributions with pure extra-fiscal purposes, "... only we are not facing taxes (unilateral revenue to cover overheads) as long as the amounts collected are allocated to compensating the damage caused by the rigidity of the behaviours that it is intended to guide".

In the case of bilateral taxes based on the principle of equivalence, earmarking constitutes a form of efficiency in the realization of the principle of benefit since they are taxes intended to compensate for certain costs and benefits. Their predetermined allocation constitutes their very foundation; however, this earmarking has to be accompanied by mechanisms to control efficiency and effectiveness, coordination, and planning.

The earmarking of environmental tax revenue in an improper sense does not always guarantee the reinforcement of the means allocated to the respective expense or purpose since it will often only allow the release of sums from the budget's common fund that were previously aimed at it as well as being an excuse to justify an increase in the tax burden.

---

[97] Dourado (2020), pp. 48, 49–79; Vasques (2008), pp. 620–647.

[98] Constitutional Court rulings No. 539/2015 of 20/10, No. 7/2019 of 8/1; No. 452/87 of 9/12/1987.

[99] The principle of non-consignment of tax revenue is contained in the State Budget Framework Law, currently, Law No. 151/2015 of 11 September which, in its Article 16, establishes the principle of non-consignment in relative terms with different exceptions.

[100] Available for consultation at https://www.tcontas.pt/pt-pt/ProdutosTC/Relatorios/RelatoriosAuditoria/Documents/2017/rel003-2017-2s.pdf.

[101] Our translation of: "...só não estamos perante impostos (receitas unilaterais para cobrir despesas gerais) desde que os montantes cobrados sejam afetos à compensação dos prejuízos causados pela rigidez dos comportamentos que se pretende orientar." Dourado (2020).

Moreover, consignment may perpetuate services and organisms that no longer have a *raison d'être*, and their continuation constitutes an unjustified and unnecessary expense resulting from consignment.

The creation of successive organisms with environmental competencies to which revenues are consigned without the control of their concrete application has implied an increase of bureaucracy and technocracy, essentially an increase of public expenditure without any environmental compensations. In other words, the consignment of revenue to autonomous funds itself does not guarantee the legal allocation of resources to the environmental objectives on which an eco-tax is based.

The positive and practical results of the existing environmental funds to which the revenues from various environmentally based taxes are consigned remain to be demonstrated. Without questioning their potential, little or nothing is known about the activity developed due to the opacity in the disclosure of the respective activities and objectives programmed and achieved. This goes against one of the main objectives of earmarking which is to inform citizens about how the resources from taxes consigned to eco-objectives are used. It makes the system more transparent and attractive to the civil community as it encourages their involvement in the pursuit of the common goal of environmental preservation.

As environmental patrimony preservation is a community interest, its rational and democratic management is inherent to its collective nature. It is not possible to conceive democracy without information and communication or to desire an eco-citizenship without knowledge. The participation of local authorities, private entities, environmental associations, researchers, and universities, through proposals, information sharing, and encouragement, can make the activity of the Portuguese environmental institutes, agencies, and funds to which a large part of the tax revenue is consigned more efficient and transparent.

On the other hand, environmental protection is doomed to failure if it is only a state task. The creation and improvement of a fiscal policy with ecological, dissuasive, or corrective objectives requires a debate, contributions of a technical nature, and decision-making instructions that are outside the scope of political and fiscal science. This can only be achieved with participation, observation, and adherence of civil society and its nuclei of knowledge.

5 Conclusions

The creation of a tax for environmental purposes should be preceded by the definition of concrete objectives—national aspirations for which planning for its implementation is based on scientific knowledge of the local reality with an effective allocation of revenues so that part of these revenues can be efficiently returned to economic investment.

Interventions by the environmental tax legislature must be rational, coordinated, and consistent with the existing tax system which requires consideration of their long-term consequences, otherwise, they will exacerbate problems rather than solve them.

After the initial assessment of the environmental tax, its implementation should be monitored and controlled in order to check its rational suitability for the objectives pursued.[102]

The use of tax law for environmental protection can also be made by modifying existing taxes based on ecological premises to include the objective of environmental protection alongside considerations of promoting development and solidarity. This can be accomplished through the reorientation of the tax system; establishing promotion mechanisms based on the creation of benefits, credits, and deductions for behaviour more ecological; and penalizing through tax increases for inertia behaviour and resistance to environmental change.[103]

It is called the method of greening tax law materialized in environmental tax policy measures, introduced in terms of corporate income tax, personal income tax, and VAT. Although they are not environmental taxes, they may prove to be more effective instruments to model and encourage behaviour with a lower potential risk of bringing unexpected and adverse effects. They may also not generate as much complexity in the tax system as happens with the proliferation of new taxes.[104]

The new demands of modern states require new interpretations, concepts, and paradigms from law, but social evolution cannot be achieved by destroying its founding values, principles, and rights.

The tax constitution has provided the political system with internal mechanisms of checks and balances, that must be respected for the legality, coherence, and understanding of the tax system.

The principle of fiscal equality in the jurisprudential interpretation of taxes with extra-fiscal purposes should not be reduced to the prohibition of arbitrariness. Although these taxes are most often selective and differentiating, this selection or differentiation must be based on objectively identified criteria, even if external to the tax law such as the polluter pays principle, of prevention or correction at the source.[105]

The control of the adequacy of tax measures to pursue extra-tax purposes cannot be minimized, based on legislative freedom and the financial imperative, and limited to the prohibition of excess. The principle of economy or efficiency should be present according to which state measures should produce the best results at the

[102] On the question of whether and how the legal process of monitoring the outcome of corrective taxes can and should be improved, see Hey (2020), pp. 360–368.

[103] In this sense, Soares (2004), pp. 459–496.

[104] Law No. 82-D/2014 of 31/12, called the Green Taxation Reform, provides several examples of tax measures with environmental purposes introduced in taxes on income and wealth; see Article 40 of the CIRC, article 88 of the CIRC, in VAT, article 21(2)(f), (g) and (h) of the CIVA, in the IMI benefited buildings with greater energy efficiency.

[105] On the relation between efficiency and the incidence base of the ecological tax, see Soares (2002), pp. 22–31.

lowest cost and with the least aggressiveness vis-à-vis the fundamental rights, freedoms, and guarantees of taxpayers.

The requirement for a solid and clear economic and financial justification in this type of tax measure is essential for the control of its proportionality and adequacy.

The Constitutional Court has reaffirmed that the prohibition of restrictions on fundamental rights, freedoms and guarantees with retroactive effect, provided for in Article 18(3) of the Constitution, does not apply to taxes, since they constitute immanent limits and are not restrictions on the right to property.[106]

However, there are constitutional limits to legislative freedom in tax matters when it pursues extra-fiscal objectives other than those derived directly from Articles 103 and 104 of the constitution. The tax, as a fiscal objective in itself, represents a burden, a duty for citizens like the other fundamental duties, and an inherent limit to the right to property. However, when the imposition of this sacrifice or burden is justified to safeguard other fundamental rights or to pursue specific tasks of an extra-fiscal nature of the state, it cannot be inappropriate, inefficient, and disproportionate to the pursuit of the extra-fiscal interest or the objective it aims to pursue because, in that case, it becomes a prohibited restriction under the provisions of Article 18(2) of the CRP.

References

Azevedo ME (2010) A fiscalidade Ambiental (Reflexões), Ciência e Técnica Fiscal, No. 426

Canotilho JJG (1995) Proteção do ambiente e direito de propriedade (crítica de jurisprudência ambiental), Separata da Revista de Legislação e Jurisprudência No. 3850 e 385, Coimbra Editora, in annotation to the Judgment of the Supreme Court of 17/1/1995

Canotilho JJG (2004) O Direito ao Ambiente como Direito Subjectivo, Estudos sobre Direitos Fundamentais, Coimbra Editora

Cardoso da Costa JM (1972) Curso de Direito Fiscal, 2nd edn. Coimbra

da Silva ST (2013) As Taxas e a Coerência do Sistema Tributário, CEJUR, 2nd edn

de Andrade JCV (2001) Os Direitos Fundamentais na Constituição Portuguesa de 1976, 2nd edn. Almedina

de Oliveira Ascensão J (2008) O Direito – Introdução e Teoria Geral, 13rd edn. Refundada, Almedina

de Vasconcelos Fernandes F (2019a) A Contribuição Extraordinária Sobre o Setor Energético, Regime Fiscal e Constitucional, Gestlegal

de Vasconcelos Fernandes F (2019b) As demais contribuições financeiras a favor das entidades públicas no sistema fiscal português – conceito, pressupostos e regime jurídico-constitucional" (incluindo a analogia com as *Sonderabgaben* alemãs) Revista de Finanças Públicas e Direito Fiscal, No. ¼, IDEEF, Almedina

de Vasconcelos Fernandes F (2020) Direito Fiscal Constitucional, Introdução E Princípios Fundamentais, AAFDL

Dias JEF, da Costa JD (2010) Breve Apontamento sobre a natureza jurídico-tributária da "taxa" sobre as lâmpadas de baixa eficiência energética, RCEDOUA, No. 25, Almedina

[106]In this sense, the Judgments of TC No. 236/86, in Case No. 56/85, Judge Councillor Raul Mateus; Judgment No. 141/85, Case No. 86/83 and 47/84, Judge Councillor Jorge Campino.

Dourado AP (1987) Direito Fiscal, Almedina
Dourado AP (2019) Foreword to: A Contribuição Extraordinária Sobre o Setor Energético, Regime Fiscal e Constitucional, Gestlegal
Dourado AP (2020) Direito Fiscal, lições, 5th edn. Almedina
Garcia AV (2020) De La Tributación Ambiental A Las Medidas Financeiras Incentivadoras De La Economia Circular, Universidade de Málaga, Editorial Aranzi
Gomes CA et al (2017) Ordenamento do Território, Urbanismo e Cidades. Que rumo?, vol I. Almedina
Guerra Filho WS, Cantarini P (2017) Proporcionalidade. Enciclopédia jurídica da PUC-SP, Tomo: Teoria Geral e Filosofia do Direito, Celso Fernandes Campilongo, Alvaro de Azevedo Gonzaga, André Luiz Freire (coord. de tomo), Pontifícia Universidade Católica de São Paulo
Hey J (2020) Effectiveness of regulatory taxes: control through proceedings v. judicial control: a German constitutional perspective. Intertax 48(4)
Lobo CB (2019) Finanças e Fiscalidade do Ambiente e da Energia, Almedina
Martins AMG (2017) Manual de Direito da União Europeia, 2nd edn. Almedina
Martinzes FA (2015) Estudios Fiscalidad Ambiental En España: Situación Actual y Perspectivas De Futuro, Thomson Reuters Aranzadi
Miranda J (2007) Constitutions Nationales et "Constitution Européenne", Revista de Estudos Europeus, No. 2
Nabais JC (2003a) Direito Fiscal e Tutela do Ambiente em Portugal, RCEDOA, No. 12
Nabais JC (2003b) Direito Fiscal, 3rd edn. Almedina
Nabais JC (2004) O Dever Fundamental de Pagar Impostos, Almedina
Nabais JC (2019) Estudos Sobre a Tributação dos Transportes e do Petróleo, Almedina
Novais JR (2012) Direitos Fundamentais e Justiça Constitucional em Estado de Direito Democrático, Coimbra
Ollero C (1991) Los fines no fiscales de los tributos, Revista de Derecho Financeiero y Hacienda Pública, Editoriales de Derecho Reunidas, EDERSA, No. 213
Pereira PR (2020) Princípios de Direito Fiscal Internacional: do Paradigma clássico ao Direito Fiscal Europeu, reprint, Almedina
Pereira da Silva V (2021) O verde é uma das cores do Direito Constitucional. In: Marcia Andrea Bühring (coord) Estudos Em Homenagem ao Prof. Doutor Vasco Pereira da Silva, FDUL
Pina CC (2006) Mercados de Direitos de Emissão de CO_2, Estudos Jurídicos e Económicos em Homenagem ao Prof. Doutor António de Sousa Franco, vol I. Faculdade de Direito da Universidade de Lisboa
Saraiva R (2009) A Herança de Quioto em Clima de Incerteza, Doctoral Thesis, Faculdade de Direito da Universidade de Lisboa
Saraiva R (2011a) Análise económico-comportamental do Direito: uma introdução. In: Fernando Araújo et al (org) Estudos em Homenagem do Professor Doutor J. L. Saldanha Sanches, vol I. Coimbra Editora
Saraiva R (2011b) Direito à Energia Sustentável. In: Estudos em Homenagem ao Professor Doutor Sérvulo Correia, vol IV. Coimbra Editora
Soares CD (2002) O Imposto Ambiental Direito Fiscal do Ambiente, Cadernos CEDOUA, 2nd edn. Almedina
Soares CD (2004) A inevitabilidade de se avançar para a tributação ambiental…também em Portugal, Revista da Ordem dos Advogados, Ano 64, Nos. ½
Vasques S (2008) O Princípio da equivalência como critério da igualdade tributária, Almedina
Vasques S (2018) Manual de Direito fiscal, 2nd edn. Almedina

MIX
Papier aus verantwortungsvollen Quellen
Paper from responsible sources
FSC® C105338

If you have any concerns about our products,
you can contact us on
ProductSafety@springernature.com

In case Publisher is established outside the EU,
the EU authorized representative is:
Springer Nature Customer Service Center GmbH
Europaplatz 3, 69115 Heidelberg, Germany

Printed by Libri Plureos GmbH
in Hamburg, Germany